Islands of Women and Amazons

Islands of Women and Amazons
REPRESENTATIONS AND REALITIES

by Batya Weinbaum

University of Texas Press, Austin

Library of Congress Cataloging-in-Publication Data
Weinbaum, Batya.
    Islands of women and Amazons : representations and realities / by Batya Weinbaum. — 1st ed.
        p.   cm.
    Includes bibliographical references and index.
    ISBN 0-292-79126-7 (alk. paper). —
    ISBN 0-292-79127-5 (pbk. : alk paper)
        1. American literature—Women authors—History and criticism.
    2. Feminism and literature—United States—History—20th century.   3. Women and literature—United States—History—20th century.   4. American literature—20th century—History and criticism.
    5. American literature—Indian influences.   6. Isla Mujeres (Mexico)—History.   7. Mythology in literature.   8. Amazons in literature.
    9. Utopias in literature.   10. Islands in literature.   11. Women in literature.   12. Indian mythology.   13. Women—Mythology.   I. Title.
    PS228.F45W45   1999
        810.9'9287—dc21   99-28867

To my daughter, Ola

Contents

Illustrations follow page 153

Preface

Myths about the separate existences of women have appeared in diverse cultures since history began. The Sirens that sang on the Aegean rocks, the Amazons in the jungles of Brazil, the islands of self-reproducing women in Polynesia, and matriarchal utopias such as the one created by Charlotte Perkins Gilman in *Herland* are only a few variants. This book will explore a range of images of the archetype as an effort to contribute to feminist, literary, Latin American, classical, and American studies.

My objective throughout is to show how these myths and the archetype from which they derive are neither progressive nor reactionary. Rather, the theme can represent different psychological needs arising from different historical contexts and forms of struggle. My research into history, popular culture, folklore, myth, and narratives referencing societies exclusively of women (or societies in which women dominate) will provide new prisms through which to view political feminist material. I discuss effects on folk life and culture as this dialectical, transformative reclamation process occurs.

My reading begins with a statement of the Amazon archetype. I then analyze various historical uses and interpretations. I explore the difference between a sign, which points to something outside a text, and a symbol, which operates within a text.

Those intrigued by the idea that women might have lived a different, more empowered sort of life at an earlier time primarily have explored the symbol of the Amazon as an archetype. Yet Amazon women also act as a symbol within other texts. I explore, for example, the archetype's initial Greek context, as Amazons are glimpsed originally in the *Iliad* and in subsequent aspects of Greek culture; how the Amazons lost their pre-Christian aspects and developed as negative representations of paganism; and the exportation of Amazonism by a European writer, Montalvo, imitating the Greeks as he wrote about the New World.

To break down the separation of "culture" from material life, as cultural critic Raymond Williams recommended in *Marxism and Literature* (1977), I explore the social production of the name and notion of an "island of women" on a real contemporary site, Isla Mujeres, in Mexico. The site of worship of the Maya moon deity, Ixchel, this "island of women," developed for North American tourism, exemplifies the changing reality behind the mythic representation. In other words, I explore how the concept of an island of women takes on a configuration as a whole way of life.

Changes in the field of popular culture on the island and in the United States proceed even as I write. For example, the last fieldwork I conducted on Isla Mujeres, discussed in Part 3, revealed trends that develop so quickly that they defy up-to-the-minute recording, even as I attempt to keep up. The NAFTA agreements, economic restructuring, the spreading effects of the Chiapas uprising, and devaluation of the peso all brought about major changes that continue to alter people's daily lives. I had the experience of interacting with some members of the local intelligentsia, who translated a piece of my work into scholarly Spanish for publication. In this process, I unearthed further research, some of which has appeared in the *Journal of American Culture* and *Literary Studies East and West* (Weinbaum 1997c; 1999).

I have not yet studied some of these most recent changes long enough. For example, although the crafts stores on the island display objects made in other states of Mexico, as well as in Hawaii and Indonesia, a movement of artisans has emerged on the island. In the spring of 1997, a handful of local crafts people were selling their own wares on Sundays in the town square, yet not many of these local crafts have reached the shops catering to tourists. Nonetheless, the movement toward economic self-protection represents a revitalization of sorts on the island.

In this same season, a bus named Ix Chel, painted with fish and sporting Mayan as well as Spanish names, toured the island, primarily for the benefit of local people. The name this bus bore is the same as that of the owners' daughter as well as that of the goddess. Here, the islanders were looking "backward" to reclaim something for themselves, the much-needed everyday transportation. Yet the trilingual signs on the bus began to break the mold in which locals primarily used forward-looking icons rather than icons representing a romanticized past. The latter, I had argued, described primarily the tourist outlook. I had indicated how islanders kept the tourist market in mind with signs addressing the tourist need to experience a romantic past.

On the home front, I cannot begin to keep up with the reclamation of Amazonian imagery in U.S. popular culture, such as the appearance of Xena, the woman warrior on horseback in the spin-off of the television series *Hercules*. I became convinced of the futility of trying to keep current on a cross-country trip to the women's music festival in Michigan in August of 1997. En route, I passed a full-length purple semi bearing the label "Amazon Trucking" on the cab. I don't know whether the drivers (women) were delivering to the music festival, but this striking visual reminded me that the processes I describe here will continue long after the completion of this book, as will the blossoming of the Internet's Amazon.com.

I hope that feminist students and scholars, having read this book, will continue with better tools to analyze those further developments on their own, just as exposure to other books on my topics motivated me.

Acknowledgments

I am indebted to Joseph T. Skerrett, Jr., Francisco Javier Cevallos, Margo Culley, Al Hudson, M. Rivka Polatnick, Robbie Pfeufer Kahn, Ruby Rohrlich, Amy Pualwan, Kate Quinn, Judith Sherts, Judy Luce, Libby Hubbard, Jan Oliver, the community of Isla Mujeres, the library staffs of the University of Massachusetts at Amherst and Goddard College, my students, and my family. Theresa May at University of Texas Press was persistent in the battle to present interdisciplinary work. The editors of *Utopian Studies* and *Journal of American Folklore* provided comments from reviewers, for which I am grateful. Students at UMass—Amherst were also helpful in providing their reader-response and working with my categories.

I also acknowledge Francis Robicsek for permission to reprint from *The Maya Book of the Dead* by Francis Robicsek and Donald Hales, specifically, the movie-like position change of the Dragon Lady, from p. 115 in the University of Virginia Art Museum production. Also thanks for permission to use Field Museum Negative no. 2157, of the statue in Cozumel.

Introduction

I first became interested in materials which led to this book in the course of pursuing ethnographic fieldwork on the hula. When I began to read the collected mythology of Polynesia, references to islands of women particularly intrigued me. I discovered many related legends in collections of Polynesian myth. Some of this folklore alluded to islands where women lived without men and reproduced spontaneously with the wind or with black eels from the sea. Occasionally myths described these islands of women as floating.

Sometimes, in these legends, male lovers flew over from neighboring islands to teach women natural sexual intercourse. Children of such matings then spent lifetimes trying to return to their fathers. Alternatively, once captured by their fathers, the children spent lifetimes trying to return to their mothers. When I did fieldwork in Hawaii, local hula teachers and folklorists told me that these ideas of islands of self-reproducing women originated in New Zealand. I expediently pursued other angles.

When I returned to the mainland, I discovered that floating island myths are universal. Moreover, I discovered that in anthropological research, natives often inform observers that whatever is noted as peculiar stems from somewhere else, and not from their own culture.

At the time, I thought I had dropped my interest in myths of islands of women. Yet I soon discovered what Christine Downing contends in *The Goddess: Mythological Images of the Feminine* (1981): we don't pick these myths—the myths pick us.

My next experience with the appeal of the myths was in the mid-1980s, at what organizers then called the Seneca Falls Women's Encampment for Peace and Justice. Women had set up the camp near an active army base in upstate New York. Operating from their own base, activists used civil disobedience tactics to protest deployment of nuclear weapons. Commonly called the "Peace Camp" in the 1980s, what now survives as the "Peaceland" provided a basis of interaction in an ongoing way for a diverse constituency of women. While participating in this live-in protest, I met a woman of mixed-blood origin who became fascinated with my research. The source of her intense enthusiasm may have been that she saw her own roots in these legends.

Sometime after this interchange, I discussed the experience with Michelle Crone. For years she had been active in the organization of women's music festivals.[1] Upon hearing that women existed separately on remote islands as recorded or alluded to in folklore and myths, her eyes lit up, too.

The myth seemed to activate something collective and quite unconscious in the imaginations of various individuals. Hence, I became interested in cultural and psychological theories of the archetypal mind. I went on to explore various revisionist creation stories that had come out in the 1970s.

Some myths claimed that women evolved out of the sea and held that only later did men come from the land to colonize them. Before impregnation evolved, some claimed, women had been able to reproduce asexually, without aid of intercourse with males, as happens in some other species.

This pursuit led me to Susan Cavin's *Lesbian Origins* (1985), a book which discusses lesbian origin myths. She analyzes how the science of patriarchal history might have distorted those myths. Cavin's work also heavily influenced the contemporary poet and theorist Adrienne Rich, particularly in the latter's essay "Compulsory Heterosexuality and Lesbian Existence" (1993).[2]

Influenced by Cavin, I read about Amazons. Particularly, her discussion of a fifteenth-century Spanish novelist who had written about Amazons in the New World intrigued me. This was García Rodríguez de Montalvo, whose *Sergas de Esplandian* later became the focus of a chapter in this book.

I had yet another route into this material. Once when I was writing a Jewish roots satire (Weinbaum 1991b), to my surprise an image emerged of an island of women off the coast of Venezuela that would somehow be God's chance to start the world over after a nuclear holocaust. I turned the piece into a separate short story, "The Women Who Won the World." Similarly, when I was revising previous materials, an island of women that floated across the horizon of a short story's pages got me a contract from a small women's press that wanted to publish a collection of mine (1993a) but whose editors had not accepted my earlier tries. Curiously enough, I received their acceptance while in residence on Isla Mujeres (Island of Women). Off the coast of Mexico in the Caribbean, this island was a place I had also been drawn to visit on a long motorcycle trip in the spring of 1971. Then, my companion and I had slept on the beach, and I had danced on the ruins, lured by the promise of working for tourism. This time, though, I had gone to the vicinity primarily to visit the site of the death of my father. He had drowned off the coast of nearby Cancún on the mainland a few years previously. In 1991, I had anxiously anticipated the shock of the experience. Before and after visiting the beach where the accident occurred, I returned again to Isla Mujeres to draw what solace I could, as the island sustained itself so very positively as a fortifying place in my memories.

This time I was living on what money I had and on what I could earn while waiting for a publisher's reimbursement. I spent a great deal of time during my self-styled "recovery" working with "the folk." The island folklore surrounding the name of the island itself intrigued me.

I was particularly aware that most islanders with whom I interacted did not know that this name derived from an international mythic theme. Nonetheless, some poetry of local writers preserved on the island referred to Greek myth where sirens reportedly sang on the rocks, enslaving men who heard their sounds.

What would the sounds of these songs be like? My imagination got the best of me. Would they be like the *ulala* sound of greeting that Middle Eastern women make? Or would they be more like the deep-throated, bellowing, low monotone chant of indigenous Hawaiian women? Would the songs approximate the soft feminine trills I had made on the upper octaves of the piano when composing delicate lullabies in secluded, empty churches in Hawaii? Or more like the sound of the tips of waves as they come to rest on shores nestling naked against seaweeded rock in the moonlight? Would they be closer to the sound of the outlawed fourths that contemporary feminist composer Kay Gardner discovered when researching women-only music? Or like the musical modes that Greek males barred, due to the disruptive nature of the sounds to their own control of culture? Would they be the same sounds that threw men into a frenzy in the streets, as declaring allegiance to the Great Mother as her religion spread? Or would they more resemble the strains of female blues singers that some say led stockbrokers to jump during the 1930s crash in desperation?

The sounds will remain a mystery. Yet the poems I found, published by the Casa de Cultura on the island, employed the same themes as the Greek myths. The word "sirens" appeared in a poem made by one of the local artists who did murals for restaurants. Did the artist have direct knowledge of the Greek legend?

Much of the island's poetry referred to the special sound made by its women. I could find no clues to the origin of this notion, other than that to this day, such a sound emerges during the festival of the patron saint of the island, the Virgin of Immaculate Conception (Conchi), through women's ritual chant and song. On the virgin's festival nights, high, sweet voices sing to the Mother of the Sea and to the Mother of Us All.

A hotel and restaurant manager introduced me to the poetry. She told me that on the day of the festival, the women not only sang but also danced together, creating their own women's space, free from men, in the houses. This seemed to contradict the macho veneer of the culture in which I was about to become immersed.

When I came back to the States, I was able to compile an extensive bibliography. This included a vast array of explorers' reports of women existing separately from men in the New World, in addition to the fictional work of Rodríguez de Montalvo.

Historically, creators of cultural works associated the idea of an island of women with the idea of the Amazons. A separate existence of women, with its many representations and realities, still has quite an appeal, even in mainstream, contemporary American culture. Diverse representations exist in American literary history and culture of what has now been canonized as the Amazon archetype, and this idea led me to explore possible reasons for such widespread appeal.

In my previous work on socialist ideology and revolutionary structure (Weinbaum 1978) and family realities and workplace relations (Weinbaum 1984a, 1984b), my primary concern was how different people could perceive the same social and cultural facts in so many radically different ways—a concern that carries over to this book. Also, in the 1970s, when western social reformers looked to utopian experiments in countries considered socialist, I did extensive research on China (1976, 1977). I noticed that even in what idealistic political activists held to be the best of all possible worlds, the structure of the economy blocked the liberation of women. Individual members pooled income across sex and age groupings in the economic unit of the household, on which the ideological unit of the family rested. I began to wonder whether other economic (and ideological) arrangements had ever existed. This turned me toward a search for the beginnings of patriarchy. When I did so, the image and archetype of the Amazon confronted me.

Had there ever been a time when women were not economically dependent on men, when economic pooling grouped women as the basic survival unit? Researching the reality behind the Amazon myth seemed like an attractive route to locate answers to our contemporary situation.

Part 1 of this book explores the archetype of the Amazon and various uses in American popular culture, literary history, and criticism. I suggest "reclamation," "revitalization," and "reaction" as categories for organizing material concerning Amazons, based on Northrop Frye's methods of critical analysis. I review the contemporary critical literature about these images, which has focused on Amazons as dying, Amazons as representing wild femininity, and Amazons as expressions of the rites of passage from puberty. This contemporary literature has condensed around whether or not Amazons actually existed and how accurately their mythic representations serve as signs pointing to something outside the text itself. Relatively little information has been maintained, either in the texts or in material civilization, concerning the types of cultural constructions the Amazons had, about the women's child rearing or conception practices, or about the Amazons' relation to other women or to goddesses.

By the 1970s, the Amazon archetype had become a puzzle of conflicting, contradictory, non-congruent images. Common cultural use had freed the signifier "Amazon" from a direct connection to the external referent. I found this process to reveal more about the colorful imaginations of the representers and the contexts in which they live and create than it does about the "truth" of the Amazons themselves.

Part 2 examines Homeric, classical Greek, and European medieval and early Renaissance literary representations of Amazons. I argue that the Amazons went through a metamorphosis from what I call a primary form, as a collective horde of fighting women, into what I call a secondary form, in which the Amazon appeared as an individuated anima figure. I argue that this change occurred in the transition from oral, collectively chanted and performed literature drawing from (and probably based on) women's lament, to written, literature authored by individual men as pens and other writing utensils developed simultaneously with the oppression of women. As civilization developed, instead of being an autonomous, collective entity, as the Amazons appeared in the *Iliad*, the Amazons became the projected animas of men. They no longer strived against men. They were no longer man-killing, man-hating, and flesh-devouring. They became beautiful, well mannered, helpful, and sweet. Though Homeric Amazons were androgynous, more warrior than woman, by the second phase, beauty, vulnerability, and other male-proscribed aspects of femininity had become dominant, all but eclipsing the original androgynous warrior.

Part 2 concludes by documenting the exportation of the Old World Amazon to the Americas. Early fifteenth-century colonial explorers claimed to have located many islands of women off coasts around the world. These explorers' reports interacted with variants of the mythic theme of an Isle of Women, a theme which was also popular in the myths of many indigenous peoples.

I argue that these reports of isolated locales expressed utopian themes in which women had extraordinary powers associated with supernatural relations with beasts and nature. Montalvo's *Sergas de Esplandian* capitalized on this interaction between explorers' reports and tales of indigenous peoples. The work infected the minds of the explorers, who sought islands of women in a futile search to satisfy infantile paradisical longings. Thus, the interplay between the utopian and dystopian aspects of such an imagined island creates what we read today as a palimpsest.[3]

Part 3 explores the real, contemporary "island of women" in the Caribbean on which I did fieldwork, where I went to test in my own life and reality the ideas from mythical history. I examine the considerable interaction between the culture of the island and the cultures of tourism in the context of the historical reclamation of Maya middle-American myth. I look at the ways in which modern tourists project through a certain lens as they search for "the primitive." I argue that this process eclipses and eventually undermines existing folk culture. I view the island as a collectively created fiction matching the unconscious needs of the tourists for a primitive, matriarchal, precolonial, untouched haven-like space. I explore the impact of such a search on local cultures by examining changing material culture, dance forms, and practices of female folk arts such as midwifery.

I show how the theme of women existing separately from men is not always progressive, and suggest reasons why. In fact, such representations of women dominating a social existence often reflect the political economics of the times. Women's striving toward their own freedom might be only one of the needs or issues represented.

I aim to demonstrate the timelessness of this abstraction, as well as its cyclical recurrence and the relation to the social and economic histories within which the idealized symbolic abstraction has been reproduced. Consequently, the study often does not reflect a linear progression of time. Rather, I show how Amazons have appeared in many types of spaces—islands, cities, tribes, countries, planets—in different times and in different social formations, as creative subjects have utilized alternative forms, mediums, conventions, and processes of writing in specific social and cultural relationships.

Yet I point to the consistency of patterns that one can observe in ideology, literature, popular literature, and "literature of the people." These patterns occur even in periods of profound transformation. I demonstrate that the Amazon archetype's constant re-emergence is not simply due to women discovering strength in their own independent existence. However, as we make our own history and struggle with visions of how to reproduce our own means of life, the Amazon takes on new forms and meanings. These, then, represent new definitions of changing practical consciousness. Amazons are elements of a continuing and changing practice, moving beyond old forms in each new set of transitions.

I start from the proposition that if social being determines consciousness, then any change in society will result in a change in the forms of literature. I find this to be so not only in the means of production and consumption of literature, but also in the representation of the Amazon within that literature. There is no singular Amazonian "ideal type," because the important characteristics and moving forces change along with the ideas and realities of the cultures in which she appears.

Hence the reader will find the range of times, genres, disciplines, countries, forms, and places covered to be diverse. I include among other references contemporary feminist novels from Europe and the United States, nineteenth-century American novels, British and U.S. twentieth-century fiction, contemporary U.S. feminist literary theory, early second-wave feminist anthropology, writings of the Beat movement, U.S. popular culture, feminist history, French writings, icons from the French Revolution, colonial accounts by Spaniards in the early days of the Americas, the writings of Marco Polo, anthropological work of Bronislaw Malinowski, early classics of Greek literature, Spanish Renaissance writings, newspaper accounts, world folklore, German writings, and Roman history and icons.

I have discovered many variations of the Amazon archetype. Yet my own spirit has been touched by those magnificently helmeted women on horseback who gallop across civilization's plains and pages. These women seem unheeding of the social mores of the societies through which they roam as they race off to construct their own society—as an artist recently represented on the cover of *The Amazon Chronicles,* a book which an independent feminist publisher was able to bring out before its recent demise (J. E. M. Robinson 1994).

In fact, many women have used this archetype in the feminist context. Among the examples are Inez Haynes Gillmore's account of nineteenth-century women's rights activists, *Angels and Amazons;* Suzy Charnas' 1970s novel *Motherlines,* about women who live without men and who ride horses and try to breed with their animals; and Ellen Frye's 1994 novel, *Amazon Story Bones,* in which an Amazon grandmother tells tales around the fire to her grandchildren about what life was like in her long-lost tribe of women.

Some readers might detect moments when the bit of my discipline breaks, a mane tosses, and my spirit reconnects with the spirit of those re-emerging Amazons. Many feminists (Cixous, Irigaray) discuss the problem of women staying within the discourse of men without changing established convention and territory. Consequently, in places I diverge from traditional abstract disembodiment. I weave in my own personal connection to the archetype. This attempt to be holistically integrative in turn impacts my creative, expressive, and dialogical form.

Part One

The Amazon Archetype in Popular Culture,
Literature, and Criticism

O N E

The Amazon Archetype

As Annis Pratt has explained in *Archetypal Patterns in Women's Fiction* (1981), the term "archetype" derives from the Greek *arche*, "a beginning or first instance," and *typos*, a stamp, which "denotes the primordial form, the original, of a series of variations" (3). Drawing from Jung, Pratt defined archetypes as "primordial forms" that "spring from the preverbal realm of the unconscious, where they exist inchoate and indescribable until given form in consciousness" (3). What we are to examine, then, are archetypal images and the popular literary forms that derive from such unconscious originals.

Pratt explained that archetypal patterns, once discerned, can be used to organize categories of particular expressions, which one can induce from "images, symbols and narrative patterns" observed in a wide variety of literary works (5). We can describe these patterns within a given text, or between texts within a larger body of literature. Pratt developed categories of analysis for the last three hundred years of women's fiction. She discovered that the quest patterns proposed by Jung, Campbell, Frye, and other archetypalist critics may work for male-authored texts, but they do not suit women's fiction.

Pratt concluded her second book, *Dancing with Goddesses: Archetypes, Poetry and Empowerment* (1994), by redefining archetypes as "elements in an interwoven matrix comprising earth, human beings, animals and other living creatures and plants" (369). According to Pratt, archetypal theory is not mind over matter, but mind constantly resonating with new matter. Such a process must occur in an atmosphere where hypotheses can be tossed about and experimented with in an unconstrained, playful way. If contemplating material from vast sources such as those indicated above can result in first describing, then categorizing, and finally hypothesizing, then archetypal theory can help us understand the world in which we live.

As Pratt herself has observed, there are potential problems with archetypalist criticism, especially if one borrows wholesale from theorists such as Campbell, Frye, and Jung. Some fear that the sexism, bad politics, or fascism that Campbell or Jung exhibit will contaminate those who experiment with archetypal criticism. For example, according to Pratt, Jung's theories about primitive peoples exemplify the mind-set of a European chauvinist. He set up an exploitative hierarchy of the world's peoples, utilizing the "primitive mind," but only to heal the suffering of the painfully civilized European (Pratt 1994, 36). Similarly, some fear that the use of free association as a method of unveiling deeper meanings might identify one with particular formulations Sigmund Freud advocated.

Others have argued that the methods developed by archetypal criticism merely serve to strengthen the existing cultural biases of the critic, who develops a pattern or understanding and then projects spectacles through which to view social facts and relations. Moreover, adversaries warn that such a process is likely to do more to obscure realities of observed cultures rather than to illuminate them. For example, the colonial "discoverers" of Hawaii perceived welcoming dances on the beaches through the lens of entertainment. However, the dances were actually ritualized religious performances of history. As another example, a tribal group in northern Mexico perceived a red-haired anthropologist doing fieldwork as the devil. This was the significance that the local informants gave to red hair in the culture he was observing. Yet the problem of perceptual blinders lies in wait for all theoretical constructs, be they anthropological, structuralist, functionalist, Marxist, or feminist. Archetypal categories are not meant to be regarded as fixed or absolute. In fact, fluidity in symbols is basic; mutation is the most noteworthy characteristic.

For example, one might ask why Diodorus says in the following account that the Libyan Amazons, who predated the Asiatics, originated from a lost island, Hespera, off the coast of Africa:

The Amazon women, mythographers say, lived on an island called Hespera [i.e., Evening] from its position toward the setting sun. . . . The island was in the marsh Tritonis . . . it was of good size and was filled with fruit-bearing trees of every sort from which the inhabitants took substance. It also had multitudes of flocks of goats and sheep, whose milk and meat their owners ate. The nation did not use grain at all, because it had not been invented. (Diodorus 3.52.4, quoted in Tyrell 58)

In addition, why did their queen Myrina consecrate a sacred space to Cybele, mother of the gods, on a towering, rocky island called Samothrace (Sobol 27; Bennett 17)?

Furthermore, why did the ancient Greek Apollonius represent the Amazons engaged in a ritual of venerating a black stone placed on an altar in an open temple on an island off the coast of Colchis (Bennett 17)?

One might also ponder the cultural history of Elephanta, an island off the western coast of India near Bombay. This area of the world offers traditions of horse sacrifice, government by queens, and female bodyguards for the royalty. What might the female statue in this island's sculptured caverns have represented to the local inhabitants in its history? The Portuguese took their traditional disdain for other religions to their usual lengths in Elephanta and did considerable damage to the sculptures. They left a palimpsest to be interpreted. The statue later discovered had a full breast on the left and none on the right. To most modern spectators, this figure would represent an Amazon warrior who had to cut off one breast in order to fight. And why did an early twentieth-century Muslim writer, who saw *purdah* from the inside and campaigned against it for much of her life in India, choose to create Ladyland, which secluded men and in which women were in power (Hossain 1905)? Was the author, in 1905 Madras, invoking some of the lost power of women in the continent's history?

We might also question why the *Odyssey,* certainly a hallmark text in Western civilization, contains tales of islands dominated by women (Circe, Calypso, the Sirens) from whom the hero Odysseus has to struggle to break free. Was there really a female-dominated civilization previously, from which the hero in an emerging patriarchal order had to win his independence?

In a similar vein, why did Herodotus discover and make note of the floating island of Chemmis on an inland lake? Was this island part of the far-flung matriarchy of Amazonian women living on islands? Apparently a temple of Latona, one of the greatest Egyptian deities representing primeval female darkness, graced the island's center. And what led Paul Friedrich to discover that cults of the Greek goddess of love were organized on islands? Why do classics scholars also discuss a place called the Amazonium on the island of Patmos? Why did the ancients report additionally that the Amazons erected a temple on the Isle of Ares?

We might also ask why Prester John, in a letter to the Emperor of Rome and to the King of France dating from the middle of the twelfth century, described the land of the Great Feminie. This land, he explained, was not precisely an island. Yet the land mass was encircled by a wide river. The women, he wrote, had three queens, each with one hundred thousand armed women. He claimed this number did not include the women who drove carts, horses, and elephants to bring supplies. He also described sexy warrior women with whom the fortunate man could stay up to nine days at a time, during which the man might impregnate them. Yet if this same man stayed longer, he would die. Sex became dangerous and the women murderous. What is the possible source of this myth? Why did John also claim that near this river that flowed from Paradise was a fountain in which all who bathed emerged not one day older than thirty-two years?

And why did Sir John Mandeville, a fourteenth-century traveler, affirm so readily the existence "somewhere in the east" of an island called Amazonia, or Feminye, "inhabited only by women" ([1240, 1356, 1481?] 1983; Pollard 103–104)?

Why did an early Renaissance Spanish writer create a craggy rock island in the Americas of black Amazons who rode multicolored steeds?

Why were islands peopled with Amazons reported in 1506 by a missionary off the coast of China? Why did they suffer "no man among them except at certain seasons, for the preservation of the race" (Rothery 120)? Why have officials in Tibetan monasteries been copying documents using the non-Tibetan words "*zug te bung*," and in Mogul, "*chutanai okin?*" Both phrases mean something like "girls together" and refer to a central Asian nation.

Modern editors of these chronicles think the documents deal with inland Asian Amazons (Real 227). Is this why an ancient women's language exists in the interior of China, a language in which the male gender does not appear?

Is this the same "Women's Land" to which Maxine Hong Kinsgston referred in *Chinamen* (1977)? In the book, Tang Ao, looking for the Gold Mountain, crosses into a Land of Women and encounters two old women who pierce his ears, break and bind his feet, pluck his face of all hair, adorn him with makeup, and turn him into a dainty server of dishes for a party for the queen. Were there really, as Kingston writes, no taxes and no wars in this Women's Land? Was this the country discovered during the reign of Empress Wu (A.D. 694–705) or as early as A.D. 441, and was it, as some scholars in China say, as far away as North America?

What is the possible reality behind the myth of El Wak-Wak, the well-known, woman-inhabited isle located either near Borneo or off the coast of East Africa beyond Zanzibar? Was this supposedly manless island to the south of China really a place where women mated with the winds?

What of the Isle of Women Marco Polo reported in his travels? On this island of females, which he claimed to have found in the China Sea, did women really arm themselves with bows and arrows, live without men, and mate with cannibalistic lovers?

Why did Columbus report in his journals (1825) that he too had found an island, Matinino, whose name and description sounded like the one Marco Polo reported? Did Columbus really think he had arrived in the east when he sighted this island, Matinino, only to miss it due to a chance, sudden change of the winds? Did Columbus really take this island to be the refuge the ancients wrote about in relation to the Themyscian Amazons (Jane [1930] 1970)? Columbus also claimed that the name meant something like "women" or "matriarchal regime" in the indigenous language of the time. Why did Fernandez de Oviedo make similar claims about the island he spotted in Las Antillas?

Why did Real report an island called Ciguatlan off the west coast of Mexico, whose name in the indigenous language meant "island of women" or "city of women?" Why did the Spanish find statues of women similar to those on the island Orocomay (40)? What can we discern about the existence of and possible relationship between such islands dotted around the American coasts? These include the Island of Women (Isla Mujeres) off the Caribbean coast of Mexico, on which colonialists discovered similar statues of women. Why has this latter island been developed so successfully for tourism since the 1970s? Was this present-day tourist paradise retreat once really a matriarchy? A convent? A harem? A site of goddess worship?

Legends of the ancients, even as colonial explorers and their receptive audiences embroidered them, continue to broaden this field of cultural study. For example, the Italian humanist Pietro Martire d'Anghiera interviewed Columbus when he returned to Spain in 1493. His *Decades of the New Worlde* greatly elaborated on Columbus' account. Translated into English in 1555, this document became one of the first books on America published in English.

Why does the document claim that a forbidden, exotic, and enticing island was "inhabited only with women to which the cannibals have accesse at certain tymes of the yeare, as in owlde tyme the *Thracians* had to *Amazones* in the Island of *Lesbos*?" This was, for the cannibals, the epitome of the one-night-stand with beautiful, sexy women, without responsible involvement (d'Anghiera [1555] 1971, Book 2, 64; Kleinbaum 104).

The variations in examples move us forward into the literary arena of culture. For example, Torquato Tasso's *Gerusaleme Liberata,* a long poem completed in 1575, includes an image of an enchantress, Armida, who lures away the hero to her island in the Atlantic (Miner 88). Shakespeare's *The Tempest* and John Fletcher's *The Sea Voyage* both contain an idealized woman, cast away on an island, who has never seen a man. Why did Thomas D'Urfey adapt this island as an Amazonian commonwealth in his 1686 *A Common-Wealth of Women?*

What of the island in *The Arabian Nights* (Zipes [942?] 1991) ruled by a queen who had her own army? In this text, women of valor and strength exhibited excellence in horsemanship, and women with long hair grew on trees. Or, according to an alternate version, the fruit of the trees looked like women's heads.

Nor is the theme limited to the ancients, to the explorers of the Americas, to Western European writers, Asian American writers, Muslim Indian writers, turn-of-the-century writers, or to the Middle Eastern folktale. Further variations continue to stimulate provocative questions, such as:

Was Java originally a women's island, as has been reported?

What possible source lies behind the legend of a woman's island off the coast of Japan?

Why did Portuguese voyagers report that they had discovered off the coast of Africa an Amazon island called Socrata?

How did Malacca, Madagascar, Seycheles, Sumatra, and Sunda gain exotic reputations as women's isles?

What, if any, relationship existed between Circe's island, the Island of Lemnos, and the Cossack island on the Dnieper where men visited once a year for rendezvous with women?

How are the above myths related to the stories reported to the Jesuit missionaries by the inhabitants of the Marianne Islands? Are those stories related to the floating islands of women that crop up in folklore surrounding various seas?

To the north, why did William Baffin, during his explorations of the Arctic region in 1616, name an island "Women Island?"

The stories of islands of women also emanate from areas throughout the Pacific. Trobriander islanders, who were studied by Bronislaw Malinowski, believe in the existence of "a mythical island on which there are a number of villages inhabited only by beautiful women . . ." (Malinowski 1929, 229). Does this belief in a women's island stem from the taboo against all males, even relatives, entering the quarters of the mother and child for two months after birth? Why, on this mythical island called "the fill of copulation," do women grow their pubic hair long enough to form a sort of grass apron? Why are these women considered fierce and insatiable? Why is it said that when ". . . they cannot have intercourse, they use the man's nose, his ears, his fingers, his toes . . ." (300)? Does all this relate to "the matriarchate"— or the rule of the mother in savage society (Malinowski 1927)?

We might also move into the arena of nineteenth- and twentieth-century popular culture to find further variations of the archetype. For example, why did *Mizora: A Prophecy*, first published in *The Cincinnati Commercial* in 1880–1881, include a zone in the earth in which women reproduced without men (M. E. B. Lane [1889] 1975)? Why did *Unveiling a Parallel: A Romance* (A. I. Jones and Marchant [1893] 1991) introduce a female-dominated planet into popular American consciousness toward the close of the nineteenth century?

Why did an American TV series of the 1970s portray an island of women that sends its Amazon queen to fight the Nazis, based on the *Wonder Woman* character inaugurated by DC Comics in 1942 (Fitzsimons and Rodgers 1977–1979)? Why is a residual Amazon Princess in the *Wonder Woman* comics still distributed in packages of Kellogg's cereal today? Why did ABC begin making the two-hour pilot *Wonder Woman* in 1974, and then follow up with *The New Original Wonder Woman* series, in which Wonder Woman takes a golden belt for strength (Wallerstein and Margolin 1975–1976)? Why does she possess a golden lariat whose movement she controls? Why did CBS do a later series, *The New Adventures of Wonder Woman*, set in the present day? What is the relationship between these previous "wonder women" and the current television series *Xena*?

The examples move us also to the arena of science fiction. Why did Leslie F. Stone, a little-known popular science fiction writer of the 1930s (Weinbaum 1997a, 1997b), create female-dominated planets—one on which women ruled from an island—in works that reached the public through mass-marketed pulp magazines (1930, 1931)? Marion Zimmer Bradley, a U.S. writer who has been publishing since the early 1950s, created another variation—a group of women who attempt to gain control over their own lives by isolating themselves from contact with men on the "Island of Silence" in *Two to Conquer* (1987). Why is it that there, on this island, shielded by their magic, women serve as healers and priestesses of the goddess Avarra, who treats the women's ailments? Why is it that from this island of women, they and other women join together to form a new Order of Renunciates, the basis of the Free Amazons?

create new values, new meanings, new practices, new relationships, and new kinds of relationships. Hence Williams would classify these authors as "emergent" (123). They are substantially alternative and oppositional to the status quo.

Barbara Walker's *Amazon: A Novel* (1992) is a prime example of revitalist rather than a pure revivalist work. Walker's main character is an Amazon undergoing a coming-of-age ritual in the cave of the Great Mother after having killed her first Greek in battle. The Amazon then time-travels to modern California. Four men nearly rape her when they find her by the side of the highway wearing nothing but an amulet belt and carrying a sword. A woman journalist picks her up. She discovers the Amazon's true, prior identity.

The Amazon from the past educates her present-day hostess on various conjectured Amazonian tribal aspects such as bisexuality, non-monogamy, and masturbation. Thus, in this revitalist, emergent work that stands in clear opposition to the dominant culture, a contemporary author comments on how the patriarchal sexuality of our own times limits women. Walker has read these aspects of fictionalized Amazonian experience backward into the revival of the legend. Her Amazon from the past also promotes women's fitness and self-defense as alternatives to women's victimization by the present culture. She tackles a talk-show host on television. In the end, she participates in contemporary women's spirituality rituals. She earns the right to return to her tribe and to her own time by saving the goddess temple in the twentieth century from destruction by a right-wing fundamentalist, whom she recognizes as a reincarnation from her own past life.

Other examples of the distinction between residual revitalization and emergent revitalization abound. Contemporary writers Eva Keuls and Abbey Kleinbaum have revived the Amazon by re-examining early artifacts and texts, as did Robert Briffault in the 1920s. Yet in the early twentieth century, Inez Haynes Gillmore did something substantively different. She wrote of an Amazon character who led a revolt of women with clipped wings by teaching them how to walk. By creating such a character, Gillmore offered opposition to the dynamic interrelations of the cultural system in which she wrote. She did not merely revive a text in which women fought as peers of men. Rather, she revitalized the Amazon concept to lend the borrowed meaning of "Amazons in the past" to her own metaphor of "Amazons in modern context." Instead of inhabiting the familiar terrain of pre-Greek wars, her creations existed on a wild, largely uninhabited island on which a group of contemporary men had been shipwrecked.

Another example taken from Gillmore's work lends meaning to the concept of revitalization: she called the nineteenth-century American feminists "Amazons" (1933). She did not mean that the women who led the women's movement for suffrage in the nineteenth century rode horses, wore armor, and fought like men in physical combat, laying siege to contemporary cities. Rather, Gillmore was revitalizing the concept more abstractly, moving the term from a residual, even archaic, basis to an emergent, dynamic category. She employed the concept "Amazon" to describe women who were taking the lead in situating women to become peers of men, using methods accepted by the current society. Education and legal training, she reasoned, might achieve the same purpose in the modern world as physical prowess had in the ancient past from which the Amazons emerged.

Likewise, in *Herland* ([1915] 1979), Charlotte Perkins Gilman did not merely revive an old Amazon tale. She employed the device of the accidental creation of a society of all women, as some Greeks hypothesized Amazonian societies came about when women who had been left during war revolted. Then she revitalized the concept by showing a positive evolution of that society free of men. In *Herland,* even the contemporary male visitors recognize the superiority of this woman-only society. They do not abduct individual women to their own world, as did various Greek males in classical myths.

Yet another example of emergent revitalization showing the strength and cohesion of women as a group is the creation of the "Amazons in Outer Space" concept by a student asked to write a paper comparing two *Star Trek* versions of planets dominated by women, "Spock's Brain" (1991) and "Angel One" (1987). When I asked the student to explain his use of this conceptual category, he replied that he hadn't meant to imply that these women on other planets rode horses, were bare-breasted or one-breasted, or fought in hand-to-hand armed combat with men, as we are given to believe the original Amazons did. Rather, he saw that the women were in charge of their own political-social structure. This seemed to him to make the women capable of being considered "Amazons." Further, another student helped his friend out of a loosely used metaphor. He volunteered that a mystery surrounded the women, as if the fact of their dominance could not be taken for granted but had to be understood in terms of the plot, pointing to what was also true of the handling of classical Amazons.

All these makers of culture, even novice ones, have revitalized the concept in a contemporary setting, rather than just reviving an Amazon from the past as closely as possible to her original meaning and context. Thus Sarah Hoagland (1988), a contemporary lesbian theorist, reaches back to old societal values. Yet she does so in order to create new values in proposing her notion of "Amazon caring." Lillian Faderman (1993), a contemporary lesbian feminist critic, has likewise performed "revitalization" rather than mere "revival" in her discussion of early second-wave writers as "Amazons." Kleinbaum, in her fine historical work on the social history of the idea of Amazons (1983), primarily revived the myths as they previously existed and traced their permutations. Yet she dedicated her book to Joan Kelly, a pioneer women's historian from the early seventies, as "the Amazon in us all." Here Kleinbaum was clearly revitalizing the concept of Amazon by using it metaphorically, not historically or literally. All of this emergent cultural practice suggests the growth of feminist consciousness in which women cohere as a new class or group.

Throughout the historical periods upon which I touch, including our own, a tension persists between the various uses of the Amazon. However, this tension has not often surfaced as a clear-cut debate. Very often, those who invoke the Amazon simply seem unaware of each other's work. Historians, critics, members of various political camps and dissociated academic fields, novelists, and poets seldom feel called upon to read outside their own disciplines or genres.

Finally, we come to a neutral category: those users of the notion of "Amazon" who don't fit neatly into any of the above, as they neither revitalize nor revive. However, they use the image of the Amazon in creative, theoretical, and historical work. Some may even have devoted some scholarly attention to the details of the Amazon's material existence. A subtle work in this regard is Samuel R. Delany's *Tales of Neveryon* (1979). Delany's *Tales* contains a women-dominated island, women warriors, women boat-people, a wise old woman telling tales while she teaches lost knowledge to children, an ancient woman-child empress, a female-centered creation story which indicates that men's free-hanging genitals are a punishment and a curse, and stories of how women invented the tools to write. But the book is not simply proreclamation. Delany embeds these detailed elements in equally significant tales about class, hierarchy, slavery, male prostitutes whom women use and discard, and male lovers relating among themselves.

One might further be tempted to assert that the reactionists are men and the reclamationists are female. The examples are numerous. To elaborate, in Federico Fellini's film *City of Women* (1980), a chance encounter with a female passenger stimulates the sexual fantasies of a male train passenger. Female police in a dream-like city of women ridicule the male. As the women in the city hold a farcical political convention, Fellini portrays the methods, art, and politics of the recent feminist movement as absurd. Hence I would consider this particular work reactionist.

Likewise, in the nineteenth century, J. J. Bachofen ([1861] 1967) fantasized that the recalcitrant Amazons were eventually put back in their male-dominated places. Bachofen articulated his view of the emerging correctness of patriarchal history, so his work, like Fellini's *City of Women,* can be placed in the reactionist category.

Similarly, in *Sons and Lovers,* D. H. Lawrence shows his Amazon character, Clara, to be assertive, athletic, and combative in the beginning. Yet she is broken, tamed, and in need of a man by the end ([1913] 1922). As Kate Millett pointed out in *Sexual Politics* (1971), an early work of second-wave feminist criticism, women's socially disruptive gains clearly provoked Lawrence's virulent attack on female and feminist characters (Clara is a suffragist). In the second half of this century, Eldridge Cleaver and Stokely Carmichael, leaders in the Black Power movement, used the epithet "Amazon" against black women in similarly reactionist ways (Wallace 1990).

But gender is not consistent in defining the pattern. For example, in the 1920s, a Marxist named Emmanuel Kanter (1926) revived Amazons as a source of women's power. He did so as a means of trying to entice working-class women to reclaim their sense of self-worth and strength. In the 1970s, Donald Sobol collected and ordered vast arrays of classical materials. He did nearly as much to revive traditional Amazon tales, in terms of sorting out the pure chronology, as Joseph Campbell had done in the 1950s and 1960s (1959, 1964, 1968) by simply acknowledging women's history as represented in mythology.

Furthermore, R. Hennig (1940), Wolfgang Lederer (1968), and Carlos Alonso del Real (1967)—all men—each devoted significant energy to the topic of the Amazon without reappropriating her for masculinist purposes, although she was not a major focus in their work. Scholarly interests in their own fields of demography, psychoanalysis, and dialectical historical material criticism motivated each more than an overwhelming need to chastise, liberate, or empower women. Similarly, Philip Slater's major preoccupation with the psychoanalytic knots between Greek mother and son (1968) led him to venture down interesting asides about Amazons, although, again, the Amazon was not the chief focus of his work. Thus, revitalist versus reactionist treatment of the Amazon does not fall strictly along the lines of gender; at least a few male writers have helped to reclaim and revive the archetype.

Latter Nineteenth-Century Uses

J. J. Bachofen was the most prolific of the nineteenth-century "maternalist" theorists (Lerner 1993, 28). He wrote during the mid-nineteenth century, a time when the reins of patriarchal monogamous morals were tightening on the upper classes. In *Myth, Religion and Mother Right* ([1861] 1967), Bachofen argued that myth is the elucidation of symbol. His theory of social development maintains that the first period of social history was matriarchal.

Bachofen charted women-dominated matriarchal rule in at least fourteen civilizations. He then explained this phenomenon away as merely a step along the road to ultimate male rule. Focusing on Bachofen's initial assertion of maternal rule, theorists of the American feminist second wave, such as Kate Millett in *Sexual Politics* (1971) and Adrienne Rich in *Of Woman Born* (1976), drew upon his work.

The growth of nationalism, the rise of the bourgeoisie, and the consolidation of the bourgeois state resulted in a tightening of societal morals which helped to produce Bachofen's perspective. After lengthy, tedious exploration of ancient myth, he hypothesized that the Amazons were in rebellion against sexual exploitation in a time of promiscuity. He theorized that at some point their mothers established matriarchal monogamy to cool the revolt of their armed Amazon daughters. His postulate is that patriarchy, the better of the systems, finally reigned when the Amazon mothers themselves called for a replacement for their monogamous, matriarchal system. In this final stage, then, men properly controlled women, in his view, even though women had known power and freedom in previous civilizations.

Bachofen cited the myth of the women of Lemnos as evidence for his thesis. In this myth, the women murder all but a few of their men for sleeping with Thracian women. Aphrodite, punishing the women of Lemnos for neglectful worship, afflicts them all with a foul smell, whereupon, when "all their menfolk were avoiding them," the women "banded together" and killed the males (Engle 1942, 512–514). In Bachofen's reading, this myth reflects a "hastily devised" matriarchy that was unstable and fated to expire. Having been established on such shaky footing as a revolt against sexual promiscuity, the make-shift system of social order would easily give over to the more sure rule of the patriarchy.

Popular culture appropriated the term "Amazon" to mean any rebellious woman fighting for the cause of women. For instance, in *Amazon Expedition* (1973) Phyllis Birkby reprinted a nineteenth-century newspaper account of Aurora Phelps, a woman who tried to start a working woman's cooperative and living community in Boston. Phelps actually took up arms against the state to protect the physical property. For this, in 1875 the *Woman Advertiser* dubbed the militant organizer "Queen of the Amazons" in an account entitled "Grand Uprising of the Amazons" (Kisner, Har, and Shumsky 1973).

Furthermore, Elizabeth Cady Stanton used Amazon references in public addresses. She additionally proposed matriarchy as the ultimate goal of women's liberation, drawing her own conclusions from the information Bachofen and others provided (Love and Shanklin 1978, 183). When the women's rights movement was proposing alternative clothing to the long, impractical, and confining Victorian attire of females, Stanton wrote in her autobiography that she thought the women with whom she organized should wear Diana the Huntress costumes rather than bloomers. Diana, the Roman version of Artemis, goddess of the Amazons, often engaged in fighting (Stanton [1898] 1993; Kelley 1994; Doll 1972).

Further nineteenth-century explorations of the Amazons concerned their relationship to goddesses. For example, in 1884 A. H. Sayce discussed how the Hittites could have served as a model for Amazonian development. He proposed that the Amazons could have had prototypes in the armed priestesses of the Asiatic goddess Ma, to whom whole cities had been dedicated. When Ma passed into Greek hands, she took the name Artemis. Amazons went on to be interpreted as a poetical transformation of her priestesses.

Another, lesser-known historical use of the Amazons occurred near the end of the nineteenth century. Tales of Celtic or Teutonic origin intersect with many factors in the story of the Amazons or of the separate island, nation, city, state, or planet of women. Supernatural realities, colonialism, racism, the censorship of popular culture, and the "preservation of the folk" all coincided to create this context. In 1891, Edwin Sydney Hartland collected tales of Teutonic and Celtic origin for his *The Science of Fairy Tales: An Inquiry into Fairy Mythology*. He inserted into his "tales of wonder" section the story of how a strain of fairy music one day lulled Bran Mac Fearbhall, king of Ireland, to sleep. On awakening, he found the silver

> branch of a tree by his side and a strange lady appeared at his court and invited him to a land of happiness. He handed her the silver branch, and the next morning with a company of several persons he sailed out on the ocean. In a few days they landed on an island inhabited only by women, of whom the strange lady appeared to be the

chieftaness. Here Bran Mac Fearbhall remained several ages before returning to his own palace near Lough Foyle. (202)

Hartland also reported an Arab tale in which the Amazons emerged in the Teutonic and Celtic realm from the Hispanic-Arabic tradition. A king's son landed on a strange island in his wanderings. There he married the king's daughter and became his father-in-law's vizier. The country was watered

by a river which flowed at certain seasons from a great mountain. Every year it was the vizier's duty to enter the cavern, having first received instructions from the king and a mysterious gift. At the end of the hour he reappeared, followed by the stream, which continued to flow during the time needed for fertilization. . . . When the prince as vizier entered the cavern he found a negro, who led him to his mistress, the queen of a people of Amazons. In her hands was the management of the river; and she had caused the periodical drought in order to exact a tribute of aote-stones which she had to pass onto an Ifrit, to purchase his forbearance towards her own subjects. The prince ingratiates himself with her: she suppresses the periodical droughts and marries him. After two centuries of wedded life she dies, leaving him ten daughters, whom he takes back . . . to the city . . . [now] governed by his great-great grandson. (202–203)

Hartland discovered a wealth of legend which associated the Amazons more with a fairyland, like an Isle of Happiness. This isle seemed akin to an enchanted underground into which patriarchal culture within Celtic civilization had displaced women of power (Markale 1986).

According to Pratt, the black virgins in Mariology are archaeological evidence for the Libyan Amazons (1994, 291). But more important here is the patriarchal displacement of women's power to the underground. This emerged as a common theme in European myth, as in the motif of Venus' home under the mountain, kingdoms under the sea, and fairy underworlds enchanting to mortals (293). Such displacement of women's power to the underground also occurs in examples from classical Greek culture. For example, in *Eumenides*, the third play in Aeschylus' trilogy *The Oresteia,* he confined the Furies underground (*Haile*). Yet he also enthroned them, which puts them in a position like that of the goddess in Celtic myth.

In all likelihood, black Moorish "marching women" who actually appeared in Valencia, Spain, in 1099 probably carried the story into Irish mythology. The memory of a classical tradition and the real passing of armed black women carrying some kind of religious symbol most likely converged. Here the black, underground Amazons held powers more like those of the Fairy Queen than those of a vast army supposedly marching on a holy war across continents en route between Spain and Feminina (Real 133–134).

Like her predecessor Demeter, the earth mother goddess, the Amazon queen in the Celtic myths still had power to withhold growth. Such a power is reminiscent of the moment in Greek myth in which Demeter refuses to return to Olympus to allow the barley to grow until Zeus sends a placating message to her through Rhea (Calasso 221). But the story has become watered down. These "Amazons" appear to behave more like nymphs. The teller of the tale does not emphasize the women's strength or their ability to fight as peers of men. The males have contact only with the women's leaders. These female leaders are often enchanting, feminine, and charming rather than strong and warrior-like. The literature of male-dominant culture has preserved these women as available to men. A substantive difference here is that peace rules rather than war, death, and disaster. The women have more magical powers than the men. They manipulate nature to get what they want.

But the Amazon queen is either black herself or has black servants. She also grants immortality not only through children but also through extended life. She manipulates nature supernaturally in a positive direction to protect her people. Hence, something positive remains. The seeds of the undated stories remained buried as culture transmitted the story west. Consequently, myth rarely associates these women who perform miracles by controlling nature with the bulk of historical Amazon material.

Early Twentieth-Century Thematic Adaptation

Partly in reactionist response to the political activism of suffragists in both the United States and England, Amazons entered the century in satirical forms, such as in Arthur Rinero's *Amazons: A Farcical Romance in Three Acts* (1902). However, more serious examinations of the Amazon archetype, image, and history subsequently began to appear. British scholar Guy Rothery (1910) wrote a survey compiling evidence regarding the myth of Amazons worldwide, through what he considered significant moments of world history.

Rothery aimed to bring to light the intriguing psychological aspect of Amazon women, which he felt other accounts obscured. Rothery saw the original warrior women as associated with female deities, comparing the Amazons to satyrs, man-bulls, and other monsters of Greek myth. Rothery argued that the origin of the myth was a "manless state" which developed when a poor group of women, deprived of their males, husbands, and children, were forced to become violent in revenge. He gave credence to the idea of matriarchal states only in his later chapters about the "women nations" of Europe during the Dark Ages.

Thus, according to Rothery, the extraordinary rage of widows and children created the first Amazons. The Amazons first fought the slayers of their husbands and fathers, and only later turned their wrath against men in general. Motivated by desperation and deprivation, rather than by their own strength, the Amazons founded a manless state. Then, Rothery contended, the Amazons developed as cannibalistic boy-killing savages who crippled the only men they kept around them. Rothery sketched the history of Amazons like this:

> Running through the works of Greek writers, we find a moving and circumstantial story of the rise and fall of a nation of women, who, having been deprived of their husbands, sons and brothers through the fortunes of battle, and then persecuted by the cruelty of their enemies, took up arms to avenge their wrongs. Thus having tasted blood, these women, we are told, acquired an unappeasable longing for the lust of carnage, and spurred on by the exaltation of victory, they decided to forswear the rule of man and become their own mistresses. Banishing, or mutilating, the few males left in their midst, they set about laying the foundations of a state . . . (23)

From here, according to Rothery, women eventually took the offensive. Such action led to constant reprisals. They organized their "manless state" on the footing of perpetual war, "which inevitably led to conquests beyond the original borders" (25).

Rothery's material is richly detailed. Yet, by and large he portrayed the Amazons as primitive and unevolved. By the time of the Homeric cycle, the women in Rothery's treatment get a touch of patriarchal normalization from the civilized Achilles. Achilles, after all, falls in love with the Amazon woman he has killed. Rothery asserted that she deserved her punishment and that Achilles killed her in self-defense. Nevertheless, in this moment, world history discovers the primitive warring savage woman as beautiful. From that point on, culture makers have tended to portray her as wounded and tender, in one way or another.

Rothery's chapters devoted to Amazons in Far Asia, the Caucasus, Europe, Africa, and America continue his original pattern of connecting Amazons with violent, vituperative, slaughter-dealing, monstrous, crude representations. For the most part, he depicted the Amazonian women as blood-curdling savages who drank from skulls, worshiped crocodiles, wore tortoise skins, adorned themselves with snakes, and practiced primitive matriarchal religions when not serving in harems or as women in militia battalions guarding either male or female chiefs of state.

Florence Mary Bennett's 1912 *Religious Cults Associated with the Amazons,* by contrast, viewed the Amazons as followers of the Great Mother, whom they revered (29). Bennett's argument—that the women who came to be known as Amazons were first associated with religious cults—appeared in an era when the pro-woman climate culminated in a victory for women's suffrage. The build toward equal voting rights included formation of the National Women's Party, efforts to ratify the right of female suffrage state by state, and mass weekly demonstrations across race and class in many major cities of the United States.

Bennett openly supported her basic thesis in these times of radical change for women. Later, the telling of history would project the original women upon other peoples and confuse them with warring women with whom the Greeks had come into contact. Bennett's scholarly work was of considerable repute, but she never mentioned the previous, charged use of the Amazonian concept in other contexts. Rather, she drew upon many classical writers, including Pindar, Pausanius, and Diodorus. They, too, saw the Amazons as worshipers of the Great Mother in various forms, such as the Phrygian Mother Cybele and Artemis of Ephesus (Tyrell 145 n.).

Jane Ellen Harrison (1850–1928) connected analysis of Amazons to questions of race, colonialism, and primitivism. Harrison, one of the first women students at Cambridge, spent most of her scholarly life there teaching classics. At Cambridge, she wrote her two great books on religion: *Prolegomena to the Study of Greek Religion* ([1903] 1962) and *Themis: A Study of the Origins of Greek Religion* ([1912] 1962). However, she found herself largely ignored in her own field.

Surmising that the mythological Amazons contained a memory of the Hittites of Asia Minor, whose societal structure was matrilineal, Harrison argued that this structure was substantively different from the descent patterns of Indo-European peoples. Her analysis held much significance for later feminists. She claimed that in Homer, the matrilineal peoples that Hera represented had different social customs than the patrilineal invaders who came down from the north.

Mary Daly, in *Gyn/Ecology: The Metaethics of Radical Feminism* (1990) would further relate Hera of the Greeks to the pre-Hellenic Triple Goddess, sometimes identified as Hera-Demeter-Kore, whom she located in both Libyan and Irish myth. In either case, Hera originally belonged to an epoch which did not recognize fatherhood (76). Daly would point to the forcible marriage of the Triple Goddess as one of the common means of legitimating the transition from gynocentric society to patriarchy, thus leading to the taking of Hera by Zeus, Demeter by Poseidon, and Kore by Hades. Others would then read the Greek "Hymn to Demeter" as Demeter's search for recognition and identity in a world of seemingly arbitrarily imposed male domination (Arthur 1977).

According to the reasoning Harrison's early work began, the Amazons represented only one aspect of pre-Homeric, pre-patriarchal peoples, or one way in which Greek myths represented those peoples. The tribes that went south (represented by Zeus) established the idea of the primacy of fatherhood and other various, imported social systems. They colonized the indigenous peoples, whose own social institutions were then hazily recorded in exotic, strange, distanced, and remote ways (491).

Harrison's contribution to Amazonism was obviously influenced by cross-cultural developments in the newly emerging field of anthropology in this period. She re-read the Greeks through their myths, characterizing them as a wild, conquering tribe with savage initiation rituals and cannibalistic practices, like many of the tribes being codified by the ethnographic fieldwork that went hand-in-hand with the colonialism of her time. This interpretation offended many in her own historical moment.

Tina Passman has argued that Jane Harrison "wrote like a dyke and lived like a dyke," as any lesbian could see. Passman argued that Harrison was the first woman with classical training and the status of an authority to indict patriarchy as a step backward in human development. According to Passman, Harrison "was also a foremother who used what would now be termed a 'Lesbian Perspective' to challenge the consensus reality. . . . In doing so, Harrison provided the perspective, background and language that contemporary radical feminisms have employed" (1993, 181). Only lately has Harrison been awarded long-overdue recognition for her development of the role of ritual in the treatment of myth, which gave rise to a whole new school of mythic interpretation (Ackerman 1991).

In contrast to the generally reclamationist treatment of the Amazon in social and historical thinking around the turn of the twentieth century, the Amazon was entering into public discourse to be embodied in literature in a reactionist way via the fiction of dominant culture. Perhaps reacting against the emergence of feminist consciousness, as women were fighting their way into arenas in which public meanings are defined, D. H. Lawrence depicted Clara, the "Amazon" character in *Sons and Lovers,* as quick to anger. Clara also favors women fighting for themselves. A socialist and a speaker for suffrage, she lives with her mother, not with her brutish husband.

Lawrence's narrator first refers to Clara as "the Amazon" because she is strong and can run. Yet in the course of the novel, Lawrence puts her back into the diminished, conquered place belonging to women. He showed her as helpless, in need of the powers of the character Paul to get her a job in a factory. Once employed, Clara obviously becomes Paul's favorite, and the other factory women, jealous, resent her. She develops no friendship ties with the other women (odd conduct, to say the least, for an Amazon). Clara is self-educated, most certainly a sign of the modern Amazon who wants to prepare herself to fight in a time when survival of the fittest no longer means strength in physical terms, but rather in intellectual terms.

Yet, in true reactionary manner, Lawrence portrayed her as wanting to submit, especially sexually, and as wanting to please men. By the end of the novel, the author reduced the so-called Amazon to begging the main male character to marry her. Finally, she returns to her brutish husband because of some inner, compelling need. Hence, Lawrence illustrated the classic reactionist plot line: a woman can try to be an Amazon, but because she is a woman first, she can be easily tamed again; ultimately she exists for men's wants and needs in patriarchal civilization.

By contrast, in Charlotte Perkins Gilman's *Herland,* written in 1915 as a feminist-utopian novel for her own small socialist publication for women, the word "Amazon" never appears. Nonetheless, Gilman was clearly drawing on the revolt aspect that Bachofen had outlined. She imaginatively created a country where virgins revolt against males, kill them, and survive by birthing only female children. Thus she was also drawing from one of the classical accounts of the origins of Amazons—Rothery's account, in which the manless nation is an "unnatural" outgrowth of the disaster of war.

Yet Gilman went beyond the concept of the individual woman removed from her own grouping. She set up the opportunity for an enclave of women to develop a society of their own. In her vision, men then visit that society, which has survived two or three thousand years. A group of male explorers hears legends told by natives about a "land of women," similar to the legends reportedly heard by the European colonizers of the Americas. The fictional explorers locate a civilization where women survive by themselves.

This concept—that of female nationalism—apparently derived from three sources. First, Gilman associated with the radical branch of suffragists. Second, Gilman's involvement with Lester Frank Ward (1841–1913), a pioneer in sociology and the first president of the American Sociological Society (in 1905), was a pivotal influence. Ward trained as a geologist and taught at Brown University. He believed that a scientifically modeled social science would educate people for intelligent action toward social reform (Ceplain 26–27). Gilman met Ward at the 1896 Women's Suffrage Convention, where participants debated Elizabeth Cady Stanton's *The Woman's Bible* ([1898] 1993) (Hill 1980, 264). Ward, who influenced Debs and Daniel DeLeon, was an advocate of a "gynaecocentric" theory that females were superior to males, arguing in rigorous scientific form that civilization had evolved from women (Ceplain 27). Gilman lavished public praise on Ward's theory in her reviews and lectures, and she herself took feminist stock of Darwin (Ceplain 28).

Third, Gilman read exhaustively on primitive culture (Kleinbaum 207–214). Gilman read on pre-historic civilization, the origin of the great eastern monarchies, and Edward Tylor's *Religion in Primitive Culture* ([1871] 1958), as well as Tylor's other works on the early history of the human race in his studies of ancient civilizations (Ceplain 1991, 12).

Gilman's *Herland* became a classic women's utopia novel, forming the first stepping stone to much feminist critical literature. Gilman's curious intellectual lineage allows us to trace one of the greatest ironies of intellectual history. That is, the impetus that led explorers to look for Amazons in the New World may have been a case of the projected return of the repressed "other," a concept analyzed by Michel de Certeau in *Heterologies: Discourse on the Other* (1986). Certeau has asserted that whatever we exclude or bury comes back to haunt us in bizarre, super-charged forms. Yet dialectically, later readings of those much-debated, word-of-mouth casual reports that passed through generations of historians' hands may have produced the very radical feminist material used in the first wave of feminism.

In Gilman's *Herland,* perhaps for the first time in the history of this genre of literature, rather than being wooed and swept off their feet by men, women do not reject their own society. Even though there is some intermingling between the visiting males and some of the women from Herland, the Amazons that Gilman created—but never named as such—remain firmly grounded in their own matriarchal norms.

With Her in Ourland ([1916] 1997) followed the first novel. One of the spouses of a woman from Herland takes her on a tour of the outside world.

There, her "naive" observations as a traveler across many borders constitute a radical social critique of early twentieth-century American sexism. Both books illustrate some of Gilman's own theories, which the cultural evolutionism of the era also influenced (see, e.g., *Women and Economics* [1898] 1966).

Between the Two World Wars

In the period between the two world wars, several theoretical interpretations of the Amazons emerged. These were aligned with social movements larger than movements for women's rights. In the United States, for example, Emanuel Kanter used the Amazons and the notion of pre-existing matriarchy which these women warriors seemed to have defended as a rallying point to attract working-class women to the proletarian labor movement.

In his *The Amazons: A Marxian Study* (1926), Kanter argued that originally, in primitive communal living conditions, egalitarian relations reigned and relations between the sexes were good. Then, he reasoned, with the accumulation of private property, men had a need to control their wives as heirs and hence started to control their wives as property.

Kanter drew this argument from the original statement by Frederick Engels in *The Origin of the Family, Private Property and the State* ([1884] 1972). Eleanor Leacock's introduction to the 1972 edition explains the ideological issues in the debates over the origins of women's oppression and the idealized notion of egalitarian society. The significance of this debate lasted throughout the 1970s feminist period (Sacks 1974), as once again women looked to the past for models as they struggled for cultural parity.

Kanter contended that women overthrew males and set up a women's state to escape slavery. Thus, the Amazons developed dialectically: they started their separate rule in defense against their exploitation as childbearers. Ruby Rohrlich, in her introduction to *Women in Search of Utopia: Mavericks and Myth Makers* (1984), stated Kanter's argument thus: "As the early class-stratified patriarchies emerged . . . as organic utopias were transformed into dystopias, women and men began their unceasing struggles to re-establish the former ways of life in new contexts—in communities separate from the mainstream" (xvi).

Rohrlich believes it likely that "the initial separatist societies were created by women who, refusing to submit to an unprecedented subjugation, escaped from patriarchies and formed homosocial communities which they defended by force of arms" (xvi). Irene Silverblatt, in *Moon, Sun and*

Witches (1987), found that this same logic applies to the dialectical development of the contemporary Amazon. She referred to the bands of women living in the Andean *puna* in South America who grouped together in response to the extremes of colonialism in Peru.

Modern Soviets later utilized Kanter's interpretation of the Amazons as an early women's liberation group. The state promoted a more progressive role model as a prototype for socialist women in order to bring about the transition to communism and to advance the role of the proletariat. Those bent on industrialization via the state idealized the Amazons because of their physical prowess. For example, the beautiful, strong, independent Elena Petushkova was a national hero—a champion affectionately referred to as "Amazonka" in the Soviet media and consequently by the public (Sobol 142).

During this same period between the two world wars, a time in which mainstream authoritarian nationalism was consolidating around the notion of "Fatherland," Robert Briffault wrote *The Mothers*. His book appeared in Switzerland in 1927, a year after Kanter published his book in the United States. Briffault explored the peasant worldview, one which looked upon physical facts differently than does modern discourse. For example, the book speaks of women's "moonblood," women's menstrual blood, which some peasants thought literally came from the moon. As art history reflects, at this time romantic primitivism and the rise of fascism clashed (Lloyd 1991). By applying critical analysis of folk and national consciousnesses as they interrelate (Fox), perhaps Briffault hoped to find a matriarchal soil upon which the flourishing nationalism for the fatherland could not take effective root (253–254), and hence, without naming them as such, Briffault conjured up the Amazons as well. In his reading of rituals such as how women presented marriage proposals in the tribes of Queensland (189), Briffault apparently laid a basis for resistance to the emerging patriarchal lines of fascistic, nationalistic leadership by re-discovering strong, assertive women.

In this era between the wars, too, the Amazon emerged in popular literary texts. She has thus influenced America as a metaphor quite removed from her original first-recorded appearances in Homeric texts. She is also cut off from a discussion of her real or projected meaning within her own preclassical Greek, historic time. For example, Inez Haynes Gillmore memorialized the Amazons in at least two texts, one from 1914 and the other from 1933. Gillmore was born in Brazil, where her parents had hoped to prosper as coffee exporters, but when these efforts failed, the family returned to Boston. Gillmore attended Radcliffe at the turn of the century and became active in the suffrage movement. She belonged to the advisory council of the National Women's Party. In 1914, before women in America had gained the vote, Gillmore published *Angel Island*. In this allegorical novel, a group of shipwrecked males capture winged women inhabiting a fictional, deserted island. The men tame the women, forcing them into motherhood.

In Gillmore's work, the word "Amazon" refers to the theoretical leader of the winged women. She leads them in revolt and encourages them first to walk and then to fly away with their children. This the women do under threat of having the men clip their daughters' wings, since they have already clipped the wings of the captured women. In the end, the Amazon character, too—the last of the women—agrees to marry and to have a baby. She dies in childbirth, her own clipped wings displayed on the wall over her head above her bed, but only after having given birth to the first winged male.

Gillmore's 1933 *Angels and Amazons: A Hundred Years of American Women* also uses the term "Amazons" beyond the context of the original Amazons who were peers of men and who frightened and attacked the Greeks. Gillmore used the name and notion to commemorate the first wave of staunch women's rights activists, such as Elizabeth Cady Stanton.

This general milieu also influenced Helen Diner, a Viennese intellectual. In the late 1920s she wrote a book that was eventually published in 1930, *Mothers and Amazons: The First Feminine History of Culture*. In her study *The War against the Amazons,* Abbey Kleinbaum credits *Mothers and Amazons* for taking great intellectual leaps for its time, yet upon its publication, scholars condemned the book, and the general public ignored it (214–216). In *Women in Greek Myth* (1986), Lefkowitz discussed what contemporary feminist classicists still see as shortcomings.

Yet most certainly the zeitgeist of the period between the two wars affected Diner more than scholarly standards. In this era of flappers, women traveled, smoked, drank, and wore dropped waistbands. They also underwent their own radicalizing psychoanalysis. Many participated in intellectual circles of their own making. Women in Europe experimented with new freedoms, as is evidenced in the short stories of American writer Djuna Barnes, such as those collected in *Spillway* (1923). Barnes' *Ladies' Almanack* (1928) presents her concept of an all-women's salon, an idea that she originally published in a stylized version earlier in the decade. Such documents attest to the supportive, counter-cultural environment in which Diner's book emerged as women struggled to find their own voices and to create new forms of expression.

Diner circulated her work *Mothers and Amazons* under the pseudonym Sir Galahad in English in the 1930s. She asked that her readers be ready, wild, able, and free to imagine what the world is like "in those areas where it is arranged by the woman, according to her nature to the exclusion of the male as a personality" (ix). Diner didn't want the Amazons used in the political polemics of others' political groupings, as Kanter did.

Interested in androgyny, Diner introduced various symbols as she sought to broaden the question of what is women's nature. She called the double ax "an androgynous symbol of all gynecratic nations," "the famous sagaris" (129). The ax is more often referred to as a "labyrus." It was actually a Minoan religious symbol associated with the Asiatic Mother of Cretan civilization, a symbol of the pre-Hellenic state (Bennett 28). Penthesilea later killed warriors at Troy with a labyrus, indicating the importance of such symbolic themes in discourse about Amazons.

Diner resurrected the mythological warriors in order to ponder how women could organize society differently than men. She asked this theoretical question at a point when the momentum of the feminist movement had foundered, having accomplished women's suffrage in most countries. At a time when most women were wriggling free of many of the strictures of the nineteenth century and heading toward modernity, Diner explored the question of what a society organized according to "women's nature" might be.

Her wording shows the obvious influence of anarchism, which was developing between the wars as a form of resistance to fascism, especially in Spain. She drew from words reminiscent of the growing heritage of subversion, defining Amazons as merely "a collective name for belligerent hordes of women with self-government . . ." (24). This loose definition allowed Diner a great deal of liberty with which to elaborate a pre-Greek view of the women of Lemnos, who were actually Aphrodite worshipers before they stepped into male-centered history.

Amazons existed around the peripheries of the Greeks. Yet Diner wrote that only bits and pieces of this woman-centered mother history come through the Greek records, like chips of broken plates. Diner reported that all of Attica used to commemorate festively the battle with the Amazons near Athens every year (120). Apparently, the tombs of Amazons lined the roads. According to Lysias, the real race of the Amazons was almost exterminated in an invasion, which is the reason for the tombs of these women in Greek lands. Florence Bennett, the classics scholar who in 1912 presented the Amazons' existence as fact, listed these tombs and locations as cited in classical texts of Plato, Plutarch, Homer, Strabo, Aristeas, and so on (7). The importance of these tombs, to which those who wish to substantiate or disprove the existence of the Amazons have given great attention, can be better under-stood in the context of Greek burial customs of the time (Kurtz and Board-man 1971). After all, scholars have discussed how the funeral practices of societies prior to Homer's era are represented in the epics, as well as those of the classical period. Pre-Homeric societies are also said to be cults of the dead. Furthermore, ancient Greeks stood in awe of their predecessors' monumental burial chambers and walled tombs, constructed to preserve as well as to shelter ritual offerings and votives. Some changes may have oc-curred in burial practices as people dispersed to refugee settlements after the Trojan War, which these scattered tombs might also represent if it were pos-sible to tell the entire story.

In addition to citing the tombs as evidence, Diner used analogies to na-tionalism to argue logically for the factual existence of the Amazons. Just as many used to celebrate the liberation of Germany from the Napoleonic yoke and the United States celebrates independence from England on July fourth, so the Greeks celebrated their independence from the terror of the Amazons by regularly re-enacting this fight. This "Amazonomachia," or depiction of the battle, still survives in the western wall of the Parthenon. The lost epic poem *Aithipois,* one of several composed in the seventh century B.C., is the first known literary rendering of the tale (Sobol 95).

In addition to pointing to the significance of this commemoration, Diner also touched upon some of the basic problems which occurred between the wars, such as the crumbling of empires and the maintenance of colonialism. As Diner pointed out, the Greeks, having heard of Amazons via Chinese annals as "a western women's kingdom" between the Black and Caspian Seas, eventually preserved mention by reporting battle with them in North Africa. In this indirect manner, some knowledge about Amazons of the far east was retained throughout the Middle Ages (27).

According to Diner, the Black Sea kingdom along the Thermodon River was more well known than the later Black African Amazon kingdom. These Amazon women survived by living on the steppes where the Greeks thought the world ended, bounded by the Urals. This was also the scene of the cre-ation of the Laura poems in Boris Pasternak's *Dr. Zhivago* (1991), a rough habitat of blizzards, bitter winters, cold winds, and deep snow.

Here, in Diner's account, evolution slowed down. The cold demanded the breeding of strong women, the Amazons. Bred in the inhospitable Thermo-don region, the Amazons were considered enemies of the griffins. The griffin, as Diner described it, "was the totem animal of the soil and represented the ancestral soil. . . . Whoever wanted to live there was to fight it" (13). Thus, a woman who could learn to live without protection was allowed to live "on the monstrous edge," or, if she could survive it, "on the climatic fringes."

Later arguments continued to reflect the concerns of the times. R. Hennig, a German, wrote in the 1930s, during a period of organized control of populations manipulated by a despotic ruler. He imagined that all the original Amazons and the subsequent women's countries, islands, and kingdoms that Muslim traders arriving in Northern Europe reported were actually female counterparts of "male only" islands, nations, and tribes (1940). He claimed that the sexes were kept separated so as to limit demographic growth, for conservationist reasons. His meticulous historical presentation is invaluable, yet he appears to have conjured up this conclusion by reasoning backward from insubstantial evidence, again merely projecting the spirit of his times.

A woman's psychoanalytic discussion published in 1942 when the terms and concepts of psychoanalysis were permeating popular culture and film reflected the growing public terror as new weapons of mass destruction took concrete form during the war. As Bernice Schultz Engle stated in "The Amazons in Ancient Greece," published in *Psychoanalytic Quarterly* in 1942, women riders in ancient civilizations, who terrified Greek men, were represented either as frightening manly warriors or as idealized Greek goddesses. Both representations of the female rider, she claimed, were defenses against the real fear—the orgiastic aspect of Great Mother practices that the Greek patriarchal religion was striving to replace.

According to his physician, Adolph Hitler also did battle with Amazons—at least in his dreams. Hitler allegedly dreamed of fighting a trio of naked Amazons riding through space, according to Kurt Krueger. In one of Hitler's dreams, he broke his spear against one of the Amazons in a vain attempt to kill her. He was sure that Amazons were really Jews, a group with whom Amazons had been connected in other contexts (Sobol 155 n.). The account of Hitler's Amazon dream might serve to illustrate the thesis that Amazons are projections of the fear of the powerful mother—whether an actual being or a social construct concretized in societal practices.

Thus it can be seen that the Amazon archetype evolved through World War II in popular culture, literature, and various forms of criticism in three modes: revivalist, revitalist, or reactionist. The next chapter discusses how these categories and trends continued into the post-war period.

TWO

Post-War Appearances

REVIVAL, REVITALIZATION, AND REACTION

After the war, post-war Americans turned inward to the privatization of the family. McCarthyism put a stranglehold on open political life. The political witch-hunt for "anti-American" communists shut off most avenues for open political protest, forcing many up against the "bedrock" of the self. As John Clellon Holmes articulated in a piece, "This Is the Beat Generation" ([1952] 1985), Beat writers were at the vanguard of this trend. Memoirs of the period, such as that of cultural and sexual experimenter Samuel R. Delany (1988), also exhibit the dialectic between political developments and cultural breakthroughs of the times. New trends in social thought emerged. These included psychologizing the world and the symbols, objects, and social relations within it as mere outer manifestations of inner life.

The Beats revolutionized the literary, political, and cultural scenes in many ways. However, although the literary and cultural movement they created in the 1950s has generally been thought of as progressive, the Beat writers were actually extremely reactionary in their attitudes toward women and sex roles. Misogynist imagery in the texts of Gregory Corso, Jack Kerouac, and Allen Ginsberg evidences this. Many remember Kerouac best for his numerous nirvana-is-a-good-woman-in-bed scenes (e.g., in *On the Road* [1957]). Gregory Corso, in *Elegiac Feelings American* (1961), discussed "Miss Christ" and the "hurricane cunt" in ways that would repel most 1990s females. Allen Ginsberg's *Collected Poems 1947–1980* consistently reveals women as psychotic, deranged, breeding machines—bitches and whores whose vaginas are nothing more than pig muscles in which to stuff money.

Remarks in memoirs and fiction by women who lived in the midst of the Beats further document such misogyny (Johnson 1983; H. Jones 1991; Cassady 1991). The proper role for a woman on the Beat scene was that of acquiescing girlfriend. As defined in *Kerouac and Friends* (McDarrah 1985), a Beatnik was a "lad" with girls following. John Clellon Holmes' *Go* ([1952] 1988) illustrated the perfect girlfriend, if only by default.

Not surprisingly, the Amazon was appropriated by the Beats in a reactionist way. Some women who crossed the male Beat norms were called "Amazon," an experience shared by women athletes today, for whom the epithet is often associated with homosexuality. In Kerouac's dream journal (1961), he recorded how Amazons haunted him in dreams. In his worst nightmares, Amazons danced rudely, pulling him from the audience and forcing him to have sex. Such a debacle haunted him even though his raison d'être in most of his life and the greater part of his fiction was approaching women sexually. If we are to believe Kerouac's prose (1957, 1958, 1960, 1966), he desired anonymous sexual encounters with many women, although in such encounters he was of course the sole initiator. Perhaps at night his soul performed the punitive displacement necessary to equalize matters for him, as his *Book of Dreams* suggests. Kerouac also suffered from anti-Semitism that interfered with his friendships at points of his life. It might be said then that scratch one vanguard male writer and you shall find the Nazi within, as both Kerouac and Hitler suffered from nightmares of Amazons and the realities of their own anti-Semitism.

Furthermore, Allen Ginsberg was notorious, as were all the male Beats, for expecting women to be available to provide him with housing "off the road." He came to rely on two tall midwestern women who roomed together, whom he referred to as "his Amazons." These women shared an apartment in New York City, which Ginsberg treated as an always-available open house for himself and his friends (Johnson 1983).

The two women were not one-breasted, virginal, or foul-smelling—all aspects that are associated with traditional Amazons in Greek literature. They did not carry battle axes. They did not fight with or kill men as most Amazons of antiquity apparently did. Yet in Ginsberg's appropriation of the Amazon archetype in relation to these women, he used some of the elements from the original Greek, including ferocity. Then he contained that ferocity. He is remembered for referring to them as "his big fierce Amazonian guardians" (Johnson 1983, 128). He thus granted them strength, but at the same time claimed them as a possession ("his" Amazons) and assigned them to the post of servants/watch dogs or gargoyles ("his . . . guardians"). They are strong but they are his. They are strong but their strength is harnessed for his personal use.

Ginsberg's use of the Amazon also illustrates another typical reactionist tendency—to apply it to women who in some way transgress the prevailing cultural norms of femininity.[1] His two "Amazons" committed the double transgression of being tall (not your diminutive Twiggy ideal) and of participating in a female friendship that outlasted the transient male use of their home for "support." The two women also both happened to be outlanders—they hailed from the Midwest—and to resemble each other in both looks and habits. Both were boyish. Both participated in psychoanalysis. These, then, were the women Ginsberg called "his" Amazons. Both the possessive pronoun and the semi-mythical namesake, in this context, diminished the women as autonomous entities, calling attention to their outsider status as well as consigning them to the limited sphere of functioning as his personal servants (guards).

Other Beat writers sought the image of the outstanding, withstanding, or returning matriarchy, if however strangely. For example, the twentieth-century American writer William Burroughs conjured up his own vision of matriarchy in *Naked Lunch* (1959). In this text, Burroughs construed matriarchies not as strongholds of female power, but as "isolated groups, like natives of the Bismarck Archipelago." He imagined that all matriarchies are "anti-homosexual, conformist, and prosaic." "Find yourself in a matriarchy," Burroughs warned, and "walk don't run to the nearest frontier" (29).

Burroughs dreamed of overcoming police and other non-liberating aspects in his world of cafes and addicts. Yet in the matriarchies that his anti-utopian anti-hero visits, he is warned that if he runs, a latently homosexual cop suffering from frustration will probably shoot him. Margaret Mead not withstanding, the place is really just another "matriarchy"—another bastion of enforced homogeneity like western Europe and the United States.

Thus, Burroughs' view of a developing pocket of matriarchy, or of a matriarchy evolving in the future, is no "haven." Clearly, his work projects the anti-homosexual attitudes of the closeted American fifties by imagining that "queers" would not be allowed and that a matriarchy would police gays.

Some theorists suggest that until the need to prove progeny arose, societies accepted a variety of sexual arrangements. Burroughs' matriarchies fit right in with how Susan Wood (1978/1979) and Sarah Lefanu (1989) argue that males create worlds of women-without-men desperate for the order of hierarchies. Thus men create matriarchies as vicious, static, crumbling societies, prone to disintegrate from within.

In this era as well, Joseph Campbell, a disciple of Carl Jung, reintroduced the concept of the Great Mother into American intellectual life through his voluminous compilations of world mythologies. The Great Mother concept itself has its own separate history that is not always linked to Amazons. This history is also clearly distinguishable from contemporary feminist uses.

In 1901, Grant Showerman was an instructor in Latin writing, philology, and literature. He argued that the Sibylline Books emanated from the vicinity of Mount Ida, thus introducing the Great Mother to the west well after the Homeric period. Showerman did not depict the Great Mother as a deity who was crushed by the emergence of patriarchy. Rather, born in a chariot drawn by oxen bedecked with flowers, she was "Mother of the Gods, Great Mother, Mistress of All, Mother of All Blest, Mother of All Gods and of All Men, All-nourisher, All-begetter . . . Mother of Zeus himself" (234). Except for the last characteristic, this description of the Great Mother fits almost precisely the image projected in the chants to the Virgin of Immaculate Conception on Isla Mujeres, as we shall see in a later chapter. Showerman claimed that it was upon this Asiatic mother figure originally from Asia Minor that the Greeks projected Rhea, their own "ill-treated mother of Zeus" (230).

Perhaps unconsciously, Campbell's move to revive such a concept at this particular moment was subtly interconnected with the "mom-ism" of the 1950s. The prevailing ideology of "mom-ism" encouraged women to identify themselves primarily through their "all-powerful" mother role, which was their only route to any power whatsoever. Campbell himself then attracted followers: the many women scholars and intellectuals eager to see any manifestation of the feminine receiving scholarly attention at all.

Learning to live with the threat of the atomic bomb that emerged in the Second World War created a generation of people forced to confront their greatest fears. Some of the appearances of the Amazon from this period reflect these fears. For example, in Aldous Huxley's *Island* (1962), the Amazon entered the decade of the sixties as a withering embodiment of mutilation and death. Huxley's strong woman character becomes an Amazon when a doctor cuts off her breast in cancer surgery, deforming her.

Given such rising fears and a new consciousness of mortality as a result of the war and the weapons employed, it is no surprise that psychoanalytic studies emerged in many arenas in this era. Wolfgang Lederer published a popularly read psychoanalytic study which attributes the existence of Amazons to a deep-seated inner fear of women that males have due to the castration complex, which haunts them throughout life. In Lederer's *The Fear of*

Women (1968), battle with the Amazons looms pivotal in the development of the male hero. Lederer showed how the hero shifts from being he who overcomes his fear of the vagina to being the great man who overcomes his fear of the vagina, destroys the fierce rule of women, and establishes the rule of men. Lederer felt that in facing the one-breasted Amazon, men also faced their castration anxiety. Also, to Lederer, the fear of menstrual flow and pregnancy which could "infect the neighbors" (32) was the basis for the evil odor supposedly emanating from the Amazon women on the isle of Lemnos. Despite Lederer's deep over-psychologizing, he reported that as late as 1966 the San Francisco papers contained an article about an Amazon tribe discovered in Australia. He still saw a sexual/erotic symbolism in the Amazon's love-object mount as played out by little girls' pleasure in the feminine sport of horseback riding (103).

Philip Slater's *The Glory of Hera*, also published in 1968, relates the appearance of Amazons in Greek texts not only to the castration complex, but also to the general problems of the Greek mother-son relationship. This relation of mother to son was the primary subject of Slater's work. Slater explained the contradiction that while Greek women were legal non-entities and were powerless in this period, they figured largely in Greek plays. To Slater, this disproportionate appearance resulted from women's near total responsibility in the raising of the boys who later became the men who wrote the plays. Sometimes resorting to case studies of contemporary patients to prove his points, Slater argued that males develop a terror of women that forces them to reduce the females to low status. The two aspects are then mutually reinforcing, he suggested. Slater also supported this thesis by citing Herodotus' description of the Athenians' resentment that a woman, Artemesia, "not even an Amazon" (10), could command a ship against them. That they offered a reward for her live capture, Slater contended, substantiates the Athenian belief that women's place was in the home.

Revival, Revitalization, and the Second Wave

Throughout the 1950s, institutions of dominant culture promoted limitations on women's roles within the privatization of the nuclear family. In conjunction with a developing psychoanalytic dismissal of women's suffering, the promotion of domesticity led eventually to the emergence of the women's movement. Many accessible accounts, both personal and scholarly, exist of the initial movement growing out of spontaneous accumulated guerrilla acts. These accounts are replete with explanations of the congruence of the many factors which led to such an outburst (Mitchell 1972; Koedt, Levine, and Rapone 1973; Echols 1989). Various authors have discussed a range of factors that include the anti-war and civil rights movements. Many credit Betty Friedan's *The Feminine Mystique* (1963) with being the first cogent statement of the previously unidentified, unnamed problem which led to the revolt.

Sylvia Plath was a key figure because she showed the silent suffering of a character who lived in an era before the women's liberation movement had adequately articulated the problems of women within the culture. In *The Bell Jar* (1971), Plath's protagonist experiences her liberating revolt against patriarchal culture by throwing her clothes off the roof of the Hotel Amazonia, where she is staying with other young women experiencing New York City as guests of a major women's magazine (Wagner-Martin 1992).

Many American second-wave writers subsequent to Plath enthusiastically seized upon Amazon myths, texts about matriarchal origins, and similar stories to revitalize the spirit of women. In Ruby Rohrlich and Elaine Hoffman Baruch's *Women in Search of Utopia* (1984), Sally Gearhart, herself a writer in this genre, commented on this phenomenon, discussing some of the futuristic visions that emerged during this period. Jessica Salmonson, another creator in this mode, collected many of these Amazon pieces and published them in popular collections brought out by a mainstream publisher of science fiction and fantasy (1979, 1981). Salmonson eventually put together an entire volume titled *The Encyclopedia of Amazons* (1992). Her work indicates the popularity of the topic of women warriors from antiquity to the modern era.

One of the earliest re-emergences of Amazonism as a reclaimed symbol of the modern women's movement came from the pen of the Spanish communist writer Carlos Alonso del Real. Perhaps influenced by the French Revolution, he saw Amazons as hailing from a society of equal rights. Perhaps he was also influenced by the same force that was pushing toward the outburst of the second wave.

In his *Realidad y Leyenda de las Amazonas* (1967), published in Madrid, Real questioned the notion of a linear development of culture, yet argued that a kernel of truth existed in the Amazon legends throughout history. Searching to identify the beginning of "amazonism," Real attempted to determine how long this phenomenon had existed before it became popularized. Real asserted that, at least, gynecratic societies with equal rights had existed in which women possibly fought side by side with their male comrades in some capacity, much as many women were being asked to fight alongside male comrades in the emerging movements of social protest and political unrest that arose in the 1960s.

The ongoing anti-war movement had become international when Real wrote. Perhaps under this influence, Real stressed that the Amazons' first resort was to attempt peaceful negotiations. He felt that the women's groups portrayed in classical representation were cooperative rather than war-like, and that betrayal and subsequent battle only transpired after other means had failed.

Real documented this process carefully and meticulously. In the end, he drew from evidence that Soviet archeologists had recently uncovered, including tombs of warrior women buried with horses and spears that they had discovered between Stalingrad and the Urals. Real suggested that these graves reflected the orientation of the early Indo-Europeans toward the seat of Chinese culture, where perhaps the original displaced Amazons had laid the basis for the early Chinese, pre-Confucian matriarchy. According to Real, the graves indicated that at least some of these women were not able to arrive at their eastern goal. Moreover, he argued that they seemed different from the surrounding people of this time zone, tracing Amazons once again to their origin at the confrontation between two cultures.

Real's presentation is really a theory of Diaspora to the East, supported by the Soviet archaeologists he utilized. Yet other theorists have marked the path of the Amazons westward through India, the Middle East, or even Asia before interfacing with the western-oriented Greeks. Real also supported his view by citing paleo-Siberian, Finnish, and Northern Danish folklore (212).

Donald Sobol (1972) argued that Soviet archaeologists further appropriated such discoveries by chauvinistically claiming that even the original Amazons were part of their national heritage. The Russian magazine *Science and Life* explained that ancient writers did not invent Amazons, but that Amazons had actually lived thousands of years ago on the slopes of the Urals.

Sobol pointed out that the Soviet historian K. Smirnov traced the Amazons back to the shipwreck Herodotus described that stranded women who then intermingled with the Scythians. The point was that these women then developed into a minority ethnic group dwelling in the North Caucasus (142). They could also have developed into the Russian "wild women" in lore Campbell described. They stalked the woods, posed as beautiful women, married men, disappeared when crossed, and otherwise terrified Russian peasants (1949, 79).

On the other hand, some writers interpreted the same stories in different contexts, such as the contemporary questionings of sexual evolution, male violence against women, and the nature of sexuality. Writers using themes such as these expanded the contexts well beyond inherited polemical political frameworks. They often came from non-scholarly, non-traditional, non-professional arenas. For example, Elizabeth Gould Davis, a librarian from Kansas, felt compelled to write a book, *The First Sex* (1971). Her work aptly documents the reclamationist spirit of her times. She declared that the Amazons in the early myths pointed to a reality outside the textual walls. She argued convincingly that her readers might consider the possibility that women were the first sex—that women had existed before men. Men, she claimed, evolved as later developments.

Davis drew her theories about the possibility of asexual reproduction by females, or parthenogenesis, from biology. Parthenogenesis ranked as an important issue to many feminist theorists and writers of the time. The same had been true for Gilman's *Herland* toward the beginning of the twentieth century, as well as for nineteenth-century American utopian fiction.

Simone de Beauvoir's *The Second Sex*, first published in 1952, contains a section entitled "Destiny" that similarly opens with a discussion of biology. In this remarkable chapter, de Beauvoir asked her readers to imagine a parthenogenetic or hermaphroditic society, claiming that sexual differences are not necessary for reproduction.

This discussion obviously impacted Davis. The latter's title, *The First Sex*, reformulated de Beauvoir's. Jill Johnston also explored the theme of parthenogenesis in *Lesbian Nation: The Feminist Solution* (1974). The notion is even discernible in ancient Greek material, as when Hesiod's Mother Earth reproduces parthenogenetically.

Davis argued that the original constitution of the human was male and female in one body, as all embryos begin as female. She contended that the "first males were mutants, freaks produced by some damage to the genes caused perhaps by disease or radiation bombardment by the sun" (35). According to David Hartwell (1984), books about mutants were popular in the 1960s when Davis was first actively researching and thinking. Science fiction begins with the idea of "cosmic men"—or actual mutations of the species—as an emergent race of cosmic, thinking people.

Davis used symbolism from classical Greek writings to support her interpretation of males evolving as mutants. In particular, she drew upon what she called Plato's "race memory" of the time of the original separation between the sexes. "Race memory" was also a popular concept at the time Davis wrote. Immanuel Velikovsky's discussion of "inherited unconscious memory" also evidences this idea (1982, 30–35). Davis used such ideas in her interpretation of the separation of the male-female single beings who broke into two halves, one male and the other female, as Plato had described in his *Symposium.*

Donald J. Sobol's 1972 *The Amazons of Greek Mythology* popularized and revived the old Amazon legends. The work collects all the sources in the classics. Sobol, a journalist, then reweaved a telling of the Amazon chronicles that was all his own. He constructed a linear narrative of the two main contending Amazon factions—those from the Black Sea and those from Libya. Both contingents, he argued, were really just equidistant from the center of the map—Greece—as drawn by writers such as Herodotus in the ancient world.

Other scholars have written books about the differences in representation between early Amazons and late Amazons in Greek culture. To them, Sobol's attempt would seem questionable. Yet Sobol presented dissenting views in lengthy, elaborate footnotes. Hence he provided a chronological lineage of development that could not have been compiled in any other effective way due to the fragmentary nature of the texts that have survived the centuries. The surviving texts from which he drew represent only a minuscule fraction of what each author had written within each period. Furthermore, Sobol distinguished two elements—the all-female community and women warriors. He pointed out that throughout history, the one concept "Amazon" has contained, condensed, and confused these two components (119–120).

Also, as Sobol himself noted, none of the ancient chroniclers told the history of the Amazons in its entirety. Each related merely the part which held special interest for him and dismissed the rest. As Sobol concluded, the Amazonian legacy has been scattered piecemeal throughout many texts and many generations. Occasional shut-downs of pagan schools exacerbated this problem. For example, Emperor Justinian closed pagan schools by decree in 529 A.D. (94). Thus, the experience of reading the remnants of remaining texts, which are fragments from different authors who lived in different periods, can be like looking at a statue of a figure missing an arm and at another statue of the same figure with a chipped nose, when they were forged four hundred years apart. One can only conjecture about the missing pieces of each body. Hence, much room remains for substantial differences in interpretation of the life of the Amazons.

Sobol extended his arguments considerably beyond common understanding of Amazonian myth, saga, or legend of the ancient Greeks. For example, in tracing the Amazons to the worship of the Asiatic goddess Ephesus, Sobol described female armed ministers working under a high priestess, to whom they refer as "queen bee." While the priestess of Artemis continued to be called a "bee," Sobol reminded us that Deborah, or Bee, was the name of one of the greatest prophets of ancient Israel. Thus Sobol suggested that in looking at the Amazons, American readers might be confronting their own Judeo-Christian past, rather than just looking at a wild breed representing barbarianism to the old Greeks (138).

Sobol also provided a useful summary of the various theories on Amazonism current at the time. One theory states that the Amazons were women who fought with men (as originally argued by Procopius of Caesarea) and that they were probably of the Sabiri Hungarian or Cimmerian tribes. Some Greek historians took the Cimmerian women to be the archetype of the Amazons. They spread out over Asia in the early seventh century B.C. However, if the Amazons really were Cimmerian women when the Priam presented in the Homeric materials remembers the Amazon attack, he would have been "remembering" an event still six hundred years in his own future, unless, following a theory of Real's, the poets of the *Iliad* were incorporating events of their own time into poetry inherited from the past.

Other theories, according to Sobol, attempt to "explain away" Amazons. One relates the stories of women fighters to forms of military organization and to the effects of war rather than to a possible autonomous existence of any integrity. Some say that the Amazons were really a handful of Scythian women serving as auxiliaries. Others argue that when Taunasis, king of the Goths, invaded and conquered Egypt, the Gothic women he left behind organized themselves into a war community and spread across Asia as the Amazons (Sobol 155–156 n.).

Finally, the main idea that Sobol presented holds more interest in light of women's subsequent positive reclamation of the legends. He explored the claim that the priestesses' war dances had given rise to the story of the nation of women practicing warlike exercises. Florence Bennett had presented a similar idea in 1912 with her assertion that the Amazons were priestesses of the Great Mother (113–147). And, in the late nineteenth century, A. H. Sayce had proposed that the armed priestesses of Asiatic goddesses in the Ma cult had set a model for the Amazons via contact with the Hittites. However, both Sobol (139) and Bennett (74) asserted that the idea of armed priestesses was doubtful, as no record of them was ever found.

Elizabeth Gould Davis was not alone in aiming to revitalize what had been said or done before. As more non-polemical sources like Sobol and Campbell made available images of Amazons and positive icons of female strength, more active revitalization began to occur. Contemporary revivalists began reclaiming an image created by men in which women were castrated, or one of their breasts was cut off so that they could fight like men.

In the early part of the second wave of the American feminist movement, Florence Rush's story, "The Parable of Mothers and Daughters," appeared in Phyllis Birkby's *Amazon Expedition* (1973, 4–10). Rush used the past garbled images of mutilated women cut up by man's fearful fantasies to create the women anew. She completely reversed the inherited image, presenting women as half-castrated men or as eunuchs. Rush began with a romantic vision of many years ago, when the world was new, when there were rivers, trees, plants, birds, animals, and people.

Rush, like others who romanticized the wild during periods of cultural crisis (Dudley and Novak 1972), posited an organic, back-to-nature "order of things" in this short piece, which was published at a time when lesbians within the Gay Liberation movement were first synthesizing gay politics with feminism.[2] In Rush's wild, anti-civilization, pre-cultural world, there were hardly any differences among people, except that there were many little people. The narrative voice calls everyone "she."

Rush imagined that everyone got to do what he or she wanted on the days when the group procured more than enough to eat for all. "One who liked music would sing and make sounds with sticks, shells and water while another made pictures in the sand or made images of birds on a smooth rock" (4). However, even though all the work was equally shared, somebody proposed that those who had breasts were better able to do the feeding and should take the entire job.

Rush related how the "breast-people" welcomed this change. Freed from hunting and gathering, they could look around their world for a better way to live. And then:

> One day the breastless ones noticed that the breast-people were getting strong and skillful and growing so much food that hunting and gathering became no longer necessary. . . . The difference and the progress of the breast-people so startled and frightened the breastless ones that they pondered for a way to overcome this fear. So the breastless ones contrived to have control over those they feared and they committed the first crime—they took possession of the lives of the breast-people and the little ones, robbed them of all they created and produced, took away their freedom and made them slaves. (5)

Thus, Rush reclaimed wild nature with her own unique perceptions, becoming a "contemporary revitalist." This category revives the historical, but also infuses new symbolic meanings. To Rush, imagistic glimpses through myth to a possible past laid the basis for hypothesizing a new reason for the current state of civilization. In this case, that reason was male jealousy of the female-centered culture that had developed around suckling the infant at the breast.

In the 1970s her statements seemed radical. However, by the 1990s, even mainstream paleontologists such as Robert Leakey were drawing conclusions supporting the radical assertions that had seemed like overstatements in the movement's earlier days (Leakey and Lewin 1992). We can only conjecture that these original ideas from within the early women's movement influenced establishment scholars. Other factors might have been subsequent feminist scholarship, the arrival in classes of students who asked questions and did research based on movement ideas, and the general spirit of the times.

Rush's parable is clearly a conceptual play on the inherited trope rather than a revived rendition of something from the past. Later, the movement claimed the one-breasted Amazon as an image that represents women's freedom to choose whether or not to nurture. The icon was valorized for placing limits on the otherwise ever-available breast. But at that time, a one-breasted woman appeared as the galvanizing female of subsequent patriarchal myths.

This could be interpreted as a reaction against women's original source of strength, derived from her capacity to provide the infant's only source of nurturance. After all, while breast-feeding infants, women establish a bonding that is so powerful that it frequently needs to be controlled (Maher 1992; R. A. Lawrence 1985; Palmer 1988). In fact, in Rush's contemporary revitalist myth, she hypothesized that the nursing imprint could have been the basis for the evolution of civilization. Campbell (1964) suggested that suckling at the mother's breast leaves an imprint on the human psyche secondary only to that of being in the womb.

Yet, many significant contemporary revitalists unquestioningly claimed the myth of the Amazon as a social charter for a new society. A salient example is Ti-Grace Atkinson's *Amazon Odyssey* (1974). This collection of early speeches and writings by a major early theorist established a position for the matriarchalists within the radical feminist movement. Furthermore, in the same volume in which Rush's parable appears (Birkby 1973), Jill Johnston's essay, "Return of the Amazon Mother," compares the situation of the young Amazons and the young Gargarensians frolicking for two months in the mountains to the situation of modern Amazons.

By "modern Amazons," Johnston was referring to the "lesbians with or without children" who were dealing with the problems of confronting the state at a gay activist center in New York, where she was writing. Drawing from Diner's *Mothers and Amazons,* she asserted that Amazon daughters had played a crucial role in the transition from matriarchies to patriarchies. She claimed, "No doubt we are presently at a juncture in history in which the Amazons return to perform a similar function as the transition is reversed" (68). Johnston first began to develop this idea when she participated in an early panel on lesbian mothering. She continued in her subsequent *Lesbian Nation* (1974).

Johnston felt that she was pushed to the limits of her creativity when she was active in the Beat scene, which attracted her with its avant garde energy and collective creativity. As she spent time in that culture, however, she gradually became aware of the misogyny at its core, discovering that she was not driven, for example, by the need to go to Mexican whorehouses, as Jack Kerouac was; rather, she was driven by her own female-centered needs, such as the need to discover the Amazon within herself. *Lesbian Nation* documents her process largely through reprinted columns from the *Village Voice.*

Johnston argued polemically that the Amazons were real, claiming that the received image of the Amazons as "warrior tribes akin to head-hunting cannibals" (260) was false. Rather, she asserted, Amazons lived in "fugitive matriarchies" (261). "Clearly the matriarchies were under siege," Johnston wrote. Furthermore, she argued, ". . . large numbers of women removed themselves from the immediate sites of their dissolution under pressure from the males to usurp their matriarchal prerogatives and formed independent exclusive communities" (261).

By the end of the decade, Evelyn Fisher (1979) was arguing, in support of Johnston, that women had been forced to live separately from men to prevent the men from eating the young. She asserted that male cannibalism had forced prehistoric women into a self-preserving separatism (see also O'Brien 1981 and de Beauvoir [1952] 1978). Fisher reasoned that the "Amazon solution" was an extreme reaction to the violence that was "the prime mode of change in the patriarchal revolution" (261) She also surmised that the Amazons had thrived quite happily apart from the male oppressor, and that "Lesbianism among Amazons was entirely suppressed in male history."

Support for this idea comes from the vast literature documenting male homosexuality in the ancient world. According to the psychoanalytic critic Slater (1968), the available sources indicate that physical homosexuality was widespread and generally accepted in Greece. Throughout society during the classical period, homosexuality competed on an equal footing with heterosexuality (10). Indeed, as Slater pointed out, Apollo had nineteen homosexual lovers.

Slater connected the predominance of male homosexuality—even among the gods—to the apparent dominance by the mother that the Greek civilization was trying to overcome, a thesis Hans Licht also discussed in *Sexual Life in Ancient Greece* (1963) and from which Slater's numerical assessments come.

Many other critics and scholars later documented the homosexuality of the Greeks, and some have discussed lesbianism. For instance, in *The Marriage of Cadmos and Harmony* (1993), Robert Calasso wrote that Spartan women were lesbian before marriage and that they trained to fight and carry swords (261–262). They trained in gymnasium, talked back to men about sexual objectification, and in other ways consistently indicated a lesbian posture and point of view.

Eve Cantarella, an Italian feminist classics scholar, devoted a whole chapter of *Pandora's Daughters* (1987) to homosexuality and love, claiming that Greeks considered homosexuality normal. In addition, Paul Friedrich explored the meaning of lesbianism in Lesbos society and life in his discussion of Aphrodite (1978). In Lesbos, groups of women artists mingled together before marriage, creating a women's culture just as Greek male homosexual youths created a male culture. Members of both these single-gender groups married later. Yet, the interim culture remained significant throughout life (117).

Nonetheless, Johnston's proof for her own assertions is not based on such historical reasoning or research. Nor did she conduct an exhaustive examination of the classics. Rather, she drew upon a concept that Davis also suggested—the experience of "cell memories." The cell memory idea is really Jungian. As Esther Harding explained in *The Way of All Women: A Psychological Interpretation* (1934), Jung theorized that "when a human being explores the hidden depth of his own psyche he finds primordial images, *pictures of racial experience,* archetypes, ancient powerful forces which have influenced his character and actions all unseen and unknown" (26; emphasis added). Johnston's argument was influenced by this concept of cell memory even though the idea that we all hold pictures of primordial experience in our cells might be questionable to many. She wrote: "Any proud contemporary lesbian would scoff at the idea that these independent tribes of women did not enjoy each other apart from their well known annual custom of descending on the male tribe for purposes of reproductive copulation" (262).

Like Johnston, Susan Cavin represented the Amazons as historical proof that the human race as we know it today hailed initially from lesbian origins (1985), drawing the strength of her conviction from other work that continues in the same vein as that of Elizabeth Gould Davis. For example, Laurel Holliday, in *The Violent Sex* (1978), stated the idea that maleness is a recessive genetic trait like color blindness and hemophilia, what Davis referred to as an accidental mutation that brought no good to the human race. She offered as evidence genetic research proving that some killers possess not one but two Y chromosomes. Thus, Holliday concluded, these criminals bore "a double dose, as it were, of genetically undesirable maleness" (35). Portions of this idea—that men were mutants and that the origin of the human race was entirely female—appeared in some of the early issues of *Amazon Quarterly*. This cutting-edge journal also published early writers such as Jane Rule, Barbara Freeman, Judy Grahn, Susan Griffin, Audre Lorde, Joan Larkin, Adrienne Rich, Jan Clausen, and Ruth Mountaingrove in the second wave's beginning years.

In her chapter "Amazon Origin Theories," Cavin documented the concept of all-female societal origin as widespread cross-culturally, across five continents. She enumerated various patriarchal theories which dismiss this evidence, such as the idea that these women were "beardless male warriors" mistaken for women, an idea that comes to us through the classics, as evidenced in Herodotus.

Cavin argued that societies which commemorated the defeat of Amazons, or the male victory over women, were societies which had "experienced the historical transition from gynosociety at origin to patriarchy, in their own geo-cultural evolution" (66). She claimed that modern patriarchal history omits Amazons because patriarchal society is *founded on the defeat of Amazons, the defeat of women*" (67).

Cavin theorized that reports of Amazons portray in actuality a high female-male ratio. She argued that sociologically, the term "Amazon" is socially coded. Cavin sketched parallels between patriarchal literature and ideology on other "mannish women" such as lesbians, whose existence is also often denied. She concluded that the origin of many forms of "gynosociety are either Amazon or lesbian society, or both" (75).

Alix Kate Shulman, an early novelist in the second wave of the American feminist movement, revitalized Amazons in a completely different although still dynamic manner. In Shulman's first novel, *Memoirs of an Ex-Prom Queen* (1972), Sasha, the young third-generation Jewish-American protagonist, is the female equivalent of Philip Roth's Portnoy in *Portnoy's Complaint* (1968). She is at the same time the Jewish equivalent of Molly in Rita Mae

Brown's *Rubyfruit Jungle* (1973). Coming of age in America, Sasha struggles through personal chaos. In the absence of non-assimilationist role models, she clings vainly to quotations from books by white men in the dominant culture. These texts include Henry James' *The Portrait of a Lady* (1882); romantic transcendentalist philosophical tracts by Emerson and Thoreau; and finally, instructions for mothers in a popular book by Dr. Spock. To the end, Sasha, the central character, remains oppressed in a cycle of repetition which finally leads to despair.

However, in Shulman's second novel, *Burning Questions* (1978), the same sort of young female protagonist clings instead to quotations from Russian revolutionary women such as left-wing socialist leaders Vera Zasulich and Alexandra Kollontai. For this second protagonist, "Amazons" are these women who led the way by being active in progressive political struggles in late nineteenth-century and early twentieth-century Europe. Taking her inspiration from these strong women, the protagonist turns to involvement in the women's movement. She marches down Fifth Avenue, leaves her husband, and becomes a speaker and teacher. The FBI even follows her.

In this context, then, the word "Amazon" entered American popular culture as a revitalizing code word that accompanied the development of the second wave of American feminism. Nonetheless, as Kleinbaum notes, the mid to late twentieth-century community of gay women, in particular, claimed the image of the Amazon as its own. This is in spite of what Kleinbaum identifies as the "rationalization and co-optation of the Enlightenment philosophers, the exorcism of the nineteenth-century social scientists, and the historical explanations of twentieth-century thinkers" (2).

In the movement in which Shulman's second protagonist becomes active—and in the midst of which Shulman herself wrote—women founded a bookstore in Minneapolis called "The Amazon Bookstore." A woman singer made a recording called "Amazon," an ode to all famous female athletes, which played first on underground and then on public radio. Just a few years earlier, in *Sexual Politics*, Kate Millett had examined previous uses of the Amazon in her analysis of Tennyson's *The Princess*. Later, Lillian Faderman, in her anthology of lesbian literature, would categorize the lesbian feminist writers of the seventies as "The Amazons."

Perhaps de Beauvoir's *The Second Sex* started this second-wave trend of dissociating the concept of Amazon from the original classical texts. Drawing from D. H. Lawrence's creation of a female focused on the use of the male purely for procreative purposes, de Beauvoir developed the prototype of "maternal minded Amazons"—women who light up "at a man that seems like a good begetter—a mature, independent woman who wants a child belonging wholly to herself" (552). De Beauvoir envisioned a "mature independent woman" prototype who looks for a begetter for a child the woman will raise herself. *The Second Sex* characterizes this particular constellation of a woman seeking freedom from patriarchal norms—as Paul's mother does in *Sons and Lovers*—as an "Amazon character." Thus de Beauvoir imaginatively reappropriated the Amazon from Lawrence's reactionist portrayal of her. This image of the independent mother was not, of course, the only element of the Amazon archetype that de Beauvoir explored. In her more traditional ethnographic section, which precedes the imaginative, literary one, she also took note of the significance of the accounts of the Amazons of Dahomey and the tales of Herodotus, which emphasize the war-like aspect of the Amazon (70).

De Beauvoir's use of the Amazon archetype no doubt influenced many later feminist theorists. For example, Sarah Hoagland called for "Amazon caring," a new value which appeared in this period, in her *Lesbian Ethics* (1988). This Beauvoirian echo extended even beyond theorists. "Amazon" has also come to mean "female cross-dresser" (Wheelwright 1989) and "the first female player to break into a sport which was previously all male" (Birdwell 1980).

Wherever the tendency started, some of the earliest writing in the North American second wave of organized ideological feminism was first printed in the journal called *Amazon Quarterly*, the same journal that published the early statements of the theory that men are mutants who evolved after the female origin of the species. This earliest writing included chapters of Rita Mae Brown's *Rubyfruit Jungle* (1973), the now-classic working-class lesbian coming-of-age novel.[3]

Furthermore, Amazons began appearing repeatedly in different forms in the period's science fiction. Kathleen Cioffi classifies this vast terrain of literature into three types: Amazon literature, in which individual heroines are extremely strong and have "psi" (psychic) powers that make them invincible; apocalyptic stories of worlds without men, in which the individual heroine does not matter as much as the type of post-disaster/holocaust women's society that emerges; and bildungsromans, in which an individual heroine again goes through a series of adventures that make her whole rather than a half-distorted, fe/male person (1985, 83–90).

The Amazon also appeared in popular culture in such forms as *Wonder Woman*, a 1974 (McKeveety) film which opens on Paradise Island. Only women inhabit the island, including an Amazon princess who leaves to help in the war against the Nazis, much as we will see later in Montalvo's romance, in which Queen Calafia leaves her island to help the Christians in their war against the pagans.

Moreover, many feminist utopias were popular in the 1970s, such as Joanna Russ' *Female Man* (1972). Russ' central character comes from a world in the future where all men have died. Marion Zimmer Bradley's "Free Amazons" on the planet Darkover (1972, 1985b) are also in this mode. Bradley presented a nucleus of sane women on the imaginary Darkover who protect themselves and their planet from the inanities of the dominant, cruel, savage men. Bradley's *The Shattered Chain* (1976) further charters this society of Free Amazons, where women offer the alternative of living without men. "To Keep the Oath" (1985d), a short story in *The Best of Marion Zimmer Bradley,* is the most direct route to understanding Bradley's Amazons. In this story, a woman joins the group. In the process, she learns what the oath is in the women's secret society. In *The Shattered Chain,* a female earth-anthropologist actually joins the Amazons as part of her fieldwork intelligence service. Bradley's Amazon works continue to be read; many have been anthologized (1985a). Yet, curiously enough, Bradley now actually disavows feminism. Perhaps consistent with this disavowal, her female-dominated planet in *The Ruins of Isis* (1978) does not pose a positive alternative for women. Rather, the female leaders run their globe so cruelly that the federation system throws the planet out—a treatment of the Amazon which has attracted critical inquiry (Hornum 1985). Finally, Suzy McKee Charnas' *Motherlines* (1978) shows how the riding women (like the original pre-Greek Amazons who were infamous for being equestrians) attempt to survive by means of reproduction with horses.

Yet perhaps the real "classic" in this genre was Sally Gearhart's *Wanderground: Stories of the Hill Women* (1979). The aesthetic of this post-modern novel derives more from traditional chant modes in indigenous cultures than from modern literary realist narratives. Gearhart's hill women escape to nest, literally, in the woods, after the "revolt of the mother," when man-made machines, civilization, cultural maps, and mechanisms begin to fall apart. Gearhart's female protagonists have moved away from all men as a group. They have reverted to living outside civilization.

One might read the whole text as a revitalized extension of the original concept of the Amazons. Yet within that image, the gentles (gay helping men) sarcastically call the hill women "Amazons" because the women react negatively to the men learning a chant step. Subsequently, men point out that even though women's ways are taking over the earth, women will still need protection in the transitional state of a crumbling patriarchy. The vision of the ecology movement motivates the patriarchal fall in a preemptive text of eco-feminism. Much modern feminism calls for guidance by the body rather than by machinery, and Gearhart's fiction shows this in that the earth revolts against the excesses of man-made technology.

Thus, the image of the Amazon weaves subtly throughout the cultural products that proliferated as a culture of pride emerged among activist lesbians. This culture and its norms have influenced the standard story line in which the world has all but ended (Penelope and Wolfe 1993). In these scenarios, women live without men in a renewed relationship to nature, much like the relationship that Rush and others envisioned for a utopian, pre-civilization past.

Rochelle Singer's *The Demeter Flower* (1980), for instance, portrays a fictional future where an enclave of women live secretly in the California hills amidst patriarchal fiefdoms after the earth's holocaust. Marge Piercy repeated the idea in *He, She and It* (1991), situated in the hills around Zefat in the Galil. Israeli and Palestinian women survive the last war in that area together in caves. Male-run "multis" in which women are at a disadvantage control nearly everyone else on the planet.

Contemporary revitalist lesbian and other narratives have refocused their perspective from dominant cultural figures to those of the subculture; that refocusing is part of their force and appeal. The focus shifts from men encountering and warring with Amazons to the Amazons surviving, whether or not they interact with men at all. However, some interaction with some men has become generally important in the plot as well. This is in sharp contrast to the long line of tales men have written in which "women are depicted as addle-brained nincompoops who are totally unable to set up viable societies of their own" and who "when confronted with real men, instantly fall into their arms" (Cioffi 89). Hence, in accordance with a tendency in emergent literature that Michele Ana Barale points out in "When Jack Blinks," the newer Amazon writings have appropriated the dominant culture's understandings for their own subcultural purposes (604).

Eventually, feminism became institutionalized within the academy. In a sense, Cavin (1978, 1985) was really a foremother of the new scholarship, on the cutting edge between the initial writings of the women's movement and the academic scholarship that began to emerge. She went on to teach "Theories of Women's Studies" and "Homosexuality and Society" at Rutgers University. New scholarship began to mushroom that took many of the feminist movement's starting points as givens.

For example, in *The War against the Amazons* (1983), feminist historian Abby Kleinbaum surveyed the literature about Amazons. Arguing from a feminist perspective, she concluded that the Amazons never existed and that the myth of an Amazonian existence has served historically to reinforce patriarchal ideology; that is, myths of a pre-historic society run by wild and unruly women have been used to rationalize the wise and just rule of men now. (Joan Bamberger had made this argument nearly a decade earlier—in anthropological rather than historical circles—in "The Myth of Matriarchy: Why Men Rule in Primitive Society" [1974]). Kleinbaum's interpretation, though still argued from a feminist perspective, is that the "Amazon is a dream that men created, an image of a superlative female that men constructed to flatter themselves" (1).

However, here and there a non-traditional, more radical feminist scholar continued to hold her own turf on a tough and sometimes inhospitable terrain, rather than incorporating inhibitions from a surrounding environment of doubt. For example, anthropologist Ruby Rohrlich (1977, 1984, 1995), who began graduate training after raising two sons, went on to make important contributions in the field, partly enabled by her training in World War II as a propaganda analyst. She interpreted Amazons as a utopian response to a growing dystopia with the development of class-stratified patriarchies. Rohrlich refused to give in to the pressures to conform within the institutions of dominant culture.

Rohrlich pointed out that the "historicity of these so-called Amazon societies was accepted by such eminent ancient writers as Herodotus, Pliny, Plutarch, Diodorus Siculus and Arrian," all of whom, as she stressed, were "considered authorities on *other* historical matters" (xvii). Although others outside the feminist arena, such as Bennett and Sobol, stated the historical veracity of the Amazons, feminist polemics turned the issue of whether or not the Amazons had existed historically into a hotly debated issue. For example, Rohrlich vehemently condemned what she considered Kleinbaum's glib dismissal of her own discussion of the historical roots of Amazonism.

During the 1980s, such debates were frequently embedded within other conversations and dialogues in academe in increasingly rich and complex examinations of the significance of the Amazon. This process illustrates what Thomas Kuhn called the process of a paradigm shift (1970). Feminism went from original breakthroughs to legitimation and complexification. A prime example of such research is Page DuBois' examination, *Centaurs and Amazons* (1982). A classics scholar, DuBois pointed out that just as the new

Amazonian myths belong to our history of liberation movements and to current changes in the sex/gender system inclusive of new ideas of community, "so the ancient myth of Amazons is embedded in a network of event, ideas, and social relations" (viii). She charted the transition in fifth to fourth century B.C. Greece from mythical to rational thinking, from poetry to philosophy, and from polarity to hierarchy. Her study shows that the "human Greek male, the subject of history and of the culture of the polis," had been defined in relation to a series of creatures seen as different. Carlin Barton's *The Sorrows of the Ancient Romans* (1993) similarly traces the relation between women and other "monsters" and "creatures" in Roman thought. Donna Haraway's *Simians, Cyborgs and Women: The Reinvention of Nature* (1991) contains similar essays associating women with the non- (or not-quite) human in modern thought, which could be used for clues in understanding what the ancient Greeks really thought.

DuBois argued that the Greek male was at first simply not-animal, not-barbarian, not-female. This put the Amazons into a different context, that of a ranking:

> Greek/Barbarian
> Male/Female
> Human/Animal

Note that the male/female difference became only one of the parameters of difference and not even the primary one in this continuum. Because French feminists also expanded the category of the "other" in which women had been placed to be more inclusive, DuBois' work fit in with developments in feminist criticism of the times.

In any case, the sum of these polarities then yielded the norm, "the Greek male human being," and the others, as the opposite side ". . . are grouped together by analogy. Barbarian is like female like animal, hence these different beings have attributes and function essentially to define the norm through opposition" (4). Within this, DuBois argued, women came to represent a potentially dangerous, poisonous force.

Maria Mies' *Patriarchy and Accumulation on a World Scale* (1986) consolidates much of the 1970s and 1980s research done in specific areas of the world on women and gender, adding new global insights. Mies constructed an even grander scale on which we might re-perceive the possibilities of Amazon civilization. Having examined much of the new feminist scholarship, she developed a broad schema of a matricentric mode of production in which women with their children were the center of civilization and the home.

Males evolved a predatory mode, Mies argued, being largely unneeded by this matricentric group. They then preyed on others for their survival—on animals, as hunters, and on other civilizations, including the matricentric ones. The "Amazons" might have been the defenders of the matricentric units who desperately bore arms to protect their neighborhoods and children, Mies argued, even if it meant at the expense of a breast in the bloody process.

Besides consolidating articulations emerging from the women's movement within the university, another outgrowth of the seventies women's movement has been what some scholars have identified as "cultural feminism" (Jaggar 1983). Considerable controversy continues over the use of this term. Some see a variety of cultural feminisms that have created women's culture as an arena in which women can strengthen and galvanize themselves to change. This would be in the direction of working to cohere a rejuvenated sense both of themselves individually and of women collectively. In this sense, women's culture operates much like a sense of female nationalism (Kimball 1981).

To understand this context, Gerda Lerner's definition of "woman's culture" is useful for clarification. Lerner's usage encompasses culture that nineteenth-century feminists created, which included a definition of the moral superiority of women as an argument for their enfranchisement. Lerner defined women's culture as "the ground upon which women stand in their resistance to patriarchal domination and their assertion of their own creativity in shaping society" (1986, 242).

Although cultural feminism growing out of the second wave began as a small offshoot of the women's movement, some of the activities initiated therein have mushroomed enough to attract mainstream media coverage. These include the women's spirituality movement (see Richard Ostling's article in *Time*, "When God Was a Woman: Worshippers of Mother Earth Are Part of a Goddess Resurgence," 1991, 73).

In this cultural feminist context, then, some write from what social historian James Clifford (1994) has called in other settings a "diaspora consciousness," operating within many uprooted, scattered, and dispersed social groupings.[4] For them, then, all lesbians are "ethnic uproots," like blacks removed from Africa, Jews from Israel, Palestinians from Palestine. As an example, Judy Grahn, in *Another Mother Tongue: Gay Words, Gay Worlds*

(1984), developed the thesis that lesbians and gays experience their own separate ethnic cultural identity, or need to.

And in Hoagland and Penelope's *For Lesbians Only: A Separatist Anthology* (1988, 489–500), Micheline Grimara-Leduc referenced the original archetype of the Amazon island in her essay "The Mind-Drifting Islands." She referred to the Amazon as a basic symbol in her known lesbian culture, where the Amazon motif tends to operate as a ground from which women could resist patriarchal domination in male culture. She explained her view that all lesbians are "mind-drifting slaves." She demonstrated how the solid image of a land or island of women was something concrete upon which she and others like herself could draw. Her basic argument runs as follows:

> The Amazons existed; their tribes were a basic primitive form of female social pattern; and if there are so many legends of female-only islands, it is because the Amazon tribes often lived on islands. When these Amazon societies were destroyed by male supremacist societies, lesbians became the heiresses of an ever-menaced culture that had to move from islands of stone and sand to psycho-spiritual shelters, to "mind-drifting islands." (497)

As K. Hess, Jean Langford, and Kathy Ross explained in a concise article, "Comparative Separatism," in the same anthology, this made the "separatism of women" different from other separatisms in that it had no regional base (125–132). Hence, this interpretation of the Island of Women/Amazon motif became very important, as a group of authors articulated in the 1974 "Addition to the 1st Printing of 'Lesbian Separatism: An Amazon Analysis'" (Hess et al., 307). This addition underlines the importance of the goal of overcoming women's separation from each other, which, according to the authors, prevents subjected women from rising up against the violence and indignities done to them under and within the "isms" of male-created cultures, cultures which they defined as "dangerous and disgusting."

In this anthology, also, writers reclaimed Atlantis from the past as an ancient matriarchy where women had to prevent mutants (men) from removing their outer genitals and placing them "bloody and warm" on the temple of Diana (J. M. Paz, 297). Thus, in this context of revitalization of the myth, the mobility of the Amazons could actually be understood as an explanatory factor rather than as a fact which is usually used to discredit the veracity of their existence.

Amazons might have appeared on islands around the world. Yet this was not because different psyches and consciousnesses produced a baseless, senseless myth everywhere simultaneously, which floated here and there, reappearing in different seas as a particular social context developed a need and took a fancy to the tale. Rather, Amazons could have inhabited the island Atlantis. They might have been the ancient matriarchal huntresses of Diana/Artemis who lived on an island that was nomadic itself. Perhaps the island floated, as myth has it the island of Atlantis did. Therefore the actual floating island of Atlantis inhabited by Amazons was actually sighted in sea after sea around the globe.

The notion that the island of women itself might have been adrift at sea, like Atlantis, was also suggested by Real to explain the presence of institutionalized queens in Japan, Polynesia, and perhaps in America. He connected the Melanesian, pre-Columbian, and Polynesian female dominance with the mysterious floating piece of Africa (217). Except for the fact that in modern times, islands themselves do not normally float outside of novels or myths, in this field of Amazonology we might have stumbled upon a universal explanation for numerous specific instances of the diffusion or spread of Amazonia around the globe.

Contemporary Reactionist Uses

Jean-Paul Sartre once suggested that anti-Semitism creates the Jew. For the contemporary misogynist, woman-objectifying stereotypical gender thinking can create the Amazon and the specter of the matriarchy, too. That is, matriarchalist Amazonian visions can be appropriated in reactionary ways. Numerous examples of this reverse trend exist.

William Burroughs, discussed earlier, is a prime example. He presented his vision of an all-women run city in a short story, writing that the women, "led by an albino mutant known as the White Tigress, seized Yass-Waddah," one of the all-women run cities in the Gobi desert set a hundred thousand years ago (153).

In this fictional world, hundreds of women can be impregnated by a single sperm collection, as the women discover in these pre-historic times. Thus, according to Burroughs, the capricious rulers reduce the male inhabitants to slaves, consorts, and courtiers, "all under sentence of death that could be carried out at any time" (155). The city council responds by developing "a method of growing babies in excised wombs, the wombs being provided by vagrant Womb Snatchers" (156). This move aggravates differences between male and female strongholds. Factional war between them seems unavoidable. Scientists invent orgasm drugs, develop a way of bypassing infancy and fusing spirits directly into adolescent bodies, and devise machines to directly transfer the electromagnetic field of one body to another.

The attempt to invent a race of supermen to explore space without the problems of human reproduction results in a time of great disorder and chaos. Cities are abandoned. People flee the cities, taking books with them over the Bering Straits; eventually these fall into the hands of the Mayan priests. A Receptacle class has been reduced to a condition of virtual idiocy. Then Yass-Waddah develops, the city that is a

> female stronghold where the Countess de Gulpa, the Countess de Vile, and the Council of the Selected plot a final subjugation of the other cities. Every shade of sexual transition is represented: boys with girls' heads, girls with boys' heads. Here everything is true and nothing is permitted except to the permitters. (158)

Others besides homosexual males such as Burroughs have negatively envisioned a matriarchy or some semblance thereof, especially in later years as a response to the outburst of the feminism of the seventies. For instance, John Irving's *The World According to Garp: A Novel* (1978), a bestseller, surely figures in this category as a reaction to the newly emerging radical feminist separatism in the 1970s.

In *Garp*, Irving satirically reported the inception of a growing matriarchy deep within the fissures of a rather badly shaken patriarchy as the moment in which, for insemination purposes, the main character's mother jumps on a man dying in a hospital. She might be called an Amazonian character, in de Beauvoir's terms, in that she considers men only for insemination purposes. This main character, Garp, is later a house-husband. His promiscuous professional wife inadvertently castrates her male lover. Then, host of the ultimate most, Garp has to attend his mother's funeral in drag. A cult group of women whose requisite for initiation is having their tongues cut out does not allow men in. By cutting out their own tongues, they symbolically protest the silencing of women in a male-run world.

Frederick Turner, too, produced negative matriarchal fantasies in his epic poem *The New World* (1985). Survivors of catastrophe on earth create a new world in which evil matriarchates rule one quadrant.

In sum, it matters very little whether the Amazons in antiquity actually existed; whether they were a return of the repressed in a reactionist male fantasy; or whether they were, more likely, a combination of both. What matters is the ambiguous Jekyll and Hyde nature of the shrouded reality behind the myth. This allows modern contemporaries to construct and project both clear versions and twisted versions. Reactionists will react; but reclamationists will reclaim and revitalize. The specter of transformed human reproduction where the sexes can develop separately from one another bears a lasting intrigue.

The appearance of the Amazon in the black nationalist movement in the United States duplicated the same dynamic by creating a dialectical reversal of the reversal. This is documented by African American women authors Toni Cade in *The Black Woman* (1970) and Michelle Wallace in *Black Macho and the Myth of the Super-Woman* (1990). As feminist sociologist M. Rivka Polatnick has pointed out, it is true that few black women identified themselves as members of the women's movement. However, individual black women did participate and did play leadership roles (1995). Yet Polatnick has stressed the importance of looking not only at activists within the "self-defined women's movement," but also at women who fought for the cause in other contexts. Some black women, she has argued, did battle male supremacy in black or community organizations in the 1960s.

In public debate over the birth control pill controversy, some black nationalist men accused some black women of dominating husbands. Some male leaders of the black power movement in Harlem labeled some black women "Amazons." These leaders had picked up on the white depiction of the black female as Amazon on account of her "ability to endure hardships no 'lady' was supposedly capable of enduring." The fact that she did so was a sign that she possessed "an animalistic sub-human strength" (hooks 1981, 81–82). Eldridge Cleaver complained about the impact on his culture of the black woman "Amazon." He added to the cultural dynamic of black women having to prove they weren't either "dominating" or "Amazon," particularly in *Soul on Ice,* in which he criticized black women as "unfeminine" and "self-reliant Amazons" (Matthews 279).[5]

Hence in this context, some black nationalist men used "Amazon" in the sense of dominating rather than in the sense of being equal to or peers with men. Such a public exchange of terminology followed the misuse of the term "matriarchy" in the report Daniel Patrick Moynihan made to the government about problems in the black community ([1965] 1981). The misapplied metaphorical usage of the word "Amazon" had occurred in popular culture newspaper print before, but contenders had not thrown the term back and forth as heatedly.

Susan Cavin cited another instance in her discussion of a newspaper account. In 1977, a large number of women became active among radicals in Western Europe. At that time, a journalist wrote that "an Amazon complex" was running out of control, as experts debated why many young women had become terrorists (Cavin, 251–252). The journalistic misuse of the term continues in the American media right up into our own historical period, as evidenced by Richard Corliss' reference to Camille Paglia in *Time* as ". . . a media Medusa, a Valkyrie for hire, Penthesilea fighting for Amazon rights" (1994, 90). His is surely a sarcastic version. Anyone familiar with the texts sees Penthesilea as seduced, carried off, separated from her people, and then killed: in other words, as a victim rather than as a fighter for the rights of her group, tribe, or people.

Yet, due to Moynihan's report, the grass-roots communities of black women in the period under discussion perceived their own women through the misnomer of a similar "Amazon complex." Consequently, some of these women began discussing matriarchy, by far predating the white feminist discussion of the term.

The largely white New York radical feminists picked up the concept of matriarchy later, under Ti-Grace Atkinson's leadership. But in 1968 "Pat Robinson and Group," a black consciousness-raising group Polatnick studied, wrote their first position paper, later published by Cade (198–210). Considerably later, "The Answer Is Matriarchy," by Barbara Love, a founder of the group the Matriarchists, and Elizabeth Shanklin, a member first of the feminists and then of the Matriarchists, called for "herstories of the matriarchal movement" (183). Love and Shanklin claimed that women had been "very effectively conditioned to feel negative about matriarchy" (183). Their article stating this position was not anthologized by Ginny Vida in *Our Right to Love* until 1978. Kathie Sarachild in "The Power of History" was still refuting Elizabeth Gould Davis at this time, cautioning against the reclamation of the concept of matriarchy (1978a).[6]

The misuse of the term "matriarchy" as applied to black communities forced black women to reclaim the concept earlier than white women had. As Wallace has pointed out, when Stokely Carmichael used the term "Amazon" as applied to "black matriarchal mamas," it was severely misused, because

the black woman, who is at the white woman's knee, under the black man's heel, and gets the back of the white man's hand [is described] as an Amazon. Didn't he [Carmichael] realize that Amazon meant female warrior? What warrior would have put up with that kind of abuse? (168–169)

Johnston saw lesbian mothers as Amazons—a view later institutionalized as part of lesbian culture under the rubric of the organization and newsletter of lesbian mothers, called "Momazons." Shulman saw Russian women revolutionaries as Amazons. Similarly, Wallace went on to reconstruct black slave history and the civil rights movement using the same terminology. Wallace wrote an intensely autobiographical book that found support in the women's movement but was not well received for the most part in the African American community.[7]

Wallace argued there that black women had inherited two archetypes from slavery: the Black Lady and the Amazon. The Black Lady was free or in a special position in the master's house, like the master's mistress. Other African American women writers later reclaimed the African Amazons of Dahomey as "highly prized, well-trained, and ferocious women warriors" in their capacity as guards and fighters under the Panther Kings of Dahomey (Lorde 1978, 119). But in this context, the black woman as Amazon in American culture meant the woman who was bigger, stronger, more rebellious, and usually poor (Wallace 214).

Wallace cited Harriet Tubman and Sojourner Truth as "the front lines of every camp of escaped slaves," bound to be "ball breakers, and unfeminine" (219–220) in the Amazon character. Wallace also placed Rosa Parks, the woman who refused to move from the front of the bus in Montgomery, Alabama in 1955, as well as Fannie Lou Hamer, another African American civil rights heroine, into her Amazon category (223). The actions of these two local women began a movement, Wallace argued. Yet given social dynamics attributed to gender, they did not give speeches considered to be major, or rise in national leadership.

In fact, such women, who were primarily local initiators, found themselves passed over and rejected, Wallace chronicled, when "black men ran off with white women." These original "Amazons," Wallace felt, started the civil rights movement. Yet they lost status when the civil rights movement gave way to the Black Power movement and what she saw as the best outgrowth that second movement had to offer, the Black Muslims.

Some did not consider Wallace's account of these developments historically accurate. Yet Wallace did point to some of the contradictions in the black woman's role within that movement, and essays that Toni Cade published in *The Black Woman* (1970) substantiate such claims. In a self-critical way, some of the black male leaders also later critiqued their own self-serving adaptation of a foreign form of gender hierarchy (Baraka 1984). The term remained current enough for Audre Lorde and bell hooks to use later in discussions of the same problem.

So the myth persists, reappearing in a different cultural scene. The outbreak of black nationalism in the United States was a far cry from Greek Argonauts being sent to retrieve golden girdles, or from foul-smelling women on Lemnos whom Aphrodite punished for turning away from her proper worship.

In essence, then, what had occurred by the 1970s with these contradictory images, including the publication of Jessica Salmonson's first collection of stories *Amazons* by DAW in 1979? The signifier "Amazon" had been freed from a direct connection to the original external referent.

Even in word plays in America, the word is not exclusively property of lesbian culture. American men coined the word "Glamazon" to designate tall glamorous showgirls and "Pajamazon" to refer to a "charmer amply constructed for night-long bouts" (Sobol 160–161 n.). The Marx Brothers movie *At the Circus* (1939) punned with their word "Pajamazon" to describe what an explorer found down in the Amazon, "Lady Godiva with her pajamas on."

From Roman times, the appellation "Amazon" has been used to refer to any woman of remarkable size and physical dexterity. According to Sobol, that reference was made to women prisoners found among the wounded during the course of Roman victory in the Mithridaic wars (155 n.). The term had been used since the time of Appian in 66 B.C. to mean war-like women. Moreover, after the defeat of Zenobia (272 A.D.), the Roman general Aurelian marched home with a parade of his many captives, each wearing placards such as Frank, Gaul, Sarmartian, Egyptian, Syrian. In the midst of this, he segregated ten Gothic women. He labeled these women "Amazons" because they had been fighting on the battlefield, not because of their separate tribal, national, or ethnic existence. "Amazon" also became an unflattering term applied to women of extraordinary physical size or skill (88–89).

But in popular usage in American culture, "Amazon" had become an experience of disconnected discontinuous material signifiers encompassing such disparate future and past elements as Russian revolutionaries, suffragettes, black women slaves, lesbian mothers, promiscuous "open door" heterosexual women, civil rights leaders, tall glamorous showgirls, islands of women in apartments who unquestioningly provide free room and board, the objects of Marx Brothers exploratory humor, and leaders of anti-Nazi fights in popular entertainment. All of these have perhaps one element in common, the independent survival strength if not always the defiance of women.

Yet, the image's referent becomes other texts, other images. In studying this subject of objectifying Amazons, it is apparent to me that as much is revealed about the colorful imagination of the representers, and the context in which they live and create, as about the "truth" of the Amazons themselves.

THREE

The Amazon Archetype

CONTEMPORARY CRITICISM

Amazons: In mythology, a fierce race of female warriors, who figure in many of the cyclic myths. Their
queen Penthesilea was killed by Achilles. Hercules
(and also Theseus) campaigned against the Amazons to get the girdle of the queen. According to a
fanciful etymology they were supposed to cut off
the girls' right breasts (a + mazos) to prevent inter-
ference in archery.   —MARTINBAND 1962

Amazon: In Greek legend one of a race of females
who supposedly dwelt off the coast of the Black
Sea and in the Caucasus mountains. Men were
excluded from their state and they devoted themselves to war and hunting. Thus a woman of masculine habits. The name means deprived of breasts,
and they supposedly cut off their breasts to use the
bow more effectively.   —JOBES 1962

The contemporary women's movement gave a name to the suppression of
women. The quotations above from two dictionaries (one from the Greek
classics and the other from folklore, mythology, and symbols) encapsulate
the image of the public symbol "Amazon," not influenced by any particular
political group or artistic community. Similarly, when Pratt conducted an

experiment with students working on the archetype Aphrodite, she reported that students discovered how Aphrodite had been degraded from a golden divinity that was a celebration of feminine sexuality to a threatening, silly seducer of men. The students returned from the library listing "trickery," "seductiveness," and "power over men" as her characteristics. Many concluded that Aphrodite was a "floozy." Yet, as Pratt pointed out, Aphrodite as the archetype of feminine sexuality represents, for men, the impact of a lover on the male's personality, and for women, on their own sensuality (1994, 101).

However, as feminist poet and literary critic Alicia S. Ostriker has made clear, a major theme in feminist theory on both sides of the Atlantic for the past decade

has been the demand that women writers be . . . thieves of language . . . though the language we speak and write has been an encoding of male privilege, what Adrienne Rich calls an "oppressor's language" inadequate to describe or express women's experience. (210–211)

Consequently, feminists have engaged in the process of reviving old myths through acts of reclamation. Thus, Barbara Walker in *The Woman's Encyclopedia of Myths and Secrets* (1983) defined Amazons as the name Greeks used for tribes that worshiped goddesses in North Africa, Anatolia, and the Black Sea Area. She mentioned how scholars now believe the name derived from "moon-woman," and how the women warriors in many of the legends made "magic battle cries" that rendered their enemies helpless (24–27).

Feminist linguists Cheris Kramarae and Paula Treichler in *A Feminist Dictionary* (1985) began the reclaimed definition simply as "powerful female." As part of a feminist movement, these authors have revitalized the old images, forms, symbols, and stories found in ancient myths. They have suggested that "the Indo-Europeans were once a matriarchal culture that worshipped the powerful female . . ." and that "the Amazons were the last of the original Indo-Europeans to remain in their homeland" (43).

Feminists reclaimed the myth of the Amazon, granting it new forms. In the process of reclamation, women demystified the appropriated image. They called forth images of the matriarchy or of separate communities of women in order to galvanize women to step outside the boundaries of society. Such change happens when competitive groups struggling for hegemony contest meanings in the public realm.

In the dialectical development of the Amazon since her initial recorded appearance in Homer, each epoch has invested the chameleon-like symbol with its own particular spirit of place and time. As I collected and contrasted the endlessly diverse forms, three dimensions emerged as crucial for understanding similarities and differences.

The first axis of comparison is the Amazon's relation or non-relation to other women and goddesses within the text. The second is her relation or non-relation to stories within the texts of other, "odd," "nontraditional," non-patriarchal parenting, including insemination, childbirth, and childrearing. The third seemingly significant axis is the relation or non-relation within the texts of Amazons to other women in war. In my work, these issues took on significance in distinguishing between the reclamationist and reactionist categories. Additionally, the general appearance, costume, and affect of the Amazon as she changed through historical place and time helped me distinguish between the basic categories.

To further develop a critical understanding of the genre of writings in which women exist separately from men, or in which the societies are women dominated, I saw that it was necessary to develop more precision in the tools used to analyze that form, even working within these three parameters.

In *The Marriage of Cadmos and Harmony* (1993), the Italian critic Robert Calasso isolated for critical attention the male hero's attraction for fallen women. He incorporated the Amazon in this character, but in a diluted, selective way, excluding all that did not help him reinterpret the myth for his purposes.

Calasso, a poetic interpreter of the classics, portrayed Antiope as singled out to be the "dying Amazon." She appears as nothing more than a dead virgin warrior to whom Achilles desires to make love as he holds her lifeless corpse in his arms. For him, this detail of near-mortality was the ultimate "turn on." Calasso's assumptions are that men are to rule, and that women exist either to help in that rule or to betray. His text presents a series of abductions, mutilating rapes, and women whose children are stolen by the patriarchy, which was an emerging system in the process of establishing its own descent lines at the time at which his story is set. Further, Calasso's criticism focuses on women who have little choice except to self-mutilate (suicide) or to support men.

Pratt's criticism in *Dancing with Goddesses: Archetypes, Poetry and Empowerment* (1994) develops a different tonality. Pratt isolated a different portion of the same texts for critical attention as she participated in the new cultural emergence of women as a class or group, building on much feminist research that traces the possible history of positive female snake goddesses from old Europe (10,000–5000 B.C.) and the Mideast (9000–7000 B.C.).

Pratt showed that in 1600 B.C. the Minoans and the Mycenaeans both had widespread domestic snake cults. In Knossos, home worship associated the Lady of the Dead with the goddess of fertility (1994, 26–27). As part of the patriarchal takeover in ancient Greece, Apollo murdered Python, who was a female seer-snake originally belonging to Mother Earth. Priestesses traditionally administered to Python, but Apollo put male priests in her temple (M. Stone 1978, 203).

The Amazons, the Gorgons, and classical Medusa, according to Pratt, then remain linked as the heirs of this female seer in the form of a snake. Pratt discovered this detail of identification when researching what she called the "deep background" of distorted images of women appearing in Greek myths. Writing about 60 B.C., Siculus pinpointed Medusa as queen of a tribe of Amazons called Gorgons, whom Hercules destroyed so as not to allow a country of women to tarnish his reputation.

These Gorgons appeared as grandchildren of Gaea, who had serpents for hair. Culture associated them with the snake goddesses of Cretan palaces. Medusa was a mother goddess of Crete. Poseidon, later god of the sea, was her consort at this stage of mythic development. Much as with the Amazons, later literature reflects Medusa in a less flattering light. Culture has also associated Amazon tribes with snakes and snake worship, even possibly with Medusa as their queen (Pratt 1994, 29). Thus, Pratt argued, a similarity remains between Medusa's treatment and the treatment of the Amazons.

To develop her sense of tonality in her critical interpretation of myths, Pratt associated the Amazons also with wild femininity. That is, they were more at home in nature than in culture. Thus, they were congruent with the Artemis archetype Pratt treated later in the book (1994, 288–289). Pratt focused her critical attention on this wild femininity in searching to identify a pattern behind the imagery.

Thus, to Pratt, Amazons are a form of "wild women." She sees wild women in lore of peasant culture expressing a healthy antithesis to the emerging Christian condemnation of enjoyment of sensuality as sin. Pratt wrote that they lived together in a group. They were healers, potentially deadly but sexually hungry, and hostile to the norms of matrimony. Contrary to the typically developed Amazon descriptions—such as Penthesilea, for example, who was stunningly beautiful to the male gaze—in European legend these women were exceedingly ugly (285). To Calasso, Amazons were acted upon, dead or dying; to Pratt, the key detail was their wildness.

In this context, we could see the Amazons as part of what Pratt has called "the fragmentary outcrop of pagan images characterizing wild and Artemesian poems in the European tradition, where pagan archetypes are more likely to occur as vaguely encoded bits and pieces, divorced from the theologies in which they were embedded" (1994, 315).

As history usually links Amazons with steeds and horses, more work might be necessary to uncover the relation to myths of the all-powerful horse goddesses who can beget children without men (299). This specter returns to haunt men in twentieth-century American poetry as well as forming the basis for many Indo-European tales. Kingdoms of fighting women often have been associated with ritual horse sacrifice (*asvamedha*).

Such Indo-European myths take on many cyclical forms. These include stories of the mare beneath the sea, Irish rites and myth where a horse goddess appears to invigorate the king in sex, the tales of the demise of the erotic goddess, the epic of the return of the mare goddess, and the lore of the demise of the mare. All of these might be associated with the Amazons.

Details from Rothery, who discussed the well-known militia of riding women in India, might further illuminate this line of criticism. The Greeks heard of the militia via Megathenes, who was ambassador to India in 200 B.C. He reported that these women rode elephants and horses, were equipped with weapons, and protected the king. They are reflected in the Maha Bharata ballads as far back as 1500 B.C.

The riding warrior women of the Indian continent were contemporaries of the Amazons in the *Iliad*. When converted into sacred books by the Brahmins, the Vedic and pre-Vedic customs remained in epic poetry in the form of the horse ceremony story (Rothery 73–78), much as the Amazons were changed once oral stories began to be written down. Today, the Amazon Princess Wonder Woman rides a winged horse in the comics. Bellerophon was sent to master a species of winged horses as well as the Amazons.

Although not all male classics scholars have been reactionist (see, e.g., Peradotto and Sullivan, *Women in the Ancient World: The Arethusa Papers* [1987], one of the first consolidations of classical women's studies), the 1980s saw a trend within academia to explain away figures of female power, including that of the Amazon. The goal of such scholarship, conscious or unconscious, was to normalize those time periods and historic places in which the image of the female showed some power, and thus to incorporate rather than to leave as potential threats the cultural insights and products of a struggling oppositional group. The aim of these writers was to rationalize the notion that even in the face of maternal mythopoetic symbols, the hegemonic belief in the pervasiveness of male domination was in fact the norm. This applies beyond the field of Greek scholarship to goddess research in general.

William Tyrell's *Amazons: A Study in Athenian Myth Making* (1984)—hailed by Ken Dowden (1992) as the "standard book" (184) about Amazons—is a prime example of this trend.

Initially, Tyrell feigned the pose of objectivity, at first stating that his research into the evolution of the Amazon in Greek classical myth exhibited more dignity than to stoop to the level of determining whether the Amazons were real or not. For the purposes of his study, the small incidental fact of whether or not the Amazons ever existed—inexplicably blown way out of proportion by unmentioned others—doesn't really matter. Those who think the Amazons existed, Tyrell asserted, are participating in myth making of their own (as if he were not). His thesis is that other than as a reversal of the patriarchy, the Amazons had no substance. He proposed that their only function was to express the antithesis of the cultural ideal based on the adult male (66). The men in charge of "the media," he claimed, then developed the Amazons, emphasizing the clash with Greek warriors. Episodes concerning Hercules' labor and the invasion of Africa were later elaborated (22).

Tyrell did provide interesting data, particularly about the appearance of Amazons in funeral orations, claiming that this touch was to add grandiosity to the oral legend about the establishment of empire. Tyrell argued, also, that the myth of conquering Amazons in war was included in funeral orations to prove the purity of the men of Athens as opposed to the "foreign nature" of women. Athenians would rather, by 338 B.C., claim that they were born of the earth, not of women (116).

Throughout Tyrell's accounts, he frequently left his Amazons nameless—another subtle means of diminishing them. For example, he wrote that Theseus raped an Amazon. Another way in which Tyrell contained the Amazon was by characterizing her as a recalcitrant daughter—a woman reluctant to enter her role as an adult. In this reactionist portrayal, the Amazon is the daughter who stays with her mother; she represents the "failure" of girls to make the transition to adulthood through marriage. Writing as a structuralist, he constructed neat formulaic equations showing how the Amazon reverses the polarity of Greek culture.

Drawing from the Cambridge school of mythic scholarship developing at

the time he was writing, Tyrell analyzed the myth of the Amazon in terms
of Greek puberty and female initiation ritual. He argued that the Amazon
as symbol in this myth existed to reify the limbo period before the Greek
woman was about to wed. The Amazons mythically represented both the
boys and girls who did not "transmit," as he put it, to adulthood (76–77).
(See also Gananath Obeyesekere's *The Cult of the Goddess Pattini* [1984],
which characterizes the mother-goddess cult as a "projective system" in the
Freudian sense, a system in which any mother goddess serves as an intense
replication of the child's attachment to the mother.)

In addition to containing the Amazon within a structuralist/psychologiz-
ing framework, Tyrell also focused on the theme of annihilation. He claimed,
for example, that the Amazons were killed as Athena's surrogates (125). If
Amazons were killed in myth, Athena could survive as a pure virgin warrior
who posed no threat. This implied that the Amazons existed only to be
killed, proving that dangerous women could be kept in their place. In this
respect, Amazons existed only to fight men and to be defeated.

Tyrell's approach is in some ways consistent with that of Kleinbaum—
whose scholarship he did not mention, even though their work was contem-
poraneous. She shared his assumption that one can do research on artifacts
and historical representations about Amazons regardless of whether they existed. However, while Kleinbaum's intent was, initially, to discover women
of power, Tyrell's was to show that women suffer eternally.

Calasso would go further in the theme of women's suffering. He traced
the moving body of imagery within the work of literature. He traced out how
dead, dying, raped, and murdered women shape the work. The dying Amazon would become only part of a whole corpus of dead bodies, not merely
one. Pratt, however, has discovered systematic, moving, vibrant autonomous
power of women, even if patriarchal culture freezes them into distorted images. She has seen under each dead or distorted still-shot the moving vitality
of women's lives as a force, not only the life force of the Amazons.

An early commentary, Esther Harding's *The Way of All Women: A Psychological Interpretation* (1934), discusses the relationships between the
women characters in various texts which reflect this underlying wholeness of
fragmented women that Pratt also detected. Harding suggested that at times
one woman is split into many parts or selves. She analyzed in particular the
relationship between the individual and the collective.

The fact that one woman is separated from the many might represent in
Harding's terms not only psychological war between men and women, but
also the conflict within a woman. This occurs because the man sees (or

carries off) only the part of her that he would like to incorporate as his "anima." The part that goes with him is not the entire woman. She, as the man's anima, engages in war with the other parts of her self that he does not recognize.

Similarly, when the Amazon queen is isolated from the rest of herself and becomes only the Greek man's anima, she fights with her female comrades. Eventually she kills them off. These comrades that she kills are really her counterparts—or other parts of herself which still fight for the totality of her existence as an integral whole. These other parts of the same woman attempt to rescue her amputated part.

Her comrades fighting against the abduction then are really other aspects of the woman who was prey to Hercules (or any of the other of the series of men)—when raped, kidnapped, or seduced. The anima portion of the woman might be naive and err. For example, Calafia, in Rodríguez de Montalvo's *Sergas de Esplandian* (or any of the other Amazon queens), decides to marry the conquering male. Yet an integrated woman, operating with all parts of herself as one, might know better and try to defend herself instead of marrying.

Man's soul cannot reduce the Amazon queen, or the individual woman, to exist primarily for its own benefit. Parts of her will rebel—even if uselessly—against this sudden death of her being. This is Penthesilea's experience. This myth of the Amazon portrays, then, in comparative symbology, the conflict and warring parts within the woman. The loss of an Amazon queen and the pursuing battle portray the woman's own battle for her lost soul.

Yet we have already gone beyond the process of looking at women as a symbol within any particular text, as in the first chapter of this work. There we looked at the symbol of the Amazonian existence as a "sign," meaning a symbol that points to something outside and beyond the text itself. Image becoming symbol and at last turning into sign creates myth. Signs are "verbal units which, conventionally and arbitrarily, stand for and point to things outside the text where they occur" (Frye 73).

In *The Reign of the Phallus* (1985), Eva C. Keuls continued to deepen the process of not taking the Amazons so far out of their original context. Rather, Keuls re-examined the original context of the Amazons in a deeper and more contextualized way. Aiming to see what they might have signified in the ongoing life of the authors who ostensibly created them, she reclaimed elements of Bachofen.

Keuls added an element of sophistication to the analysis, discussing the Amazon symbol in the context of the emergence of the "Greek phallocracy"

(1–3). For example, men carried money bags in which they consolidated their emerging power, money, and wealth, both literally and symbolically. Friezes show the bags hanging from men's belts. *The Reign of the Phallus* contains many reproduced drawings, patterns, and designs that depict Amazons aiming swords at male genitalia and men sinking knives into the breasts of females.

Keuls referred to a pre-existing "gynecocracy," of which the Amazons might have been a sign. Furthermore, she analyzed the "gynophobic" fear in myth that women will "get out of hand" and take "control over their men and their own lives" (321). She examined how, in the politics of Aristotle, the word "gynecocracy," literally, "women's rule," really describes women breaking out of the cage of binding restrictions.

There are many versions of the myth of the women of Lemnos.[1] Keuls argued that in the one in which the Lemnian women kill all their men, the female hero is really Hypsiple, who spared her father by hiding him in a chest. Antiope actually allowed herself to be captured, Keuls pointed out, to become a dutiful wife and mother. Consequently, the moral of the story is that men should put the wild woman back in the cage and domesticate her by making her into a mother.[2]

Greek ethnography serves to demonstrate that the only alternative to restrictive, male-dominated marriage was complete promiscuity and gynecocracy (324). Keuls explained that the Greeks expressed shock, for example, at the Etruscan nudity (325). Herodotus was known for registering odd facts often not substantiated by the culture's own artifacts and documents. Especially in introductory notes and appendices pertaining to women, even Herodotus' late nineteenth-century translator, George Rawlinson, felt that Herodotus portrayed women in an unusually strong light. Keuls pointed to Herodotus' observation of the Egyptians' gender roles being "topsy turvy." For instance, when the women did the marketing and selling, the men stayed at home and wove (1880, 327).[3] Keuls did not specify the Amazon as a symbolic object to be removed from her own cultural surroundings. Rather, she generalized the Amazon to be an aspect of gender within Greek society.

Another example of criticism that perceives the Amazons as more a sign of something outside the text than as an internal symbol can be found in Eve Cantarella's *Pandora's Daughters: The Role and Status of Women in Greek and Roman Antiquity* (1987). Cantarella looked at what the myths of females resisting marriage reference beyond the mythic text itself. Her study, written in Italian in 1981, translated into English in 1984, and published in English in 1987, offers further insights into cultural processes.

Pandora's Daughters starts with a tale from Hesiod about the happy time when men once existed without women until Zeus got angry with Prometheus. Out of this anger, Zeus and created Pandora, the first woman. Pandora was cruel and had a thieving heart. Thus, to start with, Greek male historians had no ambivalence about women, Cantarella insisted; they were clear that women were simply a curse—a notion reflecting women's oppression.

Cantarella then summarized another view of history that she saw as a sign pointed to outside the text. This was a history in which women developed agriculture and men went elsewhere to hunt. Because women developed agriculture, they also developed fertility rites. The female divinities took the upper hand. Yet they had male consorts. The fact that women had mysterious powers still seeped through into the Greek myths, Cantarella noted.

For example, Helen, Circe, Calypso, and Medea all had certain powerful magnetic charms. Yet, before the twentieth-century female reclamation of goddess divinities who predated the patriarchy, scholars referred to these same figures as "bogies," or witches, in a negative sense.[4]

As Cantarella encapsulated, the hoe and the need for male labor developed concurrently with irrigation. Agriculture developed to the point of trade. At that juncture, the construction of protective buildings required even more male labor for the villages. After all, the trade brought traders, but also raiders.

This matriarchy flourished from 12,000 to 6000 B.C. in Asia and became the characteristic social organization of the Neolithic period. By 4000 B.C., the civilization had spread by sea from centers of diffusion mostly identified with Syria. Therefore, female power would have characterized social relations and religious institutions at very different times and places.

In the Mediterranean, in particular, she summarized,

> female power would have continued past the end of the Neolithic to the Bronze Age and the threshold of the so-called Hellenic Middle Ages (that is, in the Minoan and Mycenaean culture). It would have left traces even in the societies described in the Homeric Epics. (13)

Thus, texts might point to many forms of female power, matrilineal law, and matrilocal social organizations outside themselves. If what is meant by "matriarchy" is strong female presence in society and religion, then matriarchy did exist for both the primitive peoples and the ancient modern societies. The Amazon is a remaining sign of these matriarchal civilizations.

Cantarella described how in Minoan society something called the "Mediterranean Culture Mother" grew. The mother figure was a female divinity of the Helladic group that existed before the arrival of the Europeans. Two serpents flanked this mother creatrix, a goddess of land and sea, on a sacred boat. Culture considered this Mediterranean Great Mother an omnipotent mistress. She served as the female generative force. She used a consort who was otherwise passive to satisfy her sexual needs. Thus, it is no surprise that traces of female descent remained in the Mycenaean society in which male gods such as Zeus and Poseidon emerged.

The myths of the matriarchy coded in myths of the Amazons and the Lemnian women were therefore possibly more than psychological, metaphorical constructs. They might have been remnants of societies where women held decisively more power. In other surrounding societies, clothing was androgynous. Women held jobs with salaries.

The organization of gender divided work into female and male tasks. The *Iliad* reflects Crete, Sumer, and Minoan civilizations, including admiring references to the "Crete of the Hundred Cities" (Rohrlich 1977, 32). Minoan women also hunted. They are often represented with bows and arrows, sometimes driving chariots, as did Athene and Hera when they stole the chariot from Zeus to try to go down to earth to effect skirmishes and politics. Mycenaean Greece invaded Crete after tidal waves, earthquakes, floods, and fires devastated its coastal towns somewhere between 1500 and 1400 B.C.

The remnants of the matriarchal Cretan civilization (called "Minoan") shine through the work of the humanist poets who composed the *Iliad* and the *Odyssey,* according to George Thomson. In his studies of ancient Greek society, Thomson noted that the brash pioneers of private property had no qualms about ransacking the previous, more sophisticated and opulent civilization of the sophisticated Minoan matriarchate (1949). Women handled the storing and distribution of cereals, and land concession belonged exclusively to women.

An Amazon society where women were warriors and men were slaves might not have sounded so absurd in the context of surroundings in which divergent cultures arranged work patterns differently according to their own distinct gendering of roles. That such a generalized pattern served to normalize the anomaly of the Amazons is also apparent in Books 1–3 of Herodotus' *History.* Although Amazons do not emerge until the fourth volume, even in the first three volumes, women figure as queens, rulers, priestesses, oracles, market workers, bakers, construction workers, authorities, musicians, goddesses, and wearers of armor. They also lead troops, direct armies, engage in battle, maintain vehicles, drive chariots, and tend shrines and animals. Women in the world Herodotus depicted are bold, noble, war-like, clever, triumphant, courageous, defiant, and very much involved as individuals in the public world.

Only later, in the context of Hesiod's hyperbole, did Amazons become an unreal phantom. Likewise, there could have been an island such as Lemnos where women actually had power until Jason and the Argonauts—the foreign conquerors—landed.

Other indications exist of women resisting marriage to men, Cantarella maintained, such as the myth of the daughters of Proteus. These women refused to take husbands even though they were sought after by all the Greeks (18). As we collect myths, we still have to look at the society that mediates them.

A myth could mean the opposite of what a nineteenth-century matriarchalist thought, or of what today's feminists think, Cantarella argued. Yet, there are still many cities whose origin legends link them to women. For example, Caulonia was supposedly founded by Caulos, the son of the Amazon Cleta, who made her way to Troy to attend the burial of Penthesilea.

The Amazons worshiped Artemis, the goddess who protected young virgin women. At puberty, the virgins were passed over to the protection of Helen, who remade them in her image (21). But this arrangement did not occur in myths until the end of the fifth century B.C. and cannot be used to say that Amazons never existed at all as independent women. Again, a serious perusal of Herodotus' *History* makes it evident that the existence of many races was disputed, not just the Amazons. We can assume that Minoan elements seeped through into the emerging Greek society. Mycenaean women lived in a transitional situation, prior to Western misogyny.

Thus, Cantarella looked outside the text to see what the symbolic signs might refer to in the outer, ongoing world. She noted the imposition of patriarchal marriage systems onto indigenous matrifocal female populations. Slater also referenced this interaction between matrifocal and patriarchal cultures as the chief reason for cantankerous relations between Hera and Zeus, between other gods and goddesses, and between women and men in Greek myth. He also discussed how the tradition of a patriarchal conquest of a matriarchal society is an ancient one in classical scholarship, "based on the evidence of early matrilineal, matrifocal, goddess-worshiping traditions being supplanted by their patriarchal counterparts."[5] Analogous to various archaeological discussions of the Amazons, Herodotus' *History* also explores at great length the possible non-Greek, Persian, Egyptian, or eastern origin of Heracles (Hercules).

In most of the various uses and interpretations in this study, we have looked at what each of the authors feels the symbol points to, outside the text. We have done so with the concerns of an archetypal critic. That is, in addition to looking at each text and author in historical context, we have looked at the relationship of each treatment of Amazons to some treatments which appear in other literature. We have looked at the relation between texts, looking at each one as part of a whole. We have seen how some observers, in the context of different social actions and different social practices, can find anarchists; others, lesbians; others, single mothers; others, followers of Artemis, Ares, or the Great Mother; others, the vanguard in working-class revolt; still others, women who seem to suffer from lack of contact with strong, heroic men; and others, the justification of Athena, or the rites of puberty for young girls.

The amount of confusion over the symbol and term "Amazon" merely expresses the essence of symbolism. According to Raymond Firth's anthropological analysis of symbols in *Symbols: Public and Private* (1973), one thing can stand for another, re-presenting a relation from the concrete to the abstract, from the particular to the general.

But there is something also to be said for looking at each isolated structural unit more closely, as Calasso did—to see each in relation to the aesthetic form in which the Homeric Amazon symbol originally occurred. In this manner, we can identify precisely what took root. Thus we can understand what grew into trends that developed two or three thousand years after. In our own times, the conceptual term has again fallen into common use and has become wildly popular with the romantic rebirth of primitivism. The past, which we still have to examine to understand how we use the term "Amazon," now becomes a repository for possible directions for hypothetically "corrected" futures.[6] This occurs when members of modern urban societies, based on their own disaffection, become fascinated with archaic and pre-historic societies.

Part Two

Amazon Archetype: Evolution in Form

FOUR

Problematizing the Greeks

TRAGIC FLAWS IN THE ONE-BREASTED AMAZON ARGUMENT

Throughout this long succession of various uses and interpretations, then, has the image and form of the Amazon remained the same? Are the Amazons fighting with griffins on Diner's Siberian plains the same as the bare-breasted ones that confronted Lederer's male readers and their Greek counterparts with castration anxiety? Do the foul-smelling Amazons of Lemnos who killed their own husbands, brothers, and fathers in a jealous rage resonate with the women who tempt men to their Land of Happiness with silver branches? Do these even closely approximate the snake-haired tribe of Gorgon Amazons whose queen was Medusa?

With such rhetorical questions unanswered, my research led me to examine the original Amazon myth a bit more closely. To re-contextualize that myth in its original mode, I looked at the original Western literary context from which she emerged.

I found that changes in the mode of production of literature removed the "Amazon" from the earlier, primarily oral mode in ritualistic chant. Only at this juncture did she become more of a projected anima figure. The male writer who had access to the papyrus and then to the privacy of composing his fantasies with his pen could create her as he pleased. She took on a distorted form only when both sexes no longer had creative interactive influence on the image produced.

Problematizing the Greeks

During the American feminist second wave, Sarah Pomeroy was the first contemporary scholar of antiquity to articulate the problematic situation of women in Greek patriarchy (1975, 1976). Building on further historical studies, many feminists went on to encompass this sort of scholarship. As mythic historian Joseph Campbell has pointed out, wherever the Greeks went in their Iron Age invasions into cultures still in the Bronze Age, "there was a local manifestation of the goddess-mother of the world" whose preexisting civilization they then had to conquer (1964, 149).

Campbell influenced early reformulaters of the Greeks. He was a disciple of Jung and remains a controversial figure. His *The Masks of Gods* (1959) impacted writers of the American second wave. Campbell's cross-cultural collection made the various forms of female deities visible to the public. His work preceded the goddess movement, the critiques of Greek culture of the classical period as a patriarchy, and the emergence of feminist theologians like Mary Daly, who, in *Beyond God the Father* (1985), had the audacity to assert that there might have been a god before the Father, and that perhaps this god had been a female. The images Campbell gathered inspired women to do research years before a profession of women's studies came into existence.

As Simone Pembroke wrote in an article on the ancient idea of matriarchy, early Greece was "dominated and contained by a feminine material principle . . . which the more spiritual period of masculine ascendancy which succeeded it had to combat for every step of its own advance" (1967, 1). Pembroke's image is like that of a male embryo trying to separate its own identity from a female womb, an experience the psychoanalytic social critic Dorothy Dinnerstein analyzed as a source of male hatred for women and thus also a source of female oppression (1977). Erich Neumann had previously declared Greek mythology to be largely a dragon fight of consciousness that struggled for independence from the mother, a struggle that was of spiritual importance to Greece (1954).

The Greeks believed a land populated entirely by women existed "on their very borders" (Monaghan 1981). Furthermore, the populace commonly held that once or twice a year, on the borders of their country, the Amazons, as these women were called, had intercourse with men from surrounding tribes. Some contended that they kept their daughters and returned the sons to the tribe of origin; others claimed that the Amazons killed the boys. At home, they supposedly lived peacefully. They were thought to supply all their own economic needs and to produce coveted artisan crafts.

Apparently for some four hundred years (1000–600 B.C.), the Greeks believed that Amazons held Asia Minor along the shores of the Black Sea. The Greeks still held this belief hundreds of years after the legendary warriors last engaged in battle. Only later did the Greeks attempt to dismiss the earlier tales as untrue. Nonetheless, the historical existence of Amazonia still provokes scholarly skirmishes.

Perhaps sufficient historical evidence does not exist to verify Amazonian reality. Yet this discussion evidences clearly the persistent hold of this first instance in a centuries-long series of cultural variations. Ultimately, as with all truth, we are confronting a question of faith and belief. If one believes angels exist, there is no need to prove their existence, let alone to corroborate this existence statistically by exercises designed to count the number of them that can dance on the head of a pin. For more is at stake than whether or not the Greeks, or these particular Greeks (for which sufficient documentation exists to undertake historical investigation) in this particular historical period, had a country of women at their gates.

What is at stake is the actual origin of patriarchy, the necessity of male dominance, as well as the possibility of the independent female, of females coexisting together separately and apart from men. Hence, we must examine the interrelation with another series of texts, those concerning the existence not only of Amazons, but also of a matriarchy. Consequently, it is impossible to discuss the archetype of the Amazon separately from debates concerning matriarchy. In these debates, the primary Amazon is merely a symbol, as can be seen in summaries of how those debates appeared in the American feminist movement in the 1970s that feminist anthropologists Paula Webster and Esther Newton outlined (Webster 1978, Newton and Webster 1975). Feminist theorists and writers Adrienne Rich (1976) and Kate Millett (1971) summarized debates over matriarchy in the late nineteenth and early twentieth centuries, particularly in the works of Bachofen and Briffault. Those late nineteenth-century works on the matriarchy had significant bearing on the outbreak of the movement.

The symbolic actors who appeared in the early Greek legends as "Amazons" entered world literature first in chant, then in drama, and then in history. They formed different relationships with different audiences as they changed convention and form. They played out the psychodrama of the confrontation between two cultures—the earth-based female-centered culture, and the culture of the newly emerging city-state of Greek patriarchy. This is what all the Greek myths of Amazons represent, according to feminist literary scholar Meredith Powers (1991).

Powers argued that epics we think to be the basis of Western civilization were really the assertion of an agnostic patriarchal tribalism which was later to become the basis of elitist Athenian civic pride. Thus, we might perceive epics as the emergent literature of a new social class establishing its dominance. Sociologist Robbie Pfeufer Kahn (1995) also analyzed how the theme of birth entered into one of the earliest stories of the West. She showed how the Homeric tradition draws an analogy between the suffering of a soldier on the battlefield and the anguish of a woman in childbirth. Thus the emerging tradition articulates itself in relationship to residues of the previous social formation.

Kahn showed how in material about war, language such as "hot blood gushed forth" carries an equivalence to menstruation. Such metaphors bring war home by comparing it to the heroic pain of women. Kahn suggested that this earliest Greek literature contains evidence of an even earlier historical period in which birth instead of war may have been at the center of significant action.

She offered this argument because the language throughout Homeric works makes these analogies with the confidence that they will be understood. She demonstrated how newly emerging Greek culture reworked the older female-centered stories that preceded patriarchy—work that is echoed by the studies of Monica Sjöö and Barbara Mor (1987), Marija Gimbutas (1982, 1991), Paul Friedrich (1978) in his work on Aphrodite, and Christine Downing (1981) in her study of mythological images of the feminine.

Particularly as we inherit tales as told by the Spartans, the subject, the male Greek hero, receives orders to conduct a quest to retrieve a chastity object from the queen of Amazonia. She herself seems to be an object, as we can see in the various forms and interpretations of Labor IX of Hercules, The Belt of Hippolyta (Gantz 1993, 397–400). Even in a story about the Amazons, woman appears as the object from which to take. Then, by accident, the queen's lover kills her. He assumes she has betrayed him when her own misled troops attack the ship upon which they are about to embark. Thus she is not at all the self-stylized, self-actualizing subject in charge of her own existence, as she appears in modern reclamations.

A few slight references occur in the *Iliad* which constitute the first known Western appearance of the Amazon. The Homeric collective voice refers to the Amazons as "the women peers of men," and the "women who fight like men." The two directly positive references are Book 3, line 189 and Book 6, line 186.

Richmond Lattimore's translations are "when the Amazon women came, men's equals" (105) and "the Amazons, who fight men in battle" (1951, 158). Lattimore's glossary defines Amazons as "a race of warrior women who invaded Asia Minor" (499). On the other hand, E. U. Rieu in *Homer: The Iliad* (1950) translated the Book 3 reference as "the Amazons, who fight like men" (122) and the Book 6 reference as "the Amazons who go to war like men" (122).

In the currently most popular translation of the *Iliad,* Robert Fitzgerald translated the phrase as "Amazons, women virile in war" (1979, 147). Michael Reck translated the Book 3 mention as "that day the dangerous Amazons came" (1994, 65). In Book 6, he referred simply to the massacre of "the last" ones (1994, 118). The translation I prefer is "Amazons, women peers of men" in Book 6 of *The Complete Works of Homer: The Iliad and the Odyssey* (Homerus 106).

Florence Mary Bennett has written about how critics class these as "echoes" from pre-Homeric saga, and how "therefore it may be inferred that the Amazon tradition in Greek literature dates from a time even earlier than the Homeric poems" ([1912] 1967, 1).

From these slight references, Bennett deduced that Homer characterized the Amazons as a mighty band of warriors to be feared, a horde of women who strive against men and who even take the initiative in battle (2). On the other hand, Bernice Schultz Engle identified sixteen negative terms for Amazons that developed amongst later Greek writers. This latter group portrayed the women as man-destroying and as having the ability to bring pain to men (518). She showed that under patriarchy, a positive image of strong women easily turns negative.

The later story of Hercules and Hippolyta does not illustrate a model of self-sufficient, egalitarian women. Such a tradition of emergent modern reclamation, which accompanied the growth of feminist consciousness, did not begin until Christine de Pizan in the Renaissance period. Rather, what Pratt has called "an ancient, unresolved tension between feminine power and feminine powerlessness in the history of human culture" survived in these Amazon stories (1981, 167).

Pratt (1981) argued that such tension typifies the general category of women's fiction. Dominant Western culture does not preserve the original imprint of the Amazon archetype, but rather attempts to incorporate her in diluted forms that glorify "bittersweet male victories over brave, noble, beautiful but squashed females" (Salmonson, 1992).

Thus most repetitions of the Amazon image uphold patriarchy. Salmonson noted that the greater body of Amazon stories do *not* reflect Greek victories. However, these are not the stories most often retold in imitations. Many mythic versions exist that reflect the Amazon in a more positive light. Yet the forms of dominant culture do not tell these alternative oppositional stories. Such stories include the recounting of wars between factions of Gorgons, the account of Lysippe's founding of Amazonia, the story of Egee's slaying of the king of Troy, the narration of Marpesia's many conquests of the Thermodontines, the stories of the founding of many cities such as the Italian colony by Clete, and the relation of the Amazons founding the Amazonium on the island of Patmos.

The great majority of Amazon tales concern the expansion of influence after success in battles. Yet, given the often unchallenged hegemony in the culture, patriarchal renditions more often tell only the tales of Hippolyta's stolen girdle, the kidnapping of Antiope, and Penthesilea's death. Like the ritual chastising rape of Calypso by an enraged Zeus and the Homeric *Hymn to Demeter*, the Amazon tales merely chronicle the imposition of the values of male superiority.

Amazon Cycle as Tragic Mode

The original Amazons occur within the context of what literary critic Northrop Frye referred to as "tragic fiction modes" (35). Frye called tragic stories "Dionysian" when they apply to divine beings, as there is some speculation the Amazons were.[1] We might read these stories, then, as tragic, Dionysian stories of dying gods.

The women are gods or beings with supernatural powers or who possess power objects. They exist in a supernatural relationship to nature, exercising control over nature. They control droughts and rivers and make waters part, rather than let nature control them. Thus, the stories demonstrate that they, too, are capable of falling and fall prey to the follies of being human. The queens lose their sacred objects. Men capture them. They die by treachery; a melancholy sets in. This contributes to a diffused, resigned sense of the dying and the passing of the time, a "changing of the old order and a yielding to a new one," as Frye (36–37) characterized Greek myths in general.

The fate of the Amazon queens in these stories also fits the contours of a general dilemma of the text. This is the problem of the leader whom the author shows to be isolated from the people and who consequently has to fall. This expresses the irony of the fallen leader which centralizes tragedy in the retold Amazon stories of the Greeks.

Often, the Amazon stories illustrate not only irony but also the general sense of pathos common throughout the tragic cycle. For example, throughout Greek myth, themes repeat concerning exclusion of the individual from the group to which he or she wants to belong. The ambush cuts off Hippolyta from her people when she wants to return from the ship.

Similarly, Aphrodite curses the women of Lemnos with an evil smell. This curse makes their men look beyond the family social grouping and excludes the women from their family relations. Finally, the divine group of enchanted women who have supernatural powers excludes Hercules. As Frye described with an attitude of a poet, texts make a "dispassionate construction of a literary form with all assertive elements implied or expressed eliminated" (40).

Thus, possibly neither the texture nor the tone implies a moral view that women are wild and must be conquered; nor, using this reading, can these tales be read as polemics about the sex war. Neither does the text itself necessarily hold that men, in doing the conquering, are either good or bad, that women are powerful, or that women must suffer. To support this move toward the less polemical, Kahn has pointed out Homeric references respectful toward the Amazons in several places. She saw this simply as proof of authorial cultural affiliation with the immediate matrifocal past. Although a strict division of labor between men and women existed, women's generative capacity did not go undervalued.

Some feminists reclaim Amazons to illustrate the possibility of female rule. Yet Amazons also survive clearly without debate as simply another instance of tragic irony. If we can abstract away from gender conflict, so important to some contemporary feminist writers, Greek Amazon stories express tragic isolation of the hero, the queen. This parallels the story of how Odysseus became tragically isolated on his islands with a series of women in the *Odyssey*.

If we read for aesthetics, then, rather than for polemics, the queen figures as the hero as much as Hercules. Also, the central principle of tragic irony is that something apparently out of line with the central character's essential nature causes whatever tragedy befalls the hero. The image of the Amazons being one-breasted aptly illustrates this.

The One-Breasted Amazon as Tragic Irony Rather Than Fatal Flaw

Here another irony regarding the Amazons occurs. Barbara Babcock (1978), writing about reversals and symbolic inversion, assumed that the word "Amazons" means one-breasted, from *mazos* (breast) and *a* (no). Babcock actually used the concept to mean "one breast"; Lederer, "without a breast" (104). The latter also claimed the word to mean "moon-woman" (103).

Yet much confusion reigns about this issue. For example, Enlightenment author Pierre Petit expressed the notion that "these women most likely used some kind of drug to atrophy the right breast" (Kleinbaum 144).[2] According to *Larousse Greek and Roman Mythology,* "no trace of such mutilation is ever seen in representations of the Amazons" (Schmidt 1980, 132). Sobol concurred (111). Keuls' reproductions of Heracles (Hercules) killing Amazons verify the same conclusion (46). One image in particular is of an Amazon with two full naked breasts, with the warrior's knife stabbing into the tip of one nipple. Other reproductions from vases and fragments show Amazons using shields and armor to protect themselves. No breasts whatsoever are apparent, let alone a mark or a gash where one should appear. In these reproductions, Heracles looks fierce. As Keuls pointed out, the fighting Amazons cautiously protecting their vulnerable spots look rather dainty (45).

According to Friedrich, Artemis of Ephesus related more to the archaic sow and cow icons of the Mother Goddess in that she was many-breasted (93). Thus according to Larousse, the prefix *a* might have contained augmentative connotations (133), which would be more in line with the view of women widespread in that time and area of civilization as active, nursing breast-feeders.

There is no doubt of the primacy of the breast in primordial imagination. Early statuettes represent the female figure with large extended breasts. Wolfgang Lederer's 1968 psychoanalytic study, which was dedicated to understanding the fear of women, reproduces plates of many large-breasted and even three-breasted statuettes (16). We can draw from Kahn's analysis that in any breast-feeding society—which all societies at that time were— the very young enter into social interaction on the maternal body. The primary focus of this for the child is the breast.

Our culture views breasts as objects of desire more than as means of nurturance. Yet the child comes to consciousness on the maternal body, of which the breast is a part (Kahn 1989). According to Kahn, culture accepted the woman's bodily part which expressed this function until patriarchal institutions censored the breast out of daily life.[3] As the infant built knowledge upon the body, these artifacts speak of a groundedness in the body and give form to representations of early vegetal goddesses.

Is it not ironic that the Amazons—women depicted as strong and fearsome—would be deprived of one of the most basic sources of their strength and consequently of their ability to withhold nurturance and instill the fear of its loss? After all, Campbell defined the imprint of nursing as the second most powerful of the earliest imprints on humankind (and probably all mammals), second only to that of being in the womb.

Some militant feminists of the seventies embraced the image of the one-breasted woman in the hopes that the public might recognize that women needn't automatically serve as everybody's nurturers. However, the symbol of the one-breasted woman might have emerged more in the line of Melanie Klein's writings. That is, the one-breasted image might have been a psychological projection of the fear that women with the power to nurture might arbitrarily withhold such privileges, as reflected in a mutilated one-breasted biology.

Mary Florence Bennett, the early twentieth-century American classical philologist, concurred with the opposite connotation and reflection of this typology (1912). She demonstrated that the Amazon goddess was represented as many-breasted on coins. However, the aforementioned Enlightenment writer who claimed the Amazons were one-breasted likewise attested to having gotten his information from preserved coins.[4]

By examining artifacts such as shrines, Bennett provided evidence that Amazons were shown with both breasts intact (34). Bennett argued that the misconception might have come from the practice of Sarmatian women burning off their right breasts (13). Philostratus, Bennett pointed out, took pains to say that the Amazons were not thus mutilated, and that nowhere among the extant remains of Greek art was there a representation of a single-breasted Amazon. All that can be concluded from artistic sources is that there was evidently a propensity for showing one breast bare in plastic and pictorial representations of Amazon women.

Still other scholars have presented other interpretations. Slater, for instance, conjectured that women who devoted themselves to goddesses at the time of the Greeks cut off one or both breasts to present their bodily parts to the deities as a sign of service. Bennett concurred in her discussion of ancient representations of female worshipers cutting off breasts in frenzied devotion to Aphrodite (27). Slater argued further that historians of culture possibly confused these devotees with Amazons who were said to have engaged in this practice at a later time (116).[5]

Also, Calasso wrote of Hippodemeia, who started the women's games. In these games, sixteen virgins ran together with their hair loose, their tunics over their knees, and their right breasts and shoulders uncovered (181). In records and documents, "uncovered" might have been mistranslated as "cut off" and passed down incorrectly through the ages. Mortal monks acting as scribes hand-copied classical manuscripts and preserved them for future study. The selective process they used can be understood by examining comparisons of hand-copied versions (Salter and Edwards 1956). Translations of translations, though overseen by master scribes, left room for numerous mythic re-creations as well as for mistakes. Additionally, Finley pointed out instances of how over the ages the process of copying and sifting through texts has possibly muddied other issues. This possibility considerably generalizes the problem beyond questions about the Amazons (1954, 9). An interesting, compelling female image evolving from mistakes in copying might have become fundamental to the Amazon archetype.

In spite of this available alternative discussion and data, Tyrell (1984), writing the book considered standard by those who teach Greek myth in the traditional classics context, continued in the mid-1980s to claim that "all the sources" depict the Amazons as one-breasted (48). Making a structuralist argument of poetics from this, rather than including all the available discussion and evidence, he asserted that movement is one aspect of the Amazon's lost breast, the opposite of which, lack of movement, the crippling of males represents (48).

By "all the sources," Tyrell referred only to the Greek classical historians. However, the ideology, method, form, and genre of these historians could also be considered subjects for historically particularizing investigation. Tyrell, in writing about the creation of Greek myth, knew this well. The classical historians, as Mary O'Brien has pointed out, were influenced by Aristotle, who believed that women were so passive that they contributed nothing whatsoever to the child that grew within except the material of arrested menstrual flow (1981, 48).

Moreover, earlier references to women—not only to Amazons in Homeric times—showed women of strength being the peers of men. They challenged and influenced men. They entered into public affairs and politics. Additionally, their role models in the early Homeric texts exhibited the wherewithal to resist from within their folk-culture roles, as Penelope did in resisting marriage. Before a suitor could claim her, she had to finish weaving a shroud for her father-in-law. Every night she unraveled the cloth that she had worked on that day, only to re-weave it the following day.

Penelope's act of marriage resistance can be re-interpreted from the perspective of feminist folklore and cultural research as the last stand for return to matriarchy within the home. Feminist folklorist Joan Newton Radner (1993) discussed the notion of acts of coding, or "covert expressions of disturbing or subversive ideas" (vii) through which we could view Penelope's rebellion, or Hera's and Athene's stealing of Zeus's chariot. According to Gilman ([1898] 1966), Penelope's economic contribution would have been significant during Odysseus' twenty-year absence; but it takes successive waves of feminist generations to draw attention to the importance of women's domestic labor and acts within that realm. In a much later text, Mary Wilkins Freeman's "The Revolt of 'Mother,'" an individual woman revolts against an individual man by moving her entire household out into the new barn he has built for the animals after he has refused to build her the new house she needs. Similarly, exploring internal domestic revolt would require an open re-reading of women in classical antiquity[6] not as passive objects and receptacles, but as lively, challenging chariot thieves and drivers who conspired in revolt against autocratic male leaders. Perhaps we would even have to see them as residual strong women from previous archaic civilizations, as feminist folklore studies have re-analyzed such previously unseen female expressive forms (R. A. Jordan and Kalcik 1985). Margaret R. Yocum in particular has introduced the concept of looking at how women subvert authority from within traditional positions. She calls for a re-viewing of acts that other researchers have seen as insignificant.

Kleinbaum has further supported the view that the most commonly given explanation for the name "Amazons" is erroneous. She studied waves of popularity of the Amazon in Athenian art, identifying three types of Amazon statues in marble copies preserved from the various periods. All three types depict an Amazon in short tunic, with one breast bared, but both intact.[7] The same is true of the Amazons on Phidias' shield in the Athenian Parthenon and in Rothery's artifact reproductions. Kleinbaum concludes that no Hellenic artistic or literary tradition supports the idea that the Amazons suppressed or removed one breast (15–16). She attributes the popular belief that the word "Amazon" derived from the women's supposed lack of a right breast to Justin, a third-century B.C. author.[8]

Kleinbaum challenged this common misconception by asserting that the word is not originally of Greek origin and can refer to a range of things in a variety of tongues: breastless, breadless, eaters of strong foods, and so on. Rothery, writing in 1910 (a source which Kleinbaum evidently consulted) had already suggested abandoning to the etymologists the labyrinthine twistings of word warfare. He, too, found a variety of interpretations, including "vestals," "girdle bearers," and other synonyms such as "game eaters" for their name (2). He argued that the word was hybrid Greek. Since it was not a native name, he suggested that it be classed as a nickname. Then, naturally, ". . . it would be as comprehensively descriptive as the ingenuity of man could devise" (2). However, many late classical and medieval authors followed Justin's theory (37), the contradiction in material artifacts to the contrary.

Real suggested another origin of the name, an origin taken from the Roman period. Some argue that the name "Amazon" stands for months. Supposedly, the women counted the days of the months with their waist belts. Hence the Romans called the Amazons *emon* (month) and *zone* (belt) (78).

Real noted that still others have taken the word to derive from the belt on which the women wore a sickle when they went to the fields to cut agricultural products. Yet the women are usually portrayed as non-agricultural, nomadic, and warring.

Others recall that *Maza* was a moon goddess among some groups in the area from which the Amazons came (the *circasianos*), and have thought that the name derived from the moon rituals associated with the female deities whom the Amazons followed. To sort out such perplexing confusion, I have compiled the accompanying chart (see Table 1).

Although there are records of Amazons fighting deep within the inland valleys beyond rivers, there are those who have said that the name "Amazon" means only the destroyers of boats used in nautical journeys. The indigenous word *amassona* is said to mean "boat destroyer" because of the treacherous currents in the rivers on which the Tapuya savages with female warriors lived.

Still further suggestions include Sobol's that the word "Amazon" derives from the Phoenician *Am* (mother) and *Azon* or *Adon* (lord) (161). Nineteenth-century views support such an interpretation (Knight 1876). Thomson attributed the word to the women of Ephesus, who, renouncing the occupations of their sex, could take to warfare and agriculture: "reap" or *amao*, wearing "girdles" or *zonai* (182).

Diner traced additional possibilities: from the Greek word *amazosas*, meaning "opposed to men"; from *azona* (chastity belt); or from *aemetzaine*, which in the Kalmuck language is the word for strong heroic women (128). Some scholars have traced the Amazons' origin to India, claiming that the one-breasted statue of a female on the island of Elephanta provided the Greeks with their first notion of an Amazon. In addition, the early Black Sea

TABLE I.   Possible Origins of the Term "Amazon"

Term	Meaning	Possible Origin
amazon	generic Persian for "warring people"	Persian origin
oyorpata	Scythian for "man killer"	Scythian origin, Greek translation
amao-zonai	to reap and wear girdles, or a belt, on which a sickle is hung to work in field	development of agriculture, not completely wild
emonyzone	months, from counting days on waist belts	Roman period
Amazosas	"opposed to men" in Greek	sexual rejection of men
azona	"chastity belt" in Greek	self-protection
aemetzaine	"strong heroic women" in Kalmuck, a language of a Caucasian ethnic group in Russia	women from Caucasus area (not a group)
Maza	"moon goddess" in the circasianos	performance of religious rituals, dispersed
amassona	"destroyer of boats, vessels" from treacherous currents on river on which they lived	Indian word in South America, origin predated European dispersion
miscellaneous	vestals, girdle bearers, game eaters, eaters of strong foods	nicknames in hybrid Greek

settlement of Amastreis translates as "Uma's women," from *uma* and *stri* (woman).

Real identified the basic problem: the Greeks themselves were only speculating, he argued, because the word was not of Greek origin, but Iranian. As other scholars have noted about all the Greeks' names for other peoples, not just their name for Amazons, the language was at that time a jumble of many languages and tongues from many interacting neighbors with different linguistic structures and traditions (Finley 1954, 5).

Therefore, according to Real, the Greeks did not know anything about the etymology, because the word wasn't really Greek (226–227). As Real concluded in his chapter on names, we can construe nothing about the national character or ethnographic customs of the women based on the Greeks' translation of their name. The Greeks were, after all, only trying to impute some meaning to a foreign word through their own common-sense reasoning.

This word was not of their own vocabulary, but only the foreign name of a group or nation of foreigners. We can't take "Amazon" to mean "less busty," or "more busty," or really anything to do with the bust at all, just because the foreign word these historians heard sounded like the Greek word for breast.

Moreover, some have even taken the name to mean the intangibility of women who did not want men to touch them. By emphasizing in their name that part of themselves that others would most desire, the women chose to be doubly cruel to men or to outsiders.

Herodotus, the original Greek historical chronicler of the Amazons, reported that they were called *eorpata*. This was a mistranslation of the Scythian *oyorpata,* which in Greek means "killer of men," or "Androctonoi."[9] Yet, as Real points out in a thorough discussion of the derivation of the name "Amazon," if the women had indeed crossed from Persia, the Greeks would have given them a generic name meaning simply "warring people." All we can say, really, is that the Amazons traced their lineage through the mother, as Real reasoned logically, and that they fought (see Table 1).

Homeric and Pre-Homeric Origins

The irony is that culture has used the most concrete of Amazons abstractly, as symbols. But can we gain further understanding by tracing the Amazons back to their Homeric and pre-Homeric incarnations? What can we learn by a closer study of the Homeric period and the pre-Homeric period reflected in that recorded literature? Can this sort of investigation shed light on how the Amazon emerged into the epic cycles in the form that male writers then exaggerated and handed down in middle-European and early Renaissance literature? Can this pursuit serve to show how truly historic our own categories of analysis are for use in the twentieth century?

In *Homer and the Oral Tradition* (1976), classics scholar G. S. Kirk argued that what we now think of as the work of an individual, Homer, was really the cumulative elaboration and synthesis of many singers of oral tradition. Though Kirk's has not always been the dominant view, he argued convincingly that, using a range of techniques, through repetition, several singers wove a series of separate tales into a collective whole to create a vision of a world of the past. They delivered what we know today as Homer's work to the audience of a world they knew. Kirk pointed to the need to understand oral poetics in order to comprehend Homer (70).[1]

The notion that the Homeric poems arose as oral, collectively composed, live performances has been working its way into mainstream classical thought since Albert B. Lord's *The Singer of Tales* (1964).[2] Lord based his own text on field recordings by Milman Parry, which the Harvard University Library houses. Some of the texts of these transcriptions are available in *Serbocroatian Heroic Songs* (Parry and Lord 1954). Kirk drew on Parry and Lord.

As Rhys Carpenter, a classicist, noted in *Folk Tale, Fiction and Saga in Homeric Epics* (1962), Parry offered "unanswerable, unassailable proof" which placed the *Iliad* and the *Odyssey* in the class of oral literature (6–7). Carpenter additionally raised the narratological issue that how the audience was being sung to and what this audience knew required the performer to simplify the text. He argued that only later did poets such as Sappho and Byron romanticize inherited images (34).

M. I. Finley, in *The World of Odysseus* (1954), addressed the world, the audience, and this interactive process of describing one world to the people of another time, of relating the world of the song being sung to the world of the audience being sung to. A summary of the complications that arose from discovering inconsistencies and changing times and aspects of material culture in the surviving text can be found in Lord's introductory chapter (1964, 8–10). He also summarized the various theories that arose to explain such complications.

In the world known to Homeric audiences, the earth was an active force. The epics often personified various aspects of the earth in female form, such as Dawn's cyclical female-gendered risings, which occur throughout. Furthermore, the collective entity then touched upon or reworked by the individual Homer (if, indeed, there was one such gentleman), represented women and feminine psychology in a positive light. In fact, although Virgil's *Aeneid*, written much later, uses exhortation *against* the goddess,[3] the *Iliad* opens with a call *to* the goddess, seeking her help:

> Sing, Goddess, the wrath of Achilles Peleus's son, he ruinous wrath
> that brought on the Achaians woes innumerable, and hurled down
> into Hades many strong souls of heroes, and gave their bodies to be
> a prey to dogs and all winged fowls. (1)[4]

Likewise, the *Odyssey* opens with an appeal to the muse, the omniscient "goddess, daughter of Zeus," to tell whatever she knows of the traveler who has wandered far and wide since the sacking of Troy (1). Throughout, the epic names the mother first when tracing the lineage of the offspring of the divine or of those dying in battle. This contrasts greatly with the later practices of the Old and New Testaments, as contemporary feminists have pointed out.

Although this is not the perspective taught in most literature survey courses or in the introductory humanities classes through which most college students first approach these texts, Book 1 of the *Iliad* already establishes matrilineality (2). The Homeric voice identifies Apollo as he to whom Leto of the fair locks has given birth. In this way, the text identifies the god by the mother who bore him, not by the father. For the purposes of arguing that other women besides the Amazons were strong and dominant in these early texts, this is not an insignificant starting point.

Leto and her children were predecessors of the ancient wooden popular cult images representing the mother in worship: Leto superseded Rhea. Leto's daughter, Artemis of the Euphesians, was the old moon goddess whom the Amazons worshiped. Slater cited Apollo as a product of an odd circumstance of birth—not of woman born (139). The very beginning of the text is situated in a matriarchal context, with its woman-centered methods of birthing and mating, in contrast to the later, patriarchal depiction of the births of gods and heroes.

On this more generalized basis, then, the Amazons became notorious. Yet their customs could also have been something as simple as the ritual Malinowski described, in which all females of puberty age leave their villages, walk to another town, and sit in the middle of the public space preening themselves until they attract their chosen short-term male-adventure mate.

Other examples exist of women in the Homeric text who are dominant and strong. For instance, Thetis appears to the gods to ask for intervention when she rises up from the sea to appeal to Zeus (15).[5] Thus, goddesses, the supra-role models for female humans, stand up for what they want and for what they believe. They are not so passive as to dutifully watch history go by without actively speaking, although those scholars still using older theoretical models of literary interpretation might continue to eclipse this articulated female struggle.

Even more interesting is that women in these classics texts are often aggressive in their manner of speaking up. For instance, Thetis pushes Zeus to act, even though at first he resists her request that he intervene among mortals on her son's behalf. Wife beating and domestic violence emerge as issues when Hera's own son urges her not to press Zeus into divulging the nature of another woman's visit (15–17). Zeus sleeps out on the couch separate from his woman's chambers when marital dispute arises, and also fears the fact that his wife might upbraid him in public if he does not obey her wishes (17). Women demonstrate courage and commit bold acts, witnessed publicly. Such acts include Thetis' leap into the deep from the heights of Ida and

Athene's darting down from the crests of Olympus to holy Ilios to intervene on the battlefield (7.116).

Other facts also challenge the prevailing preconceptions with which classics professors generally teach. For example, in the *Iliad*, Aphrodite is active in the battlefield although she gets hurt and runs back out. Women are quick moving and independent. The phrase applied to Thetis, "the silver-footed," highlights neither domestic enslavement nor captivity, but rather, heightened female mobility. Women wield political influence, as evidenced by statements about Hera's ability to turn the minds of all when making political speeches (19.20). Women contest male authority and conspire among themselves to affect the public realm (23). Women speak in public, often in loud voices. Similar to the women who appear in Herodotus' later *History*, they cross-dress, appear as androgynous, and as men. Some men even appear on the battlefield dressed as women. As Harrison noted in *Themis*, such exchange of clothing represents the transition from matriarchy to patriarchy (506).

In *Great Mother of the Gods,* Showerman also noted the effeminate dressing of priests and followers of the Great Mother. A whole tradition of cross-dressing appears in the Homeric hymns. For example, to protect Achilles from the draft, Thetis dresses him as a woman and takes him to a temple where vestal virgins surround him. Odysseus, knowing he needs Achilles' participation to win the war, dresses as a saleswoman and enters the temple. He plants a sword in the middle of a basket of yarn. When Achilles reaches into the basket and touches the sword, his heroic blood rises. He drops his dress and runs off to join the war. Men also dress as women in Aristophanes' *Lysistrata.*

Time and time again, closer scrutiny topples the traditional view of classic Greek literature as the struggle of the male hero against a backdrop of passive female seductresses and temptresses. Women also act, empowered by a god. They are strong, reliable, loud-voiced, and athletic. They command the silence of multitudes to hear their voices, leap from high places, and maintain and demonstrate physical prowess. They obey female authority, they stir assemblies to revolt, and initiate action. The text acknowledges women's influence both on each other and on the world of men.

Repeatedly, women make decisions and take actions in the context of their perceptions and the perceptions of others that they have power (12.13). Frequently, this right to power in the public realm stems from strong feelings of having brought about a mortal's birth. For example, Thetis proclaims in an attitude of lament to her own son, who has appealed to her:

Ah me, my child, why reared I thee, cursed in my motherhood?
Would thou hadst been left tearless and griefless amid the ships, seeing thy lot is very brief and endureth no long while; but now art thou
made short-lived alike and lamentable beyond all men; in an evil hour
I bare thee in our halls. But I will go myself to snow-clad Olympus to
tell this thy saying to Zeus, whose joy is in the thunder, if perchance
he may hearken to me. (13)

The attitude of lament will become significant later, when I explore what
might be an undisclosed source of the sung poetry of the Homeric chant, a
source suggested both by the prevalence of what Keuls (1985) has called "the
mourning mother" in Greek myth and by the rituals involved in preparing
the bodies of the dead for burial. Women performed this ceremony—a kind
of reverse birth—and they also performed ritual lament throughout the classical age.[6]

What seems key in the passage quoted above is that Thetis feels that the
suffering experienced during childbirth and motherhood provides a legitimate, compelling, logical motivation to act in a way that influences the
course of historical events. As other instances demonstrate, women were
expected to be strident and assertive in public. For example, heroes immediately obey goddesses like Athene (24). The goddesses change historical
events and wield political influence. Indeed, given the structure of Thetis'
speech and where it occurs in this text, the whole of the *Iliad* might just well
originally have been "Thetis' Lament."

Additionally, the collective text presents women as the sole agents who
are able to save men from their own folly, of which war is only one manifestation (123). Women act upon the gods, as when Thetis alone can approach
Zeus to attempt to loosen his bonds. Furthermore, on the battlefield women
also appear to give direction to their sons in war. Athena is right there in
many scenes of action. She bears protective armor for some and guides fatal
darts and spears for others.

The text returns to omnipotent muses throughout for plot revelations. All
true knowledge comes from females, according to the singer who proclaims,
"Tell me now, ye muse that dwelt in the mansions of Olympus, seeing that
ye are goddesses and are at hand and know all things" (2.33). The muses are
elsewhere responsible for positive, definitive acts in the real world (2.36).
Women can hurt and maim; furthermore, power breaks forth in their voice
and song. Throughout the text, the collective voice turns to Athena for counsel; a goddess with wings delivers a message. When need be, she intercedes

and manipulates characters to advance the plot. In short, women conduct heroic acts throughout the collective texts, including their role in birth. A hard division does not seem fixed between women's private and men's public realms. Women could do both child-rearing and political work.

The narrative voice sees characters derive strength by turning to women. For example, in Book 4, Helenos proclaims that the foes soon would be seen "fleeing in their women's arms" (103). He beseeches Hector to go into the city to speak to both their mothers. He wants them to activate their exclusive control of religious sites over which women reign as priestesses: to "gather the aged wives to bright-eyed Athene's temple in the upper city" where they would use their keys to open the holy house, to lay down their robes, and to perform sacrifices" (109).

Thus, the women have the power to appeal to Athena for mercy for the city and for the Trojans. Hector makes the request in full to his mother, referring to "Athene, driver of the spoil" (108). According to documents collected by Lefkowitz and Fant, even in Athens in the fifth century B.C. such a role in religion was not minor: women controlled the holy site of Dodona near the Sacred Oak and sacred rituals that would not be holy if performed by men (1992, 14).

Even within the text, cults developed around women. They gave sanctuary (2.39) and protected the earth as grain-givers. Matrilineal authority established power, reliability, and trustworthiness. One example is the explication of Achilles proclaimed by Helenos in Book 4 of the *Iliad*: "Never in this wise feared we Achilles, prince of men who they say is born of a goddess" (103).

In fact, the organizational scribes of the *Odyssey* devoted the eleventh book to a catalogue of female heroines whom the male hero meets in the underworld when going in sorrow to visit those who have died in the war (84). Throughout the book, Penelope actively seeks to maintain the cultural norm.[7]

Ultimately, a goddess, Athena, actually becomes the hero. Here I use "hero" in the modern sense as the individual whose actions save the day by resolving the conflict and contradictions in the plot.[8] As a divine female, Athena puts an end to the terrible and seemingly endless war (Finley 1954, 24). Athena personally stops the blood feud between the so-called hero, who is mortal and male, and the kinsmen of the suitors he has killed. She does this despite having appealed to Zeus as ruler in heaven to take such an action in the beginning of the second poem.

Evidently, Athena becomes impatient with Zeus' apparent ineptitude. She carries out the climactic act of resolution herself the next time he sends her down among the humans. War is seen as a ravaging pestilence and as a disease which must be stopped, not as a manly theater in which men can prove themselves with great deeds for the sake of the larger whole.

Female dominance is evidenced in the private sphere as well. More flexible arrangements existed outside the patriarchal marriage system, which considered women personal property, as when Priam's offspring, although born out of wedlock, were still accepted (*Il.* 13.230). Moreover, chronologies of slayings on the battlefield include phrases such as, "Now Boukoloin was son of proud Laomedon, his eldest born begotten of a mother unwed; and as he tended his flocks he had converse with the nymph in love, and she conceived and bore . . ." (*Il.* 6.101). Patriarchal marriage relations were still a relatively new social foundation, slow to cancel the old ways. Women were still assumed to be active participants in their own lineage. They also exhibited an active sexuality, pursuing extramarital sexual affairs. Yet they were still referred to as being "good," such as in Book 6, where Proitos' wife, "goodly Antenia," lusted after Bellerphone "to have converse on secret love" (105).

Thus the tales that tell this story in the evolving tradition assimilated much from the preceding female-dominated past both in the private and the public realm. Each singer contributed not only individually in the process of performing ritual rites, but also as part of a larger tradition, drawing from predecessors, which further established this more female-centered past. Even before the development of aristocratic poetry, presumably each epic poem singer sang with an ambition to tell it like it really was. After all, the poems represented a people's connection with their own, real past, not idle art and entertainment; that past included a predominance of active, vocal women.

Before the development of the palace-society professionals, the grassroots Homeric singer/poets remained concise. Modern readers might want emphasis and explanations, yet because of the particular oral style of the tales being sung, the references were delicate. They were delivered fleetingly with subtlety and brevity. The speakers' experience of language was not that it must simply pass information, exchange messages, or convey meaning to named objects. Rather, they were speaking and participating with others who already had such information, singing and responding with intonation. The primary purpose was not that of passing on information. In this respect, the Amazon appears in the same state of underdevelopment as do other crucial elements in the text. The texts were designed to be emotive, not primarily informative.

As Charles Rowan Beye noted in *The Iliad, the Odyssey, and the Epic Tradition* (1972), the saga background from which the poems might have come permitted poets to make allusions that are often obscure to us, but which were probably not obscure to original audiences (19). Collective grass-roots improvisers could readily assume the background of the audience and build on prior knowledge. Only now do we engage in guesswork as to what these tales contained (Kirk 66). Chanters did not need to intrude on narrative to introduce known groups or their histories (Beye 63).

Hence, when chanters mentioned Amazons, they needn't have necessarily elaborated or explained. Amazons emerged in a text already rich with incidences of female power. Like other aspects of pre-classical history, audiences might simply have accepted Amazons as fact. Hunger for verification of particular facts about the Amazons seems to be a modern need, not an ancient one.

Yet the images of strong powerful women are so unlike the usual images of women presented from the male point of view that we must ask whether the whole text might have been not only female centered but also female created. Even with scant information, it is possible to construe that the original *Iliad* and *Odyssey* might have been the work of women, as an outgrowth of Greek lament poetry.[9] Such a supposition might be imposing 1990s thought patterns on the Greek world, similar to how debate has raged in the twentieth century about how the modern Greeks relate to the ancient Greeks. These debates raise the problem of looking at Greeks as Europeans, as many do, thus reading history backwards. Such a process might obscure differences among Greek historical periods, superimposing the Greek past onto contemporary Greece, and perhaps vice versa.[10] Yet in 1891—a century before feminist scholarly thought in the 1990s—Samuel Butler, a contemporary of George Bernard Shaw, independently argued that a woman seems to have written the *Odyssey*. The assumption I argue for here allows for positing direct cultural continuity over the millennia rather than assigning Turkish or Slavic origins to the chants.

Butler based his argument on the numerous sensibilities in the text that seemed "feminine" to him (1967). For example, he found women to be drawn sympathetically in the *Odyssey*, while men appear stilted. He identified a preponderance of female interest, identifying "a fuller knowledge of those things which a woman generally has to deal with, than of those that fall more commonly within the province of man" (105).

I have already mentioned the inordinate attention to female folk culture in the texts. Weaving, "women's work," becomes pivotal in the plot and germane to much imagery throughout as well. In addition to Penelope's act of unraveling and reweaving in the *Odyssey*, Helen's weaving of "a great purple web of double fold" is discussed in the *Iliad* down to the minute particulars of the rose design (*Il.* 22.437; Fitzgerald 529). How her body feels from the inside working the shuttle and the details of how she requests her maids to prepare her a bath (*Il.* 22.438–448; Fitzgerald 529) are also well drawn. Hector seems acquainted with the details of his wife's work with her maids on loom and spindle (*Il.* 6.450–513; Fitzgerald 156–157) as well.

Moreover, the imagery used to convey the action of men's games is not based on men's pursuits, but rather on the subtle movements made by women while weaving. This indicates the possibility that the epic was composed for a predominantly female audience (*Il.* 23.756–764; Fitzgerald 559). Athene makes her own garments (5.95), although scant mention is made of any of the manufacture of clothes for males, human or divine. The fact that Athene makes her own clothes does not call into question her horsemanship; it does not jar with the fact that she also harnesses steeds and knows how to drive and how to handle the yokes of stallions—acts with which both she and Hera are very much at home.

In addition to the folk arts of weaving and sewing, women's herbal folk culture also enters the discussion. The eldest daughter of Augeias, fair-haired Agamede, "knew all drugs that the wide earth nourisheth" (*Il.* 11.206). The text also exhibits close association with the intimacies of the women's folk art of seduction, as when Hera dresses to beguile Zeus. She enlists Aphrodite to help her in her plans to effect the course of the war (*Il.* 64.254–257).

Classical scholars have also noted the presence of female folk arts in the text. Classicist Charles Beye mentioned women's menstrual stains and women's crafts and arts, both familiar in Book 4 (36–37); he also pointed out that in Book 19, women have much knowledge of war and that women lament (20–21). Kirk also noted women storytellers in Book 4 (21).

The folk art of nursing appears in the text often; in fact, this is a text in which women are active doers of simple things in daily life rather than one in which, as we will see later, women are idealized as men's animas. The commonplace act of nursing is interwoven with the most extraordinary of things in *Il.* 6, where "the nursing mothers of frenzied Dionysos" appear (104).

An argument about the likelihood that women originally authored the text cannot totally rest on the appearance throughout of women's folk culture and women's position of power, strength, and domination. Yet it is true that women tend to notice each other's abilities and to recognize what other women do in daily life, rather than just focusing on how women serve men or how they physically attract or repel them. A modern example of this mutual interest appears in the 1917 short story "Jury of Her Peers," by Susan Keating Glaspell. In the story, women notice clues in another woman's housekeeping that reveal a murder motive not evident to the official male investigators (359–384).

Furthermore, in the epic text, women's experiential reality is often the basis for metaphorical imagery as well as for action that raises further questions about locating the production of the text. The work is definitely aligned with a female point of view, as it specifically selects experience related to female situations. Various incidences even suggest commitment to or conscious alignment with a female perspective, indicating that perhaps the material social practice of writing might have happened within a female social arena.

For example, when Hector comes home briefly, obviously estranged from family relationships by the war, he is viewed through the eyes of the female household—including wife, servants, and children. Many other imagistic references stand out from the text, such as referring to mother animals with their young and to nursing. The number ten is also used to represent a time of precipitous actions, as the tenth month is the month of giving birth, after incubating for nine. Not the Judaeo-Christian "He worked hard for six days, and on the seventh he rested," but "She worked hard for nine, and then on the tenth gave forth . . ."

How could all this be? Does this mean that women formed a significant part of the poet/singer's ritual audience, an audience that contemporary criticism dubiously traces through the environment of the male-only coffee houses in the Turkish-influenced Balkans?[11] Or, given that the text must reflect lived experience to at least some degree, does it suggest that women took part in creating the epic? In many instances, a female orientation seems strongly indicated. The writing itself deeply embeds the real social relations of the female world as the relations within which audiences heard and read the text.

Beyond the references that seem to regard female folk art from a female viewpoint rather than from the perspective of the male gaze, we might attribute some of the depicted capriciousness and strength of women to their positions as goddesses, rather than to their relative position as females within the society of the Olympians. Still, the images of the Homeric goddesses definitely project models for defiant, confident, domineering, influential female behavior. This strong female role modeling might have impacted the female mortals, who, upon hearing the stories recited, would consciously or unconsciously emulate the female deities, just as men emulated male gods.

As classicist Beye has explained, the identity of an illiterate culture often depends on its oral poetic traditions. The poetry thus articulates the culture "as it is, and what it was, giving cultural stability and continuity" (Beye 204). Thus, Beye noted, it is no small fact that the Homeric epic reveals women who are free, active, and powerful (202). They often exhibit the mystical power to dispel the mists between reality and unreality. They are often represented as supernatural forces who help the men understand themselves (182). The women are also often monumental. Men approach queens as suppliants, Helen as goddess (177).

Beye, too, identified a persistent theme of the power of women (174). Women act out of a matriarchal remnant. They represent superior intelligence, one that invading patriarchal, European-oriented peoples experienced with confusion. Perhaps they resented discovering such a female-centered population in their midst as well as in their myths.[12] Beye commented that Homeric women are both sexual and aggressive. Hera sets out to seduce Zeus in the fourteenth book. Athena enters battle as a military figure (100), as well as repeatedly being a brisk, astringent aggressive problem solver (66).

Hence, when we examine the original image of the Amazon in the context of the classical epic, it becomes clear that the archetype contains elements that are characteristic of modern reclamation and revitalist reversal. Yet, this image of the female—bold, brave, and strong—clashes with our dominant culture's traditional view of the masculine origin of Western literature.

For example, Tyrell cited three lines from Hector to the effect that "war is the affair of men" as evidence that Homer's epics and the Greek world are both patriarchal, affirming "the classic gender roles of the patriarchy" (26). Tyrell seems to have missed the main sociological content of the text, failing to note that the text devotes a greater word count to the wife's critique of the way in which men's feuds and wars interrupt women's social labor.

Yet, according to Constantina-Nadia Seremetakis in *The Last Word: Women, Death and Divination in Inner Mani* (1991), this female critique of the male continues to ripple thematically throughout both contemporary and ancient Greek lament. Acknowledgment of the presence of this theme opens the way to another critical view, the possibility that the Homeric texts are related to female lament tradition.

Lament into Literature

It may be that the discrepancy between standard preconceptions of the master texts and what actually appears in them is due to the fact that the originators of the theory that the written *Iliad* and *Odyssey* might have been the product of oral chanters studied only the performances of male singers. Furthermore, these scholars conducted this study in a twentieth-century Slavic area which for centuries had been under Turkish influence. This Muslim influence prohibited women from singing in public (Lord 1964).

However, at the time of the writing of the *Iliad* in the second half of the eighth century B.C., Great Mother priestesses and oral worshipers included women leading singing, dancing, and chanting processions through the streets (Showerman 1901). Modern interpreters of the classics, such as Gregory Nagy (1990), have analyzed the Homeric poems in terms of danced and performed song rather than in terms of chanted verse.

Thus, Lord pursued the origins of the epics by studying a modern culture in which all the chanters are male. He limited his study by his focus on coffee house (*kafona*) or tavern cultures (15). From this perspective, he could not possibly have reasoned backward to the process of creation of an *Iliad* and an *Odyssey* in which women actually took an active, creative part in composing, performing, and listening. Yet, there is evidence in the text that women storytellers and singers did exist.

Parry and Lord's extrapolation from the male Muslim enclave back to the Homeric period is clearly dubious. Further, they insisted on examining only those all-night festivals in which men alone gather to listen to epics and to talk among themselves. Perhaps these researchers followed this course because at these festivals the business of singing took on a professional appearance, with collections gathered for the singers.

Yet a deeper prejudice seems to be at work. For instance, Lord and Parry's definition of "oral literature" itself excludes women's festivals, such as days set aside for singing, lamenting, and mourning. Women also told familial-folk (i.e., epic) histories at these festivals, in both ancient and contemporary Greek culture, originally as unpaid, non-professional activity. Women took on leadership roles in composition, performance, and audience only sometimes within the hearing range of men (Danforth and Tsiaras, 1982).

The shrill music of the *aulos,* or reed pipe, another influence or carry-over from Great Mother worship, frequently accompanied the performed familial-folk epics. When women musicians entered public entertainment, women's *aulos* playing was vulgarized as popular accompaniment for women acrobats (Lefkowitz and Fant 1992, 215).

In *The Ritual Lament in Greek Tradition* (1974), Margaret Alexiou analyzed the role of kinswomen performing for and with strangers in the Homeric context. In her chapter "Tradition and Change in Antiquity" (10–14), she described how the newly emergent state legislated against large, expensive funerals with lamentation (16–17). This legislation led to further restrictions of women's public roles. Yet archaeology, epigraphy, and literature bear witness to the importance attached to funeral rituals in pre-historic Greece.

Because Parry and Lord studied an art kept alive by male Muslims *after* the imposition of these restrictions on lamentation (Lord 46), they were unable to see the centrality of the role of women. Even so, the male chanters still passed down the occasional image of women mounting and charging on white horses, presumably as cavalry (Lord 46).

Indeed, what contemporary scholars studied in order to recreate the pre-Greek past could not possibly have been close to the original social context. Perspectives from other scholars might broaden the picture. For example, Jane Harrison argued in *Themis* that folk-play or fertility drama survived through the forms that they lent to world literature. It is also possible that behind the great sadness and tragedy of the *Iliad* and the *Odyssey* lies a residual element of lament poetry—an oral poetic form primarily sung by women in their folkloric role of being responsible for spiritual mediation of the dead and for grieving.

Indeed, the theory of the poem's origin in primitive ritual drama in which women were the composers correlates with a number of facts which otherwise might seem meaningless and unrelated. This set of facts includes the Athenian custom of seasonal group burials of the victims of large wars, a custom that later led to the practice of collective funeral oration. This in turn contributed to the development of the modern Greek national character.[13]

Donna C. Kurtz and John Boardman, in *Greek Burial Customs* (1971), discussed the funeral practices of societies prior to Homer's era that have been said to be referenced in the text, as well as those of the classical period. Kurtz and Boardman showed illustrations of female mourners, particularly those of Mycenaean origin, painted on sarcophagi from Tanagra (27). Some scholars also maintain that pre-Homeric societies were actually cults of the dead (22). This women's role in creating lament poetry can be said to be significant and of high status within the culture itself. Homeric texts later reified this process. The lamentations of Thetis begin the *Iliad,* and a group funeral for fallen warriors ends it.

Just as the ancient Greeks stood in awe of their predecessors' monumental burial chambers and tombs, which were constructed with walls to preserve as well as to shelter ritual offerings and votives, so they recorded their respect and piety for the dead in sung poetry. Like the monuments, the sung poetry became a way of paying tribute to fallen heroes and codifying legends into history. The Mycenaean palace sites, inexplicably razed at the end of the thirteenth century B.C., indicate that *something* must have happened. The conflict we know as the Trojan War has been dated to this age, and the great poems under discussion were originally composed about this time.

In addition, Kurtz and Boardman speculated that a change may have occurred in burial practices as people dispersed to refugee settlements. The lack of characteristic offerings suggests either invasion or the emergence of a servile class. Since much evidence exists for the invasion theory, the codifying of the funeral laments could have been the primary method by which the dispersed peoples, cut off from their monuments of material culture, kept their rich social and cultural history alive. This parallels how, during the Jewish Diaspora and the fall of the Temple, Jews kept their history alive through mournful chant and singing ritualized into daily prayer practice.

Angela Bourke, a feminist folklorist working on women's lament poetry (1993), noted that a funeral is not just a farewell to the dead; it is a ceremony of transition among the living. In many cultures, including that of ancient Greece, women composed and sang powerful and sophisticated oral lament poetry. Current studies show that this cultural trait was not confined to the Greeks, but was and is prevalent among the Chinese, Egyptians, Romans, and others. The custom of female composition and performance of lament poetry survives today among the Greeks, as well as in the Balkans, Asia Minor, and Spain. Margaret Alexiou, who has worked on ritual lament, particularly in the Greek tradition, has discussed this phenomenon (1974).

In this arena of composition and performance, women as poets formally and publicly express their own and the community's reaction to death. They piece "traditional motifs together to provide a musical and verbal accompaniment to grief and to the dislocation that follows any death," Bourke argued (160). In many of the cultures in which women practice lamentation as mourners, the singers give vent to anger at powerful people. They publicly criticize their own relatives and in-laws and give graphic accounts of personal problems. This public criticism that results in exposure of personal details is all part and parcel of the tradition of lamenting.

Folklorists Anna Caraveli Chaves (1980) and Constantina-Nadia Sere-metakis (1987) studied women, death, and divination in Inner Mani. Their analysis of contemporary Greek funeral lament indicates that women still use the lament to articulate their own worldviews in opposition to the men's. They often use poetry to air social grievances against relatives. Commonly, these grievances concern afflictions that are peculiar to women in male-dominated society. Women lamenting at funerals in surviving Greek culture create a domain of cultural power from which men must keep their distance, socially and physically.

As I reviewed the tradition of oral lament, an idea began to form. I began to weave together the insights of contemporary folklorists with the direct sources of the classics of Western literature. Did, perhaps, much of the oral poetry forming the basis of the *Iliad* and the *Odyssey* occur originally in this female-dominated, group, folkloric context? This insight does not contradict the notion that individual women poets whose names and fragmentary works still survive, such as Sappho, might have been creating as well in other contexts.

However, the insight did clash with inherited preconceptions. I noticed the generous number of references to lamentation in these particular texts, and the similarities in structure between lamentation and embedded form. Thus I began to wonder if women's oral lamentations in the folk context could be a well-tapped if previously unacknowledged source for the larger surviving documents known as the *Iliad* and the *Odyssey*.

For example, Andromache leads off the dirge for her husband Hector (*Il.* 24.724), even before he is dead (*Il.* 6.500; Fitzgerald 157). Many lament for Hector at his wake (*Il.* 24.720). Additionally, Achilles leads a lamentation (*Il.* 18.317). Hector's body is burned after a nine-day lament period (*Il.* 24.782–786; Fitzgerald 593). The burnt mortal and transient male human body disappears into the rising eternal transcendent body of the female goddess Dawn. Achilles' body is also burnt after eighteen days (*Od.* 24.63–65).

Lamenting women furthermore care for the dead elsewhere in the texts (*Il.* 23.180–184, Fitzgerald 541; *Od.* 11.27). Professional, deep-breasted mourners enter in and interact with kinswomen (*Il.* 18.334–347; Fitzgerald 446). The soul not grieved for meets with Odysseus in the underworld (*Od.* 11.72–73). The warbling of ocean nymphs mingles with the lament of the muses for Achilles (*Od.* 24.58–62). Women perform the large, grass-roots, *goos,* a kinswomen's lament (*Il.* 6.450–500; Fitzgerald 156–157; *Il.* 22.430–515; Fitzgerald 531; *Il.* 23 and 24.5).

These examples of the numerous references to the mourning process contribute to understanding the structural importance of women's role to the dramatic plot of the text. Yet the most obvious structural similarity of the text to lamentation poetry is the repeated reference to the image of a fertile earth spawning new life even as it accepts the bodies of the dead. This image is an old one, rooted in primitive fertility magic. The new poetic form offered the traditional image inherited from lament new life and vigor. Lament structure often addresses the earth directly as women ask the earth to open to receive the deceased into its [her] breast and to recall how the deceased has served her (Alexiou 9).

In the Homeric texts (e.g., *Il.* 11.196), this continual focus on the image of the receptive earth mirrors a general tradition in lament poetry. Other examples include references to "the earth's roof to the house of Death," from Hekabe's lamentation (*Il.* 22.477; Fitzgerald 531) and images of the trivial and frequently recurring pursuits of war ravaging the earth, the Great Mother (e.g., *Il.* 18.314–322; Fitzgerald 445). The narrative voice also compares lamentation groans to those of the protector of the Great Mother, the Lioness.

Also, in many instances the classic texts reproduce the structure of mourners' lamentations. Accounts often first tell how a character or personage was conceived and raised and then how he died, even in the midst of skirmishes (*Il.* 13.230). This imprint of lamentation structure would explain why, in the middle of relating how men died in battle and who killed whom, the narration will stop to tell lineage, including identification of the character's mother. Once, for example, the text stops in the very instant of a man's death to tell how a woman excelling in beauty, skill, and wisdom (not just looks or projected anima femininity) had been selected to be the dying man's bride (*Il.* 13.238).

Although there has been increasing acceptance among scholars that both the *Iliad* and the *Odyssey* are in essence oral, collectively constructed poems pieced together by repetition of known formulae (Kirk 1976, 19), as far as I know, no one has yet used this lens to examine the original formulation of the Amazon archetype in European-centered Western civilization. Yet women sing the vast majority of known laments that express the opposition of women's experiences to those of men. This cultural and social fact would seem to explain why both texts, if read beyond our own civilization's biased filters, could be seen as critical female discourse about male activity. Such critical female discourse does emerge as a central theme in the tradition that later solidified into lyric poetry. It appeared, as well, in the choral ode or the tragic lament in dialogue between chorus and actors in tragedy and theater (Alexiou 13).

Lament poetry often contains messages that would have been intelligible to an inner circle of women, but not necessarily to the rest of the audience. Thus, as Bourke has pointed out, in Irish lament women disguise those messages protesting men's violence. According to Bourke, women mourners make devastating criticism by clever manipulation of the traditional interplay of set lines. They piece together formulae and conventions of the common lament tradition and use these to convey a variety of meanings. This strategy may well operate in the Homeric context, too.

The woman singer who composes and performs each work functions as tragic actor in lament texts, songs, and prose narratives in Irish culture. She uses her appearance, voice, and emotions to provide a full catharsis for the emotions of her audience. She skillfully articulates anger and the power to shock, leading others through the emotional experience of loss. In this manner, through coding, she memorializes public statements about her own and other women's lives. In her self-presentation, she acts out the disorder brought about by the recurring cycle of death. The case could be made that such a lament tradition presided over by women characterizes many agrarian societies worldwide and thus has bearing on the case in point. This is especially so as feminist folklorists studying both contemporary and ancient materials have unearthed similar patterns in Greek culture. Furthermore, many Balkan cultures maintain a strong tradition of women's lament as well, a relevant fact for those who still wish to utilize ethnographic material from southeastern Europe to hypothesize about the form and origins of Homeric song.

Understood against this baseline, then, it becomes much easier to understand the *Iliad* and *Odyssey* as possibly springing originally from women's spontaneously improvised composition. At the very least, something formed in women's past was still active in developing the cultural processes as an effective element of the composers' present. Those composers, whoever they may have been, seem to have been drawing inspiration from feminine endeavors, with women's folk culture and work serving as key creative sources. In both texts, the original women mourners who created and sang such songs logically inserted into them the lineage (often through the mother) of each dying soldier.

Other examples abound in the texts of how the residual past of active female mourners impacted the moment of composition of the performers/ composer. For example, Thetis sings her lament to the nymphs, who beat their breasts while the goddess cries in sorrow:

> Sisters, daughters of Nereus, hear and know
> how sore my heart is! Now my life is pain
> for my great son's dark destiny! I bore
> a child flawless and strong beyond all men.
> He flourished like a green shoot, and I brought him
> to manhood like a blossoming orchard tree,
> only to send him in the ships to Ilion
> to war with Trojans. Now I shall never see him
> entering Peleus' hall, his home, again. . . .
> (Il. 18.47–55; Fitzgerald, 437)

Laments of the wife, mother, and sister of Hector (Il. 24.704–771; Fitzgerald 591–593) also illustrate this point, particularly his wife's mourning like a madwoman convulsing in the streets when she hears his death cry (Il. 22.451–515; Fitzgerald 530–531).

At the moment of the death of the soldier for whom the lamenter is grieving, the lament often recounts how the soldier was conceived and raised—in what conditions of life, and within what family relationships. The participation of the nursing mother is often touched upon (Book 6; Homerus 47).

What are we to conclude? If women's lament was not the direct source of most of this classic poetry, at least the Iliad is not solely a male landscape. In fact, the spiritual backdrop for this war-torn, embattled life is the cyclical representation of the earth, and the females upon her, giving, reproducing, and recreating life.

Women serve as the driving force in an underlying natural chain of events. They sustain the chaotic jumps and starts of war. For example, when Odysseus addresses the Argive masses, he relates a sign "freighted with trouble for Priam and the Trojans" that was noticed when the Achaian ships were first gathering (Il. 28). When he and the soldiers were at a spring making offerings to altars, he relates, they saw a great portent: a snake. In addition to reflecting the origin of the pre-Greek snake worship, the snake was the attribute of the Goddess when she took human form, as Harrison noted (267). With blood red on its back, the snake sprang from beneath the altar. Odysseus relates how the snake swallowed first eight baby sparrows and then the grieving mother. The Argives shouted and cheered as this was interpreted as a prophetic sign that the war would last nine years.

The focus on how female imagery defines the male world continues in the *Odyssey,* which juxtaposes feminine energy jarringly with masculine force. This juxtaposition highlights the disorder that force creates among relationships and natural things, as if to suggest that female sensibilities could be the righteous norm. For example, Circe gives Odysseus instructions about how to arrange a proper religious ceremony on the shore of the dead, as classicist Richmond Lattimore discussed in *Story Patterns in Greek Tragedy* (1969, 68). Female authors such as Gertrude Stein (1934) and Susan Griffin (1979) would later re-assert this aesthetic in a modernist way, as part of the wave of feminist reclamation of aspects of primitivism drawn consciously or unconsciously from female-centered indigenous chant.

Additionally, in the tradition of women's lament poetry, the lament poet asserts her identity as a woman in ways beyond society's accepted norms. In the essence of her being—her performance and her poetry—the lament poet asserts a reversal of social gender identity. Therefore, spousal relations, sexual and otherwise, might be sung about in public lamentation performances. For example, Hera cunningly seduces Zeus as a means to turn the tide of war, a manipulation she undertakes despite the couple's normal state of marital disharmony.

The women of the inner circle would have known to listen carefully for coded messages. Yet the audiences of the reified lamentations passed on through the Homeric school might not have well understood the woman lamenter as protester. After all, her performance would have occurred within a socially coded reality. Even in the late twentieth century, in death rituals studied in Potamia by ethnographer Loring M. Danforth and photographer Alexander Tsiaras (1982), men participating in a burial were soon overcome with emotion as the intensity of lamentation increased. When the men began to cry at one ritual attended by the author and the photographer, two young women took the men's shovels and continued to dig. The women's brothers withdrew to the outside of the circle of women, where they stood "quietly and awkwardly, men out of place in a woman's world of death" (19).

Like the mothers in the *Iliad* and the *Odyssey,* the mothers observed in this modern ethnography return night after night to their children's graves (14). Similarly, parallels exist in the structure and imagistic language used by lamenters in both ancient and modern times. These include Hector's mention of his brother "fallen in dust" (Fitzgerald 156) and the recorded women lamenters calling for dust to settle "so that mothers could find their children, and children may find their mothers" (Danforth and Tsiaras 17).

Moreover, Thetis refers to her son as a young plant whom she saw blossom. Similarly, a mother in Danforth and Tsiaras' study calls to her dead daughter, "You were a young plant, but they didn't let you blossom" (15). The continuity of theme, image, form, and structure from ancient to modern also includes direct address to the deceased. These women's laments reproduce aspects of language and structure in the Homeric material, down to the trip to Hades which ended the long poems. Women's folk lament today still utilizes these aspects either in poems sung in the formal reception room of the deceased's house or in procession or at the grave site. The male world of the village coffee house studied by Lord and Parry exists in a distant parallel reality. This reality is so very far removed from the women's world that we must question the validity of the thesis about the origin of the poetry as we persist in this effort to take women's participation in composition and performance of lament into account in the textual study of Homeric materials. Because the laments protest the anger related to war in "safe" ways, bourgeois patriarchal scholars have continued to interpret the Homeric texts as examples of male performance in a primarily male milieu about the adventures of men, in which women (like the Amazons) are mere male projections.

Yet, miraculously, the perspectives that seep through are those of solid, well-grounded women, rather than shadow-thin, ephemeral, wispy females: we see how women clean house, how a woman dresses in the privacy of her boudoir, how serving women relate to the woman of the house, how a child appears at the breast, and how midwives have folk knowledge of herbs.

Lament poetry expresses anger at a safe target, often through satire. In light of this argument, Zeus appears as the withdrawn buffoon, reluctant to take action lest he should miff his wife. As the other gods note, he himself actually remains unable to put a halt to battle. Lament poets also hedge their accusations of incompetence by using their poetry to express a communal rather than a personal voice. In this way, they draw attention to the treatment of any or all women by any or all men. Using traditional formulae about no-good husbands, domestic violence, and other facets of male behavior, these coded historic texts now known as the *Iliad* and the *Odyssey* pass female resistance to male dominance down through the centuries.

One of the safest ways to express anger is through humor. I am suggesting that the women characters actually lampoon Zeus, the male god who watches from above (when he manages to notice what is going on at all), as a way to protest the deaths that were the result of the Trojan War. I am also suggesting that the original women chanters used humor to protest the violence that followed the wave of northern invaders who dispersed pre-Greek society and culture. The singers, involved in a very real way as direction givers conducting liminal transits for their communities, composed and presented their performances in an upside-down world.

It is into this upside-down world of reversals that the Amazon originally entered the fictionalized poetics of Western civilization's confused, often misinterpreted history. The songs in which Amazons appear might have originally been sung at funerals as well as at the regularly occurring re-enactment rituals performed to commemorate the dead. The process of cultural evolution later removed the songs from the context of these early rituals; the songs became entertainment at banquets.

As Greek society stabilized, a specialized class of chanting poets developed, a class that was predominantly male. Even so, Mary Lefkowitz and Maureen B. Fant's sourcebook on women's life in the ancient world lists many women poets—Sappho, Corinna, Praxilla, Erinna, Anyte, Nossis, and Sulpicia, among others (1992, 2–10).

Moreover, early twentieth-century classicist Bennett related the story of poetess Telesilla, who dedicated a statue of Ares at Argos, an incident reported by Plutarch, Herodotus, and Pausanias (61). Sobol has discussed the leadership role of this female poet: when King Charillus of Sparta attacked Tegea, the women of the city made a surprise attack from ambush and routed his army. Later the poetess Telesilla led a band of women so strong in self-defense that the Spartans chose to withdraw rather than to be beaten (125).

From these examples, we can conclude that women did not disappear altogether either from the public world or from the world of written poetry. Lefkowitz and Fant pointed to an additional problem, however, that confronts all students of the ancient world: only a fraction of the writings of antiquity have been preserved. In our case, the dilemma of determining if women's voices made the switch from lament to written poetry is compounded, since much of what remains was preserved only because men of antiquity and the Middle Ages thought that it should.

From examining other records, we can see that women worked in arts and entertainment which could have been in the bardic sphere. For example, the public record thanks a Theban woman, Polygnata, for coming to Delphi to sing at the request of citizens; this indicates that women worked as traveling musicians (216).

Furthermore, Lefkowitz and Fant made note of a written record of women winning fame in many towns and cities for various accomplish-

ments, including as actresses in plays and as castanet dancers hired for en-
gagements in private houses (1992, 217). Gravestones leave a record of a
mother of thirty years who "shone forth as performer of learned songs"
(218). The authors noted other records of freedwomen working as lute players, as traveling solo singers, and as readers (218–219). Lefkowitz and Fant
also cited an official city-state list of occupations that shows women working
as scribes, flute players, and dancers (220–221). Another occupation list of
freedwomen that they provided in their collection shows Demetria, a harpist,
and two women *aulos* players.

Thus, women continued to work in the entertainment field even as the
singing of generalized professional traveling songs became separate from the
localized, specific, volunteer, folk-art ritual singing of lament. It remains difficult to determine the extent to which women were active at this phase and
the point at which they were rendered invisible.

Jane Harrison's *Ancient Art and Ritual* (1913) articulates the view that
all arts had their origins in ritual performance. Here, I merely apply her
theory to the idea that lament poetry evolved from ritual into poetry sung at
Greek banquets for entertainment. I assume an analogous relation between
these developments and the origin and reification of hula in Hawaii, and
between black African shamanistic ritual and the blues (Baraka 1963, 1980;
Keil 1968).[14]

Thus, I am re-interpreting the early appearance of the Amazon in the following manner. Feasts became separated from cult of the dead and from
funerals. At the same time, the male song of the hero emerged, originally
heard as a lament for the death of women's sons in war. Men heard and were
relieved by the women's communal songs of group grief. As bards they capitalized on the circulation of the women's poems.

The *Iliad*, then, might have originated in the expression of anti-war senti-
ment, an original "mothers for peace" action. This was the same impetus responsible for generating countless grass-roots movements of women against
war. This general point of critical analysis can be fathomed more specifically
by a close reading of Andromache's desperate, pleading speech to Hector
before he returns to battle, in which she implores him not to go: "I have none
but you/nor brother, Hector; lover none but you!/Be merciful! Stay here
upon the tower! Do not bereave your child and widow me!" (*Il.* 6.427–430;
Fitzgerald 155).

Hector then tells her that she will be comforted in her mourning. Next,
Hector's own child becomes terrified of his imposing war helmet. The child
squirms, preferring to take comfort in his nurse's bosom. He wails, resisting

his own father's arms. Hector admonishes Andromache to tend to her weaving with her maids. However, she is cast in the role of the sagacious one. She has so aptly predicted her husband's future fate that she and her womenfolk even mourn him prematurely. Divining death is also, in Greek mourning culture, one of women's social responsibilities.

The *Odyssey* might then be a continuation of the pattern detected in the *Iliad* of female lament as war protest. This focus on the havoc that war wreaks on personal relationships is aptly summed up by the goddess who responds to Aphrodite when the latter mentions how she had appeared on the field to save her son in battle: "Be of good heart, my child, and endure for all thy pain; for many of us that inhabit the mansions of Olympus have suffered through men, in bringing grievous woes upon another" (5.85).

When Athena mentions to Zeus that women suffer from men's ways, he shows his ultimate shortcomings. He utters one short, idiotic reaction, saying that females shouldn't worry about war, but rather about marriage. That his inadequacy is the point of the exchange can be inferred by textual quantitative analysis. His feeble response takes three lines. However, the goddess's complaint is a speech of thirty-five lines, followed by several pages of women's interactions on the battlefield, both with their sons and with each other. From this, it is not difficult to surmise what position received more energetic force when performed and sung, and hence made more impact on the original audience.

SIX

How the Amazon Enters World Literature

FIGHTING AND UNADORNED

Into this rather richly detailed textual tapestry enters the somewhat opaque Amazon, fighting, yet relatively unadorned. She readies herself for the history of world literature, which then arms, dresses, characterizes, marries, cloaks, kills, and buries her. At first mention, the *Iliad* couples Amazons with a phrase depicting how they are men's equals and how they have fought men in battle. The terse phrasing is analogous to that of the repetitive, formulaic, bright-eyed Athena, white-armed Hera, ox-eyed Hera, fair-tressed Helen, rosy-fingered Dawn, Iris of the golden wings, Diomedes of the loud war cry, loud thundering lord of Hera, and so forth. These terse phrases were no doubt used for mnemonic purposes. Both reciters and listeners remember a host of characters in a lengthy recitation as a simple, vivid description repeats at each mention.

The Homeric material contains no information on how the Amazons bathed, related to servants, mourned their dead, made clothes, tended their children. Nor does it tell what colors and patterns they wove, what herbs they used, whether they had feathers on their helmets, what kind of shields they carried, what kind of temples they prayed in or to what kind of deities, who was in charge of the religious services, or what gods or goddesses sent what kind of omens. Yet the text includes all such information about the Greek and Trojan women and men. As Homeric critic Rhys Carpenter argued, the Amazons appear as saga, not as fiction (32). Hence, such details of life are not needed.

Additionally, Denys Page, a classics scholar who focuses on the folktales in Homer's *Odyssey*, has claimed that there was no need to elaborate because the audience already knew the story of the Amazons (1973, 55). Kleinbaum concurred that the constructor of these tales could safely assume the listeners knew of the Amazons, as Herodotus would later also assume about his readers (15).

The scarcity of information that such a terse style produced led to other dilemmas of deciphering fact from fiction. For example, in discussions similar to the Amazon debates, some scholars are still trying to place the briefly mentioned Lotus Eaters on the map, to explain their origins, and to explain their poetical transformation. Other scholars psychoanalyze the roots of the Lotus Eater legend (Page 35, 44).

Page traced many folklores and legends to pre-Homeric Greece, to India, and out to the rest of the world, including Africa and Old Europe. Consequently, it is not clear that the *Iliad* is the first instance of the appearance of the Amazons. Chronologically, these Greek Amazons might have lived after the time of the Indian riding women characterized in Vedic and pre-Vedic ballads, whose legend might have traveled west with Indo-European expansion.

Both Ramayana and Maha Bharata texts describe India as a land where towns were scattered and where two classes of folk inhabited forests: the ascetics, and the wild women against whom Rama Arjuna, the hero of the tales, did constant battle (Rothery 80). Markale (1986) lent credence to the view that this material might have traveled west to inspire legends recorded in Greek and other Old European myths. She argued in her study of the Celts that all Indo-Europeans were migrants of Central Asian origin who came west through the valleys of the Indus and the Ganges. They crossed the high plains of Iran before settling in northern Europe, where they began a life based on agriculture and livestock breeding (21–22).

In any case, what can we say of the Amazon's first recorded entrance into world literature, at least from the Eurocentric, Western viewpoint? First, scholars class the context of the two direct references—in the story of Bellerophon (*Il.* 6.168–195) and in the passage in which Priam mentions them (*Il.* 3.182–190)—as echoes from pre-Homeric saga, thus dating the Amazon tradition in Greek literature prior to the Homeric poems (Bennett, Real).

The description is slight. Yet as Bennett noted, Greeks considered battle with the Amazons a serious test of heroic valor. The text states the scene of the battle as Lycia (1). In the second passage, Priam remembers fighting in "vine-rich Phrygia," when "the Amazons came, pitted against men," and camped on the banks of the Sangarius.

Rothery used a translation with another phrase: that Priam, in remembering their stubbornness, admired the "man-like Amazons" (42). According to Liddell and Scott, who compiled the most authoritative Greek-English lexicon, the adjective under question really means "equal to men," with no indication of either a male or female gender hierarchy. Nonetheless, later renditions added such dimensions ([1843] 1968). This reference gives the impression of a mighty band of warriors that antedated the Trojan War (2).

Bennett also noted a third reference in the *Iliad*, though it is indirect: the reference to the grave outside Troy of the woman the immortals referred to as "swift-bounding Myrina" (*Il.* 2.811–815; Bennett 2). Eustatius' commentary on this passage reveals that this Myrina was an Amazon, daughter of Teucer and wife of Dardanus, and that the city of Myrina in Aeolis was named after her. Strabo wrote that on the Ilian plain there was a hill dedicated to this Myrina. She was called "bounding" because she was a great horsewoman (Rothery 43). Critics have taken note that she is mentioned by herself, not in the context of the collective group that came to fight from Anatolia.

Yet, she was not transformed into myth, as were the Amazons fighting Bellerophon. That is, she was not discussed with the mythic dimensions of the flying beasts (Real 24–25). Myrina, the queen whose grave is spoken of with reverence in this passage, has not been canonized in world literature as has the feminine Penthesilea. She also figures largely among the Amazons of Libya, whom Diodorus of Sicily described as predating the Amazons of the vicinity of the Thermodon River. Myrina was the queen of Amazonia, which was a warrior state of this tribe. Her large island state in the lowlands of western Libya was called Hespera. These Amazons tamed their men and forced an exchange of roles. All maidens trained for war, and husbands "meekly" raised their children. Domination (of the men) excited the women into dominating more. They went on war games wearing thick, scaly reptile skins, riding horses, and shooting arrows.

Methodically, these Amazons conquered city after city on Hespera and on the Libyan mainland. Myrina gathered an army of all the women in the conquered territories. Riding in her white-horsed chariot, Myrina led her army of thirty thousand foot soldiers and three thousand cavalry to Atlantis, an island continent larger than Asia. The Atlantians were supposedly offspring of Poseidon, god of the sea and brother of Zeus.

The army forced the Atlantians into retreat. In the first conquered city, Myrina put all the males to the sword. She put women and children into slavery and burnt the city. Rulers of remaining cities surrendered to her after this example. She rebuilt on the site of the destroyed city and gave the place her name.

En route back to Atlantis, some captives stole swords from the Amazon women and started to slaughter the conquerors. Myrina raised three pyres on three tombs to bury her casualties, creating huge piles of earth called the Amazon mounds. Then she marched on Egypt, went westward through Arabia, worked her way into Syria, continued northeast to Cilicia, fought the Tauri, conquered Phrygia, and claimed the coastal lands of Asia Minor (Real 69–71; Rothery 43, 112–113).

Rothery reported how some cast the original Ethiopian Amazons as Scythian Amazons who had crossed the Mediterranean and then worked their way east through Egypt, crossing the Ionian islands to Asia, where they were finally met by Hercules (9). There Myrina founded many cities. She named some for her women generals, as indicated on coins from the area around Smyrnia bearing the heads or figures of female warriors (Bennett 8–9). Then, she launched a series of attacks on the islands of the Aegean.

On Lesbos, Myrina erected another city, this one named after her sister, Mitylene. A storm caught the Amazonian fleet. Myrina prayed to Cybele, Mother of the Gods, that her army might survive. The sea bore her ships to a rocky towering island, which Myrina consecrated to the goddess in gratitude. She set up altars. Troops offered sacrifices. She named the island Samothrace, meaning "sacred island."

For many years, the Amazons dwelt by the Aegean. Then, an army of followers of the banished king of Thrace and Sipylus, who had also been banished from Scythia (a country bordering on Thrace), marched against Myrina and defeated her. The men who had revolted from the Amazon-held territories buried her below Batiera on the plain of Troy.

When Asiatic Amazons were involved in the Trojan War, men called the site Baticia, or Thorn Hill. Nonetheless, the gods knew it to be Myrina's tomb (Sobol 19–28). From Tyrell, we learn only that attribution of the tomb on the Trojan path to the Amazon Myrina was similar to assigning the names of Ionian cities to Amazons, and that this geography alludes to an earlier tradition of Amazonian presence along the Ionian coasts (55–56).

Thus, we can conclude from the poems attributed to Homer, as interpreted by Bennett, only that the Amazons were a horde of warrior women who battled men, and "with whom conflict [was] dangerous even to the bravest of heroes" (2). They belonged to Asia Minor. They hailed from the area of Lycia, apparently opponents of the Phrygians on the river Sangarius. An aura of the supernatural surrounded one of their graves. Herodotus' *His-*

tory suggests that they could have been just one of the many bands that swooped westward, attacking settlements once the collapse of the eastern Assyrian and Babylonian empires undermined the supports of any organized, centralized civilization to the east.

Real concurred that Homer said very little about the Amazons (19–36). Nonetheless, he argued that the theme obviously was of great interest to the peoples of the time. Real also identified a poem, "Amazonia," attributed to Homer. This remains an interesting fact of association, whether or not an actual man named Homer really wrote the piece. Real theorized that this association stems from the fact that Homer supposedly came to Smyrnia at the same time that the Amazons did.

Real's own translation of the adjective applied by the Olympians to the buried Amazon queen was merely that she was "agile" (20). Later commentaries held that such an adjective could only apply to an Amazon (21). According to Real, the Homeric texts never mention that Myrina was of Amazon heritage, because the intended audience already knew this. In the same way, Real maintained, no contemporary Spanish author would have to tell his readers that Columbus is credited with having discovered the Americas.

Real also concluded that because Priam did not have to explain to Helen who the Amazons were as he related to her his memories of previous battles, the existence of Amazons must have been known and accepted at this time. The architects of the text would have known, along with the audience, that years before the Trojan War, Amazons existed to the northeast who occasionally invaded, being "rivals of men" (22).

Although here Real translated the Amazons as "rivals," he reverted to seeing them as equals, which is something different from rivals. He used the translation of Alfonso Reyes, who wrote and made note of the indomitable army of Amazon guerrillas as *"los hombres iguales"* (22). This example indicates how vastly different interpretations can emerge of even a few lines and phrases.

Real used the word "rivals" to include the double sense of comparatives, as well as to indicate hostility (23). However, the original adjective in ancient Greek (*antianeiras*) doesn't necessarily imply both senses. Likeness didn't necessarily mean hostility, but Real contended that Reyes' translation of "virile women" (*mujeres viriles*) or *"hombrinas"* does not really communicate the original intent. Instead, Real chose a translation that implies that "women fight against men," or "women, enemies of men." This situation presents a problem regarding how we respond as readers, our psyches compensating for our own particular distortions of world history.

Real also claimed that the lack of an explanation for the Amazons in Bel-lerophon's reference stems from the Homeric assumption that the audience already knew of them (23). But in the latter instance, the hero proves himself by fighting against mythical beings, whereas Priam merely performs military duties for his country in a historic battle. Here we move from history to legend, from saga to myth, from commonplace record to distortion of reality.

Tristram Potter Coffin defined "legends" in her analysis of the female hero in folklore and legend as historical stories telling about human adventures in a world made for humans by their gods. These differ from myths, which are religious stories telling how these gods regulated order in the world that they had created for humans. According to Coffin, an atmosphere of belief pre-dominates when people tell legends concerning figures like Helen of Troy; but legends can turn into myth in the course of "wandering from mind to mind and from place to place" (4–5).

Sobol argued that in the Homeric material, the portrayal of the women as raiders from the east fighting against Priam was key in the transformation. Ancient poets first writing down oral tales idealized reality in order to stress divine interventions or the deeds of great heroes. Such idealization might account for the reverent reference to Myrina's grave.

Given the Homeric nuances, the Amazons might have seemed like dogma, Sobol argued, because no recorded facts existed against which to compare the legend. An all-female state might have seemed completely plausible to Homeric audiences, while modern audiences may have been disconnected because of distortions by Hollywood writers and producers in search of sex symbols.[1]

Sobol maintained that the geographic areas the Amazons called home of-ten produced fierce hordes of women who posed a perpetual threat. The nar-rative poems might have explained tombs and other markings attributed to Amazons as they arose in Lake Maeotis and Lake Tritonis, criss-crossed Asia Minor, and disappeared in the dust mound of Troy.

After the Bronze Age, the Greeks (Achaeans) sailed again for Asia Minor. They brought their tales with them as they settled into colonies and Aeolis. These transformed tales became the Greek epics. What was relevant to the Greek recorders was that the Amazons were non-Greeks. Thus it makes sense that the earliest known representation, reproduced in Dietrich Von Bothner's *Amazons in Greek Art* (1953), shows large hefty women with black skin and raised buttocks, and that in later images, the women appear to be Semitic, with long, thin, pointed noses and dark, curly hair. For those who feel pushed out of the texts of Western civilization by thin, blue-eyed, blonde white heroines, this might be a curiously self-validating discovery.

Also, we must remember that scribes first started to write down laws only in the mid-seventh century B.C. At first they only scratched on stone, clay, and metal. These mediums did not lend themselves to lengthy works like the *Iliad*. Only in the later seventh century B.C. did Homer's disciples pen the *Iliad* and the *Odyssey* on papyrus. Many say the first poem was later grafted on, since the catalogue of Book 2 omits Amazons (Sobol 92–95, 154).

The discussion among critics is limited to how Homeric references function as what Frye would call a sign—that is, the extent to which the Amazons represent or refer to some historical reality outside the text. Yet, as a symbol functioning within the text, the Amazons do not interact with other women or with other goddesses, if they are indeed goddesses themselves. This is so even though the text features goddesses in strong positions who perform significant acts, as I demonstrated earlier.

Furthermore, the Amazons are portrayed as fighting, but so are many other women in the text. For example, Athena is actually in the battlefield guiding darts. This shows she was effective in weaponry and in war (*Il.* 5.8). In this respect, these skilled "fighting women" were not so unusual.

Additionally, the text contains no mention of child-rearing or conception practices among the Amazons, although other "odd births" or products of "odd" conception transpire, such as Helen's. The text arose historically during a period of change and uncertainty about biological paternity and social fatherhood, much of which is reflected in Coffin's discussion of the many stories of Helen's conception (38–39).

Finally, by the time of Euripides, authors would portray Amazons as having a sophisticated Ares-worshiping civilization with their own cities and architecture (Sobol 163). Yet no internal social systems of governance, religion, or weaponry can be noted. As others have mentioned, men reported the Amazons in a matter-of-fact way, without details of costume, love life, or physical appearance. Masculine civilization had not developed them as a fantasy product. Rather, they appeared in this first instance outside the drama, local color, plot, and action, like a thumbnail sketch or a crescent moon indicating the collective alter ego of women, an early slender premonition dawning in the night sky of receding matrilineal civilization.

SEVEN

The Second Phase

FOCUS ON THE FEMININITY
OF PENTHESILEA

As Kleinbaum observed, the Homeric documents tell only up to the death of the Trojan Hector. Later poets like Artinus continued the story in telling of Memnon, the King of Ethiopia and of Penthesilea, Queen of the Amazons. Artinus' version then itself only survived in fragments through a fifth-century philosopher who quoted him, although Diodorus and Justin also knew the story told in the lost cycles.

In these cycle poems, significant change occurred in rendering the Amazon. Traditional scholarship attributes this change to successors filling in many omissions in the *Iliad* and the *Odyssey* (Sobol 93). When arranged sequentially, these poems recount the pre-history of the Greeks from the creation of the gods until the final deaths of the Trojan War.

This series of poems, called the Lost Epic Cycle, recounts ancient history up to the twelfth century B.C. In hexameter verse, some of the poems tell the story of Troy. Arranged chronologically, these have been lumped together and called the "Trojan Cycle" (Sobol 94).

The Greek cycle poems do not survive in entirety. Current knowledge comes through Photius, a ninth-century A.D. patriarch of Constantinople. He collected extracts from or abridgments of 280 works of classical authors in his *Bibliotheca*. Among these was the *Literary Chrestomathy*, credited to the fifth-century A.D. Proclus. This was a handbook of classical Greek literature which dealt exclusively with the epic poets.

Photius' abstract from an abridged copy of Proclus gives stories thrice removed from the totality presumed to be available at the time under examination. The minstrels of the Achaean colonies in Ionia and Aeolis compiled them from oral material, creating even further distance from the prose of the storytellers (Sobol 94). We only know from Photius' extracts that the five-part *Aethiopis* in the Trojan Cycle, written by Arctinus Miletus (c. 750 B.C.), began where the *Iliad* was dropped in the Homeric material, actually picking up with the arrival of women fighters from the east (95).

We can only speculate how much more we would know about Amazons if works had not been lost. In addition to the cycle poems here under discussion, lost classical works about the Amazons included *Insurrection of the Amazons* (Plutarch, Theseus 28), the conjectured *Amazonika* by Onasus (Bennett 5 n.), and the *Aithis* or *Amazonides* of Hegesinus (Sobol 154 n.).

Nevertheless, from this feat of near-divination, we might make some conclusions about shifts in Greek thought concerning Amazon women. In the Homeric material, these women were raiders from the east. But by the second phase of Amazon existence, the women were a race residing in the lands along the Black Sea at the mouth of the River Thermodon. Moreover, they had established their own civilization, with a capital at Miscrya. Whereas in the *Iliad* the Amazons fought far away in time and place, in the cycles they fought center stage in the story's present action (Real 26).

Furthermore, whereas references in Homeric material were cryptic and always cautious, the cyclic successors elaborated individuated interactions. The Amazons didn't just engage in battle. They performed deeds influenced by the gods, transcending life's realities. In earlier versions, the Amazon women were fighters noted in terms of their courage, stubbornness, and prowess. Yet, here in the cycle poems, authors wove in additional elements of beautiful femininity.

Once feared as fighters, the Amazons were now loved and conquered. The barbaric raiders were humanized—dressed, made vulnerable, and softened, as well as individualized. Here the element of literary creation of the Amazons sets in, leading to later Roman romanticization.

Also, they changed from fighting the Trojans to being Troy's allies. Critics give many reasons for this change, and in ancient times classic historians debated the switch. Some motivating reasons include the admiration Amazons held for the father-in-law of Helen; the hatred Amazons held for the countrymen of Bellerophon, Hercules, and Theseus; the consequent need to vent their anger on the Greeks; the need to participate in any war with whatever allegiance in order to find men to enable them to bear children; and Penthesilea's beauty, which was so great that the Trojans wanted her on their side (Real 32, 33; Rothery, 43).

The Greek Penthesilea became a figure much represented in art and literature. The first artistic representations of the Amazons—the terra cotta shield found at Tiryns in the eighth century B.C.—were congruent with their entry into written literature (Sobol 97). They were shown as large, black, sturdy, and dominating, with no emphasis on delicate clothing. They clearly towered over those against whom they were wielding a threatening spear. Dietrich von Bothner found that classical representations of Achilles and Penthesilea contained only scenes of intense combat, without subsequent romanticization (148). Yet artists went on to portray Penthesilea in numerous variations of handsome clothing—in the short tunic, or *chiton;* armor-clad and in Athenian helmet; with a crescent-shaped shield; in Persian-style close-fitting tunic and trousers; and in a Phrygian cap (Rothery 16).

Penthesilea was probably a figure of purely literary origin, even before Arctinus wove her in to his text. Perhaps she was even a divinity (Real 36). There might have been a real woman behind the legend, but her indigenous name was translated into what was passed down in history. Like the word "Amazon" or the name Myrina, the name of the other Amazon queen about which much is known, her actual name would have been indigenous, not Greek, since she was from an opposing tribe. In Greek her name means "compelling men to mourn," like the names often chosen by mythographers which characterize the essence of the persona represented. Interesting here because of the association with lamentation, the Greeks could have fixed her name after hearing earlier versions of the stories. She still could have been indigenous (Sobol 162 n.). Even Arctinus referred to her Thracian background.

Real assumed that there might have been women warriors from a matrilineal, gynecratic people with equal rights. Yet the dramatization of Penthesilea's beauty in dying makes her particular story likely to be neither history nor myth, but simply poetry. Real felt that although Arctinus had access to many pre-Homeric traditions, this poet, like others of his generation, combined sagas or legends from the Greek middle ages or from the Crete-Mycenaean epochs (transformed into myth and popularized as folklore) with much of his own more recent experience. According to Real, since the Homeric material includes information about Scythians, it is likely that Arctinus, who wrote in biblical times,[1] creatively combined the experience of his own epoch which had to do with the armed intervention of the Ethiopians (32). Arctinus didn't really establish a relation between the Ethiopians and the Amazons in *Aithiopia*. Rather, he invented one by trying to tie together two of his own creations (Real 29). In a sense, the only real association between the Amazons and the Ethiopians was that, according to the general theme, the Greeks considered both barbarians (30).

Here again, the discussion in critical literature has condensed around whether the Amazons were real or not, or how accurately they served as signs pointing to something outside the text. Relatively little information appears either in texts or in civilization about their cultural constructions, their child-rearing or conception practices, or their relation to other women or to goddesses. In fact, in the remnant of this text that remains, Penthesilea claims to be daughter of the war god, Ares, without any reference to goddesses or to the Amazons' lineage as goddesses in their own right. The bulk of discussion takes place without reference to how the symbols of the Amazons interacted with or affected real events in real women's lives at the time, in the rest of the text, or now.

Moreover, since the entrance of the Amazons into written literature corresponded with the limitations placed on women as mourners in the storyteller, divinatory, oral history, and lament roles,[2] this impacted the way in which the symbol was transmuted and the way in which Amazons began to be depicted. The image changed from a collective of fighting women to that of a single woman so beautiful that she attracted amorous attention from important men. Indeed, the infatuation of Achilles seemed to Tyrell and Calasso (reactionist critics in the present categories of analysis) to be uppermost. However, according to reclamationist social historian Kleinbaum, the first written description of the interaction was dry and terse; only later in Roman times was the whole affair romanticized as the beautiful Penthesilea dies in the arms of the hero (22–23).

In a translation of Proclus that Bennett discussed, Achilles' love for the queen does not seem sexually exploitative. Proclus simply stated: "The Amazon Penthesilea, daughter of Ares, a Thracian by birth, appears to give aid to the Trojans. In the pride of her valor [which in the translation used by Tyrell appears as "fighting at her best"] Achilles slays her, and the Trojans bury her. Achilles destroys Thersites for speaking slander against him and carping at his alleged love for Penthesilea . . ." (Bennett 3). Later Hollywood movie portrayals added this sexual slant, building the general public dismissal of Amazons as fantastic or incredible.

Nonetheless, Quintus' description in the fourth-century A.D., which a citizen of Amazon-founded Smyrna wrote, reflected a sensibility different from those of the Homeric period and the days of classical Greece (Kleinbaum 73). Even in the version Tyrell used, Penthesilea still emerged from the female element (Dawn and the "Lovely Seasons"). This emergence from her group seems significant because Dawn was notorious for her sexual aggressiveness and for not playing the female's waiting game. Elsewhere in Greek myth, Dawn actually raped a few men, like Tothnus, Cephalus, Orion, and Clitos (78–80).[3] That is, Penthesilea still gestated in the womb of other women like herself, but the process of becoming the men's projection of anima isolated her.

Yet as Jungian analyst Esther Harding might say in applying Jung's concepts to women submerged behind the feminine characters in literature, Penthesilea fought to be seen as herself—not as a male projection (23). Harding actually critiqued Jung's concept, saying that the anima represented a "collective or universalized picture of woman as she has appeared through the centuries of human experience in relation to man" (10).

In critiquing Jung's concept, Harding carried the idea of the anima further and brought the notion into a focus which we could apply here in looking at the Amazon as primarily a symbol rather than as a sign. The anima or the woman receiving this projection has become a symbol of the man's unknown feminine soul, divorcing the woman from other aspects of herself. While the Amazon may have once existed as an independent, fighting woman, she was later transmuted into an anima figure of the man. Thus transformed, and embellished, she passed out of the realm of the believable in human consciousness.

Here, in this story, when Penthesilea becomes only the male's anima, she dies. She herself is extinguished. Only in the man's heightened sense of his own projected anima does she live on. For Penthesilea found that to be "all things to all men"—both the woman and the warrior—literally killed her. Once she received the projection of the anima, her Amazon self died; this loss of her defining aspect actually killed her.

The real source of the anger that Penthesilea brings to the battlefield is the fury she feels toward herself for accidentally killing her twin sister while hunting—which strengthens an anima-animus analysis. She had a need to atone for her own sin. She needed literally to offer more dead bodies to the Furies or Erinyes, the daughters of the night who inhabited the depths of the earth, as depicted by Euripides in *Oresteia* (47). Like the Amazons—who might be their daytime incarnations—they have no children and shun sexual intercourse with men (Slater 168–174). Also like the early Amazons, they operated as a collective female, arguing with Apollo about the usurpation of female privilege and power. Culture associated them with dragons, later aids to female power in the early Renaissance and Middle Ages.

As this stunning Penthesilea approaches the battle, she becomes glorified and god-like in her beauty. That she seems like "the blessed immortals" amazes the Argives. This emphasis on the male gaze illustrates an important aspect of the shift from the original Amazon rendition in the Homeric material.

This is part of the process of how the Amazons became divinity late in their history (Sobol 151). Since Penthesilea and her warriors do appear in the midst of the funeral rites celebrated for Hector, we can conjecture that the women's lament song had summoned up the Amazons from the other world or down from the land of the immortals on Olympus. Therefore, Penthesilea's beauty really might have been supernatural and not just a glorification of a human woman in this version.

To continue a focus on the relations among women in the text: just as Andromache's handmaidens had foreseen death, here Andromache also foresees Penthesilea's and forewarns her as she dresses to fight.[4] The Amazon Queen ignores the words of the wise matron-widow, counting on mesmerizing the Greeks with her beauty. She kills many, but sees many of her own warriors fall, too. She then doubles her attack, claiming her strength and descent from the gods as she waves her battle ax to fight back. In an enraged speech, she vows to use the power of the gods to revenge the death of her sister-warriors. Then Achilles gives a speech, saying that she may be from the gods, but his people represent the rule of the gods on earth. Then he kills her.

Thus, as much as anything, this particular Amazon story fits the pattern of tragic narrative that Lattimore has called the revenge story. In revenge stories, warnings against pride, presumption, and challenge—as in Achilles' response to Penthesilea's moment of vainglory—are common (Lattimore 1969, 26). The fact that Achilles has made her suffer generates sympathy both in his eyes and in the eyes of the readers. To Lattimore, this would fit the uncomplicated pattern of pride and punishment; he did not consider other possible issues such as man versus woman or the status of the Amazon as myth, legend, or historical reality (27).

Tyrell quoted from Quintus regarding Achilles' suffering after Penthesilea's death:

> She lay on the ground like Artemis, daughter of Zeus, sleeping when weary from chasing swift lions in the lofty mountains. Aphrodite, beautiful garlanded wife of mighty Ares, made Penthesilea radiant even in death to cause the son of blameless Peleus to grieve. (79)

That is, her relationship to goddesses is not that they help her find her own strength, as many have suggested in the revitalization movement. Rather, they make her looks a punishment to man. The strength that she used to find through the mascot of the Mother of the Gods, in nature, is only a memory—sapped, gone. The Amazon is lost, as male projection eclipses her real self.

This, then, is the reactionist version that takes over in classical and later periods. Captured, kidnapped, and raped Amazons invading the presumably male space of war become wives, concubines, and mistresses to their male masters. The mythical character Theseus rapes not only Helen and Adriadne in other myths, but also Antiope. He takes his captured Amazon back to Greece, only to desert her for his Greek wife.

Basically, then, a shift occurred. A mass, collective Amazon once vibrated through Greek mythology. Like the Furies, these women moved as one, as a group. But this mass broke down into the projection of the anima by men. In this process, the Amazon individualized as an object for man, removed from sources of her own strength and from other women. As this separation enrages and disempowers Amazons in particular and all women in general, the need for subsequent reclamation and revitalization emerges. The Amazons are androgynous in Homer, more warrior than women. Yet by the second phase, beauty, vulnerability, and other proscribed aspects of femininity become dominant, eclipsing the original androgynous warrior.

EIGHT

Amazons Go American

MONTALVO'S
SERGAS DE ESPLANDIAN

One way to understand the continuing appropriation of the Amazon motif by dominant cultures is to compare the late medieval/early Renaissance Amazons García Rodríguez de Montalvo created in *Sergas de Esplandian* ([1510] 1992, 456–503) to those Christine de Pizan created in the early 1400s in *The Book of the City of Ladies* ([1405] 1982), an early manifestation of feminist consciousness. Pizan, a Venetian in the early Renaissance, was the first to restore Amazons to power after their demise in the latter Greek and Roman empires and throughout the Dark and Middle Ages. Writing a hundred years before Montalvo, she used the term "Amazon" to designate superlative, wonderful, glorious women (Kleinbaum 64–68). In Montalvo's tale of Amazons, by contrast, all the pagans, led by the Amazonian warriors, die in a battle which is so tremendous that it "made the heavens and earth shake" (486). As Ruth Putnam wrote in *California: The Name* (1917), Christianity and male supremacy had to be victorious in this latter tale of the Amazons, written by a Christian and a man (312).

I assigned students in a class studying sex role reversals in utopian literature the task of comparing the Amazons in the works of both writers. The class developed a lengthy list of characteristics by which to contrast the two sets of Amazons. For example, Montalvo's Amazons were silly, vain, overdressed, erotic, helpless, cruel, and inept. Pizan's Amazons were intelligent, resourceful, cooperative, nurturing, strong, brave, courageous, practically dressed, and creative.

Pizan depicted Amazon women in a state of strength; her Amazons could overcome any hurdle they approached. However, Montalvo depicted the Amazons as evil giants attracted to male dominance. His Amazons wanted to participate in the domain of men even though they had their own separated island sphere with its own cultural rules. Pizan focused on intellect, prowess, and ingenuity. These were all internal attributes which dictated how they *acted* on the outside world.

Montalvo focused on looks, stature, and costume, or how the Amazons *appeared* to the outside world of the men whose notice they attracted. Montalvo's Amazons killed their male children, while Pizan's gave their male children back to the fathers. The Amazons created by Montalvo were motivated by glory; Pizan's, by self-defense.

Montalvo's Amazons came from a wild, undeveloped craggy island, which the women never left; the one time they did leave, they suffered defeat and wedded men. Pizan's Amazons developed an empire of lands they conquered themselves. Montalvo's were dictatorial in their internal relations; Pizan's counseled among themselves democratically. Montalvo's were antagonistic to men, whom they either hated or to whom they surrendered; Pizan's were not antagonistic. Marriage, if Pizan's Amazons engaged in the institution, was merely a complementary experience for the developed and established self. Montalvo's Amazon worked for evil; Pizan's worked in a self-development program to further social progress.

As with the Libyan Amazons, who were often located on islands, early colonial explorers in the period in which Montalvo was writing were reporting many islands of women which leaders of expeditions had claimed to have located on various coasts worldwide. These reports interacted with variants of the theme of an Isle of Women, which was also popular in the myths of many indigenous peoples. The utopian themes expressed themselves in the form of isolated locales where women had extraordinary powers associated with their supernatural relation with beasts and nature (Graham 1954; Murphy and Murphy 1974). Montalvo's *Sergas de Esplandian* capitalized on this thematic interaction between explorers' reports and tales of indigenous peoples, thus feeding the minds of explorers who searched for islands of women as they sought to satisfy infantile paradisiacal longings.

Interplay among layers is useful to examine given the contemporary trope of islands, countries, or planets of women, which contemporary feminist literature usually presents as positive utopian societies. Using a model like a palimpsest—as others have done to understand the Aztec nature underlying current perceptions of Mexican reality (Alarcon 181)—we can account for the concurrence of different but interwoven narrative structures within a single text and between texts, as well as the faintly visible early texts beneath the layers. What we have to learn from such an examination is that one culture's utopia—an island of women—might be another culture's dystopia.

Montalvo worked by combining Greek, Teutonic, and Celtic legends of the thirteenth and fourteenth centuries. The first four volumes of Montalvo's *Amadis de Gaul* ([1508] 1974) were amalgamated from circulating legend. These he combined with *Sergas de Esplandian* ([1510] 1992) to complete the final, more original volume. As Montalvo's most recent translator, William Little, has written in his notes to the most current edition, all the books were part of the visionary weaponry that enabled the Castillean people "to conquer Grenada, discover continents unknown to Europeans, circumnavigate the globe, defeat major civilizations, engender a new race, and propagate their language, religion and culture on several continents" (19).

The final resolution of the romance freezes all the main characters of the Old World under the sea. This closing literary snapshot represents both an end to an era and the wide-open expansiveness of the Americas. This end created an unhinged, mythopoetic zone onto which all those who desired to get away from the particular limitations of Old World culture could project their fantasies.

In *Sergas de Esplandian,* a sorceress named Urganda the Unknown enchants the frozen characters there by her "apocalyptic magic." Urganda's power is suppressed in the course of the book, just as society was suppressing Maryology (Petroff 1986, 1994; Otis 1985; Raymond 1986; Clark 1975). Magic of this sort remains in popular literature today. For example, in Disney's animated version of the Hans Christian Anderson tale "The Little Mermaid," the Sea Witch, called Ursula, uses Urganda's sort of magic (Walt Disney 1990). Such vivid enactments represent what Markale has pointed to as the submerging of women's power as the emerging patriarchy altered myths. The freezing by women's power underground *Sergas de Esplandian* also expresses the dynamic transmutation of goddess symbols, such as Pratt noted in her discussion of changes in female archetypes in the Renaissance (1994, 134–135). In debasing Amazons and the sorceress Urganda, the text reflects the sense of the Renaissance period, which in general greatly debased female archetypes.

The ending of Montalvo's romance also traces the joint exploits of an Amazon queen and her Christian, Old World husband as they enter the New World. The dynamic ending pointed toward American horizons, where men could project their fantasies of achieving the ultimate submission of women. The ending subsequently influenced many who wrote after Montalvo.

In terms of the constitution of the romance, the Amazons take up a very small portion. However, historically, the romance coincided with the search for Amazons in the New World that Queen Isabella sponsored, which in turn reflected a larger trend in early Renaissance Europe. Queen Isabella offered rewards to her explorers for discovering Amazons in the New World. Many capitalists also put the search for Amazons into their adventurers' contracts (Leonard 36; Kleinbaum 116); some instructions given to explorers refer explicitly to directives and awards of the Queen, who was interested in locating Amazons of the New World. ("Instrucción . . .") As reported in Wagner's *The Discovery of New Spain,* an early explorer, Grivalva, believed the island I examine in the next section was inhabited by Amazons that he never saw because the women went inland upon the Spanish arrival ([1519?] 1942, 31). In addition, Voltaire sent his fictional Candide, son of a decadent white world, to take lessons in civilization from the Amazons in Brazil (Biocca 13). Furthermore, original maps of the continent, such as the 1618 map from Nuremberg, show women warriors along with headless men and cannibals defending El Dorado, the City of Gold (Kleinbaum 90). Elizabethans also believed that the Amazons migrated to South America after Penthesilea's defeat (C. T. Wright 1940). Montalvo's romance, playing on this theme of discovery of the lost Amazons in the New World, purportedly led to the naming of the current state of California in the United States, after the queen of that name in the book.

Thus, because of the significance of the theme of Amazons in Western literature, Montalvo's sketchy account of Amazons (a mere 50 pages of his nearly 2,500-page narrative) has occupied a greater portion of the contemporary twentieth-century discussion of the topic than it deserves. Kleinbaum has discussed the role of the Amazons in all of Montalvo's subsequent works (99). Cavin has suggested that the amount of attention given to this aspect of the book is part of the patriarchal cover-up for possibly real Amazonian, matriarchal civilizations that might have existed prior to European discovery of the New World.

Some credit Montalvo's *Sergas de Esplandian* with having influenced Christopher Columbus when he wrote in his first voyager's journal of 1492 that he had heard of an island of women from some Indians. However, Columbus wrote the journals in which he discussed the island of women in 1492–1493—over fifteen years before the publication of Montalvo's volume. Of course, it is also possible that Columbus' account influenced Montalvo. Some of the elite might have had access to the log Columbus kept during this voyage; furthermore, the Queen had it copied and deposited in private aristocratic libraries. Nonetheless, no one actually printed the full text in Spanish until 1825. Thus the two authors must have arrived at their notions independently—Montalvo in fiction, and Columbus in non-fiction.

The influences are likely to have been quite broad. Most voyagers' journals of the time contain sightings of women's countries, cities, or civilizations (Leonard 1964, 48–63; Medina 1934). Medieval accounts already existed in which Amazons defended the gates of decent society from the masses outside, thus upholding the status quo (DiMarco 1991). Marco Polo reported seeing a similar phenomenon (Yule 1903). Indeed, when Muslim explorers first came to the north of Europe, according to Hennig, they saw evidence of kingdoms of all women (1940).

Scholars have made few efforts to extrapolate what explorers might have actually seen to lead to such observations. One exception is Hennig, who tried to surmise ethnographically why there might have been certain separated male and female populations on some sites. I have already mentioned the various people who espouse diffusion theories. The latter claim that uprooted Amazons scattered after having been kidnapped, captured by Romans, or defeated in war. These theorists suggest that Amazons then went north and established pockets and colonies in Old Europe, only later moving on to remote islands and impenetrable mountainous regions.

Most explain the Amazonian phenomenon as projected fantasy. These theorists argue that explorers had in mind images from legends of prior times from their own civilizations. Other men, this line of reasoning goes, had created these fantasies, which did not reflect any real-life existing societies dominated by women. The theorists arguing this position take as their model the projection of numerous other European themes upon the New World (Marchi 1993; Fuentes 1992; Hulme 1992; Leonard 1964). Montalvo's romance is one of those scapegoat texts used to "explain away" Amazons or islands of women that explorers reported they saw or heard about when they came to the Americas.

In general, I place the romance in the category of reactionist usage of Amazons. The book also utilizes the secondary form of Amazon, the anima for men. The text emphasizes an individual warrior queen separated from the rest of her peers because of an amorous attraction which is ultimately fatal to her Amazonian nature.

Sergas de Esplandian was taken from a story of imagination and love that was especially popular in the 1300s. It was adapted into a literary work that by 1546 had grown to twenty-four volumes. Women were individualized and debased as they became objects for men—similar to what happened with the Greek material when it was codified as a written document, removed from the living realm of circulating oral tales.

The book appeared in hundreds of editions in many countries in the Middle East and Europe, including England, Germany, France, and Holland. It achieved great popularity in numerous languages, including Hebrew, in a period which many identify as crucial in the consolidation of emergent city-state and national patriarchy.

Amadis de Gaul, the larger series that includes *Esplandian,* opens to the modern reader a window into the world of European literature and culture at the end of the Middle Ages and the beginning of the Renaissance (Malachi 1982, 6). The work had a profound influence upon Cervantes and was mentioned in *Don Quixote* ([1605] 1928). The barber in this first modern novel saves the first four volumes about Amadis, which he deems are the best books of chivalry and ought to be spared. But at the order of the priest in the early part of the book, the housekeeper throws the volume under question, which includes the Amazon escapade, into the yard, where it burns with the other trash (19, 23).

Montalvo's romance was one of the first books mass-produced in Europe with the aid of the newly invented printing press. It went into print around the same time as the book describing how to identify witches, one of Europe's other female demons. Montalvo's book enunciated a recurring interplay with witchcraft, enchantment, and changes in women's power and gender roles. These changes came about as a result of the witch-hunts and the forces that brought about such hunts in the first place (Graubert 1993).

The separate and distinct space of the island was designated to teach the audience how men should tame women from the wild to wed and become fine Christians. This Montalvo posited as a better alternative than women finding their own power or freedom with nature, beasts, and elements, at the time labeled satanic (Bernheimer 1952). Unfortunately and rather ironically, scholars have debated the book in terms of its status as a record of civilizations discovered in the New World. At the same time, others have understood the text as an imprinting model that shaped the minds of the conquerors as they sallied forth into the unknown.

Esplandian in fact delineates how the mystical female sorceress (Urganda the Unknown) and the realm of witchcraft that she represents (as well as the worship of the Virgin Mary) gradually lost power to Jesus Christ the Lord. This process was congruent with the institutionalization of Christianity and the strengthening of the monarchy in Europe. However, Marian aspects of worship were inlaid over indigenous goddesses and maintained their power in other places, such as the New World. This retention of Marian aspects intertwined with aspects of indigenous religions was particularly strong in Mexico (Carrasco 1990).

The critical focus on Montalvo has been on the Amazons who appear only at the end. But as I read the romance preparing to analyze the Amazon finale, I asked, how can the removal of Montalvo's Amazons from their textual environs lead to a full analysis? Consequently I set out to explore the Amazonian references in the context of the text as a whole and discovered that the conqueror's Amazons here wear a completely different suit of armor, dressed as they were among the demons of the Old World.

Montalvo's work moves from a record of circulating myth to a sustained fiction of his own invention, similar to the process of Geoffrey Chaucer's *The Canterbury Tales* ([1386–1399] 1951). Montalvo turned what some modern readers have reclaimed as utopian myth into his own dystopian fantasy, disempowering the women. He reduced them to subservience to men in unequal gender roles. The equality of the ruling king and queen whom he freezes at the end remains. Yet the power of individual independent women declines until the powers of a wise wild man in the Americas supersede those of Urganda.

Female power is submerged as a Medusa-like mermaid grabs the sword that Urganda had enchanted from the hero. The mermaid dives beneath the sea to disappear forever. The Amazon queens, finally married, readily give over their kingdoms to the men. These gentlemen let their wives persist in fighting with them sometimes on colonial campaigns.

Such action takes place for the most part in "remote settings and at distant periods" (Malachi 1982, 9). Consequently Montalvo provides a ritual theatrical space for the dance of the repressed. With the overthrow of the true (now utopian) power of women, the return of women's power as ghost-like phantom occurs, congruent with the overcoming of the Marian cult represented in Urganda. As a symbol, the return of the lost power of women takes the shape of a strange dystopian island of "unnatural" women who lead men into some unforeseeable but exciting future. Women's lost power also takes the grotesque forms of the fire-breathing serpentine dragons which Urganda lays aside in favor of chivalrous protection. Meanwhile, the mermaid-medusa, still wild, sinks with the old rulers of Europe under the sea.

Yet as a sign, the Amazon women in Montalvo's romance might also have represented other cultural factors present in the society of the times, in which real women were actively struggling against such a curtailment of their powers in daily life. It is in this sense that feminist reclaimers of the myth today recreate the theme of an island of women autonomously existing in nature, conducting their own civilization as a utopian model.

For example, some active resistance was recorded in the fourteenth-century tradition of the transvestite play, in which actors portrayed the "unruly woman." Before sovereignty was at stake, the portrayal of the woman who broke rank with dominant culture was not an issue because women were not kept "in line" to the degree that they needed to be once patriarchal orders of custom and society emerged. The holiday rule of women-on-top flourished in pre-industrial Europe and during the period of transition in economic and political forms. A larger pattern of cultural play with sex roles then emerged, revealing subjection of women in society. This promoted resistance. But the intent was to criticize emerging hierarchy through the expression of disorder as comic relief to pressures (Babcock 1978, 183).

Montalvo's "unruly women" ride wild beasts and fight in battle. The narrative voice chastises them moralistically and brings them into line with sex-role hierarchy as they lose their battles and select mates. One might read this as a particular exposition of overall themes expressed in the transvestite plays.

In Montalvo's American Amazons, thus, we have witnessed a successful dystopian transculturation of what was originally a utopian phenomenon and then later became so again at another point in culture.

Earlier colonial writers influenced Montalvo, particularly John Mandeville, who created the fantastic Isle of Feminia ([1240] 1983). In *Women of the Celts* (1986), Jean Markale analyzed Mandeville's oceanic Isle of Feminia as a symbol projected from the vague past to a timeless future life inside the womb. When decoding islands in Celtic myth that might have influenced Montalvo, Markale applied this imagistic metaphor. Such islands include the Isle of Avalon administered by Morgana and ruled by women in matriarchal organizations, and the island where the princess reigns in the voyages of Maelduin and Bran.[1]

Furthermore, Markale used the same framework when discussing the Island of Women or the Gaelic equivalent inhabited by Teutons on the east side of the Baltic, according to Pliny the Elder (79–80). To Markale, the remarkable thing about all these islands is that they remained outside the influence of the patriarchal structures of their times. She argued that the islands could be relics of an earlier epoch when women ruled society, the projection of an unconscious desire for uterine regression, or both (81).

Furthermore, to Montalvo, as to the original recorder of the Lemnos myth, the island the women originally inhabited might just serve as an isolated focus outlined by waters to show in a particular case what would happen to women left on their own. In general the concept of "island" has appeared this way as metaphorical allegory in many other contexts in literary history.

To name some examples, Jules Verne's *The Floating Island* ([1895] 1990) elaborates how a society of American millionaires constructed an artificial island to circulate the world as if the island were a country on its own. Verne's *The Mysterious Island* (1887) also depicts prisoners of war stealing a balloon to get out of Richmond in 1865. They go off course in a hurricane and land on an island. H. G. Wells used the image "islands of light" in the midst of darkness in *War of the Worlds* (1898). His island of beast-men produced by the male scientist in *The Island of Dr. Moreau* ([1933] 1979) was later played upon in modern science fiction by Brian Aldiss in *Dr. Moreau's Other Island* (1980), in which the hero is a castaway on a Pacific island on the eve of nuclear war.

The examples continue, specific to American cultural history. Earlier, Shakespeare's *The Tempest* had originally represented America as an island unto itself. Sol Paradiso, the main character of Kerouac's *On The Road* ([1957] 1979), floated like an island across the frothy sea of America. In Richard Wright's *Island of Hallucination* ([1959] 1963), "island" refers to an isolated place in the narrator's head. Anais Nin's island of Golconda in *Cities of the Interior* (1974) is the escape to spontaneity and primitivism from a city space.

Alex Shulman used "primitive island" to refer to the nuclear household where women and children are kept, insulated from men and corporatism, in *Memoirs of an Ex-Prom Queen* (1972). The notion of the cousin Dolly in Marge Piercy's *Woman on the Edge of Time* (1976) is that a baby conceived on an island would be blessed, strong, lucky, and wanted in time, which brought down the whole book's curse. Later in the same book, Piercy uses "island" as a metaphor for the mental hospital that traps Connie, the protagonist, in a small, insular world.

Thus in the course of literary history, moons and planets became metaphorical islands, and islands came to represent more an island of the mind. The novel *Concrete Island,* by J. G. Ballard (1974), illustrates this trend. The book stands out as an exemplary island novel because the author places the Robinson-like character on a self-enclosed piece of land formed by a highway intersection in London. The traffic island becomes the island, and the castaway is a driver whose car has plunged down the embankment (Parrinder 193–204).

Montalvo's island of Black Amazons is one of a series of strange islands. In the earlier volumes, when the text is closer to the oral stories being written down, women have greater power; later, as the production of literature moves from primarily oral to primarily written, women's power decreases.

In Montalvo's first volume, damsels ride horses, like knights; give prophecies; find babes in the sea; change form at will from being young and beautiful to being old and weak; disappear mysteriously so that men cannot find them; give birth at midnight to offspring who are ferreted away to foster parents in the middle of the night; and don't raise their own children.

Women also tell lost wanderers what to do (67). Kings turn to women for instruction and direction (311). Women serve as the object of fervent prayers (335); provide guidance to travelers (378); establish tournaments (381); and rule islands such as the Island Gravisanda, which can only be reached by moonlight (381).

Furthermore, women both pursue and reject lovers (382). Women command when knights come out, and they send forth damsels and maidens (383). Women also heal wounds received in battle (388). They act sexually. They take the sexual initiative, usually reserved for men in civilizations in which patriarchy is more advanced (389–930); withhold their names from men with whom they have had sexual encounters; force men to do what they wish (391); conceal pregnancies so that the situation of being with child won't interfere with their lives (391); and give birth riding through the forest merely by getting off the palfrey, and getting back on to resume as if nothing had happened (371).

Women also enter palaces of kings to conduct public shaming of wrongly disinherited women (394–395); they even act in matters of state (395). Thus, in the first volume, women act according to customs listed by Briffault and others as belonging to traits and characteristics of matriarchal cultures and civilizations. That is, they propose marriage (397); interact with the elements, dwarves, and giants; and swear allegiance to queens (398). In short, they represent civilization before the emergence of a stable patriarchy.

The early Greeks often portrayed the masculine character's struggle with feminization. Likewise, the tribulations of the male hero at this stage of development appear to be a trial. In the second volume, after Oriana rejects Amadis as a lover, he gives orders to establish a monastery dedicated to the Virgin Mother; the monastery is to be large enough to accommodate thirty friars. Amadis then goes off into the forest to grieve. He prays by the moon to balance fortune. He addresses fortune as "she," as in the Latin tradition when Fortune was a goddess.

Amadis, having lost his lady, seeks females reified into quasi-goddesses to placate him since he cannot have his own. Montalvo's Amadis is a man upset by emotion who tries to starve himself to death, a man overwrought with emotion who cries real tears (461) and who would like to live the rest of his life in a cave, renouncing worldly delights and pleasure since he can't have his woman lover (463). Amadis refuses to eat for three days, until the holy man orders him to do so. In a dream, Amadis sees Oriana, the lover he thinks he has lost, surrounded by fire (464). He screams, "Holy Mary, Help Her," takes a holy name, and sails off.

A cart comes along piled with dwarves, knights, and beautiful maidens. Amadis recognizes the giant behind the cart as the one who earlier had cut the throats of virgins in the Boiling Lake. The virgins tied on the cart invoke the Virgin Mary to free them (540). These virgins must be understood in the context of the awe and respect given to women who chose virginity as a way of life in the early Middle Ages (Salisbury 1982). The virgins also recall early Celtic mythology concerning water and moon virgins, which the virgins in this text also seem to represent.

Symbolically, dwarves and giants represent the distorted masculine (repressed or grandiose), and virgins and dragons represent the distorted female (also repressed or grandiose). This can be inferred from the complex relation between the feminine and the animus in tales noted by Marie-Louise von Franz' discussion of the feminine in fairy tales (1993).

Urganda the Unknown descends from Morgan the Fay and The Lady of the Lake of the Arthurian cycle. She seems to be the protector of the islands. Amadis sees her in a ship coming toward him across the sea, dressed in white and holding a flaming torch. She sits under a canopy bedecked with flowers, branches, and instruments playing sweet sounds. Ten maidens with garlands and gold wands stand behind her. She performs some kind of matriarchal prophesying ritual, throwing her fires into the sea. She predicts the forthcoming battle between pagans and Christians, which Montalvo related in the fifth book.

Meanwhile, Amadis' father, King Lisuarte, expresses his desire to attack the Island of the Boiling Lake. Again, a woman comes forth to intervene. The Giantess of the Boiling Lake comes from the sea to request in the presence of the queen that Amadis fight (607). If Amadis lives, the island will be subject to the king, and the prisoners will be freed.

The duelers arm themselves before the altar of the Virgin Mary in order to invoke good fortune. Of course, in all these battles, the insiders—Lisuarte, his son Amadis, and later his son Esplandian—always win. The outsiders—dwarves, giants, and later Black Amazons—lose. Hence, as noted by DuBois (1982), the "other" is supplanted by the "normal"—that is, white, European, and Christian—male.

A close reading of the text brings to the fore further detail about the submergence of former women's power. Magical instruments play themselves, as myths inform us ancient women's instruments actually did in the mythohistoric times of the goddess (Weinbaum 1995b). Furthermore, men construct themselves around the Virgin Mary—whom diverse scholars such as feminist reclaimer Elizabeth Gould Davis, mythic historian Joseph Campbell, anthropologist Eric Wolf (1965), feminist theologian Mary Daly, and poet-critic Robert Graves ([1955] 1975) have characterized as a hybrid of the original mother goddess.

As incongruous as it seems, Amadis prays at a hermitage to a female with divine powers. Later, he orders an even more splendid monastery to be built, when he realizes that his prayers must have been heard (655). As absurd as it might seem to Americans raised on movie and cartoon versions of invincible knights in shining armor, such prayers are within the context of pre-Christian, "pagan" (i.e., goddess) religious systems. These knights have a hermitage of Saint Mary outside their tent, and they keep a vigil to her all night, the way the Greeks used to pray to Athena when they were serious about summoning the power to win (680).

Calafia appears in the fifth volume, which centers around Amadis' son Esplandian. She represents the opposite pole of the female in this emerging patriarchal culture. Not the pure form of the mother of god—descended from the Great Goddess—Calafia is more like Penthesilea. She represents the anima figure that is gradually emerging in the developing patriarchy, if not the floozy and the whore who is coming to represent the opposite of the good and the virgin in evolving Christianity.

Calafia rides a yellow- and purple-spotted mount whose striking appearance directs attention to what transpires beneath her buttocks upon the saddle. This Queen of the Amazons appears to be colorful, daring, brave, wildly sexual, assertive, and in tune with wild beasts which she has tamed. As such she represents the "green archetype" in a patriarchal space, which Pratt (1981) has noted as a strong underlying theme and pattern.

Calafia continues to challenge the kings and knights and to give commands to men even after most other women in the book have acquiesced.

The war against the infidel was the main idea of the time. Calafia represents that current, rather than retreat to private women's civilization. She was used by the author to indicate not the battle between the sexes but "the apocalyptic war between Christians and pagans" of the time (Little 1992, 43).

Calafia's role in amalgamating and leading the pagan forces is similar to the role of Penthesilea in post-Greek versions in which she heads the confederated forces attacking Troy. When Queen Calafia sees Esplandian, she is stunned by his beauty, as is a series of women throughout the book. The model for this might have been the strong impact that Penthesilea had upon Achilles at first sight. Calafia abandons the pagan side. The pagans lose the war and she converts to Christianity.

This myth resembles stories of India related by Joseph Campbell in his *Oriental Mythology,* as well as, *The Orlando Furioso,* the Italian Lodovico Ariosto's epic poem of chivalry (1516). In such stories, the hero goes mad with passion. In the Indian tales, the woman, originally three-breasted and fighting in armor, loses the third breast, stops fighting, and falls in love with Lord Krishna as soon as she sees him.

This tale, like the Atalanta stories from Greece in which the hearty shepherdess outruns or outwrestles suitors and lovers, also derives from a period when the goddess, conquered and stabilized as "consort" at first, soon disappears, lost in the religions of newly dominant men. Elizabeth Gould Davis said of such legends that they point to a time when women were strong enough to choose their mates by who proved fit enough to challenge them in a fight. However, the message remains that men naturally and rightfully conquer women.

However one interprets Montalvo's text, his Amazon island is far from the islands that women writers would later create. For example, the island imagined in Joanna Russ' *The Two of Them* (1978) is quite different. There, Irene has a vision of all women coming together, pining for what Pratt has called apatriarchal space (1981, 144)—an uninhabited island where she can support a life with her lover. As Shinn pointed out in *Worlds within Woman* (1986), here the protagonist imagines creating her own while away on the legendary island of Wonder-Woman comic book fame, the island of Amazons (168).

Montalvo's island of Amazons as outlined above also differs greatly from Inez Haynes Gillmore's *Angel Island,* described as a feminist parable by Marion Zimmer Bradley in her analysis of responsibilities and temptations that confront women writers of science fiction.[2] Indeed, Montalvo only sketchily described an Amazon island.

Furthermore, just as the sea presents the zone from which an upper-class mermaid comes in H. G. Wells' *The Sea Lady* (1902), so the island represents a zone from which the queen and her Amazons emerge. Much as Wells placed the sea lady, Montalvo basically described the women as being out of their element. They thrash and flounder in a civilization ostensibly run by men, but they are actually politically out of the control of the men in charge.

The narrative voice scarcely describes or recalls the land the women come from. As anthropologist Peter Rigby noted, reversal of female domestic norms becomes a healing parody of the male's violent role in these rituals (1972). In the tribes Rigby described, when the world is in bad shape and male ritual leaders have failed, women dress like men and act out rituals. Their satire provides release. The women effect a cure by caricaturing men's role in war (238), similar to women's caricature of male warriors in oral work attributed to Homer.

In Montalvo's text, nearly the whole known Christian and pagan world is at war until the Amazons appear. The women don't come from a fully developed land in which reproduction, birth, familial relations, ritual, religion, the structure of work, music, science, art, and imagination are in place. Rather, they exist in the plot purely as warriors and purely to end the interminable wars being waged by men.

In this sense, perhaps the Amazons serve as a generalized Athena, who functioned as a female helper or adjunct warrior in the Trojan story. Thus, the very part that does not "fit" civilization as patriarchal culture develops returns to balance the imbalanced social cosmology. Once again, the metaphor of marriage versus war returns, which DuBois saw in Greek culture. Thus, according to the standards set forth by Diner, who defined Amazons as self-governing women resisting marriage to men, Calafia, her sister Liota, and their entourage do not count as Amazons at all.

The final volume of the Montalvo romance, in which Calafia appears, opens by claiming to have been written originally in Greek (67) and uses a word based on the Greek for labor, *sergas,* playing on the labors of Hercules in Greek fable. Also as in Greek myth, many of the natural matrilineal, matriarchal lines are broken. The "hero," Esplandian, was suckled by a lioness, a symbol of the Great Mother. After having been born at midnight with magic letters on his chest, he was raised by a hermit, not by his original birth mother.

In the opening moment, magical sounds of women's music, like the songs of the sirens which captured men at sea, awaken Esplandian. In versions of a similar story that tells of music enchanting Bran, the branch of the "otherworld woman" emits beautiful music. This sound draws Bran and his crew to the Island of Women. There the inhabitants remain for what they think is a year, though in fact it is many years (O hOgain 1991, 50).

The relation between this Spanish and Irish legend is that when the Irish learned to write, they recorded tales from Spain—in spite of the fact that the traditions of the Irish are the oldest of any people in Europe north and west of the Alps (Curtis 1990). Thus Ireland is the most likely source for the magical "sweet sound of golden horns" made by Urganda the Unknown's six damsels, seated on the wings of a great serpent.

According to William Little's introduction to *Esplandian*, the magical female creature making such sounds is "a talented practitioner of the magical arts" (70 n.). She lives alone on a small, rocky island. Yet she is more than this. The Sirens, who also lived on craggy islands, were originally winged birds with women's faces. They were bird-women, not fish-women, as depicted on Bothner's Plate 6—an Amazon with a Siren, a bird with a woman's face.

Other enchanting fish-women existed in Greek myth who seized and ate sailors. Yet the sirens did not change from bird-women to fish-women until patriarchy had submerged women's power, removing women from patriarchal space by placing them under the sea. Simultaneously, Montalvo stripped the Amazons of their ego-defining animal mascots, helmets, and armor, reconstituting them as objects for the male gaze in delicate see-through clothing. The Bird Goddess was finally reduced to Mother Goose, who flies through the air and the elements on a large goose, telling stories to children; in Montalvo she appears as the Enchanted Damsel on a craggy cliff.

The Enchanted Damsel's crag is called Doncella Encantadora. Esplandian wakes up on the Rock of the Enchantress, the spot where the Damsel's husband had killed her by throwing her over a cliff because he was bored being a lord of a desolate place. This had happened two hundred years before, and the knight/husband had taken everything back to Crete.

Esplandian ascends the cliff in full armor (72) and a serpent, awakened as Esplandian strides past, sticks out his arm's-length tongue (74). They then meet a knight whose lady had left him to marry a giant, also similar to stories in Homeric material; then she became a pagan (83–84). Esplandian's name means "Knight of the Snake." The translator, William Little, claimed that he is in metaphorical terms a fictional attempt to birth a hero to re-fight the 1453 lost battle for Constantinople (85, n.).

Thus, Esplandian is identified as the knight of the snake. This is linked with how gender roles deteriorate in this book compared to those in Books 1 and 2. Might a reference to the old pre-patriarchal, matriarchal snake goddess who still has the hero in her grip have been intended? Pratt for one has indicated that Hera and Athena in Greek myth were actually reformulations of snake goddesses in previous cultures (1994, 33). She also has written, as was previously mentioned, that the Amazons were seen as snake goddesses and/or as worshipers in the snake goddess culture. This fact gains more significance as well when we examine Mexico and middle America. Goddess statues of earth mothers wearing skirts of snakes have also been found in Mexico, also fabled to have been an area to which some post-European Amazons escaped. This identification of the hero with the snake could be interpreted as an attempt to incorporate female elements to re-balance the world.

In this final book, strong women ordering men around no longer confront us. Rather, an enchanted damsel appears in distress, and a dowager mother watches her son get killed (93). The mother, then, typifies stereotyped gender roles familiar to modern culture. She becomes so distraught that her maidens carry her inside. She points out to the knight who has killed her son that no one is stopping him from coming inside, but does not exactly extend an invitation.

This subtle touch immediately initiates the notion that women are weak and deceitful rather than strong. The mother of the deceased expects the knight to die, because the hall has been enchanted so that all who enter uninvited will fall immediately to the floor, deprived of power. Since the knight carries an enchanted sword, no other sorcery can harm him. The lady is surprised that her spell has no effect on him. The magical phallus, or the enchanted sword of the hero, then continues to undermine women's power, which is increasingly portrayed as evil and negative in medieval legendary literature, even to the point of depicting Themis, the ancient Greek goddess of justice, as an evil fairy godmother (von Franz 1993, 37–38). In Book 1, Montalvo showed women publicly shaming kings in their own courts; here, he has presented a view of kings as "ministers [who are] by God's will appointed to run a certain people" (95).

Furthermore, men who have been ordered around by women in Book 1 begin to tell women what to do. Women who once acted on their own now turn to men and kings in absolute deference. "What do you want me to do with the king?" the damsel asks (96). The knight simply says—with the expectation of being obeyed—"I want you to release him." She obeys. The knight gives his reason—"Because it pleased God, who protected me." The lady, who is the giant's mother, then comes to the king (Lisuarte) whom she has just released, and asks him to kill her (109).

Next, in a long series of incidents showing women giving up power to men, a woman wants to kill Esplandian. She tries, but stops because she falls in love with him (as Achilles had with Penthesilea) and asks the king to make him her knight (134). Esplandian overhears and agrees that the woman can be his damsel for life. Thus loss of women's autonomy is complete.

Thus Books 1 and 2 contain images of female power. But by Book 5, women kill themselves, ask to be killed, are killed by husbands, and ask to be permanently bound to men. A speech early on in the book even moralizes that it would be against women's nature to kill (125). But there have been no moralizing speeches about women's role prior to this.

If women live with any autonomy at all in this book, it is outside the law, not as part of legitimate society. The king's power even usurps that of Holy Mary (131). The woman who tries to take revenge admits it would be "against a woman's natural tendency." The same damsel, whose instincts used to be to preserve herself and fight for her rights, becomes bonded for the rest of her life to serve the knight she had earlier tried to kill (133).

Then, the entourage leaves this isle on the Great Serpent. Formed from the crag of the Enchanted Damsel, this is a boat which sails by itself with nobody at the tiller "other than the vast knowledge of her—whose powerful arts were capable of much more than this" (745). Much like primitive instruments from matriarchal civilizations reported to play themselves, this boat runs itself. The passengers finally land just before night on the twentieth day at the port on Firm Island. Amadis et al. happily receive the new arrivals, having been expecting something good because of the message Urganda had left. Esplandian, riding a white horse, looks so beautiful in the crowns Urganda sent him that no one can take their eyes off him (148). They set off to London to see the queen.

En route, a damsel dares the knights to duel with some knights of her own. They marvel at why an unknown woman would approach them, although no similar comments were made in Book 1 when another unknown woman enters and shames a king for disinheriting a woman from her fortune and throne. According to the narrator, "Oriana and the other ladies, out of shyness, did not enter into a discussion of an alien matter so opposed to their nature" (148). In pointing this out, Montalvo has reversed both the women in the earlier books and the Amazons to come later, as if women are to have no interest in affairs of war or state. The knights attack. Two are hurt.

Esplandian cries out, in warning, "Leave me alone! Whatever strength I have is from the lord, don't force me to use it!" (149). Thus, the male deity takes precedence over the female (Mary), although in reality the hero's strength derives from a female's magical enchantment of his sword. The joust turns out to have been set up by Esplandian's uncle, who tests him. The "most pleased was Oriana, who was so overjoyed by her son's good fortune that it was as if she was made Queen of the World" (151). Thus, women are shown to live vicariously, through their children, rather than dueling to defend their own thrones.

Books 1 and 2 contain popular tales that illustrate gender roles in which women have at least some degree of power and autonomy. A careful reading of Book 5, however, indicates that these roles are transformed. For example, earlier, Amadis is shown suffering greatly over a woman in a way that males in an established *macho* culture would consider to be effeminate. In Book 5, the emotional dance takes on the contour of the opposite, with emotive women and stoic men foreshadowing the emerging roles of the modern period.

When the entourage reaches Miraflores castle, the queen falls half-dead and unconscious in Esplandian's arms, "because just as her sadness over his earlier disappearance was infinite, even more so was she overcome with great joy upon seeing him now" (152–153). Having been left, this suffering lady hasn't done anything try to overcome her emotion. Such feminine immobility stands in stark contrast with the behavior of Oriana, who in Book 2 is *active* in overcoming her suffering. Oriana even writes a "Dear John" letter to Amadis to overcome her pain. The view of women as passively suffering opposes in yet another way the view of strong, active, assertive non-despairing "ladies" presented in the earlier books. Furthermore, upon return, the king thanks God, not Mary (155).

If Montalvo was really drawing on Celtic legends rather than merely raiding them to rewrite with an emerging male chauvinist delight, he would have run across Queen Mauve, one of the mighty fighting women encountered throughout the Indo-European Bronze Age. She was, like "Hippolita, an Amazon, an imperious matriarch as likely to break her suitor's neck as to submit to him" (Lederer 102–103).

Even Queen Isabella, who reigned when Montalvo wrote, did not fit the faint, frail, feminine image that he promoted. She financed Columbus, hired female antiquity scholars to instruct herself and her daughters for court, established the Spanish Inquisition, and certainly made her impact on matters of state by supporting the persecution and expulsion of the Jews (Siegel

1991), as well as the forcible conversion of the Moors (Lederer 1968, 99; Gonzalez 1992, 33–34).

As Spanish histories note, Isabella was vigorous and athletic. She rode high-spirited horses, hunted deer, and killed a boar (larger than the size of a man) with her own spear. Of energetic nature, she worked at affairs of state until late at night; she also hired an army to fight another woman's army for the throne (Descola 1963, 188–190).

Moreover, if Montalvo had read the original Greek classics, he would have read of the many actual battles that the Amazons won. According to Bachofen, Amazons were shock troops of the ancient worldwide system of mother right. If this is true, then Montalvo distorted the original picture a great deal by taking them off their horses and putting them on imaginary animals.

Thus as civilization progressed, the Amazons moved from the primary form of being an autonomous, collective entity to the secondary form of being a projected anima of men. Indeed, Montalvo's "Amazons" do not strive against men. They are not man-murdering, man-hating, flesh-devouring, lustful, and cruel to children, as previous renditions portrayed such women. The Amazons Montalvo created are beautiful, well-mannered, helpful, and even sweet. Their aim is merely to help in the pagan war against the Christians.

Ruth Finnegan analyzed and critiqued the emergence of written literature in the chapter titled "Technology and the Great Divide Theories" in *Literacy and Orality: Studies in the Technology of Communication* (1988). Focusing on the divorce between audience, speaker, reader, and author which occurs as an effect of the use of writing for communication (18–19), she argued that with oral literature, "communication depends on personal performance, on audience response and on the direct personal interaction between author and public . . ." (18).

Finnegan pointed out that the effect of oral narratives is likely to be different from that of written literature, "which facilitates the opportunity for the independent and withdrawn author, and for abstract meditation divorced from the pressures of the immediate audience . . ." (18). Media analyst Marshall McLuhan, too, in *Gutenberg Galaxy: The Making of Typographic Man* (1962), traced the way printing forms have modified experience, mental outlook, and expression.

Applying McLuhan's and Finnegan's theories about modes of production and consumption to the evolution of Montalvo's female characters provides insight into how the images of these women change as a result of technological development.[3] The women become more the products of a single individual male who withdraws to contemplate outside of the mediations of communal storytelling or previous chant/ritual activities. They become increasingly removed from avenging their own women leaders, and many steps removed from defending their own territory and ritual objects. As the private, individual points of view of the male writer were expressed (with the help of the pen), fictional women became drawn into the subservient women's role of "helping out" in the affairs of men.

Clad in beautiful costumes, tottering on dainty feet, the women fit in with the rest of the women Montalvo constructed. This transformation occurred partly as an effect of the form of the printed book. Privatization in production and consumption of images developed, thus allowing for the deep-seated fantasy life of both writer and reader to take hold.

Montalvo did not derive his stories totally from the Amazons of the Greeks. He wove in other traditions with those of the Greeks. The enchanted isle of women legend from the Celtic tradition further influenced Montalvo, for example. My reading of Hartland's *Science of Fairy Tales,* an inquiry into Celtic and Teutonic myth, suggests that many of Montalvo's stories fit more with tales of wonder than with tales of wars—the latter being the genre form of tales of the Amazons.

Indeed, northern European tradition is also filled with the type of changeling stories Montalvo wove in. Such stories, where the offspring taken from the mother at birth, are typically found with the rise of patriarchy in many cultures. The infants are suckled by spirits, fairies, elves, or beasts (Hartland 104–105). Such legends represent a mythical transformation of a breaking of maternal lines then occurring in aristocratic culture. The stories are similar to the Greek subplots telling of males who are not born of women, stories constructed to establish the dominance of men.

As anthropologist Vanessa Maher has explained, the establishment of patriarchal institutions had very much to do with the interruption of breast-feeding, even in fourteenth-century Spain. The establishment of patriarchy meant that the relation between mother and child was controlled by cultural emphasis and social institutions in which men held dominant positions. The child was in some cases removed from the mother, and the breast-feeding relationship was interrupted or prevented "in order to secure the patriarchal alignment of the child" (23).

Men in power feared that breast-feeding would create powerful maternal loyalties which would upset patriarchal institutional premises. In fourteenth-century Spain, for example, James II of Aragon surrounded his children with nurses and tutors, arranged marriages for daughters as early as age six, and separated children from each other and the mother—all to ensure that their loyalty was to himself. He did not want emotional ties to hinder his political plans.

This was the custom rather than the exception among the European aristocracy of the period. Florentine merchants often removed the infant from the mother, with the father paying for a wet-nurse, thus severely restricting the mother's influence. Thus the man's control of breast-feeding was a way of establishing the children as property of the paternal line. The breaking of mother/suckling lines—which seems gratuitous in Montalvo's romance to modern readers—thus reflects a broader, more significant trend in the culture, congruent with conquering free females and promoting marriage of the Amazons to Christian gentlemen. Montalvo had a wealth of stories reflecting this trend around him, and incorporated them into the set-up for retelling the Amazon myth.

The thesis that women's power is declining continues to be evidenced throughout Book 5. In one incident, the hero sees a huge fire on land. He goes closer and sees a ring of fire ten feet wide. Inside stands a woman with a baby. Knights surround her, threatening, "Oh Duenna, *evil* female, your *arts* will not protect you enough to keep you from a cruel death" (160).

Earlier in the book, women are not referred to as "evil"; nor are women's "arts" diminished; nor is any male brutality against women displayed. In this instance, however, the woman recognizes two of the approaching knights as her sons. She calls for their help. They are amazed to see that this is Urganda the Unknown, and vow to save her. This, too, is not characteristic of earlier parts of the book, when the sorceress hasn't needed male protection.

In the course of this final book, the dominant sorceress is rapidly becoming a displaced witch. The attacking knights approach the others and ask whether they are companions of this treacherous woman. The sons vouch for their mother's trustworthiness. The attacking knights are surprised to hear the others defending her. Urganda has to be defended for the first time in the entire series. She explains her story as the two knights win and take her to the woods with the baby.

Again, the narrative destroys more motherlines. Urganda has taken the baby from the wet-nurse; yet another baby is to be raised by others, far away from its mother. This intentional interruption and displacement of maternal authority persists throughout. They go to a ship, where "two dwarves were there to steer" (163). The "strange" begins to occur—women coalesce with dwarves to navigate.

Soon Urganda is accompanied by two strong dragons, the medieval transformation of the lioness mascots to the mother goddess figure. They take a journey with the prince (the baby) to Rome. There his arrival causes great joy. Urganda "rode her palfrey, and carried the boy in her arms, accompanied by two *very strong dragons* on either side who were breathing flames of fire from their mouths" (164). When the king of Sardinia, Don Florestan, comes before her, knowing that the "noble king" will guard her, she disperses the dragons.

These dragons that she discards so easily are the leftover relics of the matriarchy, for dragons have represented the matriarchy since Apollo fought the dragon at Delphi in the Homeric hymn to Apollo. When Apollo decides to dig into the earth to set up an oracular shrine, a spring-nymph persuades him to go to a place where a she-dragon appears and challenges him. The female serpent dragon was called Delphyne in later literature. In one story, she nurses Hera's child—born without male help out of anger at Zeus when he circumvented female power and birthed Athena from his head. From the spot where her corpse disintegrates comes the channeled intelligence of the earth shrine at Delphi. Friedrich (1978) associated the dragon with the feminine even in pre-Greek myth in his discussion of the goddess Inanna as a prototype of the Greek goddess Aphrodite.

Psychoanalytically, one can interpret the dragon icon as repressed female sexual energy writ large and becoming a monster as a result of repression when it finally returns. In any case, the shift from female autonomy to male protective identification becomes clear. Urganda willingly lays aside the symbols of matriarchy in exchange for protective male bravery.

Thus, the magical sorceress, once all powerful, dispenses with her own ability to self-protect with passionate fire-breathing female energy which can ward off men. She opts for male protection herself. The king sees that she is alone and vulnerable with a child and approaches her.

As the symbolic female acquiescence continues, they walk and talk happily, never knowing what happened to the two giant serpents surrounding her. The king even refers to the dragons as "large serpents," the two forms of beasts being interchangeable relics of the Great Mother. Later, Montalvo's so-called "Amazons" call off their beasts in the overall war plot, in which they play only a small part. This lays the basis for the theme that women are conquered by men once they have sacrificed their own supernatural relation with beasts, which represent their powerful connection with nature.

Esplandian experiences serious doubts about whether he can live up to the memory of his father as he weeps at the statues of his father's likeness and even kisses the hand of the monument. Matrilineal delineation becomes untraceable due to the motif of changeling infants, which leads to children being raised in foster care. Statues are built where men fight and kill, not where women conceive and give birth or give thanks to Ma. There is no more evidence of material culture monuments to fertility, to conception, or to moon (or any other) goddesses.

After the oedipal competition between men becomes established in the book, the competition between women becomes acute. Before this, female competition has not been an issue in any of the books. Now, however, Leonorina falls in love with Esplandian merely by hearing Carmela's story of trying to kill him. She dresses Carmela in her own clothing to meet Esplandian's ship. A true anima figure, she functions on the level of appearances. She is consoled that he will have embraced her clothes at least, if not her body. Then, later, Leonorina experiences "daggers in her heart" for having been tricked into presenting Carmela in her own clothes, and hence into increasing Esplandian's attraction to the other woman. (212)

Also in the course of this transformation of the feminine, women become sex objects. The text speaks of the "delicious fruit"—the women—with which fortune will reward a key male character in the book. A Christian readership is assumed, as the narrator's mode of address demonstrates (213–214). Carmela now travels with three knights. People are afraid of the great serpent ship, still a quasi-matriarchal symbol which gurgles with the sound of a pre-Christian Celtic god (210–211).

Midway, fights begin between Christians in the castle and Turks, whose camp is situated around the periphery (232). Esplandian's killing of giants as he cleans up "the edge" is taken as a miracle, as proof that he is a Christian god to those who hear of him (234–235). Carmela shows up wearing Leonorina's clothing. Esplandian exclaims, "Holy Mary! Either this is my damsel or I am out of my mind!" (236). Carmela delivers her message from Leonorina. The king, recognizing this state of mind, guides Esplandian to a couch.

Esplandian kisses Carmela on the exact spot on her cheek which Leonorina had kissed; weirdly, Carmela feels her desire satisfied, even though Esplandian is thinking of Leonorina as he kisses her (238). A fleet attacks; the mountain is surrounded, and a messenger forces the king to break the couple's embrace, once again counterposing love and war. The king resigns himself to living out a spiritual life and makes Amadis and Oriana rulers after the battles that follow.

Next, in one four-line chapter, it is announced that Queen Oriana has given birth to twins. The most formative event in the unfolding drama of the majority of women's lives happens outside the male plot; it has not even been announced how, why, or when she became pregnant, how she felt, what she ate, and so forth—the ordinary things that women struggle with while men struggle with each other to become men.

Hence, the list of things Montalvo did not consider when he built his women's island continues to grow. His major aim in creating these unreal anima-women characters was to show how the women were fighting against their nature. He exhibited great concern with how male onlookers perceived the women's physical appearance, with how the women dressed to present themselves to the men, with whether a woman could mount her horse without male assistance, and with other superficial matters that are only significant if the woman character is functioning more as a sign than as a representation. Not even vaguely did he represent a collective mass of women; rather, he conjectured a feminine anima expressing some buried, soulful portion of his own psyche.

At the end of the fifth book, a man has lost his sword to a wild woman rising from the sea, which has been turned into a frozen abyss, yet men as a group have brought the Queen of the Amazons under their "natural order." She has married and handed her kingdom over to a man. Women have been removed from beasts and nature so that they can be feminine and protected by men, according to the will of the dominant, monotheistic, patriarchal god. At the same time, a male sage gets his strength from beasts and nature— as women once did—thus covering over and surpassing all previous esoteric knowledge executed by wise women.

Unless conquerors' reports were also studded with giants, dwarves, and women who walk with fire-breathing dragons, lift stone buildings, and work enchantments, it is highly questionable to use Montalvo's text as a source that could support the possible existence of Amazons or other women-dominated cultures and societies in the New World. Of course, the book might have helped in what Frederick Turner (1980) has called the "defloration" and "possession" of the New World. *Esplandian* inspired Christian men to justify and rationalize the slaughter of American Indians, including the killing of the Aztecs (i.e., pagans) in the midst of celebration and ritual— just as Christians felt just in slaughtering pagans in Constantinople.

Part Three

The Island of Women as Fiction
in American Tourism

FIGURE 1. Pirate and maid on store sign.

FIGURE 2. Goddess figurines sold as versions of Ix Chel on the island.

FIGURE 3. Call for ladies' night at a disco video bar.

FIGURE 4. Functionless mermaid objects. These were probably made solely as tourist art, given small scale and prominent display of raised breasts.

FIGURE 5. Ariel. A local artist copies the image from Disney on the walls of a kindergarten for the island's children. The sources of the aesthetic are transitional, not traditional, also part of a more widely-observed dynamic in arts of the Fourth World (Graburn 30).

FIGURE 6. Postcard and T-shirt art.

FIGURE 7. Sexy mermaid.

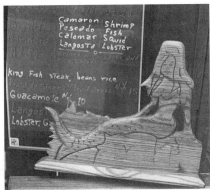

FIGURE 8. Menus.

FIGURE 9. Certified temple rubbings and T-shirts. Hand painted signs advertise Maya art of another period in English. The shop announces the stamp of authenticity from the National Institute of Anthropology. Such certification also conjures up the authority to sell the "Best T-shirts in Town."

FIGURE 10. Mermaid emerges.

FIGURE 11. *La Poza* cantina. The island also sports several private cantinas with live music, such as Kerouac described. This male enclave aspect of local culture clashes with the expectation of many visitors. These clubs are almost entirely off limits to women. Landmarks for locals derive largely not from mystical, exotic or occult realms, but from the realm of daily life practice. The cantina is named for *La Poza*, the well that used to be the watering site in the center of small inland rural communities. Male transvestites also do the serving.

FIGURE 12. *Maricon* with child: Street life. Showing other continuums with nature in culture perhaps missed by tourists, the *grasa* (high bird) or *maricon* (cross-dressing transvestite male) has access to children. The community does not ghettoize him. He openly has a husband, collects baby clothes to trade with women, makes costumes for children for spring festivals, and sits in the streets wearing female hairdo, skirt and earrings.

FIGURE 13.   Unmarked Maya temple site.

FIGURE 14.   *La Guadalupana*. The saint sells Coca Cola, indicating the primacy of Catholicism over primitivism.

FIGURE 15. *La Isleña*. The Islander.

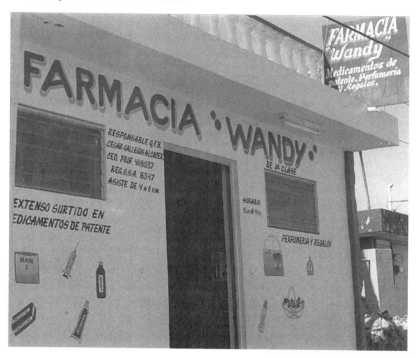

FIGURE 16. *Farmacia* "Wandy."

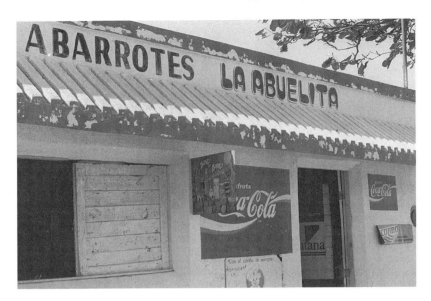

FIGURE 17. *La Abuelita*. Store name "the little grandmother" centers on family relations, not myths, exotic female creatures, nature, or beasts.

FIGURE 18. *La Colonia*. The neighborhood.

FIGURE 19. *La Lucha*. The struggle.

FIGURE 20. *Las Palmas*. The image of palm trees allures tourists.

FIGURE 21. Restaurant-bar *Zazil-ha*. *Zazil-ha* means clear water in Maya. The restaurant is situated on the side of a lagoon.

FIGURE 22. Reconstructed glyph of ancient shaman.

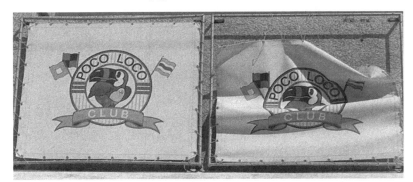

FIGURE 23. *Poco Loco* Club insignia. Tourists come to be a little "crazy," as shown in the popular insignia which a store sells immediately across from the dock. The store sells the insignia on jackets, T-shirts, and other tourist paraphernalia worn during "wild dancing" in streets and bars.

FIGURE 24. Animal spirit (*balam*). Sacred animal spirit squats in the garden of a high-priced hotel that has a lively, well-known "Happy Hour." Down a sandy path to the right, lower class tourists used to be able to stay for one third the price.

FIGURE 25. Hamburger Man. This sign expresses the local owner's desire to stand in the present to create the future, not to face backward to romanticize a past.

FIGURE 26.   Hand-painted wall. This hybrid mural in a downtown cafe combines a palm tree sporting a coconut with straws, a rainbow, a coffee cup and coffee pot marked in English only, and a gigantic shrimp cocktail cup filled with plastic beach balls and an umbrella for shade such as are rented to tourists on the horizon. The combination of images created by a Maya Cancúnite contrasts with the primitivistic "back to nature" purity of the Venetian artist whose works were on display in a nearby gallery, as high rather than popular art.

FIGURE 28. Mermaid and shark.

FIGURE 29. Thin white woman holds bilingual menu. A popular working-class menu across from the market sports a thin bare-shouldered white woman holding a sign, in sharp contrast to the workers inside who are short, plump, solidly dressed, and brown.

FIGURE 27. (Left) Primitivistic masks miniaturized elsewhere for tourist consumption.

FIGURE 30. Workers inside.

FIGURE 31. Wildcats and antelopes. These animals roam only the mural, not the island that is covered instead with taxis and hourly-rented motor bikes and golf carts.

FIGURE 32. *Jugos* in the *zócalo*. Ongoing artifacts in the Maya present.

FIGURE 33. "Wild" gringos.

FIGURE 34. New Year's celebration. In small villages in the interior, all-night dances used to be sacred to community-building, presided over by religious men. Now, on New Year's Eve, families with children still come to the *zócalo* to sit at tables and drink soda and beer, all that remains of community welcome feasts that used to be given to welcome whole towns who walked long journeys through the jungle to come to the celebrations.

FIGURE 35. Stylized couples dancing. Men "naturally" take the lead. This is in stark contrast to *jarana*, or fast-foot virtuoso dancing that women used to do as solo performers. *Torito*, gender reversal role-play dancing, has also disappeared.

FIGURE 36. Figure giving birth: Miramar, Cozumel. Courtesy of The Field Museum, Chicago, IL, neg. #2157.

FIGURE 37. Dragon Lady in ceramic fragment. This shows the movie-like position change of another image of the feminine from unearthed ceramic art which might have become an indigenously reclaimed model for the Maya mermaid icon, had local artists had access to their own heritage collected in North American museum collections (from *The Maya Book of the Dead: The Ceramic Codex* by Francis Robicsek and Donald Hales, 115).

FIGURE 38. Woman wrapped with serpent. Another possible indigenous model for sign painters on Isla Mujeres, this traditional image of the feminine from Maya culture has also been bypassed. From *The Maya Book of the Dead: The Ceramic Codex* by Francis Robicsek and Donald Hales, vessel 12a (19), this display for scholars in Taube (375) might have been abhorrent to tourists, restimulating the fear of snakes associated with women in the western Medusa image and in the Eve story. Nonetheless, the image echoes ancient snake-goddess mythology of not only Mexico, but Europe and other parts of the world, indicating either regional expression of common ancient beliefs, a result of contact in pre-colonial trade or migration patterns of matriarchal civilizations from the east as previously suggested.

NINE

How the Folk Erodes

MYTH, IMAGE, SYMBOL, AND REALITY

As I developed this argument, I named two forms of the Amazon archetype. The first I called the "primary form." By this I meant the Amazon as developed in oral literature, a collective fighting horde equal to men. The second I called the "secondary form." With this term I referred to the Amazon as developed after the invention of writing. In the second case, a lone, isolated, independent man was free to develop his fantasy. Unrestricted by the possible resistance of immediate audiences, a separated-out, anima-projected woman emerged.

In the late nineteenth and early twentieth centuries, women created a struggle for equality. More women became writers. As they did so, they forged a tertiary form of the Amazon archetype. As both reclamation and revitalization emerged, this new configuration again portrayed the Amazon archetype as a collective entity of women. The newly emerging women writers wrote for popular press newspapers, magazines, and publishers. Sometimes they saw an advantage in self-publishing. As a group, they did not depict the Amazon as men did—individualizing her for consumption purposes. Yet neither was fighting as a collective horde any longer the primary characteristic.

Most often in texts women wrote for popular consumption, women began to develop societies which showed that women were equal to men, or even superior (Albinski 1988; Bammer 1991; Ferguson n.d.). The women in these Amazonian all-women or women-dominated societies sometimes appeared to function as the exaggerated essence of goodness and social justice.

They were superior to men. They appeared as angels within or upon the earth, or on other planets.

In this tertiary form, which emerged at the early stages of reclamation of Amazonian imagery, some women writers continued to stereotype roles of women, as had occurred in early nineteenth-century English literature as well (Agress 1978). Sometimes, as in a short story by 1930s science fiction writer Leslie F. Stone, women still fought and won—but no longer through feats of physical strength (1931).[1] Rather, they beat off invading men through more advanced mental powers as well as through superior technology for warfare. Also, in this tertiary form, women writers placed women from all-women or women-dominated localities in their own territory. The outsider-men visited women's terrain throughout the novels and fictions. This stance was distinct from forms in the past in which women were fighting on other people's territories, engaging in other people's struggles as professional fighters.

The above may make sense out of changing forms in a vast amount of feminist utopian literature. But the argument in this form does not yet theorize about the entire picture. Reader response theory suggests that the same text can receive the projection of many different responses. That is, these primordial forms springing from the unconscious can be released in the same field. They interact as transactive elements brought on by the same minimalist stimuli. Hence, a complete study of the topic would necessarily have to examine a range of responses to the same text and not just compare differing forms in the texts themselves.

In previous chapters, I explained differences in moments of creation, moments of performance, technological changes in the production of literature, and the subsequent changes in the imaging of the feminine in different texts. But also in the case explored in this section, the same text alters upon examination. As different responses get played to, different art, artifacts, myths, and legends emerge.

With such a project in mind, I examined the phenomenon of a real island off the coast of the Yucatan with the intriguing name Isla Mujeres (Island of Women). This island is situated both in the context of a Maya present and past and in the context of a currently fluctuating but booming tourist industry. There, a variety of culturally placed visitors, workers, producers, and readers demonstrate the complexity of the problem.

This living artifact is located in the Caribbean. Given the name Isla Mujeres by Spanish explorers, it may or may not be the island on which Columbus reported sighting Sirens. It may or may not be the island of which he reported hearing in his conversations with "the Indians." It may or may not have been the report of this island that inspired the creation of an island of women in Montalvo's romance. It may or may not have been Montalvo's romance that influenced those who discovered and named the island.

The most straightforward account of the naming that I have found is Alfred Maudslay's translation of Bernard Díaz del Castillo's *True History of the Conquest of Mexico* ([1568] 1927). Contemporary scholars on the Cozumel Project mentioned this account in a list of examples of coastal shrines occurring in groups at some distance from the settlements along the east coast of Quintana Roo. In this version, explorer Díaz del Castillo made reference to going on shore at the bay and finding farms and maize plantations, as well as "four *Cues* which are the houses of their Idols, and there were many Idols in them, nearly all of them figures of tall women so that we called the place the *Punta de Las Mujeres*" (Maudslay, quoted in Freidel and Sabloff 1984, 45).

All that can be said, really, is that the replaying of these and similar narratives, either real or projected, influences those who go there today. Those who live and work there play to the evolutions of such narrative material in those visitors for commercial purposes, rather than delve into myths, legends, or images of their own historical origins. Anglo-Peruvian Richard Luxton mentioned after discussion with fishermen from the island that the island was said to have gotten its name from having been used as a pirate's stronghold where treasures from the Spanish Main were kept, together with mistresses and cooks—the plunder of English and European ancestors. "If apocryphal," he remarked, "the story was suitably sited amidst barnacle-covered cannon dredged from below and hauled to the surface, and it did provide the tourists with a frisson of excitement to take home . . ." (1981, 87).

Yet, such a process has the accumulated effect of creating a social space with divergent cognitive patterns imposed upon the same terrain by many different socially placed people. In this section, I connect specific insight gained in my own creative-poetic process (1993b) to existing social theory. I ask experientially, was women's folk culture a key source for the island's name? Do women's folk culture and the derived name serve as a creative source on the island today? What conditions of life among women on the island did the name express? How were women the baseline of the island's material and spiritual experience? I chose to enter the culture through writing, and also through participation in women's culture as I undertook a study. I share here, for example, my participation in divination, pregnancy, birth, and infant and child care.

Through participating in island life like this, I found two created orders

of archetypal responses. Admittedly these categories might be skewed somewhat since I did not broaden the subject to include Chicano/a as well as
Anglo-American and European tourism, although some visits to the island
by Chicanos/as are beginning to appear to supplement the record (Castillo
70–74). The categories I developed were based on Anglo-Americans looking
at Mexico as "the other," not on Chicanos/as looking at their own roots,
although that would be an interesting area for further study, especially as
such journeys begin to occur with greater frequency. Just as study of the
experience of American Jews looking at Israel would be different from a
study of American born-again Christians looking at Israel, it seems obvious
that this is a related, valid, but separate, area of pursuit.

The overall categories I found when looking at the island diverged greatly
from the realities of the island itself. A visit to Disneyland can provoke different reactions, according to the modes of apprehension of the *aficionados*
(Spinelli 1992). Likewise, what Abrahams (1986) has called the emotional
cognitive state of visitors undergoing peak experiences would vary in a situation such as a tourist island. The whole audience is expected to share a
particularly heightened emotional state. The type of archetypal reaction in
this state fits the "island of fair women" motif in folk literature. This type
emphasizes art and artifacts that depict women's beauty entrapping men,
such as the story of pirate Mundaca, and recently represented by the opening
of a bar named "Calypso," after the female sorceress in the *Odyssey*.

Yet an opposite type of reaction fits the "lost power of women" motif in
contemporary reclamationist literature. Art, artifacts, nuances, and legends
preserved for the benefit of those with this reaction emphasize roots in goddesses of ancient Maya culture. These center around a cluster of signs and
other references to the moon goddess of the Maya, Ix Chel.

Represented somewhat differently in copies from codices,[2] objects from
dedication offerings, and carvings in eccentric obsidian rocks, the Maya
sometimes referred to the goddess as "Lady Rainbow." She painted the colors of the sky after she poured the rain down. The Maya regarded her as
the protective patron of women in childbirth and of weavers. Her domain
extended through southern Mexico, the Yucatán Peninsula, and Central
America at least as far as El Salvador. In the form of a large, widespread
celebratory culture, people still actively worshiped her at the time of the
Spanish conquest of Mexico (K. Turner 1976, 43–44; Lurker 1988, 172;
Vera 1979, 34).[3]

The fair island motif represents more the Aphrodite than the Amazon
archetype. Gertrude Jobes best described the Aphrodite-like, beautifully se-

ductive "Island of Fair Women" motif as distinguished from the motif of the
Amazons, whom she described as "women with masculine habits" (81). As
Jobes explained, in dream and mythology an island usually represents isolation or abandonment, a gathering place of souls. She cited among others the
American Indian Blissful Isle, the Greek Happy Islands, the Roman Fortunate Islands, and the three paradisical realms in China. A floating island is a
celestial paradise, or utopia. The Island of Fair Women, in particular, she
says, is

> a paradise in which a mortal is in danger of dying of love by suc-
> cumbing to the enticements of the beautiful goddess. The theme is
> world-wide. The mariners who land on these islands never escape.
> Sometimes they are transformed into animals, or other shapes as in
> the Circe legend. (846–847)

Local lore seems to have attached to this worldwide theme the Isla Mujeres story of Mundaca, the invading pirate who falls in love with an Indian
woman who refuses him. In the story, he stays on the island forever, pining
after the Indian woman. He even builds a castle in which to keep her, but
she never comes. This story is an example of what Claude Lévi-Strauss in
The Savage Mind (1966) called a "bricoleur" effect upon the original plane
of the mythical thought. Victoria Reifler Bricker also attested to this view of
myth as composed of "remains and debris" of historical events arranged into
a story structure, based on evidence of performed Mayan legend (1981, 4–5).

Thus the lost power of women motif represents in this case more the fertility of the Mother Goddess archetype than the collective horde of fighting
Amazons, and remaining debris of mythical and historical events such as
these are layered. Traces of the old Moon Goddess reclaimed on the island
go back to 932 A.D., 174 years earlier than the appearance of the First
Mother, the Moon Goddess. Early Maya texts name her, and artists also
depicted her on panels at Palenque. She held the power to create gods by
calling them up from the Otherworld. She also did the Snake Dance, en-
abling the final creation and the birth of all the gods (Freidel, Schele, and
Parker 1993, 272–283). Hence, after all my research into the Amazon archetype in modern-day consciousness, I found other archetypes predominat-
ing on this particular island. This is so even though the prevailing version of
Amazon mythology during the period of Spanish discovery probably influenced the naming of the island itself.

Thus, what archetype someone projects remains a result of social conditions of the individuals projecting. The level of emerging reclamation, revitalization, or reaction in the cultural mind set of the times partly determines what surrounds the individuals concerned. Contemporary women's search for their own identity as they struggle for sources of revitalization in their own reclamation with the impetus of redefining themselves via ancient icons and myth becomes only one of a series of variants. The scanty bits of information remaining available about the island's origins, pre-Conquest, allows a confusion of projected elements to continue to occur, including both the reclaiming of the island as a lost goddess center and the allusion to mariners and other men who landed on the island and never escaped.

For example, men in search of loose, free, unencumbered women available for the taking still visit the island. At the center of the island is a national park with the monument of the house that Mundaca the pirate ostensibly built for his love object, the Indian maiden. Yet reclamationist Kay Turner claimed as her starting point that Cordoba found the island "overspread" with female idols and elaborated how the island took its name from the many feminine idols found there:

> On the island were found towers of stone with steps and chapels covered with wood and straw, on which were placed in very artful fashion idols that looked like women. In effect, Cordova found the idols of the goddesses of that island Ixchel, Ix Chelbelyax, Ixbinic, *etc.*
> (Turner 44)[4]

Turner then moved to a discussion of the rule of Ix Chel's, which extended back in time before the Conquest[5] to the very beginnings of Maya culture. Turner focused especially on Ix Chel's function as Earth Mother and the goddess of becoming (i.e., birth). She wrote of archaeological evidence that to her demonstrates the widespread influence of female fertility cults in all pre-Classical Mesoamerican cultures.

From the sketchy reports of what was discovered on the island, Turner reclaimed Ix Chel as the most prominent female deity in the Maya world. Turner stated that this goddess's reign lasted nine hundred years, spanning the Classic and Post-Classic periods (600 A.D.–1500 A.D.). Contemporary Mayas, Turner wrote, "still sense her presence in their world," calling her "The Queen," "Our Grandmother," "Our Mother," and "The White Lady."

Either form of present-day American tourism—that geared toward seduction by an island of fair women or that aimed at the lost power of women and represented in the goddess complex—might seem objectionable on several grounds. Both involve a process of appropriation of the island culture, turning island life into a consumable object, just as Mexico has been appropriated for what the country stimulates in the eye of the beholder (Alarcan). Yet, either form also reflects valid needs that have developed in members of advanced post-industrial societies in response to repressive control of sensuality in the interest of modification of fertility, reproduction, and sexuality. Thus, tourists search for a non-mechanized and non-rationalized identity on the island as they overcome depersonalization in the cultures of origin.

Visitors, including myself, tend to look for the hidden realities that lie behind the superficial appearances of the island. As we do so, we project a transference onto the island's opaque open door from our own need to compensate for loss in modern society. We juxtapose exotic and familiar customs, relating assumptions which we take for granted in our own lives to a newly discovered way of being. For example, goddess reclaimer-revitalizer Turner imaginatively hypothesized the actual use and significance of the figurines:

> Ancient Maya women knew Ix Chel most intimately as the Ix U Sihnal, Moon Patroness of Birth. Their deepest dreams and their most profound personal desires were answered through the mediation of the moon goddess. It was she who allowed conception, she who made the birth of a living child possible. The moon is the place of generation. Most probably every Maya woman owned a figurine of Ix Chel or an even more elaborate altar to her honor. A woman in labor placed the figurine beneath her bed to ease the pain and insure the life of the child. A woman desiring to get pregnant did the same. The most famous shrines to Ix Chel on the Yucatan Peninsula of Mexico and Cozumel Island were visited by thousands of women yearly from all over the Mayan world. Some must have traveled hundreds of miles, over months of time, to reach the sacred places. It was the desire of every woman to make a pilgrimage, at least once in her lifetime, to one of the major shrines. Picture hundreds of women in dugout canoes, paddling across the twenty miles that separate Cozumel from the mainland, all intent on their devotion to the one who belongs to them, who makes them the bearers of life. . . . If it is true that Cozumel was the most highly regarded site of pilgrimage to

receive blessing from the great mother, it might be true that Isla de Mujeres served as a cloister for the training and meditation of priest-esses. (45–46)

During a visit Turner made in 1976, she reflected that old timers, mostly fishermen, diminished the goddess as an old lady that the Indians used to worship down there. Turner maintained that patriarchal folklore under-mined the legacy of the goddess represented in the figurines. The pirate leg-end of the seventeenth century, she has argued, was superimposed on the reality of the island, which has had its alluring romantic name only since the Conquest.

The Spanish neatly created this tabula rasa situation, which allows others to fill in the sketchy gaps in current folklore with pictures from their own imaginations. The Spanish burned the Yucatán almanacs and architectural hieroglyphic inscriptions when they arrived, and they hoped to destroy for-ever the written record of the Maya. They committed what has been called "one of the greatest cultural crimes in history" (Marchi 1993, 43). Their cultural arrogance extended to destroying all "pagan" idols by decree and to sleeping in the temple sites they had just cleared.

Fray Diego de Landa's account of his burning of twenty-eight sacred books of the Maya sheds light on the attitude behind such acts by over-zealous missionaries:

These people also made use of certain characters or letters, with which they wrote in their books their ancient matters and their sci-ences, and by these and by drawings and by certain signs in these drawings, they understood their affairs and made others understand them and taught them. We found a large number of books in these characters and, as they contained nothing in which there was not to be seen superstition and lies of the devil, we burned them all, which they regretted to an amazing degree, and which caused them great affliction. ([1560?] 1959, 169)

Then patriarchal research continued its own form of destructive burial. Researchers in the male-dominated field of archaeology saw mostly men. They labeled women with breasts "gods," according to feminist Lynn Vera, who in 1979 made a journey through Mexico in order to reclaim female imagery (34). Caption-writers often interpreted small figures sitting on large figures as old men with young women, rather than as mothers with small children on their laps.

Furthermore, obvious birth and womb images typically have not been so identified. Explanatory texts consistently name figures which one could interpret as male or female as "he." Clearly, touristic development often left goddess-dominant sites unreconstructed, while the government, for nationalistic purposes, monumentalized shrines and sites of male activities such as the games at Palenque.

For example, excavators did not approach Cozumel until the 1970s, after the outburst of the women's liberation movement in America. Some of this feminist activity emerged in Cambridge, Massachusetts, the same site from which the Harvard team conducting the research and excavation largely emanated. Only then did interest result in the site's reconstruction, perhaps under the movement's influence. This experiential activity aptly fits with what de Certeau has said about the pursuit of the popular and folklore in general—only after culture obliterates folklore do people pursue old myths, with great mystification about what they might have been (1986).

The sense of place and the preservation of historical fabric and natural settings have occurred in the development of tourism in the last twenty years. Feminist reclaiming women might have a sense of superiority over the common "tourist." Yet they remain unaware of participation in a sort of "new tourism," such as John Rosenow and Gerreld Palsipher explored in *Tourism: The Good, the Bad and the Ugly* (1979). In an age of increasing rootlessness characterized by the proliferation of shopping centers and the homogenization of mass society, communities with tangible ties to heritage provide a sense of cultural roots and of unique environment that tourists in general now prefer to explore (39).

Women are undertaking spiritual quests for women's experience as a result of oral consciousness raising and storytelling that led to the rejection of male-written versions of women's early tales (Christ 1979). Yet also, conceivably men are also undergoing a search for a romanticized work life. The image of pirates patrolling high seas and falling in deep, unrequited love with native women might vicariously fulfill a search brought on by their own ennui, which growing workplace depersonalization has been increasing.

The search motivated by reclamation takes its impetus from second-wave feminism and yet manifests a much deeper cultural criticism of America. Whereas Walker's *Amazon: A Novel* used her narrator coming from the past to call attention to patriarchal authority structures in our present, here, the reverse occurs: we go from *our* present, and attach a critique of *their* present, from our projected need for a past. Yet, ironically, in doing so we might collide with others with radically different worldviews executing the same process from another perspective.

To begin my own study of this phenomenon, I began to look at an existing actual "island of women" to get to the bottom of what is projection and what is myth. Perhaps this effort makes about as much sense as reading an actual account of a Spanish woman whom Amazonian Indians imprisoned for years to see if there are any historical roots to Voltaire's scene in *Candide* in which an upstart son from a decadent world of white men encounters a utopian civilization of the same territory in which women warriors, the Amazons, were said to have existed (Voltaire [1759] 1957, 63–81; Biocca 1971, 13). Original maps of the continent showed women warriors in that area, defending El Dorado, the City of Gold; consequently, famous conquerors including Gonzalo Pizarro, Walter Raleigh ([1614] 1971), and Gaspar de Carvajal ([1542?] 1934) once explored the region looking for Amazons. Yet is there any reason to explore what exists there for hopes of residuals in the here and now? I initially started to grope through this territory of geography and history with such a question.

The island on which I began my work was far from the Amazon Basin but bore the same sort of allusions in legend. I was playing many roles— as a graduate student improving language proficiency, as a member of a family healing from a tragedy, and as a woman marginalized in dominant culture and its structures of education who was trying to create meaningful alternative work. More importantly, to the islanders and tourists I met there, I was a "reader." That is, I was one who had the gift to practice divination through cards.

Divination has long been an important part of Maya culture, as evidenced by anthropologist Robert Redfield's classic ethnography of a Maya village near Chichen Itza—an area in the interior of the Yucatán from which a majority of immigrants to Isla Mujeres have come. He wrote in the early 1930s with the aid of a local educated male informant, Alfonso Villa Rojas (Redfield and Villa Rojas 1934). Divination, this study revealed, was predominantly practiced by traditional spiritual healers referred to as "*h-men*." These were shamans who read codices, communicated with spirits, healed, and divined. The word *h-men* literally means "one-who-knows," from *men*, the fifteenth sign in the set of glyphs associated with the eagle, which in traditional Maya belief is the seer of the heart of the sky (Luxton 224). These *h-men* were known for their far-seeing, para-normal abilities. Classic Maya texts, like Classic Maya sculptural images, suggest complementary contributions of male and female to the construction of political power in this realm.

Reference to gender dichotomy excluding women from divination does not appear in earlier records such as that of colonialist Fray Diego de Landa ([1560?] 1959), who described women shamans and women's role in supernatural ritual (Joyce 1992, 63–69). By the 1930s, however, traditional esoteric knowledge was considered to be largely taboo to most women (except for midwives), according to Redfield and Villa Rojas. It is to the traveling Spanish fortune tellers who were chased out of Spain and who emigrated to the New World during the Inquisition that I owe the acceptability of my role as a reader. On the island, this skill I had developed elsewhere opened many doors. The appearance of these gypsies from Spain had already caused a shift in local practices of divination. Traditional shamans adjusted to the march of history—if the Spanish did not torture, hang, burn, and whip them to death—through the mutation of symbols. They shifted to the Spanish playing deck, still a cross between the Western European card-playing deck and the deck of tarot. They divined with these imported cards, rather than or in addition to reading patterns in beans and corn. Julian Steward's collection of synopses of South American Indian tribes describes inland indigenous shamans who worked primarily in dreams. Their power grew in proportion to their ability to work with this aspect of divination (1963, 177).

My identity as a reader, combined with increased proficiency in the language, gave me access to more people over time, who gradually led me to diversify my skills to include interpretation of dreams and palms as I worked with them. Many revealed their life stories and invited me into their homes. Although I initially entered the homes and lives of people to do a service, I gradually realized that as I readily transformed myself for more entrance into the culture, I could observe firsthand the mutation of symbols and the erosion of folk traditions as well as the emergence of new sorts of symbols in my own dreams.

I also observed the adaptive creation of new symbolic traditions such as display of Barbie dolls and coke bottles accompanying virgin icons in living room altars. I noticed that copied and improvised wall paintings of Walt Disney Pictures characters and drawings from other imported cartoons seemed to have actually replaced the wall paintings of the winged spirits that Redfield's photographers had seen in houses in the 1930s.

I was genuinely engaged in the practice of my livelihood. Yet questions of cultural mergers inevitably began to arise: were Mickey Mouse and Donald

Duck replacements for the spirit *balams,* the little people made of air who could appear in different animal forms? When a father painted such figures on the walls for a celebration of a child's first birthday, did they become the child's protective animal spirits? Did the images brought by the globalization of mass culture replace those of the 1930s? Redfield and Villa Rojas (189) wrote that parents presented a series of objects to the child to promote learning. Did these new figures—created by a cadre of artists working for Disney and later copied by islanders—guard the walls of Isla streets the way the *balams* used to guard the field?

Such were the kinds of questions that emerged as I lived on the island. My perceptions of both myself and the people around me changed, and kept changing. People on the island seemed to perceive me to be like most others coming from the outside to work in tourism. Perhaps many never suspected the questions inside my mind. Yet over time, as I did my fieldwork, traveled away from the island to talk about my work at conferences, and solicited assistance from islanders in translating an article I had written in English into Spanish for a professional journal, other aspects of my identity emerged. Some volunteered examples of cultural anecdotes supporting the theses they learned I had been illustrating. For example, from a local informant helping in the translation, I learned that one Christmas he had seen a nativity altar in a friend's home with a Barbie doll on each step, culminating in a scene of the birth of the baby Jesus at the top.

Workers generally offered me solidarity, including housing, food, and survival strategies. Such tactics were as important to me as the researched information; I was living and making my life, which only secondarily became "lived research."[6] For example, another "reader" used to come regularly from Mérida. She sold herbs, read candles, and did clearings of negative energy with a white dove. Once she exercised her skill for me in exchange for a card reading during my pregnancy.

My interaction with the reader gave me the opportunity to learn more about female folk culture, but, more importantly, I found the reading to be personally meaningful. In the suffused glow of candlelight, I sought answers to questions about the father of my child and the future of my relationship with him. She, in turn, offered to perform a clearing with a white dove, which she said would release the energies needed to break my water.[7] At the time, my daughter's birth was more than two weeks overdue. The reader's actions brought about the desired effect within half an hour, even if I had no faith or little belief in her process. At the time, I was immersed in lived experience; only later did this experience lead me to the whole sociological phenomenon of traveling healers and readers that came periodically to work the island and to provide their services to the community. I gradually came to understand the community's perception of me, but the understanding was produced by how I lived my life at the time, not primarily by my later research.

Moreover, via my role as a reader, I befriended visitors and tourists as well as island workers, vendors, politicians, families, and business people. Thus I had access not only to the "real life" of "the folk," but also to the worldviews and perspectives of visiting travelers and islanders, with their own varied worldviews and cultural mind-sets. I participated in divination sessions with members of distinct but interactive cultures in this border region. I built informant networks and deepened my understanding by observing the expectations held of my performance by both groups.

Throughout the fieldwork, I began interpretation by weaving in what came to me through dreaming and other unconventional ways in which signs emerged. Having deconstructed my Western ethics of rationalization during the time I spent in the field, I began to observe tourist-projected frameworks observing me. I recognized these mind-sets, but by this time I had become somewhat estranged from the worldviews of my culture of origin.

At home, in the university, many understood neither my mythic exploration nor the survival skills I utilized in my livelihood as a diviner. Yet when I returned to the island and said that I was "writing a thesis," many seemed equally skeptical about my life as a graduate student, researcher, reader, and Xeroxer of library books. To the degree that I engaged in activity that opened doors in one world, this activity demoted me in another, and vice versa. Thus during my years in the field (December 1991–June 1997), I existed on a cultural see-saw. This situation, like that confronting sociologist Carol Rambo Ronai, who wrote about childhood sexual abuse, challenged me to create a "layered account." As she pointed out, all accounts are "simultaneously lived experiences at the time of their production and ungraspable moments of reflection that escape before they are written" (1995, 398). I dove headlong into the life of the island. I then underwent a continual dialectic of experience that changed me. I had to learn to be closeted about one activity or the other that was centrally defining my life—writing a thesis, in one milieu, and working as a reader, in the other.

Then, too, I did conceive, go through a pregnancy, give birth, and deal with infant and child care in both cultures. Such a process simultaneously gave me invaluable insights into the fieldwork culture and made me more marginal in my culture of origin, the graduate department of a northeastern

North American university. I bonded with both women and men on the island. My pregnancy and motherhood made my intellectual field life that much deeper, richer, more interesting, and more grounded on the island.

Yet at home, that which naturally made me closer to the nexus of one community excluded me from the other. Since my major professor couldn't fathom how I could both do intellectual work and be a mother, I lost a year of time. I had to make a special trip back from the field at a crucial phase of my research, expend energy writing another prospectus, and arrange for a new committee under a new director.

Surviving this conflict on academic turf served both to toughen me in the face of resistance in either world and to heighten my experience of both realities. I concluded that no matter what obfuscation of historical realities had occurred, some kind of centering force—however vague—was strengthening for women on the island. Perhaps this "something" derived from the icon of the name or whatever it was that supported that name in the culture, perhaps something from the broader contours of Maya culture itself. And that "something" did not flourish except in the support fissures and cracks in the university culture.

As I completed my work, I did so wondering why on an island called Isla Mujeres bearing children did not automatically tend to exclude women from public structures of work in the way most Northern Anglo-Americans took for granted. My experience of seeking a cultural identity on the island, and of the discrediting dominant culture of the university, colors all my interpretations.

What follows, then, is an analysis of how material objects express the conflict of cultures and conflicts within island culture, particularly those items in popular culture relating to the central mythology of the island. I view the island here as a collectively created fiction matching the unconscious needs of the tourists for a primitive, matriarchal, pre-colonial, untouched haven and space.

Since the tourist is often in a child-like pre- or semi-literate guided and directed state, conditions are ripe for marketing to those infantile needs. I analyze the myth of the island of women in history, popular culture, folklore, poetry, store signs, material culture, artifacts made to promote the island (including magazines, guide books, and t-shirts), poems written on the island, songs, dance, music, religious and political processions and icons, wall murals, and paintings commissioned by hotel and restaurant owners. I explore space usage, ruins, abandoned sites, utensils, meals served in restaurants, and beds versus hammocks. I set up a series of binary oppositions (the

United States and Mexico; Cancún and the island; natives and immigrants; the artificial and the natural; the modern and the traditional; the inauthentic and the real) and then proceed to demonstrate how these oppositions don't stand up.

After all, U.S. mass culture has its impact on aspiring and modernizing native transplants from the rest of Mexico and the Yucatán, and ideas about Maya culture fill U.S. and foreign tourists, including myself as a researcher. Hence, wonderful cultural mixes or cross-cultural constructions abound, making the island an endlessly fascinating intellectual retreat. The problem is, there hasn't been a pure, undefiled folk life for a number of years. Ongoing struggle has been occurring on the inland in the jungle settlements, from which many workers have migrated to settle on the island. Turmoil and population shifts have gone on in this region for years (Redfield and Villa Rojas 1934; Redfield 1950). Maya civilization had collapsed even before the Spanish Conquest, the consequent fleeing to jungles, and the subsequent rebellions and numerous revolutions which found support there (Culbert 1973).

Yet, others come imagining a pure, untouched folk life to address their own cultural malaise. Often, the legitimate impetus for American spiritual pilgrimage involves projected fantasies that tourists might better explore at home. Sometimes casual travelers unwittingly create unromantic disadvantages for the migrating working islanders, who are not merely on a vacation. This is especially so in shaky times of economic and political crises, which tend to reduce tourist flow and hence hamper the livelihood on the island. Throughout my fieldwork, I maintained both an abstract and a personal perspective in participant observation. The maintenance of this balance also gave me invaluable insights into belief systems, power structures, and pecking order among those, particularly women, who live on an island of this name. In the following chapters, then, I utilize the whole sense of culture— both the mental, abstract, cognitive aspects of culture, and the material products of culture, which archaeologists would see as cultural artifacts.

TEN

The Island of Women as Playground for America's "Leisure Primitivism"

> When you go across the border at Nogales Arizona
> some very severe looking American guards, some of
> them pasty faced with sinister steelrim spectacles go
> scrounging through all your beat baggage for signs
> of the scorpion of scofflaw. —You just wait patiently
> like you always do in America among those appar-
> ently endless policemen and their endless laws
> against (no laws for) —but the moment you cross
> the little wire gate and you're in Mexico, you feel
> like you just sneaked out of school when you told
> the teacher you were sick and she told you you
> could go home . . .   —JACK KEROUAC,
>   LONESOME TRAVELER: A NOVEL

D. H. Lawrence thought of Mexico as the solar plexus of the Americas. In
The Plumed Serpent (1926), he portrayed British intellectuals going to Mexico for the sense of the mass, as in proletariat socialist realism "masses" that
many artists and intellectuals of the elite classes depicted in that era. He
explored as well the philosophy and history of the Aztecs and took pure
sensuous delight in Mexico's birds, smells, and sun in *Mornings in Mexico*
([1927] 1982). He wrote as a foreign writer living abroad.

Similarly, Americans have been traveling to visit Mexico for the cultural-
historic "view" for a long time—which has to do with the limiting bounda-

ries of their own culture. The "Mexicanidad" movement, particularly, influenced bohemians in the 1950s, as evidenced by Kerouac. The movement consisted of Mexican intellectuals and artists rediscovering indigenous cultural values, which were despised by most of the ruling class within Mexico itself, for the sake of revolution (Brett 1991, 126–130). This included the work of communists Diego Rivera and Frieda Kahlo. Guy Brett has argued that since the Indian in Mexico became part of Europe's argument with itself, official art circles repressed most of this movement after World War II (1991).

Allen Ginsberg, showing the same influence in *Collected Poems* (1984), revealed many self-revelatory experiences that he had over the view of Palenque in 1954 ("Siesta in Xbalba," 97–110). His poem "Autumn Gold," written in 1966, reveals how his view of the New England landscape altered irrevocably once he returned home from Mexico (1984, 461–465). Likewise, Kerouac's experiences in Mexican whorehouses and his observation that all of Mexico was one "bohemian camp" in which one was never alone in *On the Road* (1957) show how the primitive-seeking northerner can be affected by the Mexican social landscape. His *Mexico City Blues* (1959) served the same purpose. Burroughs' *Junkie* (1953) described his "view" of Mexican women as dealers. Ferlinghetti's *Mexico Night: Travel Journal* (1970) exhibited similar influence. Charles Olson's *Maya Letters* (1968) worked out of the same mode, as did Anne Waldman's peyote experiences with a Mexican woman shaman, which led to her incorporation of landscape in her book-length poem *Fast-Speaking Woman* (1978).

The middle class usually follows in the tracks of bohemians. We might have predicted, then, that the exodus of the Beats to Mexico in the 1950s would lead to tourism in the same localities twenty-five years later. Isla Mujeres, off the coast of Mexico, was, in the 1990s, one of those hotly developed new spots.

Inadvertently, a gold mine of cultural elements has emerged on the island, showing how material objects impart messages replete with meaning in the intersection of colliding cultures. As Thomas Schlereth suggested in his introduction to *Artifacts and the American Past* (1981), my approach is to use the community as a learning laboratory. Here I examine how the collective unconscious, using the image of women on the island of women, has created objects representing different aspects of that psyche, as well as how this process has influenced the lives of real women in that milieu.

As passengers fly in on American Airlines over Cancún, the pilot directs their attention to the left, to the "Isle of Women." These same excited passengers discuss enthusiastically their oxymoronic plans to "rent a car and go somewhere really primitive." According to Fray Diego de Landa's *Relación de las cosas de Yucatán* ([1560?] 1959), Francisco Hernandez de Cordoba gave the name to the island in 1517 when he left Cuba with three ships to collect slaves. He supposedly then found the four goddess idols on the island. They were all dressed from the waist down.

I have found no contemporary references to two of the names given for these goddesses. However, according to Lynn Vera, the syllable "Ix" means "woman" or "lady" and usually was included with the name of a goddess (34). Manfred Lurker's *The Dictionary of Gods and Goddesses, Devils and Demons* (1988) says that Ix Chel was regarded as moon goddess of the Maya as well as a protective patron of women in childbirth and weavers. *The Book of Goddesses and Heroines* (Monaghan 1981) further notes that Ixchebeliax was, among the Maya people, the name given to the daughter of the moon, the goddess who taught weaving, spinning, and dyeing to the women of the Yucatán, Guatemala, and Honduras (158).

According to this source, the Maya of the Yucatán gave the name Ix Chel to the snake goddess of water, the moon, and childbirth and weaving. One tale has it that she took the sun as her lover but her grandfather hurled lightning to kill her. Dragonflies sang grieving over Ix Chel for thirteen days. She emerged whole to join her lover. The jealous sun mistreated her, and she took to wandering in the night, making herself invisible when he appeared. She spent her energies nursing the women of earth through pregnancy and labor as well as taking special care of those who visited her sacred isle of Cozumel.

The explanation given at the recently constructed museum on the nearby isle of Cozumel describes Ix Chel as the "goddess of pregnancy and childbirth, and the protector of the child in the womb and during birth. Every Mayan supposedly visited her once in a lifetime; she also models the face of the child in the womb." During a visit in 1993 with two women from California who were seeking information on the history of the site, the taxi driver elaborated the museum's statement to mean that ancient Maya women came to the island knowing they were pregnant and stayed to give birth. The tour guide at the site renovated in 1980 insisted that women came to the full moon fest to participate in the animal sacrifice attended by priests. However, he felt that they only came if they were having problems with fertility.

There are numerous reasons for considering these conjectural statements somewhat dubious. A contemporary Maya woman from Guatemala said that any of the above claims were unrealistic. The notion that any woman of traditional Maya culture would have the time, freedom, or resources to travel such a distance was, she said, patently absurd. She felt that these ungrounded claims were pure hype, manufactured for the tourists by those expecting a big tip for saying what their customers wanted to hear.

My own observation of cultural folk ways in *la colonia* tend to corroborate this contemporary Maya woman's doubts. When on Isla Mujeres, I interacted with a pregnant woman whose boyfriend did not allow her to go out for a walk alone. She could not walk the streets at all unless he accompanied her. His jealousy was part of it. But the community ethos about protecting pregnant women and babies—particularly from the evil eye and from bad spirits contained in numerous winds—conflicted with the notion of long-distance travel away from the home when a woman was pregnant or with a new born. In particular, during an eclipse, the entire family of this woman's boyfriend was involved in trying to shield her stomach from the special energies that they thought might affect the fetus negatively. Besides, a native custom persists that does not allow recent birth mothers out of the home for forty days after giving birth.

Part of the confusion stems from the fact that Cortés ordered the destruction of the goddess-dominant sites in 1519, so no one really knows what might have transpired there. On Cozumel, he actually declared the beautiful shrine to Ix Chel idolatrous and ordered his men to tear down the images. He further instructed them to construct a statue of the Virgin and wooden crucifixes on the same spot. He acted in accordance with those carrying out a decree from Lima to destroy all such idols. Spaniards carried out this destruction all over Mexico. The desecration went as far as the men taking over altars and shrines as general living quarters. One of the large wooden crosses that Cortés' men erected now stands in the National Museum of Mexico.

Modern reconstruction destroyed the principal existing structure, photographed in 1895, which featured a figure giving birth as one of its columns. The column survived, and is now in the museum started on the island after the Harvard/*National Geographic* Project. More recently, common looting has become an ongoing problem for those engaged in archaeological work.

Furthermore, some scholars theorize that the Mayas themselves may have deliberately destroyed some artifacts which could have enlightened historians and researchers. Some consider that a "racial pact of silence" before the white man is still in effect. Some hope their own silence and evasiveness will discourage those who would be invasive enough to ferret out every detail in the violent disruption of the indigenous peoples of the Americas (Reed 1966, 342).

Nonetheless, colonialist Landa reported that these figurines, about whose identity we can merely guess, had their breasts covered "in the manner of the Indians" (7). They were "richly adorned and flower-bedecked" (Reed 1966, 343). However, *The Islander,* a magazine written on Isla Mujeres explicitly for tourists, misquoted this as "*un*covered at the breasts in the manner of the Indians . . ." (1992, 4)—an example of how the meaning of artifacts undergoes continual mythical transformation.

Thus, distorted confusion over the name of the islands feeds the needy cultural imagination of tourists. This activates a grip on the imagination that is very compelling. The oldest record of the myth places it first with the Andaman Islanders. According to Joseph Campbell, the Andaman Islanders had what they called a "woman island" formed by an all-woman creator (1959, 318).[1] Their island also sported female figurines, the earliest discovered graven image before the costumed shaman replaced the naked female (Campbell 324). Campbell also associated those female figurines with mother-goddess spiritual activity.

It remains unclear whether the discovery of the *diosas* signified the existence of a pre-Conquest, goddess-dominant religious structure on the island akin to matriarchal periods in other parts of world history. Alma Reed, writing about the ancient past of Mexico, suggested association with Isis, Astarte, Venus, and other goddesses of fertility worshiped in the ancient world. A male Maya immigrant from the jungle offered a more practical explanation: the point now a spot for fantastic tourist speculation was merely an observatory to watch for boats coming. This down-to-earth contemporary Maya informant's view is that the goddesses served a function similar to that of the Virgin of Guadalupe in the contemporary marketplace. He conjectured that the idols only stood as Catholic images do, for psychic protection. On Cozumel, beyond the southern lighthouse on the tip of the island, a platform stood twenty feet high, formed by conch shells that created a loud roaring sound when stimulated by southeast winds. Analogously, perhaps he was right that these outposts were signal stations to warn approaching boats of a land mass. They could also have been signal stations to warn islanders of continuing storms.

However, Irene Silverblatt, historical anthropologist, has clearly outlined the existence of "nunneries." There the conquering Inca placed young women of pre-Inca tribes whom they had rounded up to live together as mystical brides to the Inca Sun King (1987). Silverblatt attributed these structures to the necessity of control of reproduction and sexuality for the empire. Although she focused on a geographic area further along the land mass to the south, her research remains relevant because religions did travel, particularly through trade and commerce, along shores and inland from shores. The ruins of former coastal cities in Quintana Roo, as well as the styles of living that the Spanish encountered, provide ample evidence of a flourishing Maya maritime empire. Merchants as connectors to the outside world remained a special substratum in developments that scholars studied in the 1930s (Culbert 351; Scholes and Roys 123; Folan, Kintz, and Fletcher 12–15; Redfield and Villa Rojas 9).

Thus not only does the naming of a site at Chichen Itza "The Nunnery" indicate that such a structure reminded the Spanish of their own nunneries at home. Here also the pre-Conquest populations might have used the structures for sex-segregated religious purposes like the ones Silverblatt described to the south. Also, according to Silverblatt, hordes of women banded together and fled to remote areas in colonial resistance. The women fought to re-create their moon-goddess local community worship rather than to adopt the oppressive strictures of an abusive Catholic colonialism. Thus we might also conclude that the discovered goddess statues might have been part of a real, dialectical response to the march of Spanish colonial history which dealt out much abuse to women, as Silverblatt has documented.

Silverblatt's fascinating historical anthropological account of pre-Inca, Inca, and colonial social structures can be used as a model for clues and as background to the present work. Basing her work on archival research as well as on fieldwork, she referenced islands that women set aside in Lake Titicaca for women's worship of the moon goddess. These women's religious practices included the use of conch shells. The conch shells discovered in the area that could have been used for ritual in Cozumel do suggest a connection, whatever mutation has occurred by now.

Yet if that connection were through trade and commerce, as historians have suggested, the existence of this "Island of Women" could be explained in other ways than as a center of worship. The common-sense explanation that workers, shopkeepers, and long-term community residents on the island often gave as to why Spaniards discovered only women there is simply that the men were out fishing. In an earlier stage of my research, this answer befuddled me; I thought of it as a deliberate or confused burial of a long-lost women's history. Yet gradually the kernel of common folk wisdom began to make sense, once I had befriended wives of fishermen whose husbands were gone eight days at a time on lobster boats based out of nearby islands. This commonsense explanation also exhibits possible synchronicity with the practical explanation of the same observed phenomenon in Sumatra. There, men involved in trade would leave their matrifocal communal dwellings and be gone for weeks or even months (Kato 1981; Sanday 1990). Obviously, this common-sense explanation would not be such an intriguing attraction in the booming tourist industry.

Touristic travel constitutes an important form of expensive American recreation. A large literature exists on the subject. But most of this writing directs attention to tourist flows and to economic impact, rather than to what the multi-billion dollar industry has done to the appearance and morphology of the land's cultural and social "scapes."

Clearly, the impact of American aesthetics and consciousness through its imperialistic tourism abroad is enormous. Without going into an in-depth review of the literature on this topic, I merely accept the general idea that the eye of the beholder rearranges the molecule which it observes, something the scientific community refers to as the Heisenberg Principle. Here I will show how the eye of the beholding tourist rearranges what occurs on Isla Mujeres, an island five miles long and a half mile wide off the coast of the Yucatán in Quintana Roo, Mexico.

The typical promotional maps show only tourist sites, not local neighborhoods or sites of importance to the daily existence of the inhabitants. This official obscuring of reality constitutes an incidence of "Fourth World" invisibility to visitors to the Third World. Although problematic, the term "Fourth World" has been used to refer to the invisible life of indigenous cultures even though a national identity influenced by colonial impact has been formed.

Taking a different approach to American tourism, I studied the island in the capacity of a shrine that Americans have created abroad. Some Americans ritually travel to sites that re-stimulate a basic sense of awe, as in a pilgrimage. The tradition of talking statues that supplicants visit in this area goes back far in Maya culture. In pre-Columbian times, supplicants visited the life-sized clay statue as the oracle of Ix Chel on Cozumel (Freidel, Schele, and Parker 178). Freidel and Sabloff described the ruins they explored in a project that the National Geographic Society funded in 1971. The Harvard-Arizona Cozumel Project expressed the view that the situation of the idol in a sacred pilgrimage just before the Conquest in the center of criss-crossing trade lines was a manipulated factor. The scholars conducting the project felt that the site of the talking idol led to the accelerated rise of mercantilism and the religious decline of Maya lowland society, which had become greatly secularized by the end of the Classic period. Cozumel, they argued, as a port of trade, "was an ideal location for a talking idol since the inhabitants

could maintain a flexible ideology through Ix Chel's continuous pronounce-
ments . . ." (111). These researchers suggested that there had been an evolution from altar-bound silent idol to altar-bound talking idol to life-sized
talking idol. Such flexibility might have allowed those who lived on Cozumel
to adjust rapidly to changing political currents flowing through the island
with trade.

Perhaps pilgrims in need also visited the statues on Isla Mujeres. I want
to suggest that when travelers visit such sites, they project their imaginations
and let the island as a whole do the talking. We should thus include these
sites in a conceptual expansion of Melville Herskovits' often-cited early definition of material culture. In *Cultural Anthropology* (1955), Herskovits defined material culture as the totality of artifacts generated to cope with the
physical world. The functional aspects of this include the facilitation of
social intercourse and the creation of symbols of meaning (119). Even if
juxtaposing the abstract and the material in a different sense, we can see
that tourists seek and receive a different sort of "channeling" to create their
own personal symbols of meaning that help them cope with their individual
physical worlds in a way that their own traditional culture's religion does
not. For some, relating to these sites generates new sorts of invigorated social
intercourse. This regeneration and redirecting of social intercourse and personal expectations of the physical world includes the stimulation and release
of archetypes in the mind.

When I was doing my principal fieldwork, there were at least three main
ways to "enter" the island for a day trip. Many visitors to the Zona Hotelera
(hotel strip) in Cancún go to the island with the idea of "getting close to the
people," to "the real Mexico." They seek to have a "genuine folk experience," to "get back to" something they have lost in what Stanley Diamond
has called society's "devolution" (1987).

The visitors who come to the island for day visits from Cancún stay in
time-shares, condominiums, and skyscraper hotels on the mainland. They
take modern busses to American-like shopping centers and plazas. They
typically spend dollars, not pesos. Since much of this enterprise is foreign
owned, it is as though these tourists in Mexico have never left home. This
nightmarish transplant from America has developed—as has Isla Mujeres—
over the last twenty-five years.

Such development on Cancún incited fierce populist protectionism on the
island, which is near Cuba. Like its socialist neighbor, Isla Mujeres has a
long tradition of grass-roots politics. A Cuban restaurant, a Cuban cigar
specialty store, a gallery showing work by contemporary Cuban artists, vis-

iting Cuban musicians, and frequent travel to and from Cuba all serve to establish cultural links with that country. Cubans periodically move to Isla to live and work. The political activity on the island has included the controversial involvement of Armenta Concepción. Nicknamed Conchi, she was a woman who ran as a candidate for president of the island, representing the leading establishment party (the Partido Revolucionario Institucional [PRI]). However, she experienced the same kind of resistance to women taking political leadership roles that so negatively affected a female candidate in Mérida, the nearest major city, during my sojourn in the field.

The opposition to Conchi voiced the opinion that a woman's place is "*abajo*" (under). At night, opponents painted "*Estamos con* Picho" (We are with Picho) in large graffiti over walls, backs of trucks, and campaign posters throughout the island—even on tourist blocks. Such actions forced PRI to invest in a continual whitewash job to cover up the signs and symbols of real life on the island. It was in the leading party's interest to preserve the dominant signs and symbols that promoted the tourism-inspired idyllic fiction of the island so as not to negatively impact business. Conchi's supporters marched in the streets, chanting slogans such as "*No hay democracía en la isla*" (There is no democracy on the island) and "The people, united, will never be defeated." I associated these phrases with left-wing politics. However, bystanders I approached on the streets didn't tend to agree with me or to have the same political orientation as someone like myself, with Anglo-European-American categorization.[2]

Eighty percent of the island's population has immigrated from the Yucatán to work in tourism over the last twenty-five years. This movement reverses the trend seen after the Spanish takeover, when people fled to the jungle. Famine in the interior, which had already promoted some migration to the eastern coast, where those who could found work as fishermen, also fed this trend. Alfonso Villa Rojas, the local informant who worked with Robert Redfield in an earlier study inland, went on to write in his own book (1945) how Quintana Roo served as a refuge for rebelling Indians. They were organized in the cult of the Talking Cross; the masses assembled to hear the direction of God, which stimulated them to revolt against the whites. Quintana Roo was even separate from Mexico for awhile. Before the North American Free Trade Agreement (NAFTA),[3] both formal laws and informal behaviors on the island—in contrast to those in Cancún—made life very difficult for foreigners attempting to own or to construct properties or businesses. Such restrictions had the effect of continuing the ways of a culture that according to Villa Rojas emphasized group solidarity and hostility to all outsiders and required subjugation by the military to achieve pacification (1945, 25, 28).

The foreign entrepreneur or worker often needed some means to circumvent deportation, such as marrying an islander. Legal papers were and are very difficult to obtain. Empty stores, abandoned restaurants, condominiums, hotels, and half-completed construction sites once presented newcomers with visual reminders of the difficulty of accomplishing ambitious ideas such as renovating properties and opening businesses.

By contrast, in the new urban sprawl of Cancún, which developed without such insular cohesive identity, the hurdles to foreign ownership were more easily overcome. On Isla Mujeres, potential developers frequently just gave up because they were unable to obtain permits to build on what was once *ejido*, or common land. Islanders only had to look across the bay toward Cancún to be reminded of what would happen if they relaxed their protectionist politics. Even in Playa de Carmen, a beach settlement one hour down the coast on the mainland, foreign owners of the restaurant "Chicago" have gone so far as to put up street signs in English (State and Madison) reminiscent of street corners in the windy city. This plays into the nostalgic provincialism of American tourism, eclipsing Mexican national identity on its own territory.

In spite of the general resistance to the forces of development, however, the face of the island has changed significantly since I began my work there in 1991. An international corporation has opened a film store, even though Mexican nationals manage the site. A sandwich shop with the international corporate logo "Subway" opened on a main street of a small town in which there are no subways. Those attempting to flee American corporatism are disappointed to find a sign advertising that "Dunkin' Donuts" are now sold right downtown, across from a more traditional *panadería*.

Also, a Venetian couple opened an art gallery to sell the wife's large, expensive oil paintings to the increasing numbers of Italian tourists over the last several years. Stafania Zuanella had formed a group of women painters in Venice before coming to the island. On the island, her works have become primitivistic "windows to nature." The painting of a simple hammock slung between two trees on the beach offers an idyllic paradise that actually no longer exists. Such paintings illustrate the artist's primitivistic longings more than they reflect the reality of the island itself.

Foreigners have opened and started operating increasing numbers of largely short-lived businesses such as nightclubs, beauty parlors, and specialty shops selling luxury items like incense, essential oils, and nutritional supplements. As the island became more sophisticated, more Mexican-foreigner marriages have been made for more legal businesses. Developers from Can-cún have built condominiums where foreigners can live for longer periods of time—even year-round—which has led to the growth of a new expatriate, English-speaking, more or less moneyed community. A large Mexican cor-poration with foreign money, Xcaret, has bought a national park, thrown out the local businesses, and has plans to develop a site for "eco-tourism." Where once Mexicans could enter their own national park for fifteen pesos (then $2 U.S.), in the future they will be charged a day entry fee of at least $50 U.S. This increase will have the result of making the facility largely in-accessible to the majority of locals and Mexicans, as has been pointed out by local political candidates in opposition to the development. Also, the god-dess site itself will be part of the corporations' eco-tourist site. Even local residents will not be able to visit the point where the statues were found without paying the high price. Chain stores frequently purchase vases in Guanajuato for twenty-five pesos, and then sell them for 450 pesos on the island. Because of over-development on Contoy—which was once the home island of many fishermen, the government has opened another island to habitation that was previously protected from settlement for ecological rea-sons. A de-radicalized politics led toward co-optation on the island.

The normal day-tripper entering the island is very fluid with cash. Con-sequently, the locals gear up toward attracting group expeditions. One at-traction is to take a special yacht to the restaurant-hotel María Kankin. There the establishment serves the tourist special foods like lentil soup and apple pie—not exactly *típico* (typical) dishes. Restaurant managers arrange seminars throughout the island for cooking staff on how to cater to Ameri-can taste. Menus routinely show items exclusively for outsiders. Tourists sit on the beach under constructed *palapas,* in imported chairs replete with buttons to push to attract the attention of the waiters. All over the island, *palapas*—traditionally, one-room huts made from palm leaves from the mainland jungle—have become luxury structures. Tourists come practically naked to sip exotic drinks and cold beer near the beach as they watch the sunset, dance, or participate in Happy Hour, a tourist folk ritual. On the other side of the island, where foreigners have only recently begun to settle, the *palapa* roof on a house is a sure sign of foreign ownership. Frequently such a house will sport other luxury items, like a mahogany door and a gold or brass door knocker. Workers live in tin-roofed shacks made from unro-mantic cartons—building materials that have emerged organically from the changing environment. If they can afford to do so, they build more permanent houses of cement. Gone are the stone foundations used a thousand years ago, which have led archaeologists to believe that thatch-roofed buildings originated in ancient Maya culture (Freidel, Schele, and Parker 52).

The day-tripper, unaware of this ironic twist, usually doesn't climb to the road that circles the island. Often organized into a package day shopping tour, in all likelihood such a visitor does not visit the Maya ruin site or discover the Mexican *colonia* (colony, neighborhood) from which Conchi, the woman presidential candidate, drew most of her following. The day visitor goes shopping and does not pass the dump, which during most of my fieldwork was smoking with dead dogs, used disposable diapers, and other garbage generated by tourists and locals overrunning the infrastructure of what was once a small fishing island.

A day visitor might also hit the middle-class beach, itself an artificial creation. Fledgling palm trees have been imported from Southeast Asia as they are more blight and disease resistant than the island's own. Most of the island's own trees either perished from pollution or from Hurricane Gilbert in 1989, a very destructive storm, as the classic guide book *Baedekers' Mexico* discusses (1990, 26).

A second choice is to take a boat which lands two thirds of the way from downtown to the Maya ruin, on a public beach where workers serve fish cooked right on the beach to visitors in group package tours. This group experience could be considered more "folksy." At least the establishment serves food the folk might actually eat—freshly caught and fried fish, rice, black beans. However, the cost of the meal, at least thirty thousand pesos in 1992, was approximately a day and a half's wages for a waiter, and Mexican inflation continues at a rampant rate.

One becomes aware over time that restaurant owners and managers price the "popular" food way out of range for the "popular" people to pay. Even the utensils are different. Deep into the interior of the mainland jungle, where the majority of workers originate, people use tortillas as utensils; silverware is a luxury item. Yet on the island, as elsewhere in modern Mexico, restaurants serve tortillas as a substitute for bread on a table set with standard Western utensils, spoons, and forks. Workers who themselves use a tortilla at home to scoop up rice, runny bean sauce, and pieces of barbecued chicken, serve the group visiting the island "for a genuine folk experience" along bench-like tables. There, tourists often strike up conversations with the fishermen, who feed the island's fictional image.

Craft vendors also sell items in stands—the same items sold in shops downtown in the developed commercial district of four blocks. Like standard folk items, tie-dyed t-shirts and batiks are common and repetitive rather than unique. Some are manufactured at home in the family compound on the island, one of the few cottage-industry craft productions that still exist.

However, whereas university students in the States buy and wear t-shirts proudly declaring their university, locals seldom buy Isla t-shirts. Instead, all but the elders tend to wear t-shirts from the United States with insignias such as the Statute of Liberty. Thus, batik t-shirts of fish and coral are not traditional crafts in the sense of being handed down, and they are not worn to proclaim a belonging that the people feel. Tourists often experience the urge to merge and to take home a keepsake showing membership in an island community, such as one of these t-shirts produced particularly for them. But I found when doing readings that the people who live there more often experience the longing to get out to see the United States. They want to try something urban and to broaden their life experiences. The United States has represented progress to the Maya-Mexicans at least since the study by Redfield and Villa Rojas in the 1930s. The t-shirts with popular icons from the United States express all these cultural tendencies.

Shopkeepers sell hammocks and clothing made off the island, as well as sponges from the sea that are caught and cleaned, and other items which have nothing to do with the folk life of the island. For example, when I visited friends' homes, they didn't display masks or mermaids from other provinces in their own homes. The people's homes were more likely to display coke bottles and tall, white, blond, skinny Barbie dolls, which are heavily marketed throughout countries with populations of different racial origins in the Third World (Urla 1993), along with porn calendars, statues of virgins, and crucifixes of Jesus. I even found that Barbie dolls adorned some traditional Christmas altars, with Barbies wearing all the different costumes of the nativity scene.

Shopkeepers also sell tourists items based on traditional handiwork such as clothes and miniatures or full-sized head masks. At the same time, ironically, islanders buy clothes and other items imported from Miami that are imprinted with English words, at prices well beyond workers' salaries. They wear t-shirts with English words, sometimes pornographic, sometimes proclaiming names of U.S. colleges and universities. They also adorn their walls with mass-produced white Santa Clauses and even reindeer, snowmen, and evergreen trees for Christmas. This is so even though it never snows on the island, the natives are not white, and evergreens don't grow there. But again, this cultural colonialism through material artifacts is a truth behind the fiction not readily apparent to most day-trippers.

A third choice for the day visitor is to take a day's shopping tour. Those making this decision take the normal slow ferry or the new speedboat for two and a half times the price and lands on the pier downtown. These people walk the three or four blocks of paved street, buy folk clothes imported from Guatemala and other provinces of Mexico, look at clay and wooden miniature masks (also not from the island), and have the opportunity to sit in bars and listen to old Beatles songs as well as to Bolivian *folklórico* music played by professional musicians who come from Guadalajara and other major cities. Those who stay on the island longer often feel superior and avoid these groups. Yet they are an important source of revenue to the island. The day-trippers might also photograph the three slender females who sit silently on tall stools modeling jewelry in front of a shop a half a block from the pier, guarded by security men who, according to nearby shopkeepers, punish the women if they move. Or, the day-trippers might watch U.S. football games on color television, in English, in a video bar also a block or so from the waterfront, which advertises a bilingual "Ladies Night."

A foreign traveler staying on the island for a longer time would need to be highly motivated to seek out the source of the island's name. At first I had much of this eager, enthusiastic ambition, and used to ask many people what was the story behind the name—workers, restaurant owners, storekeepers, other travelers. But soon I found that little material evidence indicated that the islanders had much to do with the source of this history. Second, on the historical level, most of the people involved in the initial archaeological re-discovery were adventuresome rugged males with conservative ideas about women. Thus they tended to obscure the female side of the area's history even further.

An observer can easily deduce the ironic condition of the islanders being in the dark or at least withholding their own cultural information just by cataloguing the visual representations of women in the island's popular culture. These are visible in objects made to sell, insignias over restaurants, presentations in the names of businesses, and other advertising promotion similar in form and intent to the gimmick of the live models cited previously. We might classify all these as visual artifacts in that they are all things made by one psyche in an attempt to appeal to another.

Tracing these patterns of alternation reveals what folklorists call "intercultural dynamism" in folk tradition. Some indigenous stories of the Americas do indicate the original existence of women as the ground and substance of all things, showing some strength. For example, one popular description exists of grandmother as manifest in the "Sacred Woman" (Neihardt, *Black*

Elk Speaks (1961, 3–5). Victoria Bricker provided another example from her work with a male storyteller in his eighties in Chiapas. Analyzing the Amazonian theme of women and war, she found out that the women were shot only in the behind with bullets. The women were strong, as shown by the fact that they survived. But they participated in the story only as objects to be shot. They suffered and survived, but not as successful, full-fledged warriors (293). Bricker was also told that the Chamulan women exposed their genitals to cool the guns in a 1911 war (149).

However, reading secondary literature around the island and along the Amazon basin, I haven't been able to find the motif in indigenous mythology of kingdoms and lands of women to coincide with legends reported by the explorers, as I thought at first I would. One might attribute such absence partly to errors of research. Such stories are not likely to surface where one male anthropologist working with one male informant investigates a culture at a distance, such as Gerardo Reichel-Dolmatoff's *Amazonian Cosmos: The Sexual and Religious Symbolism of the Tukano Indians* (1971).

Nonetheless, Alfred Métraux, in his study of the Guarani (Steward 69–94), did report a deity called Our Mother who was the first woman, named Nandecy. Though wife of the Great Father, she survived in the Land-without-Evil, separate from her husband, who lived elsewhere. Moreover, a series of messianic cults and revivalist movements in the territory reclaimed this female deity when various leaders declared the end of Spanish rule and wanted the people to head off for the Land-without-Evil, where she reigned, somewhere to the east beyond the sea. Neo-Brazilian folklore also has a Mother of Water, a supernatural being along the Amazon Basin (Steward 145). All this indicates that perhaps an ongoing mystical female presence existed in the base of indigenous mythology available for reclamation and commodification.

But an infusion of Anglo-Euro-American culture transmuted the meaning of the old Maya statues. They became mermaids, a very popular European motif since the Middle Ages, as in Montalvo's romance of the fifteenth century. Authors and artists have often depicted mermaids as representing mortal passions that must be resisted. Mermaids have long hair, undulating movements, and close association with music, semi-bestiality, temptation, and culpable sensuality (Berger 43–44).

Nelson Graburn's analysis of how dominant cultures render indigenous legend and myth invisible is useful in this regard. In *Ethnic and Tourist Arts: Expressions from the Fourth World* (1976), he used the term "Fourth World" as a collective name for all aboriginal or native peoples whose lands are within the national boundaries of First, Second, or Third World countries. The people identified in this group rarely produce art for their own consumption or according to their own unmodified tastes (1–2).

In the Maya case, the elaborate code-breaking necessary to reveal the meaning of surviving Maya codices led to interpretations of some myths which might have been apropos to utilize instead of such accommodation. For example, artisans could have used the Old Moon Goddess in the flood that ended the last creation in the Dresden Codex as a theme on the island. This would have been similar to the way some inland artists have modernized representations of another feminine divinity in the Maya cosmology, Lady Unique.

I did not discover any myths indigenous to the vicinity about separate realms of women. However, there were portraits of women rulers and of noblewomen of high rank who had been elaborately buried. To archaeologists, these signs indicate that status transcended gender in ancient Maya society. Furthermore, offspring traced through the women had claims to the throne and enjoyed royal prerogative, not always the case in histories of royal lineage. Some interpret the glyphs to mean that the mother's name came first in tracing lineage (Closs 1989).

The tracing of descent from grandmothers in Maya myth, reflecting the time when there were women rulers at Palenque, suggests a similar possibility (Schele and Freidel 133, 177, 220–223, 236, 244, 266). In oral renditions of such tales, even in Quintana Roo in the contemporary period, when heroes leave they address grandmother spirits (Luxton). Of particular interest is Lady Zac-kuk, named like an in-kind mother of the gods and kings at the beginning of the present creation. This goddess was mother of the three central gods of Maya religion. She "very probably kept the real power in her own hands" in the Palenque period (ca. 640 A.D.; Schele and Freidel 225). Drawings depict her as a screaming bird with feathers in her mouth, affectionately dubbed "Lady Beastie" by Schele and Freidel (227). Moreover, women were principal actors in some myths, such as the release of the Vision Serpent through Lady Xoc's blood-letting ceremony (268). The Maya apparently worshipped Ix Chel herself as "Mother of Us All" on her sacred isle (377–378).

Furthermore, businesses in tourism might have commercialized myths about water people, legends concerning the Blood Girl arriving from the underworld, and stories of the children of the old goddess Xmucané, sent by one of the underworld lords. All are available at least in English sources such as *The Maya Book of the Dead* (Robicsek and Hales 1981). The wild woman as demon monster X-tabai also exists in Maya folklore. According to the story, a prominent demon appears in the form of a beautiful young woman. She dresses in a fine native dress with gorgeous embroidery and has long hair. She induces a young man to follow her to the bush. Unless he is lucky enough to escape, she strangles him to death (Redfield and Villa Rojas 121–122). Vera furthermore reported female stone sculptures in the Maya and Aztec rooms of the Museo de Arqueología in Mexico City; these, too, could have provided models for newly produced images of the feminine that could have been utilized for tourism. These statues include Chalchiutlicue, the lady of the water and goddess of the sea; Coatlicue, the earth mother who encompasses all dualities and appears as the woman of the serpent skirt; the Cihuateteo goddesses, representing women who have died in childbirth; the women of the western paradise; and thousands of clay figurines (34–35).

However, what transpired on Isla Mujeres in terms of construction of images by the populace was not a case of art created for the sake of art— which folk art essentially isn't. Pleasing the mind of the traveler profitably was the motive rather than reclamation of Maya culture for the sense of self-preservation, or re-invention of tradition for the sake of a modern search for ethnic identity.

Additionally, local artists lacked access to the glyphs, ceramics, vases, and other archaeological materials being examined by scholars, who frequently removed such items from their original site. Therefore, given the dynamism of the relevant cross-cultural elements, a more or less successful superimposition of myth of European origin transpired instead.

Thus reproduction of more authentic images did not occur—such as those of the Moon Goddess sitting in a half-moon holding a rabbit, appearing as an aged woman with a toothless smile, or dancing as an old woman with skull head, as she was found at her oracular sanctuary at Cozumel (Schele and Freidel 412–413, 502 n.).

As Graburn has observed in other Fourth World populations, an assimilation occurred in Maya popular arts. Producers began copying foreign art traditions from schooled and stratified civilizations, like those produced by employees of the vast international Disney empire. Graburn has characterized societies in this process as being in "a painful period of rank imitation that follows a people's loss of independence" (11).

A justifiable criticism of Graburn's thesis is that he listed indigenous cultures in a hierarchy as if they were "fourth" when they might have been "first" or "simultaneous." In the unfortunate ranking system he utilized, his model reflects the one he was criticizing, as if the cultures of the world descended on a hierarchical scale downward from Western Europe. Yet his analysis does provide some useful insight into the images of women that entrepreneurs choose to market on Isla today.

The choice of the use of Anglo-European images, which has been made repeatedly, reflects the islanders' projection of a fiction. Although the tourist is visiting a multi-dimensional expressive world, the tendency is not to apprehend the totality, but only these isolated, manufactured elements. The tourist understands these parts, like the image of the mermaid, not in the context of the flux of experience of the island, but in the context of the tourist's own reality.

Thus the representation, which is a symbol to the tourist without being a sign of anything particularly significant to the islanders' experience, provides the tourist with a pre-existing familiar mode of order, giving the visitor a sense of ease or comfort, with its transplanted icons from home. For example, there is a *lonchería* (lunch shop) called *La Sirenita* with a mural that a Cancún artist painted of a mermaid—half-woman and half-fish—even though the traditional siren was half-woman and half-bird (Powers 1991). The mural shows this white, bare-breasted mermaid eating a shrimp cocktail with a spoon, from a crystal goblet.

Neither crystal goblets nor spoons were traditional items of material culture on the peninsula, yet to my knowledge, this is the longest standing image of a mermaid on the island. She was already in place at the initial stages of my fieldwork. The café owner's wife, who used to take in tourists' laundry, related that her husband had had the mermaid painted by Pancho, a painter from Cancún now deceased from AIDS. The husband asked for a mermaid because "he liked them." They used to exist on the island "in history," the woman recalled. The woman's laundry business was cut into by *lavanderías* with machines. She turned to selling whole cooked chickens, a superior business until competition over-ran her.

Another shop selling Guatemalan and Mexican folk items, bearing the name *La Sirena*, commissioned a sign from the same painter. This sign sports a slinky, white mermaid in a girlie pose. The painting accentuates large bare breasts and shapely hips. The white mermaid above the new shop makes no demure attempt to hide her breasts. She lounges sexily as in a pin-up poster above a new store of luxury imports. Flat-breasted replicas of mermaids from other states, particularly Guerrero, are sold inside and at the owner's other store of a different name on the *zócalo,* as well as elsewhere. In front of *La Sirena* one year, a cameo artist from Italy set up one season to carve shells.

Just as "inauthentically," as cameo carving is by no means a local indigenous art, shopkeepers import mermaids from another province in Mexico, Guerrero. Businesses import these luxury items, produced for a yearly festival of fisherman and mermaids that happens on the other side of the country, hoping to satisfy the tourist demand to "get close to the native spirit" by having "genuine," "authentic" artifacts to take home, a trait in culture change through contact that Graburn has also observed in other areas (14). The roots of the festival memorialized by this sale of imported goods are not even clear to the sellers (often indigenous mixed Maya), as the tradition is not theirs.

The mermaid of Disney Classics, Ariel, also adorns the wall of a kindergarten for island children. She illustrates Graburn's thesis that symbols of identity are borrowed, stolen, or exchanged (27). Another, more "modest," mermaid with moon clearly in front has nature under control. She also reveals the economic forces that led to miniaturization and the production of small, doll-like, modern "idols." These are more simple in form and decoration than imported souvenirs from Guerrero. The pre-colonial, pre-Inca moon goddess described by Irene Silverblatt might be surprised if she were to return to this island instead of to the island women once dedicated to her worship on Lake Titicaca. Conch shells like those once used to adorn her shrines are here alternated with this series of mass-produced iron mermaids to mark the tourist's path to a luxury bar. Before desecration and commodification, scribes transcribing codices, a sacred act in Maya culture, also used conch shells as ink pots.

Moreover, two very small oil paintings considerably tattered with the years used to hang in the entrance way to the Osorio, one of the relatively inexpensive hotels near the pier. These pictures were visual replicas of the famous pirate Mundaca, who was trapped by the beauty of one of the island's women. There he pined in unrequited love after all sorts of ambitious schemes failed to win her heart. There is a rich history of piracy in the high seas of this area (Reed 1966).

Patricia Gomez, one of the descendants of the woman Mundaca supposedly courted, runs a small food and clothing shop downtown. She says that many years ago her aunt simply married somebody else. The alleged pirate ostensibly ignored this fact when he built a home for her. The foundation of the house he built still stands, a crumbling monument in the park in the center of the island, today a tourist attraction.

But the owner has not displayed two small, damaged paintings commemorating the moment of this event in the island's history prominently.

Rather, the owner has exhibited the pictures in a darkened area to the left of the stairs next to a pin-up calendar of a scantily clad woman in a sexually suggestive position. A buried, dusty remnant of a nearly forgotten piece of island history, this shaky artifact imparts a rather accurate impression of just how sacred the name of the island is to the islanders. The year-round inhabitants of the island include a woman who works as a traditional healer, cleansing *aire* (air, not meaning "air" literally, but more "energy" or "aura") with eggs. She has never even visited the spot of the Maya goddess to which was once dedicated a holiday of healing.

The catalogue of artifacts reproducing cultural dynamism of imported Anglo-European images also includes a pair of brightly colored murals depicting the pirate Mundaca on the wall of one side of a shop, faced on the other side by a mural showing his attractive, island-Indian, would-be spouse. The two pose in a style reminiscent of a Pocahontas story, as the poems published in the magazine *Juegos Florales,* put out by the House of Culture on Isla Mujeres, relate. Published annually, these results of a local poetry competition depict pirates trapped by sounds of the island heard only during the feast day of the Virgen de Concepción.

But the legend has a further basis deep in the roots of Maya culture. For example, a story exists about how the spirits who lived under the ruins used to come out and play music at night on the site at Tulum. Old-timers in the coastal village of Tulum, a few hours south—a town that has also mushroomed due to tourism in the last twenty years—have also reported such tales (Luxton 1981).

The wife of the owner of one of the largest beach-front bungalow colony hotels hired an American woman artist. The artist had married into a local family and developed her own business. The hotel commissioned her to paint a series of works now displayed at the front desk and in many guest rooms. In this repeated image, a young, slender, white woman pines romantically. She walks on the beach clad in shoes (even though she is walking in waves by the rocks). The artist depicts the figure of the painting in a pensive pose, remembering a lost lover. A white sea captain in a cloud hovering and shimmering above her in the sky represents the archetype of the ghostly lover.

The artist did not agree with the politics of the painting. The politics shifted to the less-than-feminist depiction of an abandoned woman, a shift from the focus on the rejected man in the Mundaca tale, in which the woman takes the upper hand. The painting also illustrates the theme of the woman staying at home while the man travels, a motif which, as Cynthia Enloe has discussed, is portrayed as the norm in the mass marketing of travel (1990).

This depiction, however, contrasts with the spirit of the island, which attracts many active women who come to the island seeking adventure. These women are unlikely to identify with the woman shown spending her time pining, passive, and alone, defined by her rejection by a lost male lover. The man painted above the waiting woman resembles the archetype of the Ghostly Lover, which catches women in the air the way the siren captures men in the sea. He does not carry her away with him but disappears when she doubts him, leaving her to experience her fate of abandonment (Harding 17).

Many have observed striking similarities between eastern sacred architecture and that of Mexico. Some have hypothesized that what we think of as Asians (and also Hindus and Buddhas) were originally here. Even if the cult of Aphrodite, which spread between Sicily and Asia Minor, did not reach this far by migration or diffusion, the island bears striking resemblance to the type of place in which Aphrodite's followers located themselves in ancient Greece. Centers of Aphrodite worship were generally on islands, as Friedrich has noted, "interstitial between land and water" (74). Just as the practical local people viewed the temple spot as a navigational outpost, so Aphrodite was a goddess of water and navigation; in the Asherah form in Phoenicia, she performed patronage for sailors, as the pirate in the enchantment myth intended the woman on the island to do.

Aphrodite cults often located centers so as to emphasize wild nature and horn-shaped crags. Friedrich quoted a description of an ancient shrine high up with a view, a temple built on solid rock overlooking the constantly shifting ebb and flow of the tides below. This description also fits the ruin sites on the tip of Isla Mujeres and Cozumel. The unexpected violence of contrasting states juxtaposed in such a site, with waves hitting the formation of rock, in ancient times was to the Greeks considered expressive of the Helen-Aphrodite complex (Scully 1962, 97).

Although different origins may have been attached in ancient Mayan culture, about which little is known, the similarity is worth noting. Congruent stages of cultural evolution may be indicated by such apparent overlap. Similarities have also been noted between Ix Chel and Aphrodite, both of which present a synthesis between sexuality, sensuousness, and motherliness often divorced in other goddess constructs (Friedrich 1978, 182; J. E. S. Thompson 1939). Some have also speculated that Maya pilgrims used Isla Mujeres as a resting place when traveling to pay homage in Cozumel to Ix Chel, just as Christians make pilgrimages to Jerusalem and Rome. Reed has called Ix Chel the "Isis" of the Mayan pantheon, along with Itzamna, "the Supreme

Initiator." These were wholly Mayan deities whose cults most likely achieved a peak of influence long before the Mexican-Toltecs covered the territory (343–344).

Nonetheless, this is all conjectured past, juxtaposed to a jarringly different present. As an example of the popular deterioration of the possible sacredness of the island is a T-shirt made in Cancún which informal vendors sell on the dock from which one leaves Puerto Juárez for the island. Under the saying "Island of Women—I'm Hot," an industrious artist has stenciled a cartoon of a cave woman and a curly-headed cave man joining hands on the beach. In 1993, this sold for approximately $3.30 in U.S. dollars. Numerous other postcard, towel, and T-shirt artifacts display similar sexualized female images.

More non-traditional, mass-produced images of women began to appear during my fieldwork. These included the all-leg women on a Budweiser towel, nicely "cooked" (turned from nature to culture) or leisure tanned. These items, marketed to Europeans and North Americans, increasingly emphasize a theme of eroticized women. The same is true of the postcard, a staple of sexualized female images since colonial days (Enloe 42). For example, a beast-ape pictured writing on the postcard is free to enact his higher nature, while bare-bottomed "Mexican Girls" pictured wearing nothing but *sombreros* seem to have no higher natures; they function merely as a visual artifact for male travelers to send home.

Colonial stimuli in culture continue to express modernizing identities in this emerging, commercialized ethnicity. Congruent with the introduction of "Hawaiiana" cuisine in some restaurants in the years I spent on the island, the plastic "hula girl" image has appeared in the shell sculptures sold on the street alongside the pier. A family orders them from the Philippines to cater to island-hopping travelers. Only a year previously, the craft sculptures this family marketed sported only plastic Jesus crucifixes and Virgin of Guadalupe statuettes on the half shell, catering not to international island-hoppers but to Mexican national tourists.

Obviously the profit motive (and the need to eat) has greatly over-run aesthetic folklore standards. Especially with the new rash of imports of batiks from Indonesia, the new items do not even pretend to have any relation to the traditional arts of the creator culture, a situation which, according to Graburn, is also typical elsewhere (10). A short, hefty woman—the matron of the family—whose own physique and costume contrast greatly with what she sells now markets plastic hula dancers poised within shells amidst green plastic leaves and imitation flowers. The day I photographed her, she wore a

T-shirt sporting slogans about workers and peasants uniting for struggle and modernization.

The goals stated on her T-shirt expressed a force opposed to the nature of the things she was selling—individuated, objectified women from another part of the world. Her own socialist-realist T-shirt, done in an art style originating in Russia in the 1920s, was in Spanish. She used to work near the dock, out of her makeshift stand, under a tree on the beach that she had planted herself years ago; in 1995, a wave of repression forced her, as well as other vendors, to move across the street. She embodied the dual sign system of one group of people speaking to another which bypasses those signs pointing to the nitty gritty of present-day realities in favor of their search for archetypal, symbolic meanings in the past.

In another example of the way in which the influx of tourism has impacted local art, the menu in one restaurant near the pier exhibits a "hula-girl" wearing nothing but a starfish shape to cover her pubic area. The owner of this restaurant commissioned a local artist to make a mermaid statue in wood to attract customers, and soon a mermaid appeared on the menu also. She says, "The people like them." Between menu one and menu two, the image of "woman" became dark, a part of nature, as if she herself were an outgrowth of nature, rather than the white, barefoot, exposed woman, who exhibited how nature was separate from herself.

The mermaid figures also contrast greatly with the owner herself, who commissioned them. She was a large, stout, independent, and very popular down-to-earth woman who befriended customers with her frank, off-color style of joking. For example, during my pregnancy she kept insisting that I had become so large in the stomach by eating beans in her restaurant. Afterward, she continued to joke that I had conceived my child by eating her beans. Getting pregnant by eating beans was one of the many forms of conception believed in by those who believed in the goddess. Other beliefs included impregnation by a glance, a dream, sunlight, falling rain, bathing, wind, a falling star, charm, thunder, lightning, flowers, trees, lettuce, shadows, magic trees, spittle, blood, fire, feathers, and scarification (Weigle 80, 252 n.; Graves 28). In fact, women such as this joking proprietor own 40 percent of the island's businesses, although this should not be taken as an indication of liberation. This owner and others like her promote the thin girlie image which clashes with their own reality and identity as much as the English which takes over their signs in an encroaching bilingual system. In fact, in a year this owner lost weight to get down to the size of the tourist women who patronized her locale.

One of the founding sisters, who had opened the fourth restaurant to ever exist on the island, once posed for me in front of a painting with a bikini woman on a beach in 1993. The daily fare on the blackboard used to be all Spanish; the menu brought to the table is in both languages now. The woman in the painting was thin, at leisure, and white. She comfortably lounged in nature. The woman responsible for producing this bicultural event was stout, brown, and an elder. The image of the young woman was barefoot, vulnerable, and exposed. The real woman had dressed herself for working in civilization down to her mechanical wristwatch and practical, sturdy, flat-soled supportive shoes. In 1994, the owners changed the words on the same restaurant's re-painted sign to completely English, dropping the Spanish entirely. Furthermore, the new sign depicted a mermaid holding a star as birds flew over the lighthouse, indicating a heightened return to the mythos of nature. The tree-lined beach in the new sign painting portrayed only palm trees and a single shack constructed with a palm-leaf roof. In reality, on the beach a few blocks away, over the years plastic boats, floats and beach chairs for rent, electrified discos, and waiters serving drinks from nearby restaurants have considerably eroded this romanticized beach image that the painted sign represents.

Chicki Mallan, author of *Yucatán Peninsula Handbook* (1986), has noted the greater importance of the island's name to foreigners, suggesting two directions for the ambitious researcher. One legend claims that the name comes from the buccaneers who, while they were conducting business on the high seas, stowed female captives. A more probable version is that "the island was a stop-over for the Maya Indians traveling to Cozumel to worship Ix Chel, female goddess of fertility and an important deity to Maya women" (243).[4] The Spanish found female-shaped clay idols there. About the Maya ruin site, Mallan reported that Francisco Hernandez de Cordoba first described it in 1517 as being a temple of worship to Ix Chel, but also a place where sophisticated astronomical observations were made (246).

These highly romanticized conjectural "hooks" in the guidebook draw people to the site. Modern tourists used to perform rituals on the unmarked ruin, bypassing the opportunity to buy traditional tourist items, hammocks, and Cokes en route. The guidebook which promotes such "hooks" is itself another artifact embodying the intersection between two cultures. The locally produced video sometimes shown on the fast boat to the island repeats the two standard hooks as well. On the slow boat, a singer plays his original guitar songs about the isle of women; playing for tips, he competes with a small three-piece band. On the fast boat, for two or three times the price, the motor is too loud for live music. Sometimes an island-made video displays tourists sites and shops, and restaurants, speculating in English that the island once housed either a "Maya harem" or a "convent to the sacred virgin." More often, the passengers view music videos or Mexican television broadcasting cartoons, news, and soap operas.

Evidence of Ix Chel is not lacking. *Ritual of the Bacabs,* an ancient book of Maya healing chants (Roys [1879] 1965), tells of invocations to the goddess Ix Chel, who appears in the form of a virgin who, through incantations in which she gathers to herself the power of the spider, can cool the poison from a spider bite. Furthermore, there is a sanctuary dedicated to Ix Chel. Many have speculated that this sanctuary served a function much like that of the shrines to Aphrodite in the ancient world, where vestal virgins prayed for women to successfully conceive and give birth (see, e.g., Lefkowitz and Fant 286–288).

But those who composed the brief plug in the island-made promo video emphasized only the continuum of sexuality. The idea of a "sacred convent dedicated to the spider of healing" might not have been as much an enticement to the island. Kay Turner, however, noted in her discussion of this chant that spider power was in ancient times an attribute of women's power in both South and North America. Likewise, according to Turner, the Navajo Spiderwoman sits atop eight-hundred foot Spider Rock in Arizona, managing the world as she sees fit from her isolated promontory. In the Maya chant, the chanter identifies the spider with Ix Chel and then becomes Ix Chel in another one of her aspects, the Goddess of Waters. Then she assuages the stings—thus the goddess is weaver, stinger, and reliever with water (1976, 45).

Such real bases in the possible roots of the island might not stimulate the same mesmerizing appeal. Nor might the idea have been nearly as enticing that this spot could have been a site to which women came to pray and to sleep, like sites memorializing the Greek women's goddesses who sought to overcome women's diseases. I would also guess that the sexualized romantic story might be more appealing to today's traveler than would a representation of Ix Chel in all her fierce glory, pictured as the moon goddess of Classic and pre-Classical Mesoamerica, with a serpent entwined in her hair or with her Mexican counterpart, Coatlicue, in a skirt of snakes embellished with skulls. As Pratt has noted, there is a common abhorrence of the Medusa image; thus such authenticity would repel rather than attract customers to the island more interested in satisfying themselves along the lines of the island's commercial purposes.

The image of Ix Chel represented in the Dresden Codex probably would be even less of a draw. The codex shows her both as goddess of suicide speaking to death, with a noose around her neck, and as a goddess of healing, carrying off pestilence in her bag (Turner 47). Neither image would serve as much of a hook, even though those suffering from ulcers, diseases, infections, and the range of psychological and physical diseases might benefit by her ability to haul off their problems in the bundle on her back, as prayed for by shamans who utilized her blessings on their divinations. The image of the Moon Goddess as a young woman, reproduced from a ceramic vase in *Lord of the Underworld* (Coe 1978), would probably create even more anxiety and fear. The arc of the half-moon sticking out of her broad back appears to be a large serpentine tail at first inspection.

Thus, these are two highly selective hooks presented in the island's commercial promotion, ignoring or bypassing much of the island's possibly more authentic mythos and history. These images attract two tourist types. Many come to stay for longer than the day-tripper purely to experience a sense of wholeness from belonging to an apparently spiritually coherent small-town community. The annual cycle of religious festivals as well as the fact that one can easily enter on a first-name basis with local dignitaries such as the island's president evidence the apparent wholeness. This intimacy factor becomes especially significant for those who must follow national news magazines to get what "feels" like an insider's personal view on White House politics at home (Clift and Cohn 1993).

For those whom the name "Isla Mujeres" attracts, two types arrive. One type, which the intrigue of the buccaneer legend attracts, consists of beach boys looking for easy pick-ups and a beach full of "bikini women," as if pirates still stored female captives there. The other type, drawn by the Ix Chel legend, tends to consist of women: single women; bisexual and/or lesbian women; women traveling alone with or without children; women looking to have children. I also spent a considerable amount of time interviewing, participating with, and observing women who came to the island trying to affirm their sexuality, which might have been undermined psychologically and/or emotionally by battering, rape, abuse, relationships with dysfunctional partners, incest memories, or menopausal experience. I met some doing readings, others at tourist spots like the local youth hostel, and others through friends.

Feminists also come in search of a vaguely reassuring past conveyed in the existence of some sort of lost utopia—that is, a source of women's once-separate or at least independent and spiritually empowered existence. They seek something in the tradition of the Isle of Lesbos, where women of the Greek empire apparently came in large numbers to gain strength.

A cross-national resurgent cultural identity seems to motivate those in this latter group. Popular texts that are read in restaurants or on the beach promote this collective history. The list includes Jean Shinoda Bolen's *Goddesses in Every Woman* (1984); Clarissa P. Estes' *Women Who Run with the Wolves* (1992); Judy Grahn's *Another Mother Tongue* (1984); Camerin Grae's *Edgewise* (1989); and Judith Plaskow and Carol Christ's *Weaving the Visions: New Patterns in Feminist Spirituality* (1989).

The first type—the male in search of women—includes a quasi-permanent dweller in the inexpensive youth hostel. He has a reputation for sexually pressuring newly arriving women, to whom he offers massages in his room upon arrival, and then tracks down in search of free gropes on the beach. But higher class sorts also emerge. Some men eventually make the short leap to nearby Cuba to find prostitutes if they can't find free sex on the island.

These men respond to the archetypal image of the island as a planet of women to be raided—where there is no competition from other men, as Kleinbaum described in her discussion of the Amazon as a dream that men have conjured up. Montalvo's fiction aptly portrays this dream, as noted. Buck Rogers' discovery of a planet of women in the 1930s movies and the Amazon planet episode in *Star Trek* on American television, "Angel One" (1987) repeats such a scenario.

The second group—women seeking a world of women—includes two lesbians from a women-spirit music-fest group in New Orleans who raise money for the Red Cross in the Mexican community. They started a women's craft collective on the island as a project for some island women to support themselves. This group also includes the white Red Cross doctor, a woman in her early forties who, rumor has it, came to the island, fell in love with a locally entrenched gringo, and decided to change her life accordingly; a Chicana fleeing an abusive relationship in the United States, who came to the island to heal and became involved with a series of local fishermen; and a white pre-school teacher who had lived with a white female partner in the States and started a second family relationship with a local man who became the father of her first and only child. Between the poles of realism and romanticism lie returning tourists. These include a vacationing feminist university professor and her politically active female mate, who have an interest in following how women candidates fare in local electoral politics. Women recovering from childhood abuse, domestic violence, career crises, or breakdowns induced by post-traumatic stress also visit frequently.

In addition, women come to buy land or business properties to use for women's retreats, artists' colonies, or bed and breakfast establishments for women only; and women come who want to start cancer support groups through natural healing or to open beauty parlors, specialty stores, health retreats, restaurants, or natural healing centers focusing on increasing conception through health and safe water birth, modeled after popular books on water delivery and water birth practices in the United States (Cunningham, n.d.). Some women come who want to conceive in the sea, based on the archetypal notion apparent in world legends that women came from the sea, and men from the land. In fact, *La Ovogenesis* (Estallita et al., 1986) reports cases of parthenogenesis in South America and in the Caribbean; thus the area has a particular appeal in this regard. Some are attracted to the island because of its association with parthenogenesis and virgin birth, which they see as a compelling myth for women. Concern with such issues has emerged in a significant range of feminist writers who are searching for a vision of women being able to live free of male domination. (de Beauvoir [1952] 1978; Johnston 1974; Rich 1976; Hoagland and Penelope 1988; Gilman [1915] 1979, [1916] 1997).

This group of women visitors to the island further includes those who are galvanized by the idea of the previous existence of the fertility goddess in Maya culture. Although not much exists on the island to memorialize this aspect, those making the pilgrimage sometimes keep journals, some of which have been published (see, e.g., Kay Turner's record of her journey).

In the course of such pilgrimages, certain artifacts operate as cultural releasers. A real-life sensory engagement with such artifacts leads to a heightened emotional response on the part of the viewer. Another reclamationist pilgrim, Lynn Vera, wrote:

> We reached Isla Mujeres on March 8, International Womyn's Day, the day of the New Moon. We walked the five miles from the ferry landing to the shrine as a way of personalizing, and extending, this long pilgrimage. As I walked I thought of the thousands of womyn who had done the same thing, as it was an important part of a Mayan's woman's [sic] life to journey to Isla Mujeres at least once. There, where only womyn gathered, she would celebrate the moon, herself and her friends. We found the shrine on a cliff, surrounded by crashing surf on three sides. . . . To the shock of the tourists, we moved right in. For two days we talked about, ate in, slept in, photographed and absorbed the energy of the shrine. We danced and

chanted on the night of the new moon, we named all our womyn friends in a ritual inside the small ruins. I sat and thought and felt for long hours in the hot sun, the Caribbean ocean crashing all around me, the structure of the rock, shells and sand speaking of a presence of womyn thousands of years old. From my journal then, March 9, 1977: ". . . I feel sure that this and all *diosa* shrines must be represen- tations of self-celebration. . . . To build a shrine of and to womyn, to designate such a place as this is to name a spot of community, of com- munications, of meeting and of sharing. The specialness of this place rushes into every part of me and I know that with all of this energy I absorb, I am also emanating lots that will sink back into this land, rocks and air and join with so much accumulated womon energy to fill other womyn, maybe 1000 years from now." We left Isla Mujeres feeling touched by and connected with the specialness of womonspirit and gynergy. My own self-image was deeply effected by the process I went through and the validity of womonspace and womonritual I experienced while on Isla. (35)

Vera went on to write of the shock of returning to men's culture and her disappointing visit to Cozumel. There, an airport now covers the original spot of the large "talking" statue of Ix Chel (36). Vera's responses provide grist for the ongoing analysis by those who question whether artifacts "have politics" (see, e.g., Winner 1980).

A very different gestalt prevails among locals. For example, only one of the makers of batik t-shirts represents Ix Chel. T-shirts with images of Ix Chel are available in the Cancún airport, but obviously such crafts work is not traditional. One hotel on the island bears the name Ix Chel, which might give the impression to tourists that the goddess meant something locally. Also, a university-educated man born and bred on the island has initiated a short-lived crafts store which he named Ix Chel, perhaps signifying a begin- ning wave of reclamation after twenty-five years of touristic development.

The only local batik worker who uses Ix Chel in his t-shirts got his design from books. While I was renting a space in his family compound, in which many generations lived together, I disclosed that I had once made and sold batiks. Consequently, this young man, whom I had met working in a beach clothing store downtown, talked to me like a fellow craftsperson. He later moved on to a batik display halfway up the island on a beach. There he was allowed to display and sell his own batik t-shirts, which took second place to the flamboyant Indonesian batik sarongs that had crept into the local merchandise. He revealed that his teacher was actually from Mérida, a city six hours away. He maintained that the goddess was not the goddess of fertility for humans, but only for corn.

Such an attitude is similar to that of Hawaiians who are engaged in nationalist reclamation; in their reconstruction of dance and chant, they also often deny the female-centered nature of local deities (Weinbaum 1988). Similarly, in this case the modernized drawings sexualize the etchings of archaeological sites, emphasizing breasts. The craftsman's choice on the sheet he showed me was between immortals in positions of sexual play, like eastern representations of Shiva in kundalini positions with consorts, and Ix Chel testing the quality of water as she goes forth to water corn. Having never seen the originals, he chose the latter image, perhaps because of the modesty instilled in him by his cultural upbringing. The rejection of the sexually suggestive images is dialectically produced and acts as a countervailing force against the production of the girlie image in their local communities by the foreign tourist onlooker.

But these symbols remain most malleable. For instance, one *folklórico* store sells a figurine of a woman squatting to give birth, an image which feminist folklorist Marta Weigle identified as Aztec in her study of mythologies of cosmogony and parturition (1989). A Mexican from Vera Cruz said that the figurine did not represent Ix Chel, but was merely a goddess from another state in Mexico that the female store owner sold marked "Ix Chel" to cater to the interests of tourists. The store owner herself—non-national, white, and German—related a different version. She claimed that the family producing the statuettes near Mexico City was not clear about the actual history of the products. She explained that three different peddlers of Mexican manufactured wares came to her door selling statuettes and images that they told her portrayed Ix Chel. On the one hand, since there was substantial contact between the Maya Yucatán and the indigenous empire centered to the north in what is now called the state of Mexico, this could have been a case of the diffusion of a single goddess who took many forms as she traveled. On the other hand, this could have been an instance of the subsuming of many local goddesses under one unifying archetype or name as the centralized empire spread, as J. E. S. Thompson (1939) discussed.

But history doesn't seem to be the issue in marketing to suit tourists' taste. In one of the research photographs I took, the woman crafts store owner proudly displayed all three statues I discussed alongside a wall mural of a brown Indian girl holding a cactus. This she had commissioned from the same local artist who had copied white mermaids from Disney reproductions for *loncherías* owned by local business people. While this artist's murals show busty, bare-breasted mermaids, the traditional mermaid masks used in fishermen's dances in the Pacific coast state of Guerrero show flat-chested mermaids with their hands across the front, breasts hid modestly behind a head of hair (Cordry 171). Hence, the process of impact of on-looker on visual artifacts and material culture continues. What one examines in this sort of research expands quickly to include the meanings imparted by those looking as well as the meanings attached by those selling.

ELEVEN

Dialectical Interaction with Island Versions of the Feminine

*The Maya cosmos is a place that is still alive to-
day. The Maya still play ballgames; still dance; still
stand prepared to battle for their cultural autonomy; and still nurture their gods with holy objects,
food, and the places they make.... The Maya
people ... want to be part of the modern world
around them.... We think the people who want to
know about the ancient Maya should know their
descendants.* —DAVID FREIDEL, LINDA SCHELE,
AND JAN PARKER, *MAYA COSMOS*

American tourists look for "bikini women," remnants of the fertility goddess, or the goddess of safe birth to make up for repressed aspects of their
own culture. But more visible in material representations of women that islanders themselves have created are Marian aspects of the island's version of
Catholic religion. In these images, they also express the trace of the ancient
Maya worldview remnant they still maintain.

Jacques Lafaye has written about the interaction of indigenous and Catholic images in the formation of Mexican national consciousness. He discussed
Ruben Vargas Ugarte's *Historia del culto de María en Ibero-América* (1947),
which indicates that Mexican creoles have created at least 1,756 toponyms
invoking the Virgin Mary (224). Concepción and Guadalupe are the dominant two represented on this island. Such information provides a deepened

understanding of how the Catholic religion still allows for expression of indigenous Maya worldviews (Oakes 1951).

In spite of the infamous Mexican macho veneer, these feminine icons can perform the function of teaching respectful attitudes toward women. Robert Bellah has said that Marian devotion doesn't worship God but rather mediates through the divine image of the Mother of God. Nonetheless, relative to the divine goddess, this remains a patriarchal image. Even so, however, such devotion retains a dimension of religious experience that Protestantism ruthlessly represses and that seems to Bellah to offer an alternative to replace the experience of nothingness of America (1973). This feeling of the mother behind God re-emerges, and perhaps becomes compelling. Perhaps this is what grips either category of visitor. Much of Catholic piety is redolent of earth religion. The cults of the saints localize and concretize this. Hence when I asked the midwife with whom I worked (whom I describe in more depth later) a simple question such as what herbs she uses at birth, she answered, "*canela, yuerba buena, y Díos*" (cinnamon, mint, and God).

To the tourist, usually only there for a short time, the questions of history seem important—the past, the naming of the island, the possible existence of mermaids and sirens, the whereabouts of the statues of the goddesses, and the sexuality of the pirates. But to the people who live there, the female icons appearing daily primarily via their Catholicism have more importance. The people exhibit the series of female icons in shrines similar to those honoring deities in the pre-Columbian religion of the area, as many scholars have discussed (e.g., Picard, Wolf, Freidel). Shrines to Guadalupe, the manifestation of the Mother to a young Indian boy four hundred years ago (which galvanized the Mexican revolution as a national symbol) adorn market and home.

In sharp contrast to tourist girlie picture postcards, t-shirts, trinkets, and towels, these female icons in religious shrines provide a model for Mexican women to emulate, creating cultural modesty. One can explore this aspect more in depth by consulting works which discuss the Virgin and her Mexican cultural meanings in relation to roles played by women in Catholic ritual (see, e.g., Arnold).

The series of locally produced female images is synchronicitous. The images occur within a systematic cycle of year-round appearances, particularly the festival cycle. The festival cycle has the function of maintaining the cyclical notion of time, which the cycle of 256 years as time's principal measuring unit used to reflect in the Yucatán peninsula at Conquest (Bricker 8). The ecclesiastical year also reproduces the Maya cycle. This cycle, transmuted by Catholicism, provides a backdrop to tourism, indicating the considerable importance of women, including their central role at the initiation of the Lenten season, when the queen of carnival reigns. Throughout Carnaval week, women walk the streets in long Spanish dresses with black lace head-dresses and other archly feminine costumes. Competing groups dance in the streets night and day the entire week in flashy, revealing, elaborate clothing.

Expressions of the feminine in dance are also key. Dance was an important component of Maya society, politics, and religion and survives through festivities on the island and elsewhere today. In ancient Maya culture, kings, nobles, and the people danced to create community in sacred places (Freidel, Schele, and Parker 1993). They danced to open the doorways to the beyond as well as to release the dead. Dance has even been called the soul of Maya cultural ritual (292). Therefore, a true depiction of women on the island would justly include kinesthetic images of women as well as iconic representations. The image of women on the island would expand to include women who dance in groups for tips to loudspeaker music. Some wear three-foot tall plastic headdresses with fruits and flowers trailing long skirts in front of tourist restaurants.

During the carnival season, Maya on the island and Mexicans elsewhere dance their history of the Spanish intrusion into their world. Numerous unexpected images of women appear at this juncture as well. Elderly squat female shopkeepers dance on stage in a group replete with finery. The island's transvestite culture emerges, sometimes even competing with the teenage girls for carnival "queen." Drunk men dance in the streets with bulging stomachs stuffed with pillows to appear as pregnant women.

During my last carnival season on the island, in 1997, a female impersonator—a man dressed up as a young boy's mother, with another man dressed up as the boy—won the adult costume award after some humorously enacted skits in the zócalo. This award was congruent with the tradition of carnival and its history of introduction by the Spaniards into highland Maya, where the Lacandon also use a female impersonator as one of the stock characters (Bricker 129–154). When the traveling Yucatec circus comes to town, the circus plays the same riff of "Tommy's mother" when supposedly the mother of one of the performers comes on stage without understanding the danger of the heights from which her son performs, only to turn into one of the stunt players as a man dressed as a woman swinging a purse in full drag on the high trapeze. During carnival I have also seen men impersonate Spanish ladies wearing veils of black or purple topped with large black hats with bands of gold, sporting peacock feathers.

This fluctuating image of women transposing gender then influences what happens in other arenas. In political campaigns, women emerge in important positions. They perform "miracles" or save the poor. They grace dilapidated neighborhoods through confronting corruption in politics, as occurs elsewhere in Central American politics (Brentlinger 1992, 1995). Expressing the omnipresence and value of the divine female—as occurred in the early parts of the Montalvo romance, before the rise of the Christian gentleman—Virgins of Guadalupe adorn homes and the marketplace. Individuals, both men and women, further display gold medallions of principally the Virgin Guadalupe around their necks. Female icons also bedeck the downtown cemetery, where whispering angels point upward to the heavens. The patron saint of the island, the Virgin of Immaculate Conception, stands in the central church. People have buried another replica of her under the water where boats take divers.

Stores that market to islanders rather than to tourists are more likely to carry the names of female saints, relational names of elder females, or acronyms formed by connecting names of daughters in a nuclear family rather than girlie images, Indian princesses, alluring pirates, or goddesses. If their self-promotion includes the feminine, this is more likely to be a case where a new young shopkeeper will name the shop after herself. Then, she usually uses an Anglo-based and not a Maya name.

Such are the seriously contested codes and representations that create the criss-cross culture of the island. The islanders struggle to hold on to their own sense of internally created rather than externally imposed meaning. Stores named for islanders express their tendency to make significant shrines to their own emerging present selves. Acronyms made up of letters of the family members' individual names form other signs. So do declarations of the sense of the neighborhood, expressions of respect for elders, support for the struggle to create community, and the honoring of various saints, the last of which expresses the predominance of Catholicism over primitivism. One store sign made by Coca Cola expresses this last category. The lettering under the trademark logo says "La Guadalupana," as if the saint sold Coca Cola.

These signs are monuments to the self-creation of the island's present. Struggling islanders in this way more generally express themselves through combining aspects of imported culture. These "impure" inventions then indicate their desire to go forward. This expressed desire contrasts sharply with the visual symbols which speak for the benefit of tourists hankering after the past, the wild, the crazy, the exotic, and nature. The latter sentimental, nostalgic visitors express their desires to go "back" through what they observe, the artificial environments toward which they gravitate, and the material objects they purchase.

This found quality of ongoing material culture and popular expression emerges from symbols of importance to the people themselves. Such cultural icons often contrast starkly with indigenous elements, much as their own body size, popular folk items, skin color, and stature contrast with what the observer applying a taste for recovered utopian scenarios might crave in the interest of fictive cultural authenticity. The expressive nature of the "ancient lost" Maya surfaces as well in the ongoing artifacts created by the present Maya and Maya mixtures. It is necessary to perceive the images of women which the islanders do produce for themselves in this broader context of their own sign system, apart from the symbols produced for tourism. In their own local sign system, they indicate their own aspirations for cultural change and survival on a local basis.

For islanders, the patron saint of the island, Concepción, is still the strongest female symbol. She wields a distinct galvanizing force. People report that she works miracles for those who pray to her. Once a year, volunteer representatives from cooperatives remove her statue from a case in the church and carry it around the island. They raise power imbued with the same sort of soul force that anthropologist Evon Vogt (1969) found in remnants of the ancient Maya festivals in Chiapas. As Catholicism has spread the ritual of processions throughout other countries, on the island a particular synthesis between Catholic and pre-Conquest rituals takes place.

Colonialist Diego de Landa described the sixteenth-century New Year's Yucatec rituals, in which processions carrying the gods moved from the center of the community to the periphery and back again (Freidel, Schele, and Parker 164). Similarly, a series of cooperatives carries the symbol representing the saint, affectionately called "Conchi," out to sites of importance to the life of the island community, and back again. This occurs daily from November 30 to December 8. Representatives of key components of the town carry the female icon to the pier. They place her on a boat to circle the island. She returns to the church in the center of the town square on the last night. A teeming swarm of islanders and visitors participate by following.

Likewise, Maya towns throughout mountainous southern Chiapas and northern Guatemala, where each village has a patron saint, create similar demonstrative processions. On the island, fishermen claim Conchi for protection as their own patron saint. Some believe that when Hurricane Gilbert came and water covered the entire surface of the island, no one was killed because Conchi protected them all.

Islanders rarely go to the archaeological site of the temple of Ix Chel. This is expressed by the route of the local busses, which don't even travel to the craggy, rocky end of the island with the stupendous view of swirling and crashing waves. Yet throughout the life cycle, most visit the Virgin of Conception and participate in processions for her and for Guadalupe.

At the end of the fiesta week of the Virgin of Immaculate Conception (also nicknamed Conchita), not only have people paraded her around the town, she has also stood on the central altar in the church in a long white gown. There people approach the saint's figure in long lines during the day. They enter late at night to pray in privacy to her verbally, just as Yucatecan Maya once verbally addressed their idols as living beings (Freidel 1976, 109). During a special mass dedicated to Conchi, islanders sing songs to her, calling chants to Conchita at the end of late masses. Individuals leave objects of personal importance attached to her costume in the same magical way that ancient Maya left offerings of their own substance to connect to the power realm of their deities (Freidel, Schele, and Parker 213–219). They pin money to her dress or crown. The people take her on a procession of boats around the island but also, late into the night throughout her feast week, women gather in their houses to sing beautiful lyrical songs to her about the mother of God and the mother of all coming from the sea. She has another "sister"— a similar statue—buried beneath the sea at the base of a lighthouse. Popular foods, such as sweet breads made in the bakery, bear her name, and many, many girl-children are named after her.

The statue in the church wears a multi-tiered jeweled crown. She also sports a silver crescent moon slung across her hips. Based on similarities in the architecture of sacred sites, those engaged in speculative history have traced the Maya to Egypt. The moon across the hips of female icons also represents the fertility sign for other goddesses from that far-distant area of the world, such as the Egyptian Isis.

However, when I spoke with the local priest in charge of the centrally located Catholic church on the island, he expressed the view that the virgin's costume did not have to do with surviving aspects of the moon fertility goddess, alternately described as the goddess of healing and the protector of poets and the mad. Although similar combinations of indigenous goddesses and women in Christianity appear in the Catholic churches in inland Mexico, Guatemala, and elsewhere, the priest of this parish insisted that there is no connection. He said that all replicas of the Virgin Mary stand on this half-crescent moon, concluding that this attribute cannot be taken to signify any remnant of a pre-Christian deity. He further supported his view by referring to prophecies in the Bible which specified that Mary was to stand on a half-moon in just this position.

This priest's insistence in the face of evidence to the contrary is intriguing. I have seen other images, including the Mother Virgin Mary, standing on the head of a serpent; the serpent, rather than representing the devil, as in Christianity, was a powerful, positive religious symbol in the Americas and throughout Mexico. As Redfield and Villa Rojas observed in the interior, the Maya adapt by simply attaching indigenous elements to the Christian gods and religious symbols, thus preserving their own pre-existing spectrum of icons and deities (107).

But this local priest defended the non-pagan identity of the icon. He claimed that the virgin only appeared to have the moon strapped across her hip because her dress was too long (twice her size). As an observer of women's icons and imagery on the island, I wonder if this priest had too much to defend in the hierarchical representation of patriarchal structures to recognize what some scholars have referred to as the "Indianizing" (Bricker 1981, 5) that obviously has occurred.

Some leading Mexican intellectuals have argued that indigenous belief in goddesses and appearances of deities was used to assist in European conquest (e.g., Usigli 1971). Jacques Lafaye, however, in *Quetzal-cóatl and Guadalupe: The Formation of Mexican National Consciousness 1531– 1813* (1974), traced the interaction between Holy Mary and Tomantzin, the mother-goddess of Mexicans. Lafaye argued that the Indians re-discovered in the new religion the mother-goddess of their old faith (227).

Others have presented additional hypotheses on the surviving goddess aspects in the various forms of the Virgin Mary. Davis, for example, claimed that the Virgin of Guadalupe was an appearance of the original Mother, a hypothesis corroborated later by the 1980s and 1990s guru the Mother from Southern India. She stood standing in the same position as Guadalupe but on white elephants, rather than cherubs, and appeared on similarly shaped pendants and icons.

Nonetheless, the colonial ambivalence about goddess influence pre-dating Conquest has a long history which is represented by the local Catholic priest's position. For example, a Spanish churchman discovered a five-ton, six-foot, six-inch figure of the powerful earth-goddess Coatlicue in 1790 under what had been the main plaza of the Aztec capital, Tenochtitlán. Fearing her power, he buried the imposing figure immediately. Alexander Von Humboldt re-discovered the statue in 1803. Alma Reed wrote that this goddess, who has been compared to Zeus, had snakes for a head, conceived immaculately, and heard her child speak to her from the womb (68–73). Coatlicue was the mother of the stars and conceived when sweeping the mountains.

Reed reported that Coatlicue was a priestess and also mother of Coyolxauhqui, the moon. For those who support the migration hypothesis, Coatlicue's association with snakes is interesting. As noted, snakes represented the goddess in pre-Greek culture as well as in ancient Greece. These overlapping indications make it possible that she is a spin-off of the Amazons as they migrated west, following both the dispersion theory and the theory that Medusa was an Amazon queen. Reed also summarized the literature since 1950, expressing the view that through analysis of archaeology it is possible to ascertain Asiatic influence on Middle American cultures in Mexico (266–271).

Nonetheless, perhaps due to his social position, the priest could not afford to readily admit that the white light shining through Conchi, this female representation reigning in the spiritual sense on the island, might truly represent an embodiment of *sakti,* the embodiment of the original eastern force, which was a vestige of goddess culture. After all, the mother of the gods also wore white, as described by Sahagun when he wrote his general history of New Spain between 1558 and 1569 (Lafaye 142, 213). White represents the fertility goddess even in some black groups, such as Marian devotees in Brazil or Haiti. Such a force shows in the whiteness of her dress; and in the whiteness of the lace-like cakes made to sell on the first day of her feast day; in the whiteness of the children's fancy dresses and shoes and bonnets. This ritual finery may also suggest purification and the ritual of dressing in white that honor the goddess (Lafaye 212–213).

Furthermore, this feast day arrives after a series of days lasting longer than a week, similar to traditional celebrations of such feast days inland, described by Redfield and Villa Rojas in various documents written separately or together. Also, December 8, the actual day of the Virgin of Immaculate Conception and the final day of the feast week, is in fact registered on the calendar in other parts of the world as both the day the Buddha reaches enlightenment and the day of birth of the Japanese Shinto sun goddess. The day of the feast for Conchi was set by the Catholic Church in Rome, but it was the first to be established in this area and became one of the two biggest holidays of the post-Conquest Maya year.

The feast cycle exhibits several aspects of matriarchal celebration. These include the emphasis on women and the passing of the life force through women, as through the mother of God, to be embodied in the children. This reverses the emphasis of phallus cult religions, downplaying the need for men and emphasizing the unity of women with their children. The statue of a mother and child in the town center in front of the church embodies this emphasis in material culture, approximating the Hera-and-child artifacts of pre-patriarchal Greek culture.

Furthermore, the culture publicly values what women by nature do. The culture does not perceive children as obstacles to participation in culture for their makers, whereas Anglo-American culture removes children from earshot and banishes them from sight as deemed necessary for smooth cultural functioning.

Immediately after the Virgin of Immaculate Conception is removed from the altar, the Jesus baby replaces her. Dressed in white, the figure is the actual shape and size of a baby, and is displayed in a cradle. As others have noted, the hand positions of Jesus Christ are similar to the *mudras* of eastern yogis; the hands of the baby seem to be placed in one of the meditative postures of Buddha. He is displayed in a cradle.

The similarity seems significant in this study in terms of the transmutation of symbols and images of women. Lafaye noted that the Mexican goddess Cihuacoatl-Tonantzin was surrounded with stories of vanishing while in a crowd of women, leaving behind the cradle of her child, just as Conchi does on this altar (212). Visiting tourists often marvel at how babies and children are thus placed at the center of the culture on the island, partly attributable to the island's particular form of Catholicism and in stark contrast to much of the experience of tourists at home in the United States.

However, since the majority of the tourists are Christian, strong responses are easily evoked by the overlapping imagery. Tourists marvel at the beauty of the children and at the finery considered necessary in children's everyday presentation. Tourists often remark how everyone—even the dogs and cats—seem well fed. Some also marvel at the apparent lack of conflict between family and work situations of managers, workers, vendors, and owners. Children are often included at the workplace rather than routinely segregated out of public and social spaces.

However, some of this glowing, naive admiration of life on the island highlights the need to pursue the intersection of the unconscious need and the conscious projection of a fiction by and to the islanders. Two-way transference can happen. Mary (in her different forms) can be understood simultaneously as an icon and as a projection of the unconscious for both men and women in Catholic culture (Maeckelberghe 1989).

In fact, most of the dogs downtown seem well fed—because of a town ordinance, for practical reasons like health and sanitation. The municipality requires the poisoning of stray dogs at least once a year toward the beginning of the tourist season for the simple reason that if too many stray, sickly, dogs are begging, some tourists become disturbed. Rather than risk the loss of some tourism, the town inhumanely kills the dogs. Since all the downtown dogs that remain alive seem to have enough to eat, the result of this systematic animal poisoning is the projected image of a maternal nurturing, what Erich Neumann described as an aspect of "primitive" matriarchal conscious-ness in his *The Great Mother: An Analysis of the Archetype* (1954). Uptown, on the workers' side of the island, starving, sickly, homeless begging dogs abound.

The Marian aspects of the island also greatly enhance the stimulation of this projection in the imaginations of tourists, even though the projected fic-tion might conflict greatly with the underlying reality, and if asked, the na-tives might articulate a substantially differing view. For example, one North American tourist who bought hamburgers in a luxury restaurant to feed the dogs once expressed her impression that "the government took good care of the people." "On the contrary," a waiter grumbled in Spanish outside her range of hearing, "the people take good care of the government." When asked, he explained that those in government smile, making promises. "We give them applause and an audience, we elect, we pay, and we get nothing," he said through gritted teeth and unbeknownst to the tourist. Given revolt that broke out in Chiapas in January of 1994 and the continuing national political-economic crisis thereafter, the opinion he expressed was not one isolated waiter's worldview of the country's political reality.

Directly opposite the image presented by the local variant of Catholicism, however, are the images presented in dance. Women perform ritualistically in the *zócalo,* the town center or square—actually added to modernizing villages in this area only with the advent of Spanish architecture, according to Redfield and Villa Rojas' study of life in the interior. Ancient Maya rulers and their courts affirmed and raised their power dancing in their ancient cities, as we know from interpretations of the glyph "to dance" made in 1966 (Freidel, Schele, and Parker 258–259).

In this modern "post-Maya" town, dance, feasts, live music, and celebra-tions rotate around the *zócalo* throughout all seasons. The result is that no matter how briefly tourists stay, they nearly always get to pass through and experience some kind of "spectacular." The ultimate examples are the post-adolescent, college-age American "spring breakers" organized on U.S. col-lege campuses to fly to Cancún for a week. From there they boat over to a dance spot on the other side of the island. Two to three thousand at a time, they drink beer while dancing to a stage show in English. This gives everyone the opportunity to feel the sense of being fully present and totally there, a quality of the island that also probably contributes to the tourists' high rate of return, as well as to the tendency of some of those who come to want to remain there.

In my time observing the island, the dance forms as well as the plastic idols sold at the pier and the images on restaurant menus transformed at a rapid pace. For example, on New Year's Eve, families used to come bringing their own food and drink, setting up on collapsible tables and chairs, and go from house to house, where potlatch feasting occurred. No restaurant stayed open; all participated in the ritual, which left most tourists out, even hungry. But now at downtown dance festivals such as New Year's Eve, a raised stage has been introduced. On this, both the members of bands imported from Mexico City or Cuba and short-skirted go-go "girls" perform, with the seemingly necessary blaring speakers. Many bars, restaurants, and discos are open until dawn, radically changing local tradition.

Needless to say, this transformation alters both form and view. People watch the go-go girls dance. Audience transforms from participant to spectator. This transition constitutes yet one more step away from local culture, especially as contrasted with descriptions by Redfield and Villa Rojas of fiestas in settlement towns in the interior in the 1930s. Then, whole towns visited each other. Visitors and hosts danced, partying all night, camping in the *zócalo* or in host family houses after being served community feast-like banquet meals.

In these dances, the point was more reciprocal community building than performance dancing for commercial purposes. My personal interest in attending the Isla Mujeres dances dwindled during the 1993 Mardi Gras season. The municipality set up a disco area with flashing lights in the middle of the *zócalo* in front of the raised band. People had to pay ten pesos to get in. In 1997, people had to pay to sit at reserved tables where waiters served beer. This commercialization is the ultimate debasement of community festivities, which are turned away from their original religious and social significance in favor of commodification; this process has been observed to occur as communities move from the folk to the urban pole (Press 1975, 5).

Generally, after the dance performance, a few Americans or European tourist women—congregating individual women, myself often included—would dance freely in wild forms. Next, single men start to invite the single women to dance. Some wrongly interpret the energetic display of the women as cues meaning that we (the women) are not really interested in dancing with each other or in individualistically expressing ourselves, but are only advertising our availability to men. This is only one incidence of the cultural confusion that often occurs, since different cultures have different socially transmitted rules for behavior for onlooker and receiver, in this case some of the Mexican men.

As the evening further progresses, largely heterosexual couples form and take over the floor. First, Americans and Europeans rise. Often older couples still dance as they did as teenagers in the 1960s with the obvious aim of "breaking loose," "getting down," and "getting out." Frequently, they are living exhibitions of Anglo and Euro interpretations of primitivism. Their faces often exude an orgiastic, frenzied, blissful enthusiasm as they enjoy the pleasure of shaking out their own bodies in whatever way that feels good.

Then, Mexican couples gradually enter the picture. They dance in tightly structured forms, such as positions representing the riding of the fish on the waves of the sea. In these forms, the challenge is for the woman to follow the man perfectly without tripping and falling, with one partner representing the fish and the other the sea. Both men and women tend to dance with a rigid body position, although hips and feet might be rotating, and to look straight ahead with a dead-pan facial expression, showing no spontaneity or deviation from the structure, as they return to a dance form which has been instilled as early as pre-school. The emphasis for women is on their ability to bend gracefully, to follow the male lead rather than to experiment independently, as is typical also in U.S. Latin ballroom. This gender stereotyping holds sway on the island now even though in the Redfield and Villa Rojas' study of inland Yucatán festivals in the 1930s, women played the part of the bullfighter, and men played the bull. In some cases, folk popularity at that time formed on the basis of how well women took the violent, aggressive lead. Nowhere now, of course, is the less sexually suggestive regional dancing performed, in which women in traditional costume do fast, fancy foot work which was and in some places is "*típico*" in the Yucatán. Sometimes women dance together as couples in the structured forms of the Mexican portion of the events, but basically the gringo presence dominates the dance floor until well into the night. By 2 A.M., most tourists retire to their nearby rooms; at that point, the local ritual continues until 4 or 5 A.M. because the predominantly Mexican families, some of whom have come all the way downtown to participate in the festivities, remain until well after the tourists have returned to their rooms to sleep. Until that time, the dance floor is usually speckled with some of the tourist dancers, who are generally a head or two taller than local participants. The height difference is something the designers of newer hotel rooms have had to take into account when purchasing and positioning tourist-suitable furnishings.

TWELVE

Material Items in Women's Culture

AN ON-ISLAND BIRTH EXPERIENCE

Ix Chel followed the sun to his palace. He accused the goddess of taking a new lover, his brother, the morning star. When he threw Ix Chel from heaven, she found sanctuary with the vulture divinity. He pursued her and lured her home; he then immediately grew jealous again. She wandered the night as she wished, making herself invisible whenever he came near. This night-riding goddess spent her energies in nursing women of the earth through pregnancy and labor. —PATRICIA MONAGHAN, "STORY OF THE GODDESS IX CHEL," IN *THE BOOK OF GODDESSES AND HEROINES*

So far we have seen how tourists come "to get back to the primitive" via getting close to a folk experience. In reality, they participate in eclipsing the folk. Sometimes this process undermines the folk position of real women of the culture that the tourists visit, even when tourists do so out of avid curiosity about the women themselves. I had the opportunity to do participant observation as a first-time birth mother and saw how the material items used in pregnancy, birth, and infant-care culture changed as well.

The objects women need to survive, to wrest children and even food from their own bodies, seem apropos for examination on the island of women. Some speculate that the island was so named because it had once housed a shrine to the goddess of safe birth. The island is touted as having been protected by such a deity, the goddess of safe birth, prior to both Spanish colonialism and to U.S. imperialism. I chose to experiment with tapping into the possibility of such remaining power.

I gave credence to the sacred spot over which the reigning Maya deity guarded. After all, many systems of indigenous belief hold that visits to historic local sites evoke particular energies. For example, Hindus believe that shrines to mountain goddesses preserve the sacredness of power locales that built or received *sakti*, the original creative power. Consequently, to evoke the blessings of their goddesses, Hindus think that repeated ceremonial visits to the shrines of the mountain goddess are in order. In giving birth on the island, I opened myself to the influence of possible deities I knew little about. Tourism frequently produces such a mind-set, even if my particular bent happened to be anthropological.

Few have developed the theme of women on the island at all, except for popular advertising which led to the girlie images marketed on T-shirts. Yet the artifacts of birth and the story of its dislocation could form an exhibit in a museum about women and island culture. The material items which women use in pregnancy, birth, and post-partum care tell a story as much as pots and pans can in social history, or the evolution of other home objects on the island.

During the course of my study, I had the opportunity to view a similar process in women's folk culture. I conceived employing the power of the artifacts of the Virgin Conchi. I spoke to the virgin's idol in the church, focusing my will, making offerings, lighting candles, and receiving counsel in the process of trying to conceive. I also gave birth on this island of women as it is formed in present-day reality, in which aspects of the female protection of the indigenous fertility goddess have been appropriated into her Catholic patron saint form. Others prayed to her for me during a delayed period in my daughter's birth.

Many women experience childbirth as a major turning point in their lives (Belenky 33). I sensed that this act would usher in a whole new view of myself in relation to society and culture, and I chose to work the process into my field research on folklore and folk life on Isla Mujeres. I decided to work with a traditional midwife (the *señora*) who had been born in a village in the Yucatán. She operated out of an unspoken theme that she was there to take care of me. She held the assumption that if the mother is taken care of, the baby will be, too. I also worked with a young nurse from the island and a British doctor.

All were women, but they were bringing together incompatible worlds. The latter two in the team were imposing their own medical meanings. A young male pediatrician entered the all-women's birth scene once. The attending female doctor summoned him for support in asserting modern health care's symbolic ritual. At face value, he explained the importance of at least taking antibiotics if I did not agree to enter a hospital twenty-four hours after my water first broke. This is a period that those trained under the medical model consider dangerous. They perceive birth as a mechanical production process with a timed script that birthing mothers must follow. Lay midwives, however, working with a more organic model, have experienced assisting perfect births seven or eight days after waters break.

I engaged in an informal learning process about birth culture with the midwife as key cultural worker. I participated in island habit, daily life, sense of expected outcome, and customs. In the process, I learned much by cross-cultural interactions with the *señora*. I attempted to find and further define what feminist critic Angelika Bammer (1996) has identified as the links between the bodies we discuss theoretically and the flesh bodies we actually occupy.

My perseverance stemmed partly from the fact that I found that the *señora's* life history illustrated a larger emerging pattern in contemporary folklore research. That is, the process of seeking what is already remiss in more developed and industrialized countries unfortunately often eclipses the life of the "folk" observed. Only when the unfolding of civilization through changes in culture, technology, demography, and ethnicity drives the spontaneity of the folk and the ideas in tradition into extinction do efforts begin to collect, record, and archive that which has begun to disappear.

Folklore records until recently depicted women as silent. Areas of women's material and popular culture were left out of accounts (Kodish 1993). However, I found some record of Maya midwifery in an earlier period. For example, Bridgitte Jordan's account in *Birth in Four Cultures* (1983, 11–31) documents her anthropological fieldwork filming and assisting births. Also working in the Yucatán, she likewise focused on social-interactional and socio-ecological aspects of the birth process.

These aspects, apropos to establishing a baseline for the folk life of women, are hard to miss in rural areas, where the medicalization of health is rapidly displacing the elder indigenous healers. There were similarities between Jordan's process and the work which I discuss. However, Jordan's observed midwife was less deferential to the doctors, even though she acknowledged medical expertise. I found it useful to read this piece in conjunction with historical accounts for insights into the impact of economic development on birth culture.

Jordan, who published the first record of birth in the literature on the Yucatán, noticed that births in the community traditionally took place in the home. The site was typically either in the woman's own compound or, especially for the first birth, in her mother's. As opposed to the rapidly developing practice of hospital births, the daily life of the family continued outside the birthing, only separated from the rest of public space area by hanging a blanket from the rafters (18).

Villa Rojas is a helpful source in regard to healers' roles in general on such sites. His study of the Maya of East Central Quintana Roo (1945) notes similarity in the predominant beliefs among the natives of the interior and the residents of Quintana Roo, of which Isla Mujeres is a part. Furthermore, Lois Paul, in "Careers of Midwives in a Mayan Community," discussed the role of women as both ritual and obstetrical specialists in small indigenous Maya communities of the Highlands.

I did not just happen to get pregnant in the field, and then seize the opportunity to deepen my research out of a sense of deepened commitment to cultural studies praxis. Contemporary feminist anthropologist Ruth Behar has stressed the importance of writing how identities are shaped in the process of getting a university education in *Translated Woman: Crossing the Border with Esperanza's Story* (1993, 340). Hence I share the understanding here that the source of my felt empathy toward an elderly woman, displaced by the rationalization of a process which she practiced intuitively, stemmed from a feeling that she mirrored a process not unlike my own.

I returned to the university on the doctoral level in 1989, after having been active since the seventies as a feminist researcher, activist, writer, and thinker. I spent the first few years of return to the university noticing that women's experience was no longer a baseline for practical thinking about women's lives. I had lived in the realm of activities that some scholars designate "cultural feminist." That is, I lived outside of the university, committed to keeping radical feminist principles alive. Once I returned, I discovered that most thought of radical feminists as outdated leftovers of the past. I experienced the isolation of many so-called older women (I was thirty-eight) returning to school. I had the experience of administrators passing me over for teaching assistantships, the positions often held for younger incoming students perceived as having more of a productive future. Both male and female older students often experience this discrimination in higher education in the United States.

After a few years of paid positions that did not materialize, I felt that I was not being taken seriously, and I left the university to go back to making a living from writing and practicing a folk art I had undertaken while participating in the women's renaissance, the reading of cards. At that time, I went to the island that eventually became the subject of the present book. Approaching forty, I no longer felt that I could postpone childbearing on the dim hope of a promised position.

In this situation of freedom, having reclaimed my marginality from the dominant culture, I sought out what psychological theorist Carl Jung—with all his theoretical shortcomings and problems—would have called the universal mind strength of the symbol of the Virgin of Immaculate Conception. In the dialectic between imposed Catholicism and indigenous belief, the people had superimposed the goddess of healing and safe birth onto the virgin concept. They forged a strong patron saint of the island, combining icons from Catholicism with the statuettes found on the island at Conquest and from which the island officially derived its name. Thus I had the opportunity to work positively with the archetypal pattern of available female iconography to reshape my destiny with my own psyche interacting with the island. I found that my extended visit was successful. I came back from my pilgrimage pregnant, confident that if called upon, the positive associations of female archetypes actually worked.

When I returned to the States in my first trimester, the director of graduate studies finally offered me a teaching assistant job, which would have given me the support to continue on campus. However, at this point I consciously decided to look upon my experience at Isla Mujeres as an opportunity for study. I had suffered previous anguish with an accidental, medically induced miscarriage in the States. This time, a hospital doctor proclaimed me part of an "at risk" population with which no midwife should work with at all; unmarried and forty, I had apparently come to my first pregnancy at a so-called life-threatening age.

Such a prognosis clashed with the still vivid memories I had of the strength I had felt on the island, where I had reclaimed the integral relation between my body and psyche. In the States I was also submitted to invasive testing. Such tests are only the tip of the societal iceberg. Women are often treated as wombs at the end of reproductive technologies in the battle over women's rights and freedoms. This in turn is itself only a case in point of the thoroughly machine-mediated environment in which those in the United States live. The logic of the production line has become the foundational approach to almost all human and societal relations.

The system treated me as the sort of "fly in the ointment" client that professionals abhor. Doctors often deal out such treatment to women who for whatever reason have been marginalized—considered deviant or "substandard" by the dominant culture, and hence poor and often without substantial insurance. I decided at this point, mid-pregnancy, to intentionally use the birthing process in another culture as an opportunity for research, even though this meant deferring the offered university position for a year to return to the field.

The midwife I found to work with in this social, political, and economic landscape was elderly (sixty-seven). However, she couldn't remember the year that she was born. She was married to a seventy-three-year-old juice vendor. He was self-employed at the time. He worked in the tourist section selling juice. He worked from his bicycle, which had a wooden cart constructed over the two wheels on the front end, on which he kept the fresh fruits and the squeezer.

Like his wife, he was being displaced by rapid, mechanical commercialization and modernization. In his case, due to the erection of vending machines selling canned Coca Cola and other imported sodas on downtown street corners, in January of 1995 he was hawking newspapers. By December of 1996, he was selling lottery tickets. Like the story of the midwife, his case history indicates larger social trends. The large, cumbersome vending tricycles like the one he used are increasingly available as toys for island children.

Together, the midwife Doña A. and he were mother and father of twelve children. Additionally, the midwife was raising a granddaughter whom she had breast-fed. She had stimulated her milk production with orange leaves without even having undergone the pregnancy. Grandmother to many, Doña A. had delivered most of her children's children herself in her own home. She was also illiterate, later putting what she called her *firma* (signature), a thumbprint, on my child's birth certificate.

As was also the custom in Maya communities studied by Marxist-feminist anthropologist June Nash (1970, 110), the couple immediately identified themselves as "grandmother" and "grandfather" to my child as soon as she was born, and bragged about my daughter in the community. Honoring the goddess of birth as protective energy coming from within, Doña saw birth as a sacred event that contained the life force. She attempted to honor the wisdom within me, tapping into whatever forms the goddess of birth took within myself. Although I had sought her out to assist in water birth, and she agreed, I soon gave up my own authority as the one who would know intuitively what was best for me by looking to her for this guidance. Hence, although a real person, she became for me a projected, idealized hope for organic, holistic union. As I made such a projection, I lost touch with much of the capacity for that intuitive quality within myself which had led me to find her in the first place. Instead of turning to my own sensations, or my own intuition, in early stages of labor I would turn to her.

From the "modern" component of the team was the doctor at the Red Cross, who was thirty-nine when helping me deliver. She was familiar with modern birth technology. She made herself available for low-tech home delivery (but not low-tech ideology) for donation when requested, usually by women like myself in the *gringa* (foreign) community. Under her leadership, the Red Cross met the island culture on its own terms, serving the culture of women birthing right up through their fifties.

Sometimes pregnant women who were already themselves grandmothers sat in pre-natal classes with their own pregnant daughters. The doctor's husband was also a *gringo;* he worked in the boat business originally and increasingly dedicated himself to full-time fund-raising, ostensibly for the Red Cross. The doctor brought with her the ideology of the clock. She imposed this on the body along with a regimented ideology of medicalized, technocratic birth. To her, a home birth could be construed as just a different place to enact a process—that is, to export her ideology of technology. Yet home, as Judy Luce, an extraordinary lay midwife in Vermont pointed out to me, is about more than just being a place, any old place in which the same things can be done repetitively as if one were in a hospital.

The nurse was the only member of the team born and raised on the island. Although modern and educated, the ways of traditional folk culture survived in her lifestyle in various ways. For example, she was in her mid-twenties and had a toddler who had been born out of wedlock. The father of the child was younger than she was; he worked as an auto mechanic and a taxi driver. She and her immediate family sometimes took refuge in her grandmother's compound. This was also congruent with residential patterns described in archaeological remains showing Maya households to be composed of many structures, implying extended family grouping (Kintz 1983). Beyond this, the nurse and her boyfriend, the father of the child, did embrace some of the ideals of modernization. For example, they named their dog "Gringo." Additionally, for a short time they maintained their own small place together before moving back to the young woman's mother's house.

The midwife was normally excluded from all white culture on the island by virtue of being Indian, a process which occurs in other parts of Mexico,

according to Ruth Behar, who studied a woman flower vendor in the north
(10–11). The midwife attending me came to the birth first with nothing but
a bottle of vegetable oil to give massages. Her ways were imprinted by the
fact that massages were often considered curing by indigenous American
tribal medical practices. She also brought a good heart, two strong hands,
advice, patience, respect, songs to sing, stories to tell, the ability to create
spontaneous poetry, and strength to lend. She, like other more traditional
Maya midwives observed by Jordan, considered massage an essential part of
her skills. She gave pre-natal massages as well as various types of curative
and diagnostic massages to both men and women.

Like indigenous midwives in the Highlands, she gave the strong impression of relying on her own ingenuity, nerve, and ability to lend strength
rather than on the wonder drugs, anesthetics, and forceps of the nearby
modern delivery room. The seemingly simple stories she told were in dialogue form. She recited by changing voices and parts, as did the subject
called Esperanza in telling her life story to Behar in the north. The largely
unsolicited stories had mostly to do with the importance of faith in God.

The folkloric parables she told me during the birth process were full of
humor and vitally picaresque. They demanded participation of the listener/
observer in a way that unsettled boundaries, also like the stories of Esperanza the flower vendor confided to Behar. Sometimes, the stories exhausted
me as a listener. They certainly distracted me from any pain as much as
heavy breathing would have done. Her stories were a raw form of neurolin-
guistic programming, particularly the Ericksonian hypnosis technique, in
which the hypnotist/counselor gets the person to let go of fear enough to
think creatively by telling stories, and telling tangents of stories, and then
telling new ones until the listener, frustrated, exhausted, and bombarded
with ennui, can't focus. The hypnotist/programmer has distracted the lis-
tener/client to such a state that new suggestive interjections can be made at
that point, such as the midwife's to me about expanding my perception of
the universe to include the metaphysical and the spiritual and not just the
anxiety of my own timing or pain.

These performances, in which she skillfully used language, drama, and
intense interaction, had the opposite effect of the rationalization, commodification, and obsession with linear time that characterizes the modern delivery room. The latter elements have dominated the white, Western, Anglo-
American process of birth as immigrants and their descendants were cut off
from folkways and centralized in hospitals. What once was an intimate, private, and family-centered experience became seen as merely an obstacle to
the proper practicing of obstetricians.

Like the Native American midwives studied by Mulcahy on Kodiak Island in the Gulf of Alaska, Doña A. coded her divinatory power and "knowing" as religious. She perceived birth as sacred. She covered her wisdom under contemporary ideology like religion. This coding most likely derived from an attempt to protect herself from delegitimating attacks on so-called primitive practices. This is so although what is known as "primitive" is really a rather complex way of being in the world, perhaps more complex than what modernized, atomized Western individuals can know.

Yet at the same time, the depths to which Doña A. had truly incorporated the inspiration and guidance of the post-Colombian-imposed Christian god also demonstrated the readily observed capability of the Maya for adaptation and absorption of new ideas into the vision of their cosmos. For example, the *señora* explained that when a client needed her, God sent her psychic messages to stay at home to await the arrival of the taxi sent to fetch her, even though she might have prepared five turkeys to take to a fiesta and dressed for the occasion. Doña A. would follow her story of how this had occurred with parables from the Bible, emphasizing various similar tests of one's belief in the proper God.

Thus, upon receiving supernatural notice from the deity in which she believed, she showed willingness to step outside the usual space or time boundaries applicable to other women. In this gender-bending orientation, she was not unlike midwives of the Maya Highlands.

My first experience of being a birth mother started with my water breaking in the lobby of a tourist hotel on a Saturday, at 5 P.M. The first night, Doña followed me with her minimal equipment. I took the nurse's suggestion and went to dance in the town square in order to get some exercise to build up my physical stamina. My contractions only went from every forty-five minutes to every twenty minutes the first night. They stopped in the day when the sun came up, and started at dark the second night at every twenty minutes. The contractions (called "*dolores*," or "pains" by the doctor) had gone down to every five minutes before stopping at dawn.

As the birth progressed, Doña's stories shifted gradually to the encroachment of the medical profession on her business. In the middle of this process, I was increasingly immersed in the performance of her storytelling as a way to cut the extraordinary social focus on myself, which I found excruciating. Stray members of the tourist community had a lot of leisure time to drop in, inquire if I had birthed yet, and continue on to the beach; I longed for more privacy. Even to go out and walk around meant encountering numerous islanders and tourists who seemed up on my progress and inquired if there was yet any news. The doctor came in a borrowed car to leave off the nurse, an assistant with no prior experience in delivery, along with a walkie-talkie so the doctor might be called in case of emergency or at the right moment. Midwife Judy Luce later pointed out that this was a setup for the nurse to be in fear, waiting for disaster to happen.

The doctor also left a kit. The low-tech kit contained sterile gloves, gauze, disinfectant, injections to bring down the placenta after the baby was born, equipment for sewing stitches, and other medical paraphernalia. The nurse was thus armed to make charts with a fetal heart monitor, and with something to measure blood pressure.

Thus as the doctor's pawn, the nurse was symbolically asserting technological domination over body and spirit. Her constant plotting and charting documented a culture in the mind of a vision of human activity as an extension of the mechanical, rather than the other way around. This view of human as extension of the mechanical is a social atomism increasingly predominant in American culture (Gorer). The doctor also came with ideas for guiding meditations, information on how to get boats to get to the local hospitals, and a letter of introduction in Spanish to officials in case she felt I needed more advanced technology to have a safe delivery and birth.

This clash in physical material realities represented different relationships and attitudes to authority. Levels of equipment and availability of time considered necessary furthermore reflected issues of proper birthing territorial space. These issues in turn were indications of larger social change in medicine as part of modern industry, discussed in the numerous critiques I sought out due to my alienation from the medical system during pregnancy. These included studies about how the baby becomes the product and the mother merely a birthing machine to be handled efficiently in the process of mind over body in the politics of everyday American life.

To the midwife, I was the authority. She was my servant, or, as she saw it, God's servant. She had placed herself at my disposal from the onset. Her fee covered everything from pre-natal massages to eight days of post-natal staying with me in my home to cook, to clean, to help care for the infant, and to normalize my experience of an extraordinary event when returning to every day "real" life. Feminist folklorist Joanne Mulcahy also found this inclusive fee traditional among native midwives in Alaska, where it served similar purposes (1993). Doña A. followed me everywhere—to dance at the *zócalo*, to the beach. She brought one of my towels to receive the baby with us everywhere we went, and a sterilized razor from the doctor's kit "just in case." She wanted to be ready to cut the cord, although my contractions were forty-five minutes apart and mild that first night.

To the doctor, she herself was the authority. She positioned herself thus as a result of her socialization in training, although for the sake of politics, friendship, and spiritual kinship, she endeavored to act otherwise. I had studied and made decisions about methods. We had shared books and reading on alternative delivery methods. Yet I was the object to be watched and reported on.

I was to be warned about the technical ineptitude of the *señora,* even though the *señora* was respectfully supportive of the doctor. The doctor became angry as I did not take her advice and follow her authority when she decided it was time for me to go to the hospital. This was a retraction of her prior agreement to follow my lead in birth process and technology, including birthing position, birthing site, and the use of herbs for pain (motherwort, St. John's wort, skullcap) rather than drugs.

Statistically, of the women whose water breaks before labor begins, 80 percent will go into labor in twenty-four hours; 10 percent in forty-eight hours; and others go on for days. If there are no internal exams, and little or no active labor, the body makes more amniotic fluid and safely flushes it all out. I knew some of this from having consulted herbalists such as Susun Weed (1985). Thus I was armed as an informed consumer, and wanted to participate in the creation of my own birthing. Yet in my insistence to stick it out, I violated the production-line clockwork model with which the doctor worked. This model dictates a Cesarean after twenty-four hours.

Furthermore, the repeated visits necessitated by off-and-on-again prolonged mild labor were demanding on the doctor, perhaps more than she was able to deal with. She had to come and go from her own job and family in the borrowed car when summoned on the walkie-talkie as the nurse became confused, ambivalent, alarmed, or fearful.

The young nurse was caught in the middle of the protracted conflict in all our roles, which in turn reflected conflict and change in the larger birthing industry. She was at once deferential to the *señora* as her elder, to the doctor as her modernizing role model and employer, and to myself as experimental traveler, an intriguing, adventuresome woman "of the streets" who seemed to live and survive independently outside kin networks, rather than as a woman tied by family to the home.

The young nurse's behavior consistently replicated patterns of deference in the traditional, age-ranked curing hierarchy, although she was not without conflict. The breakdown of the authority of elder curers among the Maya in Chiapas and their attempt to reinstate themselves had become a focus for the community Nash studied as well. Similarly, the nurse's loyalties here were split because she also worked for her modernizing role model, the doctor. The doctor was approximately a quarter of a century younger than the elder, disempowered midwife-healer to whom the younger nurse would have naturally looked to as an authority in the traditional order of curers in the interior. As in Indian communities Nash studied, the old cultural forms often persist even while the community responds to changing cues in the environment (1970, xxiv, 137). Hence, the nurse continued to honor the midwife almost to compensate for conflicting reactions of the doctor and myself to the traditional, intuitively practiced ways of the elder, outmoded healer.

During the course of post-natal follow-up work, I heard many stories from Doña A. without much prompting. She provided me with numerous narratives critical of the historical displacement of her values, knowledge, and beliefs. She communicated freely her insight into how aspects of her cultural identity were being questioned.

Discouraged, she spoke of retreating inland to the peninsula because of her poverty. She explained that most first-time mothers these days had long births like my own. One interpretation of the "folk's" tendency to spend hard-earned pesos on expensive hospital births is that they want "the best" as a status symbol for those living in a modernizing culture. Yet Doña's interpretation was that out of fear, they or their families panic and cross over to Cancún hospitals. Often, in this case, the families do not pay the midwife for her assistance. "This happens more and more, not in the old days," she recalled. Kodiak Island women in Alaska insisted also that they had short labors and few complications in the days of their own traditional midwifery (Mulcahy, 187). Although one reason could be that women are built differently now because of evolutionary pressures, another explanation might be the instillation of fear by the medical system.

The señora's approach to birth was natural. She said that she learned birth from watching the pigs. Since in her world, there is a close connection between the births of humans and the births of animals, her comment expressing this worldview was not surprising.

However, highland Maya midwives studied by Paul reported learning their trade from midwives in spirit. Just as they recounted being called mystically to do their work, perhaps Doña's brief answer to my direct probe as to how she learned her ways was another instance of self-protectionism already observed in the larger historical culture.

Only 5 percent of births require intervention as an emergency event. Yet "good" medical training requires the instilling of fear that one might be in the small percentile category of births that do not go well. Fear interferes with the process of labor. Thus this instilled fear often interferes with safe natural birth. The fear can even exacerbate the situation to the point of emergency. Thus medical prophecies become self-fulfilling. Admonishment of the mother who "feels" that she and her baby are OK occurs in the form of accusing the mother of taking risks not only with her own life but with the life of the baby. Such intimidation might unduly stress others involved even though the woman might herself feel most attuned with her child still inside. Hence, encroachment onto the *señora's* territory by the Red Cross came about even with a doctor on staff who ostensibly aimed to overcome most of the restrictive aspects of her own training. A modernizing infrastructure developed as tourism and the economy grew. With this development, the *señora* was losing her calling, income, and valued cultural identity.

Other devastating restructuring effects result from the proliferation of the larger centralized health system, such as the Centro de Salud; the Red Cross, which relatively speaking operates under what are called "primitive," under-supplied conditions; the naval hospital; the social security system with its downtown family medical facility; hospitals in nearby Cancún; and the emergency water taxis to rush the mother to an ambulance. Women on the island are losing their right to low-tech birth embedded in the ways of mid-wifery, just as the women studied in Nash's account of the highland Maya in the 1950s and 1960s still used to deliver kneeling, a custom which has also disappeared (1970, 110).

Women delivering into the hands of a midwife sitting before them on a stool while they squat over the edge of a hammock in a corner of the family compound was traditional in Maya culture. Older women still delivering with Doña A. repeat this continuity. Change occurs with the introduction of the Western position of women delivering flat on their backs with their legs spread.

The latter position actually developed in France for King Louis XIV to watch the birth experience of his mistress (Arms 1975, 20). The traditional position for birthing in the system is not at all woman centered, but literally man-made, having been initiated at the request of the seventeenth-century king of France. The procedure, with the delivering mother flat on the back with the legs lifted and spread, has continued from its initial start as a convenience to doctors worldwide; the Maya women also now suffer.

Thus, for Maya women, in the move to the hospitals, the switch is not only from herbs to drugs, from family support to hospital staff, but also from hammocks to beds. The woman delivers in the Western European tradition minus the positive aspects of the tradition of indigenous midwifery and early relational mothering of the mother by the midwife.

I later found out at another stage that the ways of midwifery were waning.

Late weaning had been typical of indigenous peoples like the Tupinamba studied by Metraux (Steward 116). Inland Maya like those studied by Nash weaned at a year and a half. But on the island, either a mechanical weaning after three months, or bottle feeding by formula immediately upon delivery has replaced late weaning.

Jordan discovered in 1983 that the notion of keeping a baby on schedule had been foreign to most Maya women. The universal response to a distressed baby was to offer the breast (30). But on Isla ten years later, doctors incorporating U.S. medical practices had trained nineteen-year-old Maya mothers to breast-feed mechanically every three hours, fifteen minutes on each side, even if not yet substituting the bottle. One mother of one, surprised to see my daughter still suckling at five months, simply said she thought the breasts of Mexican women had less milk, or dried up sooner than did the breasts of American women. She was of the younger generation, who would have crossed to Cancún to deliver her first child. The system bred her to be suspicious of the midwife's services and the traditional suckling practices such an elder healer might have taught.

Yet another area of the reduced impact of traditional folkways passed on through the midwife is in the handling of the newborn. The carrying of newborns and smaller children in slings (Steward 249) or shawls around the back, neck, or hip (Steward 474) was also common among *mestizo* and indigenous peoples of the Americas and evidenced among the highland Maya. The latter swaddled their children for the first year to assist the mother or elder siblings in carrying the child in cloth on their backs (Nash 1970, 111). This created a closer bond.

The *señora* could show me how to carry the baby without the aid of a shawl. Yet the prestigious baby carriages and strollers available at the import stores where products sold are largely from the United States have replaced the folk custom of women carrying their tiny babies wrapped in *rebozos* (shawls). I had to travel eight hours inland to a market to find a suitable carrying *rebozo* to reclaim this valued feminine cultural identity. Then I journeyed overland twenty-four hours to find an Indian woman actually using one for this purpose who could show me the proper way to mount the child on the back and to tie it.

She also showed me the second position, moving the child to the side in order to easily feed even while engaging in other tasks. Visiting citizens from the United States, as well as acculturated Mexican women, expressed fear that I would drop my child when they saw me in the market practicing this technique. A seller of tortillas who worked in front of the market but was actually from Chiapas where I had learned the trick explained the artful custom to disbelievers on my behalf.

This usurpation of the pouch-like effect of inexpensive woven or net slings and shawls by man-made machines will, most likely, as it has in Anglo-European culture, lead to a separation between mother and child that diminishes an important bond. This cuts the powerful influence of the individual mother's role. For this reason, the manufactured Snuglis have been invented and successfully marketed in the northern modernized countries. Yet islanders looked skeptically at any form of these as well as backpacks and convenient American carrying devices.

Most tragically, when the *señora* dies, much additional folk knowledge will also go with her as cultural continuity is in the process of being untied. Too often, ethnographic accounts written before the women's movement, such as most of the material in Steward's *Handbook of South American Indians*, rarely mention the role of women in birthing. The life cycle begins with infancy, not birth. Birth is mentioned only if men participate in the *couvade*. Kathryn Mackay, as a nurse, did contribute information on birth customs in Chichen Itza in the 1930s in the study done by Redfield and Villa Rojas (vii, 181–182, 357–362). But by and large, the waning of the ways of female curers is occurring at a faster rate than the influx of new forms of feminist participant observers and women's baseline ethnographers. Thus the *señora*'s story is valuable in duplicating the pattern of waning of the community status of curers reported in Maya fieldwork elsewhere in the 1950s and 1960s in Chiapas.

Doña A. instructed me with much knowledge she was eager to share. She is not able to pass much on, debunked as she is from her position as learned authority. She taught me to divine the number of births a mother is to have through the number of slashes on the removed umbilical cord and to divine the sex of the unborn children from this. She showed me where to throw the piece of the cord when it falls off the button of the baby—to the sea, if it is a girl, so she won't be afraid of the sea; and to the mountains if it is a boy, so presumably he won't be afraid of the mountains. Together, we buried my daughter's placenta under a palm tree on the beach behind my apartment shortly after the birth.

Additionally, she showed me how to lactate by sleeping with a hot towel dipped in the tea made from boiling orange leaves, as she did herself to nurse her own grandchild. Such knowledge has been sadly eclipsed with large corporate systems making breast-feeding a choice more women do not make without extended campaigns and re-education (R. A. Lawrence 1985).

Doña A. can also stop a baby's hiccups by putting a string on the third eye in the center of the forehead, like the tried-and-true method of female shamans in the jungle who routinely suck a thread that has been in contact with a patient's body to remove disease. Plus, Doña A. still retains the eso-teric knowledge to explain that when a child who does not want the breast and is not wet cries at night, a bird must have flown over, making a call that sounds like the cry of a child. Her remedy is to find one of the bird's feathers to burn under the hammock, so that the child can rest. She furthermore maintains that a child's birth guarantees a mother's entrance to heaven. She therefore cannot conceive as sensible giving up a child for adoption, even if a woman already has eight children.

This loss in women's genuine folk culture is one resultant effect of the appearance en masse of seekers of Mexican-Maya primitive folk experience on this Island of Women. When Doña dies, aspects of "the folk" pass a bit further into archaic extinction. Unfortunately, this *señora* will leave no other record. She still resists photographing, taping, and transcribing, perhaps be-cause she has too little comprehension of what happens on the other side.

I have no illusions that the *señora* who attended me actually represents Ix Chel in her aspect of goddess of safe birth, to whom the shrine was suppos-edly dedicated on the island, pre-Conquest. This imagined essence, real or experienced, draws many like myself to the island in search of women's lost powers. Yet the *señora* believes in the male god (Díos) forcibly imposed at Conquest, and is furthermore an Evangelical Christian.

Sometime after the birth, the midwife defended herself, saying, "I am not a witch—I believe in God." Her defensive anti-witch stand perhaps comes as a result of "good" healers differentiating themselves from "evil healers" who deal with negative forces (Nash 1970, 146–147). But also, this comes as a result of derogatory opinions of witches expressed by members of the medical profession.

Such opinions are expressed in relation to midwives, but also in the con-text of any major health condition which might lead people seeking medical help also to seek help from traditional healing sources to cover all the bases. The pediatrician, sometime after the birth when I was teaching English, said there were no midwives on the island. He claimed that they were "*casi brujas*" (almost witches) who used smoke, incense, tapes, and magic. He himself used imported North American statistics, which can be seen as an-other divining method predicting probabilities and futures. He was com-pletely unaware of Doña and what role she played during my labor, or even of her existence on the island. This is so even though she had been there delivering babies in homes on the island twenty years before he came to do the same in the naval hospital.

To prove she was not "a witch," as medical colleagues purport her to be, she told me that in 1983 the health center asked her to qualify for a license. She perceived the examination and subsequent presentation of a plaque as an "award." This lovely, positive person interpreted the questioning of her methods not as a "check" on her medical standards, but as her examiners really wanting to know how she attended a birth naturally without injections, so they might do so themselves. Such interactiveness between traditional healers and practitioners of modern medicine has often been observed in other studies, even though people try both avenues of support when in great need or undergoing crisis (Redfield and Villa Rojas 1934).

However, in her methods of working with me, she could possibly have been the embodiment of the wisdom of deep-rooted Maya folklore. She showed a clear flexibility in the symbols and traditions. Hence, she was able to provide me with the cohering symbol I seemed to need as someone fleeing mechanized birth in our culture. Hundreds of years later, Ix Chel has not disappeared. Rather, the stories, hands, advice, service, and attitude toward birthing mothers of Doña A. have gradually transformed and transmuted the goddess of safe birth. The divinity Ix Chel devoted herself to serving women in labor, as the devoted *señora* attempted with me.

In doing so, Doña A. demonstrated what others have identified as the Maya ability to view the cosmos as a dynamic model combining historical myth, knowledge, and practical experience as perpetually re-created in ritual performance (Freidel, Schele, and Parker 39). In my labor, as I said, I had two nights of mild, well-spaced contractions. Then, my labor would stop with the sunrise. The midwife was assuring me by the second night that my labor was coming with the moon, which helped me at night, and that by the third night I would give birth. I actually did so. But the doctor dismissed the prediction. She had no means of understanding the basis of Doña's knowledge.

In a sense, the *señora*'s reassuring folklore in the form of stories, poetic metaphor, and song broadened the field of perspective to include all the miracles of creation. She evoked the way trees blew in the wind, the way the three Marias appeared in a constellation in the sky, the way the morning star appeared. These gentle evocations had the desired effect of relaxing me. She even encouraged me to feel that the birth was a natural part of the process of all things. The natural unity of all things, the sense that all things are connected rather than isolated and separated, reveals a key element in indigenous Maya culture. The basic characteristic of that culture was, and continues to be, "life as an integral, holistic and complete dynamic," as described by Hunbatz Men, who was born, raised, and educated in a small Maya village in the Yucatán (1990).

The calming folk-technology of spoken ethno-poetry during the birth and labor, as well as the tradition of selecting names, also reflects such an attitude. This worldview flows from a more matriarchal, primitive, rather than patriarchal, individual cultural mind-set. For example, traditionally parents do not select the name of the child beforehand. Members of the surrounding community make suggestions for forty days, perhaps representing the Maya principle *k'ex,* making the new out of the old. The tradition certainly embodies a reciprocity and tension in transformation and replacement (Freidel, Schele, and Parker 285) The names offered usually reflect something organic, something related to the time of the season of birth, rather than reflecting individuality or linear family history. For example, the family often selects a name of a flower that blooms in that season or the name of a saint day the child was born.

The Maya emphasize structure rather than personality in their folklore. The timelessness of oral tradition and ritual holds no place for individuality (Bricker 1981, 8). Individuality is in itself a Western and Anglo-Euro-American modern concept. Every time someone on the island calls my daughter "Conchi," short for the Spanish name Concepción, further underscores this concept. Although that was not the name I as the individual birth mother selected, my daughter was born on the feast day of Concepción, and thus, the islanders unilaterally dubbed her Conchi.

In contrast to this broadened perspective heightening a sense of community and promoting relaxation into the sense of a higher order of things, pressure from the knowledge of medical technology had the effect of intimidating me. The knowledge that if I didn't give birth in twenty-four hours I might be cut off from the natural process of all things, all alone among strangers in a hospital, even prolonged the labor. These were the doctor's wishes, stemming from her fear that infection would set in or that there would be other medical consequences if I dallied longer in delivering, even by natural means. With my fear of such a specter, I constricted. Thus, the instilled fear actually resulted in delaying the process rather than in my obedient submission to her medicalized authority.

By contrast, I remember one painfully stressed moment sitting on the beach with the midwife in broad daylight. I wondered aloud if I should drink my herbs for stalled labor to bring on the birth rather than go to the hospital.

Why did my contractions stop? I asked Doña. "Why do trees blow in the wind?" she answered. Giving up control and letting go of anxiety, I put my herbs down. I relaxed and enjoyed a walk on the beach with her. I felt the pores of my feet open to absorb the earth.

In this heightened state, which is not atypical of pregnancy, I realized how absurd the silly acts of my individual egotistical mind were in the face of the cosmos of things as ordered spiritually. In effect, Doña A. had activated a component of Maya curing ritual. She tried to bring about spiritual re-adjustment rather than to treat the "problem."

Hence in my participant observation, I sought the fast-disappearing ways of traditional indigenous midwifery. Many of her folkloric aspects came to be considered part of the "primitive" birth technology, when pitted against the ultimate opposite, those products of a larger technology—anesthesia, forceps, and statistics. These included folklore, storytelling, the oral development of meta-nature narratives to soothe me, and the singing of folk songs as we sat at night looking at the stars on a windy beach.

I was in the process of reclamation. Everything I had read should have fortified me. I knew the statistics about the higher rate of complications in hospital births. Yet, there were moments in which the part of my culture in my mind would eclipse the wisdom of the *señora*. Consequently, the Red Cross doctor finally delivered my daughter with two American friends in my home, at 2 A.M. on Tuesday, although my waters had spilled on that tourist hotel floor on Saturday.

Compared to any hospital or U.S. birthing center, this birthing situation would still classify as low-tech. I had my own bottled, brewed, and bagged herbs which I had brought from the States to help me. The doctor and the rest of the birthing team did not understand these. Likewise, I did not understand directions or suggestions made by Doña A. under the stress of the pain and conflict over the materials to use—the methods, territory, language, and authority. I was not able to follow the *señora*'s advice to take the position of delivery during each contraction. I did not understand her use of the word *aire* to mean energy and not air, literally. Traditional healing models in the Yucatán focus on holding air or energy in, but I panted. First developed as a childbirth technique by Lamaze, this Western technique developed for "natural" childbirth has been shown to take oxygen away from the baby. To say the least, this method had no basis in Maya reality. Although the *señora* tried to respect where I was coming from, I confused her as I followed the Lamaze technique of choosing a spot to focus on, staring at masks of angels and doves I had bought at a *folklórico* shop to distract myself from the pain.

Jordan's account of this crucial moment in terms of the handling of breath and air, so different even from liberated birthing practices in American culture, clarifies why imported Lamaze techniques ultimately served to confound the *señora,* exacerbating the cultural conflict between us:

> While the mother is on the chair, the physical involvement of the "head helper" is at its most intense. Most of the weight of the woman giving birth rests on her. When a contraction comes on and the woman begins to push, there is a matching exertion visible in the helper's body. She covers the laboring woman's nose and mouth with her hand, holds her own breath, and pushes herself until they both run out of air. She may also, for the length of the contraction, press her mouth on top of the woman's head and blow into her hair to give her strength and endurance, or stuff a cloth (or the woman's own hair) into her mouth to force her to push. (27)

Thus eventually, due to the layers of culture clash, I gave in. I followed the doctor's guided meditations about bringing attention down to the source of discomfort when I felt pain, instead of panting or trying to get away from the searing pressure with other distractions. In truth, when Doña A. repeated the advice with each contraction that unless I took the position of birth there would not be enough air for the baby, I rejected what she said immediately. I lost my patience and ability to believe her.

After all, I had heard the doctor speak questioningly of this tactic. Further, I had read Jordan's account about how a midwife she studied did not know that it wasn't necessary to push until the end (1983). Participating in the changing image of the curers, who often undergo unfavorable comparisons (Nash 1970, 141), the doctor told me that the midwife had "scared a poor girl, and her whole family" by asking her to push throughout the birth process. They rushed the delivering mom to the hospital after several hours of following this procedure at home and the baby had not come out.

In retrospect, I see that the *señora* was merely endeavoring to get me to take the form of birth. She wanted me to begin to visualize the process positively and concretely. A spirit healer from Mérida, about whose knowledge the doctor also expressed skepticism, had already advised me to put something in my mouth during labor to bring the *aire* down so there would be enough for the baby.

I dismissed this advice as incongruous. The notion that enough air would not reach the baby if the mother breathed out also did not make sense to me. But during labor, I kept asking for oranges to bite to quench my thirst and to quiet me for the sake of the neighbors. The spirit-healer, I finally realized, was right—when I had something in my mouth, the energy (*aire*) went down, as well, instead of dispersing, and helped push the baby out.

In other instances, my "advanced" Western mind rejected the "primitive" folk wisdom of the maternal body I was seeking, until I understood the system of the natural world—the material, psychological, social, and spiritual dimensions embedded behind the folk advice. Machines only measure the physical. Yet birth and the advice pertaining to its enactment originate from more dimensions than the physical world. For example, someone suggested that I take a ritual bath three times a day during the last week of the pregnancy to make myself clean and to rub myself with oils and powders. The reason he gave was that doing so would ensure the cleanliness of the arriving baby. Self-help books suggest stimulation of the oxytocin, which brings on the birth. Thus two reasons, from two different worldviews, can lead to similar recommendations. Wisdom lies behind the primitive knowledge, but we have to be ready to receive what we seek.

In spite of the doctor's role in my birthing process, the *señora* was able to proclaim proudly that she had helped with the birth when we walked in the streets during the eight days she served me post-delivery. Thus my attempt to take her folkways seriously might have helped a bit to restore her beleaguered status on the island. Like Behar validating Esperanza, I had taken Doña's life story seriously. I had, however fleetingly and momentarily, inverted the positions in the island borderland social hierarchy where tourists with more money and social mobility than most natives come and go. I had done this by inviting Doña A. into the birth process of a *gringa*. Thus I had reversed the racial and class domination in which she lived in daily.

In such a way we bonded. We forged a relation of mutual caring, reciprocity, and trust which outlasted the immediate process of my own daughter's birthing. For example, over three years after the moment described here, I returned to the island. As usual, on my first night I was deluged with requests for readings, which I usually put off. But this time, in a pink-and-white hotel facing the sea, decorated with mural paintings of fruits and flowers renewed each time I have returned, I was asked to read for the whole family of immigrants from the interior who had recently arrived and who were employed in managing the restaurant of the modest establishment.

On a small rickety table under a ceiling fan, pressed between the second row of tables facing the balcony to the sea and the large television showing risqué Mexican romances, I read cards for a father, an expectant mother, and her sister. The expectant mother was under pressure by the doctors on the island at that very moment to cross the water and enter the hospital for a Cesarean, as I had once been. The pregnant woman wanted to deliver naturally. She had turned to the medical establishment only for backup and advice. The sister wanted to be by her birthing sister, which the hospital would not allow. The husband did not want his wife cut, or to pay the money.

Yet they had no access to the folk healers they had left far behind them at home when they migrated to find employment on the island. I substituted as best I could. I read the cards. I predicted no problems, but I also suggested a consultation with the *señora*. This was for assistance in the birth, but also for confirmation of my intuition. I myself went for the *señora*. She arrived next morning with the usual assemblage of daughters and grandchildren. They stayed in my hotel room on the second floor during the *señora*'s long consultation in the single room in which the family lived behind the restaurant for which they worked.

Doña assured the pregnant mother that the signs were right and that everything seemed normal. She advised against rushing to the hospital just for being twenty-four hours late or because the expectant mother had bled at two previous births and was now thirty-five. The consultation was lengthy. The family paid the *señora* twenty pesos, although I knew they had paid two hundred for an ultrasound the day before. I knew the mother was hearing long apocalyptic stories about suffering and redemption by the Lord. After the several hours the *señora* spent massaging the woman, assuring her there would be no problem, she came to my room. She gave me the twenty pesos she had just earned and asked me to read cards for her granddaughter, who was contemplating a marriage proposal at the age of fifteen. That night, the woman birthed on the island, naturally, without any problem—which had been the family's desire. To this day, when Doña A.'s husband sees that I have arrived on the island, he hails me, greets me, and takes me to visit his wife and family. My daughter, who was five at the time of this writing, still referred to the elderly couple as her grandmother and grandfather in Mexico.

I suggest that to truly embed one's research in the body in this fashion exposes the politics of ethnography. Limitations of the vicarious manifestations of the "urge to merge" are definitively made known. This might be so in spite of one's generous intentions, when the distance required to observe is obliterated by instilled fears of life and death in the stress of participation. Although I came for ancient wisdom and indigenous traditional folklore, by and large, what I got was nothing quite so profound as Doña A.'s relating of her own story of eclipse by the medical profession. Ironically, my own participation in that story reproduced the same process of which she complained. We are, after all, part and parcel of what we study.

Conclusion

*A little girl and a one-legged old sailor go in search
of a magic plant which grows on an island in the
middle of a lake. The plant blooms continuously,
eternally and ever changingly of whatever the
beholder wishes, either fruit or blossom. The
moment the pair set foot on the island, however,
they take root in the earth and begin to sink, as
the ground usually absorbs them through the roots
of their feet. Giving "earth" maternal significance
usually assigned to it, we have a fantasy in which
dust onto dust, the earth reclaims it sown, the
mother absorbing her children back into herself as
a result of their insatiable and immoderate desire
for nurturance.* —PHILIP SLATER, ON
THE MAGIC OF OZ BY L. FRANK BAUM

Thomas More in *Utopia* (1516) gave the word for no-where to an island
with a forgotten name. As Peter Fitting (1991) has discussed, identification
is the process of temporary merging of the reader's identity with that of a
character in the fiction, and includes the attendant psychological processes
which the text replays as buried or repressed fantasy scenarios (158). History has rendered the origin of Amazons and islands of women invisible.
Consequently, all readers or visitors have become free to display their own

buried, repressed fantasy scenarios with respect to Amazons and islands of women. This feature of identification involves the tourist as a seduced reader of the story in the real Island of Women, as well as readers of the fictional and mythological ones examined in this study. I have demonstrated how linking the theme of the island of women to suppressed fantasies seduces the visitor or the reader as audience. Thus, those who go to the island—which has been developed for tourism so as to create the projected fiction—and then become islanders, participate in transforming the unfolding myth out of what was a static symbol originating in the attachment of the name to the island by the European conquerors. Without much reference to whatever actually once occurred, the visitors project split and contradictory images, to which business has aimed its marketing. Now the "reader" of current projections and marketed images must draw conclusions.

The fact that the island, as I examined in the previous section, can bear fruit or can bring to blossom whatever the onlooker desires to behold seemingly evidences a contradictory process. But this is so only if one expects a hard-and-fast, absolute reality. To the contrary, the number and variety of evoked sensations in readers, visitors, writers, and creators of culture actually validate the mythic dimensions that spring from the same stuff as dreams. Seekers of both the Amazon and the Island of Women fantasy pursue the insatiability for nurturance from which to derive strength; the forms that takes may vary across class, race, culture, gender, and history.

In fact, I have shown in this study that as the modes of production and consumption of literature alter, and as meanings are contested in public when cultural hegemony begins to change, so do the variations of the Amazon motif. I have not studied all of the objects, events, and processes available for examination; in this book I have examined only a few. Nor have I studied every instance of the island of women phenomenon. Yet at least I have established a common ground for exploring the multiple, subtle, inexhaustible, complex manifestations of the phenomenon in cultural history.

In conclusion, if what I uncovered on Isla Mujeres indicates what might have been transpiring in the realities behind the myths in history, I can only end with the insight that we might pursue more profitably whatever references exist in world literature as symbols of the unconscious rather than as signs pointing to realities outside the texts themselves, even if some substantial pre-history preceded patriarchy. The perplexing reproduction of this debated problem, as if true answers could ever be found, in itself only reflects the need for nurturance of those undertaking the creation and the argument. This in turn reflects the state of a largely mismanaged world.

As Darko Suvin has written in *Metamorphoses of Science Fiction* in his discussion of estrangement and cognition,

> Whether island or valley, whether in space or . . . in time, the new framework [in the mythological localization of utopian longing] is correlative to the new inhabitants. The aliens—utopians, monsters, or simply differing strangers—are a mirror to man just as the differing country is a mirror for his world. (1979, 5)

As I studied the images of Amazons and islands of women in nineteenth- and twentieth-century polemic, debate, and popular culture, as well as in the pre-Greek, Greek, Roman, non-Western indigenous, Indian, Chinese, Pacific, medieval, and Renaissance worlds, and in the writings of those who interpreted and applied earlier usages, I had to learn myself how to manage this most unexpected outcome of my own contribution to the controversy.

Nevertheless, the island where I lived and worked can help many along in the process of becoming what they aim to achieve. As Octavio Paz has written in *The Labyrinth of Solitude and The Other Mexico* (1985), when a society is in crisis, people look to the past for myths of origin that are also myths of fertility. In this regard, I merely link Americans in crisis to members of other cultures that look to the past or to the utopian "others" as their own empire underwent significant changes in history.

In doing so, I have found Joseph Campbell to give the best handle to understand what occurs in these attitudes and expressions. In the first two volumes of his *Masks of God*—*Primitive Mythology* and *Oriental Mythology*—Campbell discussed the concept of the mytho-genetic zone. To Campbell, this represents a large geographic area in which the sociological roots are cut and people are "seized" by images of a new innovative myth that spreads "like wildfire." Campbell was referring to the change between the shamans and philosophers in the spread of the mythic shape of a culture.

In the literature that influenced American history, both the queen and the explorers were innovators. All searched for a way to understand what was found in the New World. Most certainly, both the conveyers of psychic myth and the ideological substance that makes a society's disparate members cohere had been cut. Many dreamers or explorers reported sightings of unicorns, feathered monkeys that sang like nightingales, and blue men with squared heads.

Those who credited indigenous Americans with Amazonian origin were only following the example of the Greeks in their attempts to comprehend the customs and practices of cultures that were new to them. The assumption that Amazons were present in America also indicated a time when the particular theme was highlighted for the sake of audiences, as many of those funding expeditions put the search for Amazons as well as gold into their contracts (Kleinbaum 116). Yet, U.S. readers or visitors still accept today the theme that connects gold and women as buried treasure, in the popular, sexualized rendition of the island, which asserts that pirates kept both treasure and women there to have festive retreats between bouts of victorious plunder.

Plus, countless Americans raised their children with the mythic theme expressed in the popular folk ballad, "She'll be coming 'round the mountain when she comes, she'll be ridin' six white horses when she comes . . . and we'll all go out to greet her when she comes." Numerous avenues for spontaneous intuitive improvisation on the epic imagery captured in this popular song come to mind. However, according to *The Great Song Thesaurus* (Lax and Smith 1989), the song originated in 1899 based on the traditional black American melody "When the Chariot Comes," a hymn of the same year or earlier (365).[1]

Yet does the imagination this image captures respond to a reflection of warring Amazons, astride horses? Did this traveling myth spread westward on the same psychic substance that bore Muslim lore of women astride white stallions who descended upon a city, as recorded by Lord and Parry? Was the woman a rider returning as reincarnated from pre-Vedic legends? Did many English-speaking North Americans learn a song in childhood that represented the dawning of the New Age by the victorious return of the powerful Mother Goddess? Was this an imagistic appeal to a strong powerful woman enthralled in her own sexuality?

The founding of the United States indeed unhinged the belief systems of large numbers of people. "America" in both its expanded and limited sense became a large mythopoetic zone in which images could still take off like wildfire. Now, we turn to the dislodged shamans with respect. We debunk philosophers and bomb state capitols. Lawmakers legislate that women and children should do without milk and food and that the homeless shall live without adequate shelter.

In this mish-mash of an unhinged culture, new conglomerates emerge. Yet we find it practically impossible to trace the origin and appeal of legends such as the ones this study explored. Hence, much fun and pleasure remains in the field of American Studies. Like our predecessors, we too make up our own reality to connect to the situation before us. We too utilize what Herbert

Marcuse has called the id, freed from forms and principles which constitute the unconscious social individual, as we revitalize, through Eros, a most un-nurturing, atomized, spiritually depleted, and materialistic civilization. A commodity economy, the patriarchal state, and public control over individuals' private existences all necessitate deflections of instinctual energy. Thus many, male or female, will enthusiastically connect to an island representing a civilization somewhere in our imaginations where our mothers were strong, met our instinctual needs, and were able to cater to us exactly as we wanted. Sometimes these feeders will destroy, as when Amazons successfully went on warpaths, or when Kali ate men. Yet our need to imagine an Eden of sustained nurturance cannot be kept completely in check by this countervailing apprehension.

Notes

INTRODUCTION

1. Michelle Crone donated documents surrounding the building of the original women's music festival community to Duke University as the Crone Papers.

2. Cavin's *Lesbian Origins* originally reached Rich in dissertation form (Rutgers, 1978).

3. "Palimpsest" is a term appropriated from archaeology into cultural studies which means a superimposition of different narratives. The term usually implies the obliteration of earlier texts still faintly visible beneath the upper layers.

CHAPTER TWO

1. Reactionist literary descriptions of Amazons tend to depict the women as very tall. See, for example, F. A. M. Webster, *The Land of Forgotten Women* (1950). There, a surviving offshoot of the old Viking Norse women are discovered to have their own civilization in the middle of Africa, where they control black and mulatto male and female slaves and mine diamonds. See also Susan Bordo's "Anorexia Nervosa: Psychopathology as the Crystallization of Culture" (1988), which explores how large body size clashes with America's cultural ideal.

2. See Birkby's *Amazon Expedition* for path-breaking articles by Ti-Grace Atkinson, Joanna Russ, Esther Newton, Jill Johnston, and Bertha Harris.

3. Both excerpts from Brown's *Rubyfruit Jungle*—"Violet Hill Elementary School" and "Fort Lauderdale High"—appeared in *Amazon Quarterly* 1, no. 2, published by Amazon Press of Oakland, California, February 1973 (6–16).

4. Clifford discussed the many "contemporary invocations of diaspora," cross-culturally, in "Diasporas," a manuscript in process presented at the Buckham Lectures, University of Vermont, Burlington, March 4, 1994.

5. See Tracy Matthews' discussion of Black Panther gender politics in her article, "No One Ever Ask, What a Man's Place in the Revolution Is: Gender and the Politics of the Black Panther Party, 1966–1971." She argued that while Cleaver was a self-described and convicted rapist, and his book was widely read by blacks as well as whites, discussions within the party about gender roles were responded to in various, sometimes contradictory, ways.

6. For this understanding, I am indebted to ongoing discussion with M. Rivkah Polatnick concerning her important scholarship. Consult Alice Echols, *Daring to Be Bad: Radical Feminism in America 1967–75* (1989). See also Pat Robinson and Group's paper (1970), which discussed matriarchy. Major studies of the early movement of this period include Cellestine Ware, *Woman Power* (1970); Judith Hole and Ellen Levine, *Rebirth of Feminism* (1971); Jo Freeman, *The Politics of Women's Liberation* (1975) and *Social Movements of the Sixties and Seventies* (1983); Barbara Deckard Sinclair, *The Women's Movement* (1975); and Sara Evans, *Personal Politics: The Roots of Women's Liberation in the Civil Rights Movement and the New Left* (1979).

7. For more information and analysis, see Cynthia Griggs Fleming, *Soon We Will Not Cry: The Liberation of Ruby Doris Smith Robinson* (1998), and Vicki Crawford, Jacqueline Anne Rouse, and Barbara Woods, *Women in the Civil Rights Movement: Trailblazers and Torch Bearers. 1941–1965* (1993).

CHAPTER THREE

1. Gantz compared and contrasted all the versions of the Women of Lemnos story, including the early play in which the women refuse to allow entry to their island unless the men promise themselves in sexual union (345–347).

2. The "wild woman" archetype is similar to but not always exactly congruent with the archetype of the Amazon. Stith Thompson delineated Amazons and wild women as separate categories in his *Motif-Index of Folk Literature* (1958). For insights into this relation, see also Clarissa Pinkola Estes, *Women Who Run With the Wolves: Myths and Stories of the Wild Woman Archetype* (1992).

3. However, Martin Bernal interpreted Egypt as the known predecessor for a basically Greek-Semitic culture. Only later did modern classicists interpret Greek culture as Aryan. This makes Herodotus' writings on the Egyptians, whom Bernal claimed Herodotus knew had colonized the Greek areas in previous millennia, even more interesting. See Bernal's *Black Athena: The Afroasiatic Roots of Classical Civilization* (1987, 1991).

4. On "maternal bogies," see Slater 63–70; see also H. Blumner, *The Home Life of the Ancient Greeks* (1893, 88); Martin Presson Nilsson, *Greek Folk Religion* (1961, 97); H. J. Rose, *Primitive Culture in Greece* (1925, 95); John C. Lawson, *Modern Greek Folklore and Ancient Greek Religion: A Study in Survivals* ([1910] 1964) 130–190.

5. For further discussion, see H. D. F. Kitto, *The Greeks* ([1951] 1987); Gilbert Murray, *Five Stages of Greek Religion* (1955).

6. Evidence supports the notion of a universal transition of this kind in all civi-

lized societies. See Briffault, *The Mothers* (1927, 84–90); Campbell, *The Masks of God* (1959, 315 ff.); Erich Neumann, *The Great Mother* (1954).

CHAPTER FOUR

1. Ellen Frye, in *Amazon Story Bones* (1994), illustrated this creatively in her fictional vision of how nature and deities conceived Amazons. See also Florence Mary Bennett for a historical perspective on Amazons as divine in the classics. Carlos Alonso del Real also indicated that some thought the Amazons were descendants of matings between the deities Artemis and Ares. For evidence, they pointed to the language used by Artino at the end of the *Iliad* (52). Real's own thesis is that all the world of subterranean female divinities and minor figures mixed with the Great Mother and the god of death and were transformed into heroes. The only way to this heroic transformation, however, was to become Amazons. Thus, the tombs some identified as Amazonian might have really been sanctuaries (53). Elsewhere he has argued that the Amazons were devoted to Artemis, sister to Apollo, as both deities hunted with arrow and bow (96). Therefore, sanctuaries to Artemis and Apollo could have been taken for Amazon tombs as well.

2. Kleinbaum reproduced two 1687 drawings from Amsterdam that are now maintained in the Rare Books and Manuscripts Division, New York Public Library. Yet, without the caption declaring that they are one-breasted, it is hard to ascertain this fact.

3. I have found this censorship of the breast out of daily life further evident in the choice of the term "nursing" in the English language as compared to the Spanish term, *dando pecho* (which means literally, "giving breast").

4. See Showerman (1901) for a detailed description of the Great Mother coins in the pre-Greek, Greek, and Roman civilizations.

5. For verification of Slater's thesis, see George Grote, *Mythology of the Greeks* (n.d., 159–161); Apollodorus of Athens, *The Library* (1921, vol. 2, ii, 5, 9); and E. Weigert-Vowinkel, "The Cult and Mythology of the Magna Mater from the Point of View of Psychoanalysis" (1938).

6. See Miriam B. Peskowitz's "Introduction: Stories about Spinners and Weavers," in her *Spinning Fantasies: Rabbis, Gender and History* (1997); see pp. 1–26 for various interpretations of Penelope through the ages, moving from traditional to feminist.

7. See also Dietrich von Bothner, *Amazons in Greek Art* (1953, 208–214).

8. Additionally, according to Real, the Spanish scholar who published his study of what he called "*Amazonismo*" in 1967 in Madrid, Diodorus, the Greek historian, initiated the one-breasted idea. Diodorus did this apparently by attributing the name of the Amazons to the idea that women burned their breasts off to shoot arrows (72–74). But this occurred in 50 B.C., very much later than the original tales and glimpses of stories. Then, during the Spanish Dark Ages, the ethnographies of San Isidoro, archbishop of Seville, exhibited a wide-reaching spirit more flexible than that of Diodorus. San Isidoro wrote that the name "Amazons" was traced to mean "*unimamas*," as in "one-mama'd," with mama standing for breast, the smallest outstanding signi-

fier of mother in the Spanish tongue (113–114). "*Mamita*" or "*mamilla*" similarly stands for a little bottle used in nursing. These phrases are commonly used in Spanish as a substitute for "mama"—that is, mama's breast. Yet according to Real, the Spanish author of the Dark Ages attributed to Ticiano, apparently a Roman, and not to Diodorus at all, the notion that these women—whom Hercules (Heracles), Achilles, and Alexander exterminated—had burnt their breasts off so as not to interfere with the pulling of the string back on the bow to shoot arrows.

9. According to Herodotus, in the Scythian language, "man" was *oior* and *pata* was "to kill" (6.110.1, as discussed in Sobol 152 n. and Tyrell 23, 134 n.).

CHAPTER FIVE

1. I refer the interested reader to current related research on Homeric epic that touches upon similar issues in the more recent scholarship of Lillian E. Doherty, *Siren Songs: Gender, Audiences and Narrators in the Odyssey* (1995); Gregory Nagy, *Poetry as Performance: Homer and Beyond* (1996); Erwin Cook, *The Odyssey in Athens: Myths of Cultural Origins* (1995).

2. Much has been published in this area since the work I discuss here, both within the Parry-Lord school and outside it. For those who wish to consider ethnographic literature on sung epic performance, a few important works to consult include Stuart H. Blackburn, *Singing of Birth and Death: Texts in Performance* (1988); John M. Foley, *Traditional Oral Epic: The Odyssey, Beowolf and the Serbo-Croatian Return Song* (1990); Dwight Reynolds, "The Interplay of Genres in Oral Epic Performance: Differentially Marked Discourse in a Northern Egyptian Tradition" (1991); Christiane Seydou, "The African Epic: A Means for Defining the Genre" (1983).

3. "No goddess was your parent, nor Dardanus the ancestor of your race, traitor, but the hard rocks of craggy Caucasus engendered you and Hyrcanian tigresses gave you suck!" (Book 4, *The Aenid of Virgil*, 1972, 365).

4. All citations unless otherwise noted are from *The Complete Works of Homer: The Iliad and the Odyssey*. Trans. Andrew Lang, Walter Leaf, and Ernest Myers (1947).

5. The suppressed power of Thetis possibly derives from her roots as the Indo-European goddess of dawn. See Laura M. Slatkin, *The Power of Thetis: Allusion and Interpretation in the Iliad* (1991).

6. Furthermore, Keuls has pointed to the fact that mixed-gender lamentation choruses did not develop until the seventh century, as shown in the Attic vases. Moreover, she feels that the mourning image of the Greek mother lamenting over her slain son anticipates the Christian motif of the Virgin Mary mourning over the body of Jesus (147–150).

7. See Helene P. Foley's discussion in "Reverse Similes and Sex Roles in the *Odyssey*" (1987).

8. See also Lee Edwards' feminist re-visioning of the concept of hero in *Psyche as Hero: Female Heroism and Fictional Form* (1984). Actually, according to Finley, there was no feminine gender for the word "hero" in Greek at this time. According to Jane Harrison's discussion of the hero, in the Greek times under examination, "hero" was defined as an office. The term referred to a designated function, capable of being

filled by a series of representatives. "Hero" was thus a blank frame, which anybody could fill (259). Yet women are never thought to enter the picture, even if in fact in the plot they perform a heroic function. Furthermore, the term referred more technically to a class of the mortal aristocracy. To the Greeks, the age of the heroes on which Homer was an authority referred to a time after the Bronze Age. Then, a race existed which was half mortal, half divine. Some of these heroes died in the war of Troy; others kept living on "blessed islands along the shore of the ocean" (Finley 18–25).

9. For a feminist re-interpretation of the role of women in lament poetry, see Angela Bourke, "More in Anger Than in Sorrow: Irish Women's Lament Poetry" (1993). Several studies of lament poetry in Greece are useful for developing this insight: Margaret Alexiou, *The Ritual Lament in Greek Tradition* (1974); Anna Caraveli Chaves, "Bridge Between Worlds: The Greek Women's Lament as Communicative Event" (1980); and Constantina-Nadia Seremetakis, "Women and Death: Cultural Power and Ritual Process in Inner Mani" (1987), and *The Last Word: Women, Death and Divination in Inner Mani* (1991).

10. See Michael Herzfield's *Anthropology through the Looking Glass: Critical Ethnography in the Margins of Europe* (1987). Herzfield has criticized survivalist tendencies in Greek ethnography. See also Louis Gernet, *The Anthropology of Ancient Greece* (1981); Sarah Humphreys, *Anthropology and the Greeks* (1983); John C. Lawson, *Modern Greek Folklore and Ancient Greek Religion: A Study in Survivals* (1964).

11. This is not to dispute that Turkish epic tradition, which I describe as the source for Bosnian epic, predates the arrival of Islam in southeastern Europe. Turkish epic can be seen as related to other epic traditions in the region, despite the modern image of Turks as markedly different in tradition and art.

12. As to the clash between European listeners and imported myths, Herodotus indicated that Hera and Zeus were of Egyptian origin. He also wrote that Egyptians permitted brother/sister marriages, another possible reason for the obvious antagonisms between them (Book 3, Chapters 30 and 31, 433). In discussing Hera's pre-Olympian origins, Pratt cited an account which relates Hera's rebellion against her patriarchal husband, Zeus, to her snake-Gorgon connection (1994, 29). According to Gimbutas, originally both Athena and Hera were Old European snake goddesses: Hera used to be sculpted with her hair curled like snakes, as the Amazons-cum-Gorgons and Medusa were.

13. See Tyrell, who discussed how the Athenians buried their dead from the previous summer's military campaigns in a common grave in the public cemetery, presumably in autumn. According to Thucydides, this was an ancient ancestral custom (131 n.). This was particularly a common occurrence in the years after the Persian Wars, in which participants made common formulaic speeches and laments for group consolation.

14. In the theorized evolution from women's lament to male memories of lament to solidified epic performed by professional male singers, consult other researchers in the area for further interpretations. For example, Doherty (1995) accounted for the predominance of women's viewpoints and voices in Homeric epic through the concept of allusion. Seydou (1983) and Reynolds (1991) used the concept of multigenericity rather than formal evolution. Doherty characterized such textual inscrip-

tions of female views as part of a rhetoric of contrast giving women's values symbolic force; Seydou and Reynolds both pointed to the tendency of the epic genre in Africa and Egypt to fold other genres into itself, so that a performative framework and genre dominated by men could have subsumed or "folded in" a women's genre. These models might possibly work for Homeric epic as well.

CHAPTER SIX

1. See, for example, *Hercules and the Amazon Women* (1997). Renaissance Pictures. Director Bill L. Norton. Universal City CA MCA Home Video 1997.

CHAPTER SEVEN

1. At this time, as Real explained, the Ethiopians reigned in Israel, and Egypt reigned over Syria. To Homer, the Ethiopians were remote, while to Arctinus, the Ethiopians were real, which is why Arctinus brought them in to his plot (28–29).

2. Although discussions on the oral nature of the origin of the stories do not take note of woman as storyteller, Seremetakis related how women lamenters are/were weavers of oral histories in inner Mani, a location more geographically germane to the discussion than the site of Parry's fieldwork. Indeed, several aspects of the domain are repeated—including the tower houses, the prescient divinatory knowledge of Hector's death as foretold by Andromache's house maidens (*Il.* 6.115), and the ongoing social labor of women during war feuds that is reflected both in the ancient texts and in performed lament today. That women's role in death became negative rather than transformative is evident in Kirk's account of Virgil (88).

3. Tyrell further argued that just as Amazons assumed the male role in war, so Dawn assumed the male role in rape. He cited Apollodorus' *Biblioteca* (3.12.4; 1.94; 1.4.4–5) and Homer's *Odyssey* (15.250–251).

4. See Seremetakis on foreseeing imminent death via signs in Greek culture.

CHAPTER EIGHT

1. For more on the Celtic legends, consult Tom Peete Cross, *Motif-Index of Early Irish Literature* (1952).

2. See Marion Zimmer Bradley's (1985c) discussion of *Angel Island* in her "Responsibilities and Temptations of Women Science Fiction Writers." However, Marleen Barr's discussion in *Feminist Fabulations* is more current (1992). See also Ursula Le Guin's introduction in a recent edition of Inez Haynes Gillmore's *Angel Island: A Novel* (1988).

3. See also Walter J. Ong, *Orality and Literacy: The Technologizing of the Word* (1982), for discussion of impact of technology on dissemination of the word.

CHAPTER NINE

1. See William Sims Bainbridge, *Dimensions of Science Fiction* (1986), for the context of the early years of the science fiction mass market magazines, when this

story was published. For a discussion of women fighting in modern science fiction, see Rosemarie Arbur's "Fights of Fancy: When the 'Better Half' Wins" (1991).

2. The term "codex" refers to the large number of books made in Maya culture by folding up long sheets of paper like a screen. The Maya made paper for these from roots of trees enclosed between two boards, although some books with ancient texts were made from the bark of a certain tree and were nine inches high and six inches wide. Only four codices from the Post-Classic era (900 A.D. to mid-fifteenth century) survive, although ceramic vases from as early as the fifth or sixth century A. D. show individuals painting codices, which led to a quest for the "Books of the Dead." The Dresden Codex is the earliest manuscript, probably written in the twelfth century, but believed to have been copied from a text written earlier. See Francis Robicsek and Donald Hale, *The Maya Book of the Dead* (1981), pp. xvii–xix.

3. For a sense of Mexico as a whole at the time of conquest, see H. R. Wagner, trans., *The Discovery of New Spain in 1518* ([1519] 1942), and A. M. Tozzer, trans. and ed., *Relación de las cosas de Yucatán* ([1560?] 1941).

4. For a discussion of female-centered shrines dating from the Conquest, see also David A. Freidel, "The Ix Chel Shrine and Other Temples of Talking Idols" (1975).

5. Francisco López de Gómora also recorded Ix Chel's existence at Conquest on nearby Cozumel. See his *Cortés: The Life of the Conqueror by His Secretary* ([1552] 1964).

6. See Mary Margaret Fonow and Judith A. Cook, *Beyond Methodology: Feminist Scholarship as Lived Research* (1991), on the relation between lives and research in feminist scholarship, which I found most helpful in developing this discussion.

7. I had actually been on the island praying for immaculate conception in the hope that there was some reality behind the myth. I refer readers who want to know more about this process of seeking motherhood outside patriarchal marriage to my fiction—"Isaac's Dream" (1991b), "Rainbow to the Moon Goddess" (1993b), and *Sasha's Harlem* (forthcoming). Although feeling pressure to conceive, I was reluctant to participate in the structure that seemed to be the founding nexus of the patriarchy and the downfall of many Amazons, as most of this book and many other authors (e.g., Daly) have discussed.

CHAPTER TEN

1. For more on these islands, see also A. R. Radcliffe-Brown, *The Andaman Islanders* (1948). He recorded many themes and motifs indicating vestiges of pre-patriarchal civilization.

2. See June Nash et al., *Ideology and Social Change in Latin America* (1977), and *Popular Participation in Social Change* (1976) for a different contextualization of these politics, events, and activities.

3. For analysis of the effect of NAFTA on the area as a whole, see Dan La Botz, *Chiapas and Beyond: Mexico's Crisis and the Fight for Democracy* (1994), and his later *Democracy in Mexico: Peasant Rebellion and Political Reform* (1995).

4. For examples of other touristic development of pre-patriarchal goddess sites, see Anneli S. Rufus and Kristan Lawson, *Goddess Sites: Europe* (1991). For more on Maya civilization in the Yucatán to provide a framework for examining the legiti-

macy of these claims, consult Ramon Osorio y Carvajal, *Yucatán en las luchas liber-tarias de México* (1972), especially with regard to sex roles and clan traditions among indigenous Indians. The reader should be forewarned that this unreconstructed so-cial history discusses gods, not goddesses. See also Victor Von Hagen, *En Busca de los Mayas: la historia de Stephens y Catherwood* (1979); Diego Lopez de Cogo-lludo, *Historia de la Yucatán* ([1688] 1957). Also, to understand the possible signifi-cance of female deities to past Maya women and women today, see Linda Schele and David Freidel, *A Forest of Kings: The Untold Story of the Ancient Maya* (1990), and David Freidel, Linda Schele, and Jan Parker, *Maya Cosmos* (1993). They pursued among other elements of Maya culture the significance of the original Lady in Maya cosmogony.

CONCLUSION

1. See also the program notes of recordings of the song on the Folkways label.

Bibliography

Abelove, Henry, et al., eds. *The Lesbian and Gay Studies Reader*. New York: Routledge, 1993.

Abrahams, Roger D. "Ordinary and Extraordinary Experience." In *The Anthropology of Experience,* edited by Victor W. Turner and Edward M. Bruner, 45–72. Urbana: University of Illinois Press, 1986.

Ackerman, Robert. *The Myth and Ritual School: J. G. Frazer and the Cambridge Ritualists*. New York: Garland, 1991.

Agress, Lynne. *The Feminine Irony*. Rutherford: Associated. University Press, 1978.

Alarcan, Daniel Cooper. *Aztec Palimpsest: Mexico in the Modern Imagination*. Tucson: University of Arizona, 1997.

Albinski, N. B. *Women's Utopias in Nineteenth and Twentieth Century Fiction*. London: Routledge, 1988.

Aldiss, Brian. *Moreau's Other Island*. London: Cape, 1980.

Alexiou, Margaret. *The Ritual Lament in Greek Tradition*. Cambridge: Cambridge University Press, 1974.

Alice, Gordon, Debbie, and Mary. "Addition to the First Printing of 'Lesbian Separatism: An Amazon Analysis.'" 1974. Reprinted in *For Lesbians Only: A Separatist Anthology,* edited by Sarah Lucia Hoagland and Julia Penelope, 307–308. London: Onlywomen, 1988.

"Angel One." Written by Patrick Barry. *Star Trek: The Next Generation*. Created by Gene Roddenberry. Directed by Michael Rhodes. Paramount Pictures, 1987. Airdate: January 25, 1988. Stardate: 41636.9.

Apollodorus of Athens. *The Library*. Translated by Sir James George Frazer. Cambridge, Mass.: Loeb Library, Harvard University Press, 1921.

Arbur, Rosemarie. "Fights of Fancy: When The 'Better Half' Wins." In *Fights of Fancy: Armed Conflict in Science Fiction and Fantasy,* edited by George Slusser and Eric Rabkin, 79–91. Athens: University of Georgia Press, 1991.

Ariosto, Lodovico. *The Orlando Furioso.* 1516. Translated by William Stewart Rose. 1864. Indianapolis: Bobbs-Merrill, 1968.

Arms, Susan. *Immaculate Deception: A New Look at Women and Childbirth in America.* Boston: Houghton Mifflin, 1975.

Arnold, Marigene. "Célibes, Mothers and Church Cockroaches: Religious Participation of Women in a Mexican Village." In *Women in Ritual and Symbolic Roles,* edited by Judith Hoch-Smith and Anita Spring, 45–54. New York: Plenum, 1978.

Arthur, Marilyn. "Politics and Pomegranates: An Interpretation of the Homeric Hymn to Demeter." *Arethusa* 10 (1977): 7–47.

Atkinson, Ti-grace. *Amazon Odyssey.* New York: Link, 1974.

At the Circus. Produced by Mervin LeRoy. Directed by Edward Buzzell. Metro-Goldwyn-Mayer Corporation, 1939.

Babcock, Barbara, ed. *The Reversible World: Symbolic Inversion in Art and Society.* Ithaca: Cornell University Press, 1978.

Bachofen, J. J. *Myth, Religion and Mother Right.* 1861. Translated by Ralph Manheim. Princeton: Princeton University Press, 1967.

Baedekers' Mexico. Stuttgart: Baedekers, 1990.

Bainbridge, William Sims. *Dimensions of Science Fiction.* Cambridge, Mass: Harvard University Press, 1986.

Ballard, J. G. *Concrete Island.* London: Cape, 1974.

Bamberger, Joan. "The Myth of the Matriarchy: Why Men Rule in Primitive Society." In *Woman, Culture and Society,* edited by Michelle Zimbalist Rosaldo and Louise Lamphere, 263–280. Stanford, Calif.: Stanford University Press, 1974.

Bammer, Angelika. "The Inevitability of the Personal." *PMLA* 3, no. 5 (October 1996): 1150–1151.

———. *Partial Visions: Feminism and Utopianism in the 1970s.* New York: Routledge, 1991.

Baraka, Amiri. *The Autobiography of Leroi Jones.* New York: Freundlich, 1984.

———. *Blues People: Negro Music in White America.* 1963. Greenwood, Conn.: Greenwood, 1980.

Barale, Michele Ana. "When Jack Blinks." In *The Lesbian and Gay Studies Reader,* edited by Henry Abelove et al., 604–615. New York: Routledge, 1993.

Barnes, Djuna. *Ladies' Almanack.* 1928. New York: Harper, 1972.

———. *Spillway.* 1923, 1929. London: Faber, 1962.

Barr, Marleen. *Feminist Fabulations: Space Post Modern Fiction.* Iowa City: University of Iowa, 1992.

Barton, Carlin. *The Sorrows of the Ancient Romans.* Princeton: Princeton University Press, 1993.

Baum, L. Frank. *The Magic of Oz.* 1919. New York: Ballantine, 1985.

Beauvoir, de Simone. *The Second Sex.* 1952. New York: Knopf, 1978.

Behar, Ruth. *Translated Woman: Crossing the Border with Esperanza's Story.* Boston: Beacon, 1993.

Belenky, Mary Field, et al. *Women's Ways of Knowing: The Development of Self, Voice and Mind.* New York: Basic, 1986.

Bellah, Robert N. "Liturgy and Experience." In *The Roots of Ritual,* edited by James Shaughnessy, 217–234. Grand Rapids: Eerdmans, 1973.

Bennett, Florence Mary. *Religious Cults Associated with the Amazons.* 1912. New York: AMS, 1967.

Berger, Pamela. *The Goddess Obscured. Transformation of the Grain Protectress from Goddess to Saint.* Boston: Beacon, 1985.

Bernal, Martin. *The Archaeological and Documentary Evidence.* Vol. 2 of *Black Athena: The Afroasiatic Roots of Classical Civilization.* London: Free Association, 1991.

———. *The Fabrication of Ancient Greece 1785–1985.* Vol. 1 of *Black Athena: The Afroasiatic Roots of Classical Civilization.* London: Free Association, 1987.

Bernheimer, Richard. *Wild Men in the Middle Ages.* Cambridge, Mass.: Harvard University Press, 1952.

Beye, Charles Rowan. *The Iliad, the Odyssey, and the Epic Tradition.* Gloucester, Mass.: Smith, 1972.

Biocca, Ettore. "Author's Preface." Helena Valero, *Yanoāma: The Narrative of a White Girl Kidnapped by Amazonian Indians as Told to Ettore Biocca.* Translated by Dennis Rhodes, 11–16. New York: Dutton, 1971.

Birdwell, Cleo. *Amazons: An Intimate Memoir by the First Woman to Ever Play in the National Hockey League.* New York: Holt, 1980.

Birkby, Phyllis, ed. *Amazon Expedition: A Lesbian Feminist Anthology.* Washington, N.J.: Times Change, 1973.

Blackburn, Stuart H. *Singing of Birth and Death: Texts in Performance.* Philadelphia: University of Pennsylvania Press, 1988.

Blumner, H. *The Home Life of the Ancient Greeks.* New York, London: Cassell, 1893.

Bolen, Jean Shinoda. *Goddesses in Every Woman: A New Psychology of Women.* New York: Harper, 1984.

Bordo, Susan. "Anorexia Nervosa: Psychopathology as the Crystallization of Culture." In *Feminism and Foucault: Reflections on Resistance,* edited by Irene Diamond and Lee Quimby, 87–118. Boston: Northeastern University Press, 1988.

Bothner, Dietrich von. *Amazons in Greek Art.* Oxford: Clarendon, 1953.

Bourke, Angela. "More in Anger Than in Sorrow: Irish Women's Lament Poetry." In *Feminist Messages: Coding in Women's Folk Culture,* edited by Joan Newlon Radner, 160–182. Urbana and Chicago: University of Illinois Press, 1993.

Bradley, Marion Zimmer. *The Best of Marion Zimmer Bradley.* Edited by Martin H. Greenberg. Chicago: Academy, 1985a.

———. *Darkover Landfall.* New York: DAW, 1972.

———. *Free Amazons of Darkover: An Anthology.* New York: DAW, 1985b.

———. "Responsibilities and Temptations of Women Science Fiction Writers." In *Women Worldwalkers: New Dimensions of Science Fiction and Fantasy,* edited by Jane B. Weedman, 25–37. Lubbock: Texas Tech, 1985c.

———. *The Ruins of Isis.* Norfolk, Va.: Donning/Starblaze, 1978.

———. *The Shattered Chain.* New York: DAW, 1976.

———. "To Keep the Oath." In *The Best of Marion Zimmer Bradley,* edited by Martin H. Greenberg, 303–330. Chicago: Academy, 1985d.

———. *Two to Conquer.* New York: DAW, 1987.

Brentlinger, John. *The Best of What We Are: Reflections on the Nicaraguan Revolution.* Amherst: University of Massachusetts Press, 1995.

————. "Socialism and the Sacred." *Monthly Review* 44, no. 5 (1992): 27–41.

Brett, Guy. "Unofficial Versions." In *The Myth of Primivitism: Perspectives on Art,* edited by Susan Hiller, 113–136. New York: Routledge, 1991.

Bricker, Victoria R. *The Indian Christ, the Indian King: The Historical Substrate of Maya Myth and Ritual.* Austin: University of Texas Press, 1981.

Briffault, Robert. *The Mothers.* London: Allen, 1927.

Brown, Rita Mae. *Rubyfruit Jungle.* 1973. New York: Bantam, 1983.

————. "Violet Hill Elementary School," and "Fort Lauderdale High," from the novel *Rubyfruit Jungle. Amazon Quarterly* 1, no. 2 (February 1973): 5–16.

Burroughs, William. "The Cities of the Red Night." In *Cities of the Red Night,* 153–159. New York: Holt, 1982.

————. *Junkie: Confessions of an Unredeemed Drug Addict.* New York: Ace, 1953.

————. *Naked Lunch.* 1959. New York: Grove, 1992.

Burton, Richard F. *A Mission to Gelele, King of Dahomey.* London: Routledge, 1966.

Butler, Samuel. *The Authoress of the Odyssey.* 1891. Chicago: University of Chicago Press. 1967.

Cade, Toni, ed. *The Black Woman.* New York: Signet, 1970.

Calasso, Robert. *The Marriage of Cadmos and Harmony.* New York: Knopf, 1993.

Campbell, Joseph. *The Hero with a Thousand Faces.* 1949. Princeton: Princeton University Press, 1968.

————. *Occidental Mythology.* Vol. 3 of *The Masks of God.* New York: Viking, 1964.

————. *Primitive Mythology.* Vol. 1 of *The Masks of God.* New York: Viking, 1959.

Cantarella, Eve. *Pandora's Daughters: The Role and Status of Women in Greek and Roman Antiquity.* Baltimore: Johns Hopkins University Press, 1987.

Carpenter, Rhys. *Folk Tale, Fiction and Saga in the Homeric Epics.* Berkeley: University of California Press, 1962.

Carrasco, David. *Religions of Mesoamerica.* San Francisco: Harper, 1990.

Carvajal, Gaspar de. *The Discovery of the Amazon According to the Account of Gaspar de Carvajal and Other Documents.* [1542?] Edited by W. L. G. Joerg. Introduced by Jose Toriba Medina. Translated by Bertram T. Lee. New York: American Geographical Society, 1934.

Cassady, Carolyn. *Off the Road: My Years with Cassady, Kerouac and Ginsberg.* New York: Viking, 1991.

Castillo, Ana. *The Mixquiahuala Letters.* New York: Anchor, 1986.

Castillo, Francisco Fernandez del. *Tres conquistadores y pobladores de la Nueva España.* Vol. 12. Mexico City: Publicaciones del Archivo General de la Nación, 1927.

Cavin, Susan. "Lesbian Origins" (Ph.D. diss., Rutgers University, 1978).

————. *Lesbian Origins.* San Francisco: ISM, 1985.

Ceplain, Larry, ed. *Charlotte Perkins Gilman: A Nonfiction Reader.* New York: Columbia University Press, 1991.

Cervantes, Miguel de Saavedra. *The Life and Exploits of That Ingenious Gentleman Don Quixote de la Mancha.* 1605. Translated by Charles Jarvis. New York: Dodd, 1928.

Cevallos, Francisco Javier. "*Inventando el mundo desde el centro de realidad: Fray Gaspar de Carvajal y la aventura amazónica.*" *Atenea* 1–2 (June–December 1989): 61–70.

Charnas, Suzy McKee. *Motherlines.* New York: Berkeley, 1978.

Chaucer, Geoffrey. *The Canterbury Tales.* 1386–1399. New York: Penguin, 1951.

Chaves, Anna Caraveli. "Bridge between Worlds: The Greek Women's Lament as Communicative Event." *Journal of American Folklore* 93, no. 368 (1980): 129–157.

Christ, Carol P. "Spiritual Quest and Women's Experience." In *Womanspirit Rising: A Feminist Reader in Religion,* edited by Carol P. Christ and Judith Plaskow, 228–243. New York: Harper, 1979.

Cioffi, Kathleen. "Types of Feminist Fantasy and Science Fiction." In *Women Worldwalkers: New Dimensions of Science Fiction and Fantasy,* edited by Jane B. Weedman, 83–90. Lubbock: Texas Tech, 1985.

Cixous, Hélène. "The Laugh of the Medusa." In *Feminisms: An Anthology of Literary Theory and Criticism,* edited by Robyn R. Warhol and Diane Price Herndl, 334–349. New Brunswick: Rutgers University Press, 1991.

Clark, Gracia. "The Beguines." *Quest* l, no. 4 (Spring 1975): 72–80.

Cleaver, Eldridge. *Soul on Ice.* New York: Dell, 1970.

Clifford, James. "Diasporas: Transcultural Practices in the Late Twentieth Century." The University of Vermont Department of English 1994 Buckham Lecture. University of Vermont, Burlington, March 3, 1994.

Clift, Eleanor, and Bob Cohn. "Seven Days: *Newsweek* Goes Behind the Scenes at the White House to Chronicle What President Clinton Calls 'Hell Week.'" *Newsweek* (July 12, 1993): 19–29.

Closs, Michael P. "The Dynastic History of Naranjo: The Late Period." In *Word and Image in Maya Culture: Explorations in Language, Writing and Representation,* edited by William F. Hanks and Don S. Rice, 244–254. Salt Lake City: University of Utah Press, 1989.

Coe, Michael D. *Breaking the Maya Code.* New York: Thames and Hudson, 1992.

———. *Lord of the Underworld: Masterpieces of Classic Maya Ceramics.* Princeton: Princeton University Press, 1978.

Coffin, Tristram Potter. *The Female Hero in Folklore and Legend.* New York: Pocket, 1975.

Columbus, Christopher. *Journal of the First Voyage to America.* 1825. New York: Albert and Charles Boni, 1924.

Cook, Erwin. The Odyssey *in Athens: Myths of Cultural Origins.* Ithaca: Cornell University Press, 1995.

Cordry, Donald. *Mexican Masks.* Austin: University of Texas Press, 1980.

Corliss, Richard. "Hurricane Camille Blows Again." *Time* (December 12, 1994): 90.

Corso, Gregory. *Elegiac Feelings American.* New York: New Directions, 1961.

Crawford, Vicki, Jacqueline Anne Rouse, and Barbara Woods, eds. *Women in the Civil Rights Movement: Trailblazers and Torch Bearers.* 1941–1965. Bloomington: Indiana University Press, 1993.

Cross, Tom Peete. *Motif-Index of Early Irish Literature.* Bloomington: Indiana University Press, 1952.

Culbert, T. Patrick, ed. *The Classic Maya Collapse.* Albuquerque: University of New Mexico Press, 1973.

Cunningham, Rima Star. *Water Birth and Dolphins.* N.p.: Cunningham/Copia Publications, n.d.

Curtis, Edmund. *A History of Ireland.* New York: Routledge, 1990.

Daly, Mary. *Beyond God the Father: Toward a Philosophy of Women's Liberation.* Boston: Beacon, 1985.

————. *Gyn/Ecology: The Metaethics of Radical Feminism.* Boston: Beacon, 1990.

Danforth, Loring M., and Alexander Tsiaras. *The Death Rituals of Rural Greece.* Princeton: Princeton University Press, 1982.

d'Anghiera, Pietro Martire. *Decades of the New Worlde, or West India.* 1555. In *The First Three English Books on America.* Translated by Richard Eden. Edited by Edward Arber. New York: Kraus, 1971.

Davis, Elizabeth Gould. *The First Sex.* Baltimore: Penguin, 1971.

Davis-Floyd, Robbi. *Birth as an American Rite of Passage.* Berkeley: University of California Press, 1992.

de Certeau, Michel. *Heterologies: Discourse on the Other.* Minneapolis: University of Minnesota Press, 1986.

Delany, Samuel R. *The Motion of Light in Water: Sex and Science Fiction Writing in the East Village 1957–1965.* New York: Morrow, 1988.

————. *Tales of Neveryon.* New York: Bantam, 1979.

Descola, Jean. *A History of Spain.* New York: Knopf, 1963.

Diamond, Stanley. *In Search of the Primitive: A Critique of Civilization.* New Brunswick: Transaction, 1987.

DiMarco, Vincent. "The Amazons and the End of the World." In *Discovering New Worlds: Essays on Medieval Exploration and Imagination,* edited by Scott D. Westrem, 69–90. New York: Garland, 1991.

Diner, Helene. *Mothers and Amazons: The First Feminine History of Culture.* 1931. New York: Julian, 1965.

Dinnerstein, Dorothy. *The Mermaid and the Minatour: Sexual Arrangements and Human Malaise.* New York: Harper, 1977.

Doherty, Lillian E. *Siren Songs: Gender, Audiences and Narrators in the Odyssey.* Ann Arbor: University of Michigan Press, 1995.

Doll, Caroline. *Margaret and Her Friends, or Ten Conversations with Margaret Fuller upon the Mythology of the Greeks and Its Expansion into Art.* 1895. New York: Arno, 1972.

Dowden, Ken. *The Uses of Greek Mythology.* New York: Routledge, 1992.

Downing, Christine. *The Goddess: Mythological Images of the Feminine.* New York: Crossroad, 1981.

DuBois, Page. *Centaurs and Amazons: Women and the Pre-History of the Great Chain of Being.* Ann Arbor: University of Michigan Press, 1982.

Dudley, Edward, and Maximillian E. Novak, eds. *The Wild Man Within: An Image in Western Thought from the Renaissance to Romanticism.* Pittsburgh: University of Pittsburgh Press, 1972.

D'Urfey, Thomas. *A Common-Wealth of Women.* London, 1686.

Echols, Alice. *Daring to Be Bad: Radical Feminism in America 1967–75.* Minneapolis: University of Minnesota Press, 1989.

Edwards, Lee R. *Psyche as Hero: Female Heroism and Fictional Form*. Middletown, Conn.: Wesleyan University Press, 1984.

Edwards, Lee R., and Arlyn Diamond, eds. *American Voices, American Women*. New York: Avon, 1973.

Engels, Frederick. *The Origin of the Family, Private Property and the State*. 1884. Edited by Eleanor Leacock. New York: International, 1972.

Engle, Bernice Schultz. "The Amazons in Ancient Greece." *Psychoanalytic Quarterly* 11, no. 7 (1942): 512–544.

Enloe, Cynthia. *Bananas, Beaches and Bases: Making Feminist Sense of International Politics*. Berkeley: University of California Press, 1990.

Estallita, et al. *La Ovogenesis: Wimmin's Creation*. June 1986. Drukijole Brand Weervnovm, Prinsengacht 237 Amsterdam.

Estes, Clarissa Pinkola. *Women Who Run with the Wolves: Myths and Stories of the Wild Woman Archetype*. New York: Ballantine, 1992.

Evans, Sara. *Personal Politics: The Roots of Women's Liberation in the Civil Rights Movement and the New Left*. New York: Knopf, 1979.

Evertz, Kathy Jo. "Selling the Lady: Commercialization and the 1986 Statue of Liberty Centennial" (Ph.D. diss., University of Minnesota, 1992).

Faderman, Lillian. "The Development of Lesbian Literature." Unpublished talk, Gay, Lesbian, and Bisexual Faculty Seminars, University of Massachusetts, Amherst, October 6, 1993.

Fellini, Federico. *City of Women*. With screenwriters Bernardino Zapponi and Brunello Rondi. Music directed by Glan Franco Plenizio. With Marcello Mastroianni. Gaumont SA, Italy: Opera Film Produzione, 1980.

Ferguson, Ann. "Herland or Our Land: Feminist Utopias as Models for Social Change." Unpublished paper, Department of Philosophy, University of Massachusetts, Amherst, n.d.

Ferlinghetti, Lawrence. *Mexico Night: Travel Journal*. New York: New Directions, 1970.

Finley, M. I. *The World of Odysseus*. New York: Viking, 1954.

Finnegan, Ruth. *Literacy and Orality: Studies in the Technology of Communication*. New York: Basil Blackwell, 1988.

Firth, Raymond. *Symbols: Public and Private*. Ithaca: Cornell University Press, 1973.

Fisher, Evelyn. *Women's Creation: Sex, Evolution and the Shape of Society*. Garden City, N.Y.: Anchor, 1979.

Fitting, Peter. "Utopian Effect/Utopian Pleasure." In *Utopian Studies IV*, edited by Lise Leibacher and Nicholas Smith, 90–96. Lanham, Md.: University Press of America, 1991.

Fitzgerald, Robert, trans. *The Iliad*. By Homer. Garden City, N.Y.: Doubleday, 1979.

Fitzsimons, Charles B., and Mark Rodgers, prod. *The Return of Wonder Woman*. Written by Stephen Kandel, Alan Brennert, and Anne Collins, with Lynda Carter. New York: CBS, 1977–1979.

Fleming, Cynthia Griggs. *Soon We Will Not Cry: The Liberation of Ruby Doris Smith Robinson*. Oxford: Rowman, 1998.

Folan, William J., Ellen R. Kintz, and Laraine A. Fletcher, eds. *Coba: A Classic Maya Metropolis*. New York: Academic Press, 1983.

Foley, Helene P. "Reverse Similes and Sex Roles in the *Odyssey*." In *Women in the*

Ancient World: The Arethusa Papers, edited by J. Peradotto and J. P. Sullivan, 59–78. Albany: SUNY Press, 1987.

Foley, John M. *Traditional Oral Epic:* The Odyssey, Beowulf and the Serbo-Croatian Return Song. Berkeley: University of California Press, 1990.

Fonow, Mary Margaret, and Judith A. Cook. eds. *Beyond Methodology: Feminist Scholarship as Lived Research.* Bloomington: Indiana University Press, 1991.

Fox, Jennifer. "The Creator Gods: Romantic Nationalism and the En-genderment of Women in Folklore." In *Feminist Theory and the Study of Folklore,* edited by Susan Tower Hollis, Linda Pershing, and M. Jane Young, 29–40. Urbana: University of Illinois Press, 1993.

Franz, Marie-Louise von. *The Feminine in Fairy Tales.* Boston: Shambala, 1993.

Freeman, Jo. *The Politics of Women's Liberation: A Case Study of an Emerging Social Movement and Its Relation to the Policy Process.* New York: McKay, 1975.

———. *Social Movements of the Sixties and Seventies.* New York: Longman, 1983.

Freeman, Mary Wilkins. "The Revolt of 'Mother.'" In *American Voices, American Women,* edited by Lee R. Edwards and Arlyn Diamond, 165–180. New York: Avon, 1973.

Freidel, David A. "The Ix Chel Shrine and Other Temples of Talking Idols." *A Study of Changing Pre-Colombian Commercial Systems: The 1972–1973 Seasons at Cozumel, Mexico.* Edited by Jeremy A. Sabloff and William L. Rathje. Monographs of the Peabody Museum, no. 3, Harvard University, 1975. 107–113.

Freidel, David A., and Jeremy A. Sabloff. *Cozumel: Late Maya Settlement Patterns.* Orlando, Fla.: Academic Press, 1984.

Freidel, David A., Linda Schele, and Jan Parker. *Maya Cosmos.* New York: Morrow, 1993.

Friedan, Betty. *The Feminine Mystique.* New York: Norton, 1963.

Friedman, Susan Stanford. "Creativity and the Childbirth Metaphor: Gender Difference in Literary Discourse." In *Feminisms: An Anthology of Literary Theory and Criticism,* edited by Robyn R. Warhol and Diane Price Herndl, 371–396. New Brunswick: Rutgers University Press, 1991.

Friedrich, Paul. *The Meaning of Aphrodite.* Chicago: University of Chicago Press, 1978.

Frye, Ellen. *Amazon Story Bones.* Minneapolis: Spinsters, 1994.

Frye, Northrop. *Anatomy of Criticism.* Princeton: Princeton University Press, 1957.

Fuentes, Carlos. *The Buried Mirror: Reflections on Spain and the New World.* Boston: Houghton, 1992.

Gantz, Timothy. *Early Greek Myth: A Guide to Literary and Artistic Sources.* Baltimore: Johns Hopkins University Press, 1993.

Gearhart, Sally. "Future Visions, Today's Politics: Feminist Utopias in Review." In *Women in Search of Utopia: Mavericks and Myth Makers,* edited Ruby Rohrlich and Elaine Hoffman Baruch, 293–309. New York: Schocken, 1984.

———. *The Wanderground: Stories of the Hill Women.* Watertown: Persephone, 1979.

Gernet, Louis. *The Anthropology of Ancient Greece.* Baltimore: Johns Hopkins University Press, 1981.

Gillmore, Inez Haynes. *Angel Island.* New York: Holt, 1914.

————. *Angels and Amazons: A Hundred Years of American Women.* Garden City, N.Y.: Doubleday, 1933.

————. *The Story of the Woman's Party.* New York: Harcourt, 1921.

Gilman, Charlotte Perkins. *Herland.* 1915. New York: Pantheon, 1979.

————. "With Her in Ourland." 1916. Reprinted in *With Her in Ourland: A Sequel to Herland,* edited by Mary Jo Deegan and Michael R. Hill. Westport, Conn: Praeger, 1997.

————. *Women and Economics: A Study of the Economic Relations between Men and Women as a Factor in Social Evolution.* 1898. New York: Harper, 1966.

Gimbutas, Marija. *The Goddesses and Gods of Old Europe: 6500–3500 BC Myths and Cult Images.* Berkeley: University of California Press, 1982.

————. *The Language of the Goddess: Unearthing the Hidden Symbols of Western Civilization.* San Francisco: HarperCollins, 1991.

Ginsberg, Allen. *Collected Poems, 1947–1980.* New York: Harper, 1984.

Glaspell, Susan Keating. "A Jury of Her Peers." In *American Voices, American Women,* edited by Lee R. Edwards and Arlyn Diamond, 360–381. New York: Avon, 1973.

Gonzalez, Ray, ed. *Without Discovery: A Native Response to Columbus.* Seattle: Broken Moon, 1992.

Gorer, Geoffrey. *The American People: A Study in National Character.* 1948. New York: Norton, 1964.

Graburn, Nelson. *Ethnic and Tourist Arts: Cultural Expressions from the Fourth World.* Berkeley: University of California Press, 1976.

Grae, Camerin. *Edgewise.* Tallahassee, Fla.: Naiad, 1989.

Graham, David Crockett. *Songs and Stories of the Chuan Miao.* Smithsonian Miscellaneous Publications cxxiii no. 11. Washington, D.C.: 1954.

Grahn, Judy. *Another Mother Tongue: Gay Words, Gay Worlds.* Boston: Beacon, 1984.

Graubert, Karen. "Imagining the Wicked Poor: Poverty, Gender and Witchcraft Persecutions." Paper presented at Marxism and Its Others: Antagonisms, Resolutions, Reversals, University of Massachusetts, Amherst, October 29, 1993.

Graves, Robert. *The Greek Myths.* Vol. 1. 1955. Baltimore: Penguin, 1975.

Griffin, Susan. *Woman and Nature: The Roaring Inside Her.* San Francisco: HarperCollins, 1979.

Grimara-Leduc, Micheline. "The Mind-Drifting Islands." In *For Lesbians Only: A Separatist Anthology,* edited by Sarah Lucia Hoagland and Julia Penelope, 489–500. London: Onlywomen, 1988.

Grote, George. *Mythology of the Greeks.* New York: Allison, n.d.

Haile, Edward W., trans. *Oresteia of Aeschylus: Agamemnon, The Libation Bearers, The Eumenides Fragments.* Lanham, Md.: University Press of America, 1994.

Hanks, William F., and Don S. Rice, eds. *Word and Image in Maya Culture: Explorations in Language, Writing and Representation.* Salt Lake City: University of Utah Press, 1989.

Haraway, Donna. *Simians, Cyborgs and Women: The Reinvention of Nature.* New York: Routledge, 1991.

Harding, M. Esther. *The Way of All Women: A Psychological Interpretation.* London: Longman, 1934.

Harrison, Jane Ellen. *Ancient Art and Ritual.* New York: Holt, 1913.

———. *Epilegomena to the Study of Greek Religion, and Themis: A Study of the Social Origins of the Greeks.* 1903, 1912. New Hyde Park, New York: University Books, 1962.

Hartland, Edwin Sydney. *The Science of Fairy Tales: An Inquiry into Fairy Mythology.* New York: Scribner, 1891.

Hartwell, David. *Age of Wonder: Exploring the World of Science Fiction.* Hastings on Hudson, N.Y.: Ultramarine, 1984.

Hennig, R. "Über die voraussichtlich völkerkundlichen Grundlagen der Amazonen-Sagen und deren Verbreitung." *Zeits für Ethnologie* 72 (1940): Trans. V. DiMarco and E. Brewer. n.p.

Hercules and the Amazon Women. Renaissance Pictures. Directed by Bill L. Norton. Universal City, Calif.: MCA Home Video, 1997.

Herodotus. *History of Herodotus.* Translated by George Rawlinson. Vols. 1 and 2. London, 1880.

Herskovits, Melville. *Cultural Anthropology.* New York: Knopf, 1955.

Hess, K., Jean Langford, and Kathy Ross. "Comparative Separatism." In *For Lesbians Only: A Separatist Anthology,* edited by Sarah Lucia Hoagland and Julia Penelope, 125–132. London: Onlywomen, 1988.

Hill, Mary A. *Charlotte Perkins Gilman: The Making of a Radical Feminist 1860–1896.* Philadelphia: Temple University Press, 1980.

Hiller, Susan, ed. *The Myth of Primivitism: Perspectives on Art.* New York: Routledge, 1991.

Hoagland, Sarah Lucia. *Lesbian Ethics: Toward New Value.* Palo Alto, Calif.: Institute of Lesbian Studies, 1988.

Hoagland, Sarah Lucia, and Julia Penelope, eds. *For Lesbians Only: A Separatist Anthology.* London: Onlywomen, 1988.

Hoch-Smith, Judith, and Anita Spring, eds. *Women in Ritual and Symbolic Roles.* New York: Plenum, 1978.

Hofling, Charles A. "The Morphosyntactic Basis of Discourse Structure in Glyphic Text in the Dresden Codex." In *Word and Image in Maya Culture: Explorations in Language, Writing and Representation,* edited by William F. Hanks and Don S. Rice, 51–72. Salt Lake City: University of Utah Press, 1989.

Hole, Judith, and Ellen Levine, eds. *Rebirth of Feminism.* New York: Quadrangle, 1971.

Holliday, Laurel. *The Violent Sex: Male Psychobiology and the Evolution of Consciousness.* Guerneville, Calif.: Bluestockings, 1978.

Hollis, Susan Tower, Linda Pershing, and M. Jane Young, eds. *Feminist Theory and the Study of Folklore.* Urbana: University of Illinois Press, 1993.

Holmes, John Clellon. *Go.* 1952. New York: Thunder's Mouth, 1988.

———. "This Is the Beat Generation." *New York Times Magazine* (November 16, 1952). Reprinted in *Kerouac and Friends: A Beat Generation Album,* edited by Fred W. McDarrah, 21–27. New York: Morrow, 1985.

Homerus. *The Complete Works of Homer.* Translated by Andrew Lang, Walter Leaf, Ernest Myers, S. H. Butcher, and Andrew Long. Edited by Bennett A. Cerf and Donald Klopfer. New York: Modern Library, 1947.

hooks, bell. *Ain't I a Woman: Black Women and Feminism.* Boston: South End, 1981.

Hornum, Barbara. "Wife/Mother, Sorceress/Keeper, Amazon/Renunciate: Status Ambivalence and Conflicting Roles on Planet Darkover." In *Women Worldwalkers: New Dimensions of Science Fiction and Fantasy,* edited by Jane B. Weedman, 153–163. Lubbock: Texas Tech, 1985.

Hossain, Rokeya Sakhawait. *Sultana's Dream and Selections from the Secluded Ones.* 1905. New York: Feminist Press, 1988.

Hulme, Peter. *Colonial Encounters of Europe and the Native Caribbean 1492–1797.* New York: Routledge, 1992.

Humphreys, Sarah. *Anthropology and the Greeks.* Boston: Routledge, 1983.

Huxley, Aldous. *Island.* New York: Harper, 1962.

"Instrucción que dió el capitán Diego Velazquez, en la isla Fernandina, en 23 de octubre de 1518 al capitán Hernando Cortés . . ." *Colección de documentos ineditos para la historia de España.* Edited by Martin Fernandez Navarrete, Miguel Salva, and Pedro Sainz de Baranda. Madrid: Imprenta de la Viuda de Calero, 1842. Vol. 1. Vaduz: Kraus, 1964. 385–409.

Irigaray, Luce. "This Sex Which is Not One." In *Feminisms: An Anthology of Literary Theory and Criticism,* edited by Robyn R. Warhol and Diane Price Herndl, 350–356. New Brunswick: Rutgers University Press, 1991.

Irving, John. *The World According to Garp: A Novel.* New York: Dutton, 1978.

Islander: Tourist Information of Isla Mujeres. Isla Mujeres: COPROTUR, December 1992.

Jaggar, Alison. *Feminist Politics and Human Nature.* Totowa, N.J.: Rowman, 1983.

James, Henry. *The Portrait of a Lady.* 1882. Harmondsworth: Penguin, 1986.

Jane, Cecil. ed. and trans. *The Voyages of Christopher Columbus.* 1930. New York: DaCapo, 1970.

Jayaker, Pupul. *The Earth Mother: Legends, Ritual and Goddesses of India.* San Francisco: Harper, 1990.

Jobes, Gertrude. *Dictionary of Mythology, Folklore and Symbols, Part I.* New York: Scarecrow, 1962.

Johnson, Joyce. *Minor Characters.* Boston: Houghton, 1983.

Johnston, Jill. *Lesbian Nation: The Feminist Solution.* New York: Simon, 1974.

———. "Return of the Amazon Mother." In *Amazon Expedition: A Lesbian Feminist Anthology,* edited by Phyllis Birkby, 66–76. Washington, N.J.: Times Change, 1973.

Jones, Alice Ilgenfritz, and Ella Marchant. *Unveiling a Parallel: A Romance.* 1893. Syracuse: Syracuse University Press, 1991.

Jones, Hettie. *How I Became Hettie Jones.* New York: Penguin, 1991.

Jordan, Bridgitte. *Birth in Four Cultures: A Cross Cultural Investigation of Childbirth in Yucatán, Holland, Sweden and the United States.* Montreal and London: Eden Press, 1983.

Jordan, Rosan A., and Susan J. Kalcik, eds. *Women's Folklore, Women's Culture.* Vol. 8. Edited by Martha Weigle. Publications of the American Folklore Society New Series. Philadelphia: University of Pennsylvania Press, 1985.

Joyce, Rosemary. "Images of Gender and Labor Organization in Classic Maya Society." *Exploring Gender through Archaeology.* Edited by C. Claassen. Madison, Wis.: Prehistory Monographs in World Archaeology 11 (1992): 63–69.

Jrimara-Leduc, Michelle. "The Mind-Drifting Islands." In *For Lesbians Only: A*

Separatist Anthology, edited by Sarah Lucia Hoagland and Julia Penelope, 489–500. London: Onlywomen, 1988.

Juegos Florales. Isla Mujeres: Cultural Center.

Kahn, Robbie Pfeufer. *Bearing Meaning: The Language of Birth.* Champaign: University of Illinois Press, 1995.

———. "Mother's Milk: The 'Moment of Nurture' Revisited." *Resources for Feminist Research* 18, no. 3 (1989): 29–36.

Kanter, Emmanuel. *The Amazons: A Marxian Study.* Chicago: Kerr, 1926.

Kato, Tsuyoski. *Matriliny and Migration: Evolving Minangkabau Traditions in Indonesia.* Ithaca: Cornell University Press, 1981.

Keil, Charles. *Urban Blues.* 1966. 2d ed. Chicago: University of Chicago Press, 1968.

Kelley, Mary, ed. *The Portable Margaret Fuller.* New York: Penguin, 1994.

Kerouac, Jack. *Book of Dreams.* San Francisco: City Lights, 1961.

———. *The Dharma Bums.* New York: Viking, 1958.

———. *Lonesome Traveller: A Novel.* 1960. New York: Grove, 1988.

———. *Mexico City Blues: (Two Hundred Forty Two Choruses).* 1959. New York: Grove, 1987.

———. *On the Road.* 1957. New York: Penguin, 1979.

———. *Satori in Paris.* New York: Grove, 1966.

Keuls, Eva C. *The Reign of the Phallus.* Berkeley: University of California Press, 1985.

Kimball, Gayle, ed. *Women's Culture: The Women's Renaissance of the Seventies.* Metuchen, N.J.: Scarecrow, 1981.

Kingston, Maxine Hong. *Chinamen.* New York: Vintage, 1977.

Kintz, Allen R. "Household Composition: An Analysis of the Composition of Residential Compounds of Coba." In *Coba: A Classic Maya Metropolis,* edited by William J. Folan, Ellen R. Kintz, and Laraine A. Fletcher, 133–148. New York: Academic Press, 1983.

Kirk, G. S. *Homer and the Oral Tradition.* Cambridge: Cambridge University Press, 1976.

Kisner, Arlene, Lois Har, and Ellen Shumsky. "The Vision and Persecution of Aurora Phelps." In *Amazon Expedition: A Lesbian Feminist Anthology,* edited by Phyllis Birkby, 55–65. Washington, N.J.: Times Change, 1973.

Kitto, H. D. F. *The Greeks.* 1951. London: Penguin, 1987.

Kleinbaum, Abbey. *The War against the Amazons.* New York: McGraw, 1983.

Knight, Richard Payne. *The Symbolical Language of Ancient Art and Mythology.* New York: Bouton, 1876.

Kodish, Debora. "Absent Gender, Silent Encounter." In *Feminist Theory and the Study of Folklore,* edited by Susan Tower Hollis, Linda Pershing, and M. Jane Young, 41–50. Urbana: University of Illinois Press, 1993.

Koedt, Ann, Ellen Levine, and Anita Rapone, eds. *Radical Feminism.* New York: Quadrangle, 1973.

Kramarae, Cheris, and Paula A. Treichler. *A Feminist Dictionary.* Boston: Pandora, 1985.

Kuhn, Thomas. *Structure of Scientific Revolutions.* Chicago: University of Chicago Press, 1970.

Kurtz, Donna C., and John Boardman. *Greek Burial Customs.* Ithaca: Cornell University Press, 1971.

La Botz, Dan. *Chiapas and Beyond: Mexico's Crisis and the Fight for Democracy.* A Solidarity Pamphlet. May l, 1994.

———. *Democracy in Mexico: Peasant Rebellion and Political Reform.* Boston: South End, 1995.

Lafaye, Jacques. *Quetzal-cóatl and Guadalupe: The Formation of Mexican National Consciousness 1531–1813.* Chicago: University of Chicago Press, 1974.

Landa, Fray Diego de. *Relación de las cosas de Yucatán* [1560?], edited and translated by A. M. Tozzer. Mexico City: Ed. Porrua S.A., 1959.

Lane, M. E. Bradley. *Mizora: A Prophecy. A Manuscript Found Among the Private Papers of the Princess Vera.* 1889. Boston: Gregg, 1975.

Lattimore, Richmond, trans. *The Iliad of Homer.* Chicago: University of Chicago Press, 1951.

———. *Story Patterns in Greek Tragedy.* Ann Arbor: University of Michigan Press, 1969.

Lawrence, D. H. *Mornings in Mexico.* 1927. Salt Lake City: Smith, 1982.

———. *The Plumed Serpent.* 1926. New York: Penguin, 1985.

———. *Sons and Lovers.* 1913. New York: Random, 1922.

Lawrence, Ruth A. *Breastfeeding: A Guide for the Medical Profession.* St. Louis: Mosby, 1985.

Lawson, John C. *Modern Greek Folklore and Ancient Greek Religion: A Study in Survivals.* 1910. New York: University Books, 1964.

Lawson, Kristan. *Goddess Sites: Europe.* San Francisco: Harper, 1991.

Lax, Roger, and Frederick Smith, eds. *The Great Song Thesaurus.* New York: Oxford University Press, 1989.

Leakey, Richard, and Roger Lewin. *Origins Reconsidered: In Search of What Makes Us Human.* New York: Doubleday, 1992.

Lederer, Wolfgang. *The Fear of Women.* New York: Stratton, 1968.

Lefanu, Sarah. *Feminism and Science Fiction.* Bloomington: Indiana University Press, 1989.

Lefkowitz, Mary. *Women in Greek Myth.* Baltimore: Johns Hopkins University Press, 1986.

Lefkowitz, Mary, and Maureen B. Fant. *Women's Life in Greece and Rome: A Source Book in Translation.* 1982. Baltimore: Johns Hopkins University Press, 1992.

Le Guin, Ursula K. Introduction to *Angel Island: A Novel,* by Inez Haynes Gillmore. New York: New American Library, 1988. vii–xii.

Leonard, Irving. *Books of the Brave: Being an Account of Books in the Spanish Conquest and Settlement of the Sixteenth Century New World.* New York: Gordian, 1964.

Lerner, Gerda. *The Creation of Feminist Consciousness from the Middle Ages to 1870.* New York: Oxford University Press, 1993.

———. *The Creation of Patriarchy.* New York: Oxford University Press, 1986.

Lessa, William A., and Evon Vogt, eds. *A Reader in Comparative Religion: An Anthropological Approach.* New York: Harper, 1965.

Lévi-Strauss, Claude. *The Savage Mind.* Chicago: University of Chicago Press, 1966.

Licht, Hans. *Sexual Life in Ancient Greece*. New York: Barnes and Noble, 1963.

Liddell, Henry George, and Robert Scott. *A Greek-English Lexicon*. 1843. London: Oxford at the Clarendon Press, 1968.

Little, William Thomas. Introduction to *Sergas de Esplandian: The Labors of the Very Brave Knight Esplandian,* by Rodríguez de Montalvo. 1510. Translated by William Thomas Little. Binghamton: Center for Medieval and Early Renaissance Studies, State University of New York at Binghamton, 1992. 1–62.

Lloyd, Jill. "Emile Nolde's 'ethnographic' Still Lifes: Primitivism, Tradition and Modernity." In *The Myth of Primivitism: Perspectives on Art,* edited by Susan Hiller, 90–112. New York: Routledge, 1991.

Lopez de Cogolludo, Diego. *Historia de la Yucatán*. Prologue by J. Ignacio Rubio Mane. 1688. Mexico City: Editorial Academia Literatura, 1957.

López de Gómora, Francisco. *Cortés: The Life of the Conqueror by His Secretary*. 1552. Translated and edited by Lesley Byrd Simpson. Berkeley: University of California Press, 1964.

Lord, Albert B. *The Singer of Tales*. Cambridge, Mass.: Harvard University Press, 1964.

Lorde, Audre. *The Black Unicorn*. New York: Norton, 1978.

Love, Barbara, and Elizabeth Shanklin. "The Answer Is Matriarchy." In *Our Right to Love: A Lesbian Resource Book Produced in Cooperation with Women of the National Gay Task Force,* edited by Ginny Vida, 183–186. Englewood Cliffs, N.J.: Prentice-Hall, 1978.

Lurker, Manfred. *The Dictionary of Gods and Goddesses, Devils and Demons*. London: Routledge, 1988.

Luxton, Richard, with Pablo Balam. *The Mystery of the Maya Hieroglyphs*. San Francisco: Harper, 1981.

Machado, Manual A., Jr. *Centaur of the North: Francisco Villa, the Mexican Revolution and Northern Mexico*. Austin, Tex.: Eakin, 1988.

Mackay, Kathryn. "Notes on Maya Midwivery." In *Chan Kom: A Maya Village,* edited by Robert Redfield and Alfonso Villa Rojas, 357–362. Washington, D.C.: Carnegie Institute, 1934.

Maeckelberghe, Els. "'Mary': Maternal Friend of Virgin Mother?" *Motherhood: Experience, Institution, Theology*. Edited by Ann Carr and Elisabeth Schlussler Fiorenza. *Concilium* 206(1989): 120–127.

Maher, Vanessa. "Breast-Feeding in Cross-cultural Perspective." In *The Anthropology of Breastfeeding: Natural Law or Social Construct,* edited by Vanessa Maher, 1–36. Oxford and Providence: Berg, 1992.

Malachi, Zvi. *The Loving Knight: The Romance: Amadis de Gaula and Its Hebrew Adaptation*. Petah Tikva: Haberman Institute for Library Research, 1982.

Malinowski, Bronislaw. *Sex and Repression in Savage Society*. London: Routledge, 1927.

———. *The Sexual Life of Savages*. New York: Harcourt, 1929.

Mallan, Chicki. *Yucatán Peninsula Handbook*. Chico, Calif.: Moon, 1986.

Mandeville, Sir John. *The Travels of Sir John Mandeville* [1240, 1356, 1481?]. New York: Braziller, 1983.

Marchi, Dudley M. "Montaigne and the New World: The Cannibalism of Cultural Production." *Modern Language Studies* 23, no. 4 (1993): 35–54.

Markale, Jean. *Women of the Celts.* 1972. Rochester, Vt.: Inner Traditions International, 1986.

Martinband, James H. *Concise Dictionary of Greek Literature.* New York: Philosophical Library, 1962.

Matthews, Tracy. "No One Ever Ask, What a Man's Place in the Revolution Is: Gender and the Politics of the Black Panther Party, 1966–1971." In *The Black Panther Party (Reconsidered),* edited by Charles E. Jones, 267–304. Baltimore: Black Classics Press, 1998.

Maudslay, Alfred P., trans. *True History of the Conquest of Mexico,* by Bernard Diaz del Castillo. 1568. New York: McBride, 1927.

McKeveety, Vincent, dir. *Wonder Woman.* Written by John D. F. Black, with Cathy Lee Crosby. New York: ABC, 1974.

McLuhan, Marshall. *Gutenberg Galaxy: The Making of Typographic Man.* Toronto: University of Toronto Press, 1962.

Medina, Jose Toribo. *The Discovery of the Amazon, According to the Account of Friar Gaspar de Carvajal and Other Documents.* Translated by Bertram Lee. New York: American Geographical Society, 1934.

Men, Hunbatz. *Secrets of Maya Science-Religion.* Translated by Diana Gubiseth Ayala and James Jennings Dunlap II. Santa Fe: Bear, 1990.

Mies, Maria. *Patriarchy and Accumulation on a World Scale: Women in the International Division of Labor.* London: Zed, 1986.

Millett, Kate. *Sexual Politics.* New York: Avon, 1971.

Miner, Karl. "The Wild Man through the Looking Glass." In *The Wild Man Within: An Image in Western Thought from the Renaissance to Romanticism,* edited by Edward Dudley, and Maximillian E. Novak, 87–114. Pittsburgh: University of Pittsburgh Press, 1972.

Mitchell, Juliet. *Women's Estate.* New York: Pantheon, 1972.

Monaghan, Patricia, ed. *The Book of Goddesses and Heroines.* New York: Dutton, 1981.

More, Thomas. *Utopia.* 1516. Mineola, N.Y.: Dover, 1997.

Moynihan, Daniel P. *The Negro Family: The Case for National Action.* 1965. Westport, Conn.: Greenwood, 1981.

Mulcahy, Joanne B. "How They Knew: Women's Talk about Healing on Kodiak Island, Alaska." In *Feminist Messages: Coding in Women's Folk Culture,* edited by Joan Newlon Radner, 183–202. Urbana and Chicago: University of Illinois Press, 1993.

Murphy, Yolanda, and Robert Murphy. *Women of the Forest.* New York: Columbia University Press, 1974.

Murray, Gilbert. *Five Stages of Greek Religion.* Garden City, N.Y.: Doubleday, 1955.

Nagy, Gregory. *Pindar's Homer: The Lyric Posession of an Epic Past.* Baltimore: Johns Hopkins University Press, 1990.

———. *Poetry as Performance: Homer and Beyond.* New York: Cambridge University Press, 1996.

Nash, June. *In the Eyes of the Ancestors: Belief and Behavior in a Maya Community.* New Haven: Yale University Press, 1970.

Nash, June, et al., eds. *Ideology and Social Change in Latin America.* London: Gordon and Breach, 1977.

Radisich, Paula Rea. "Evolution and Salvation. The Iconic Origins of Drvillef's Monstrous Combatants of the Night." In *Fights of Fancy: Armed Conflict in Science Fiction and Fantasy,* edited by George Slusser and Eric Rabkin, 103–113. Athens: University of Georgia Press, 1991.

Radner, Joan Newlon, ed. *Feminist Messages: Coding in Women's Folk Culture.* Urbana and Chicago: University of Illinois Press, 1993.

Raleigh, Sir Walter. *History of the World.* 1614. New York: Macmillan, 1971.

Rawlinson, George. *History of Herodotus.* Vols. 1 and 2. London: 1880.

Raymond, Janice G. *A Passion for Friends: Toward a Philosophy of Female Affection.* Boston: Beacon, 1986.

Real, Carlos Alonso del. *Realidad y Leyenda de las Amazonas.* Madrid: Colección Austral, Espasa-Calpe, S.A., 1967.

Reck, Michael, trans. *Homer: The Iliad.* New York: Harper, 1994.

Redfield, Robert. *A Village That Chose Progress: Chan Kom Revisited.* Chicago: University of Chicago Press, 1950.

Redfield, Robert, and Alfonso Villa Rojas. *Chan Kom: A Maya Village.* Washington, D.C.: Carnegie Institute, 1934.

Redstockings of the Women's Liberation Movement. *Feminist Revolution,* edited by Kathie Sarachild. New York: Random, 1978.

Reed, Alma. *The Ancient Past of Mexico.* Crown, N.Y.: 1966.

Reichel-Dolmatoff, Gerardo. *Amazonian Cosmos: The Sexual and Religious Symbolism of the Tukano Indians.* Chicago: University of Chicago Press, 1971.

Reinharz, Shulamit. *Social Research Methods: Feminist Perspectives.* Pergamon: Athena, 1993.

Reynolds, Dwight. "The Interplay of Genres in Oral Epic Performance: Differentially Marked Discourse in Northern Egyptian Tradition." In *The Ballad and Oral Literature,* edited by Joseph Harris, 292–317. Cambridge, Mass.: Harvard University Press, 1991.

Rhys, Jean. *After Leaving Mr. MacKenzie.* New York: Harper, 1931.

Rich, Adrienne. "Compulsory Heterosexuality and Lesbian Existence." In *The Lesbian and Gay Studies Reader,* edited by Henry Abelove et al., 227–254. New York: Routledge, 1993.

———. *Of Woman Born: Motherhood as Experience and Institution.* New York: Norton, 1976.

Rieu, E. U., trans. *Homer: The Iliad.* New York: Penguin, 1950.

Rigby, Peter. "Some Gogo Rituals of 'Purification': An Essay on Social and Moral Categories." In *A Reader in Comparative Religion: An Anthropological Approach,* edited by William A. Lessa and Evon Vogt, 238–247. New York: Harper, 1965.

Rinero, Arthur. *Amazons: A Farcical Romance in Three Acts.* London: W. Heineman, 1902.

Robicsek, Francis, and Donald Hales. *The Maya Book of the Dead: The Ceramic Codex.* Charlottesville: University of Virginia Art Museum, 1981.

Robinson, Jane E. M. *The Amazon Chronicles.* San Diego: Clothespin Fever, 1994.

Robinson, Pat, and Group. "A Historical and Critical Essay for Black Women in the Cities, June 1969." In *The Black Woman,* edited by Toni Cade, 198–210. New York: Signet, 1970.

Rodríguez de Montalvo, Garci. *Amadis of Gaul. Books I and II.* 1508. Lexington: University of Kentucky Press, 1974.

———. *Sergas de Esplandian: The Labors of the Very Brave Knight Esplandian.* 1510. Translated by William Thomas Little. Binghamton, N.Y.: Center for Medieval and Early Renaissance Studies, State University of New York at Binghamton, 1992.

Rohrlich, Ruby. "Feminist Anthropologist Anointed Foremother!" In *Feminist Foremothers in Women's Studies, Psychology and Mental Health,* edited by Phyllis Chesler, Esther Rothblum, and Ellen Cole, 391–406. New York: Harrington, 1995.

———. "Introduction." In *Women in Search of Utopia: Mavericks and Myth Makers,* edited by Ruby Rohrlich and Elaine Hoffman, xv–xxvii. New York: Schocken, 1984.

———. "Women in Transition: Crete and Sumer." In *Becoming Visible: Women in European History,* edited by Renate Bridenthal and Claudia Koonz, 36–59. Boston: Houghton Mifflin, 1977.

Rohrlich, Ruby, and Elaine Hoffman Baruch, eds. *Women in Search of Utopia: Mavericks and Myth Makers.* New York: Schocken, 1984.

Ronai, Carol Rambo. "Multiple Reflections of Child Sex Abuse: An Argument for a Layered Account." *Journal of Contemporary Ethnography* 23, no.4 (January 1995): 395–426.

Rosaldo, Michelle Zimbalist, and Louise Lamphere, eds. *Woman, Culture and Society.* Stanford, Calif.: Stanford University Press, 1974.

Rose, H. J. *Primitive Culture in Greece.* London: Methuen, 1925.

Rosenow, John E., and Gerreld L. Pulsipher. *Tourism: The Good, the Bad and the Ugly.* Lincoln: Century Three, 1979.

Roth, Philip. *Portnoy's Complaint.* New York: Random House, 1968.

Rothery, Guy Cadogarn. *The Amazons in Antiquity and Modern Times.* London: Francis Griffiths, 1910.

Roys, Ralph Loveland, trans. *Ritual of the Bacabs.* 1879. Norman: University of Oklahoma Press, 1965.

Rufus, Anneli, and Kristan Lawson. *Goddess Sites: Europe.* San Francisco: Harper, 1991.

Rush, Florence. "The Parable of the Mother and Daughters." In *Amazon Expedition: A Lesbian Feminist Anthology,* edited by Phyllis Birkby, 4–10. Washington, N.J.: Times Change, 1973.

Russ, Joanna. *Female Man.* 1972. Boston: Beacon, 1987.

———. *The Two of Them.* New York: Berkeley, 1978.

Sacks, Karen. "Engels Revisited: Women, the Origin of Production, and Private Property." In *Woman, Culture and Society,* edited by Michelle Zimbalist Rosaldo and Louise Lamphere, 207–222. Stanford, Calif.: Stanford University Press, 1974.

Salisbury Joyce E. "Fruitful in Singleness." *Journal of Medieval History* 8, no. 2 (June 1982): 97–106.

Salmonson, Jessica. *Amazons.* New York: DAW, 1979.

———. *Amazons II.* New York: DAW, 1981.

————. *The Encyclopedia of Amazons: Women Warriors from Antiquity to the Modern Era.* New York: Anchor, 1992.

Salter, F. M., and H. L. R. Edwards. *The Bibliotheca Historica of Diodorus Siculus.* Translated by John Skelton. Vol. 1. London: Early English Text Society, Oxford University Press, 1956.

Sanday, Peggy. "Androcentric and Matrifocal Gender Representations in Minangkabau Ideology." *Beyond the Second Sex,* edited by Peggy Sanday and Ruth Goodenough, Philadelphia: University of Pennsylvania Press, 1990.

Sarachild, Kathie. "The Power of History." In *Feminist Revolution,* by Redstockings of the Women's Liberation Movement. Edited by Kathie Sarachild, 12–43. New York: Random, 1978a.

————. "Redstockings of the Women's Liberation Movement." In *Feminist Revolution,* by Redstockings of the Women's Liberation Movement. Edited by Kathie Sarachild. New York: Random, 1978b.

Sayce, A. H. *The Hittites: The Story of a Forgotten Empire.* 1884. New York: Scribner's, 1925.

Schele, Linda, and David Freidel. *A Forest of Kings: The Untold Story of the Ancient Maya.* New York: Morrow, 1990.

Schlereth, Thomas. *Artifacts and the American Past.* Nashville: American Association for State and Local History, 1981.

Schmidt, Joel. *Larousse Greek and Roman Mythology.* New York: McGraw, 1980.

Scholes, Frances, and Ralph L. Roys. *The Maya Chontal Indians of Acalan-Tixchel: A Contribution to the History and Ethnography of the Yucatán Peninsula.* Washington D.C.: Carnegie Institute of Washington Publication 560, 1948.

Scully, Vincent. *The Earth, the Temple and the Gods: Greek Sacred Architecture.* New York: Praeger, 1962.

Sered, Susan Starr. *Priestess, Mother, Sacred Sister: Religions Dominated by Women.* New York and Oxford: Oxford University Press, 1994.

Seremetakis, Constantina-Nadia. *The Last Word: Women, Death and Divination in Inner Mani.* Chicago: University of Chicago Press, 1991.

————. "Women and Death: Cultural Power and Ritual Process in Inner Mani." *Canadian Women's Studies* 8, no. 2 (1987): 108–110.

Seydou, Christiane. "The African Epic: A Means for Defining the Genre." Folklore Forum 16 (1983): 47–68.

Shakespeare, William. *The Tempest.* Edited by George Lyman Kittridge. 1623. Waltham, Mass.: Blaisdell, 1966.

Shepherd, Simon. *Amazons and Warrior Women: Varieties of Feminism in Seventeenth-Century Drama.* New York: St. Martin's, 1981.

Shinn, Thelma J. *Worlds within Women: Myth and Myth Making in Fantastic Literature by Women.* Westport, Conn.: Greenwood, 1986.

Showerman, Grant. *The Great Mother of the Gods.* Madison: Bulletin of University of Wisconsin no. 43. Philology and Literature Series 1, no. 3, 1901.

Shulman, Alix Kate. *Burning Questions: A Novel.* New York: Knopf, 1978.

————. *Memoirs of an Ex-Prom Queen.* New York: Knopf, 1972.

Siegel, Thyme S. "The Jewish Connections to the Voyages of Columbus." *Creation Spirituality* (September/October 1991): 13–15.

Silverblatt, Irene. *Moon, Sun and Witches.* Princeton: Princeton University Press, 1987.

Sinclair, Barbara Deckard. *The Women's Movement: Political, Socioeconomic and Psychological Issues.* New York: Harper, 1975.

Singer, Rochelle. *The Demeter Flower.* New York: St. Martin's, 1980.

Sjöö, Monica, and Barbara Mor. *The Great Cosmic Mother: Rediscovering the Religion of the Earth.* San Francisco: Harper, 1987.

Slater, Philip. *The Glory of Hera: Greek Mythology and the Greek Family.* Boston: Beacon, 1968.

Slatkin, Laura M. *The Power of Thetis: Allusion and Interpretation in* The Iliad. Berkeley: University of California Press, 1991.

Slusser, George, and Eric Rabkin, eds. *Fights of Fancy: Armed Conflict in Science Fiction and Fantasy.* Athens: University of Georgia Press, 1991.

Sobol, Donald J. *The Amazons of Greek Mythology.* New York: Barnes, 1972.

Spenser, Edmund. *The Faerie Queene.* Glasgow, 1894.

Spinelli, Maria-Lydia. "Fun and Power: Experience and Ideology at the Magic Kingdom" (Ph.D. diss., University of Massachusetts, Amherst, 1992).

"Spock's Brain." Written by Lee Cronin. *Star Trek: The Original and Uncut Television Series.* Created by Gene Roddenberry. Directed by Marc Daniels. Paramount Pictures, 1991. Airdate: September 20, 1968. Stardate: 5431.4.

Stanton, Elizabeth Cady. *Eighty Years and More: Reminiscences 1815–1897.* 1898. Boston: Northeastern University Press, 1993.

———. *The Woman's Bible.* 1898. Boston: Northeastern University Press, 1993.

Stein, Gertrude. *Making of Americans.* New York: Harcourt, 1934.

Steward, Julian, ed. *Handbook of South American Indians.* New York: Cooper Square, 1963.

Stone, Leslie F. "The Conquest of Gola." *Wonder Stories* 2, no. 111 (April 1931): 1278–1288. Reprinted in *The Best of Science Fiction,* edited by Groff Conklin, 752–763. New York: Crown, 1946. Also reprinted in *New Eves: Science Fiction about the Extraordinary Women of Today and Tomorrow,* edited by Janrae Frank, Jean Stine, and Forrest J. Ackerman, 29–42. Stamford, Conn.: Longmeadow, 1994.

———. "Women with Wings." *Air Wonder Stories* (May 1930): 985–1003.

Stone, Merlin. *When God Was a Woman.* New York: Harcourt, 1978.

Suvin, Darko. *Metamorphoses of Science Fiction.* New Haven: Yale University Press, 1979.

Taube, Karl. "Ritual Humor in Classic Maya Religion." In *Word and Image in Maya Culture: Explorations in Language, Writing and Representation,* edited by William F. Hanks and Don S. Rice, 351–382. Salt Lake City: University of Utah Press, 1989.

Tennyson, Alfred. *The Princess.* London: King, 1874.

Thiébaux, Marcelle, trans. *The Writings of Medieval Women.* 2d ed. New York: Garland, 1987.

Thomas, Henry. *Spanish and Portuguese Romances of Chivalry.* Cambridge: Cambridge University Press, 1920.

Thomson, George Dewert. *Studies in Ancient Greek Society.* New York: International Press, 1949.

Thompson, John Eric Sidney. *The Moon Goddess in Middle America.* Washington, D.C.: Carnegie Institute, 1939.

Thompson, Stith. *Motif-index of Folk Literature.* Vols. 1 and 6. Bloomington: Indiana University Press, 1958.

Turner, Frederick W. *Beyond Geography: The Western Spirit against the Wilderness.* New York: Viking, 1980.

———. *The New World: An Epic Poem.* Princeton: Princeton University Press, 1985.

Turner, Kay. "Ixchel: Biography of a Maya Moon Goddess." *Lady Unique Inclination of the Night Cycle* 1 (Autumn 1976): 5–51.

Tylor, Edward. *Religion in Primitive Culture.* 1871. New York: Harper, 1958.

Tyrell, William Blake. *Amazons: A Study in Athenian Myth Making.* Baltimore: Johns Hopkins University Press, 1984.

Urla, Jackie, with Alan Swedlund. "Anthropometry of Barbie: Unsettling the Ideal of the Feminine Body in Popular Culture." Unpublished talk, Women's Studies Faculty Lecture Workshop Series, University of Massachusetts, Amherst, October 20, 1993.

Usigli, Rodolfo. *Crown of Light.* In *Two Plays.* Carbondale: Southern Illinois University Press, 1971. 1–108.

Vargas Ugarte, Ruben. *Historia del culto de María en Ibero-América y de sus imágenes y santuarios mas celebrados.* Buenos Aires: Huarpes, 1947.

Velikovsky, Immanuel. *Mankind in Amnesia.* London: Sidgwick, 1982.

———. *Mankind in America.* London: Sidgwick, 1982.

Vera, Lynn. "A Reclamation of Womonspirit: My Journey through Mexico and into Myself" *Womonspirit* 5, no. 20 (Summer Solstice 1979): 34–36.

Verne, Jules. *The Floating Island.* 1895. London: Kegan, 1990.

———. *The Mysterious Island.* Chicago: Belford, 1887.

Vida, Ginny. ed. *Our Right to Love: A Lesbian Resource Book Produced in Cooperation with Women of the National Gay Task Force.* Englewood Cliffs, N.J.: Prentice-Hall, 1978.

Villa Rojas, Alfonso. *The Maya of East Central Quintana Roo.* Washington, D.C.: Carnegie Institute of Washington Publication no. 59, 1945.

Virgil. *The Aeneid of Virgil.* 6 vols. London: Macmillan, 1972.

Vogt, Evon. *Zinacantan: A Maya Community in the Highlands of Chiapas.* Cambridge, Mass.: Harvard University Press, 1969.

Voltaire, Francois Marie Arouet. *Candide.* 1759. New York: Fune Editions Press, 1957.

Von Hagen, Victor. *En Busca de los Mayas: La historia de Stephens Catherwood.* Mexico City: editorial diana, 1979.

Wagner, Henry R., trans. *The Discovery of New Spain in 1518 by Juan Grijalva.* [1519?] Berkeley, Calif.: Cortés Society, 1942.

Wagner-Martin, Linda. *Bell Jar: A Novel of the Fifties.* New York: Twayne, 1992.

Waldman, Anne. *Fast-Speaking Woman.* San Francisco: City Lights, 1978.

Wallace, Michelle. *Black Macho and the Myth of the Super-Woman.* London: Verso, 1990.

Wallerstein, Herb, and Stuart Margolin, dir. *The New Original Wonder Woman.* Produced by Wilfred Baumes. Written by Jimmy Sangster, with Lynda Carter. New York: ABC, 1975–1976.

Walker, Alice. *The Color Purple.* New York: Washington Square, 1982.

Walker, Barbara. *Amazon: A Novel.* San Francisco: Harper, 1992.

———. *The Woman's Encyclopedia of Myths and Secrets.* San Francisco: Harper, 1983.

Walt Disney Company. *Ariel y el Misterioso Mundo de Arriba.* Burbank, Calif.: Walt Disney Records, 1990.

Ware, Cellestine. *Woman Power: The Movement for Women's Liberation.* New York: Tower, 1970.

Warhol, Robyn R., and Diane Price Herndl, eds. *Feminisms: An Anthology of Literary Theory and Criticism.* New Brunswick: Rutgers University Press, 1991.

Webster, F. A. M. *The Land of Forgotten Women.* London: Skeffington, 1950.

Webster, Paula. "Matriarchy: A Vision of Power." In *Towards an Anthropology of Women,* edited by Rayna Rapp Reiter, 127–156. New York: Monthly Review, 1978.

Weed, Susun. *Wisewoman: Herbs for the Childbearing Year.* Woodstock, N.Y.: Ash Tree, 1985.

Weedman, Jane B., ed. *Women Worldwalkers: New Dimensions of Science Fiction and Fantasy.* Lubbock: Texas Tech, 1985.

Weigert-Vowinkel, E. "The Cult and Mythology of the Magna Mater from the Point of View of Psychoanalysis." *Psychiatry* 1 (1938): 347–378.

Weigle, Marta. *Creation and Procreation: Feminist Reflections on Mythologies of Cosmogony and Parturition.* Philadelphia: University of Pennsylvania Press, 1989.

Weinbaum, Batya. "Bapka in Brooklyn." In *Tales of Magic Realism by Women: Dreams in a Minor Key,* edited by Susanna J. Sturgis. Freedom, Calif.: Crossing, 1991a.

———. "The Bird Serenade." *Quill* 1(Spring 1995b): 12–14.

———. *The Curious Courtship of Women's Liberation and Socialism.* Boston: South End, 1978.

———. "Disney-Mediated Images Emerging in Cross-Cultural Expression on Isla Mujeres, Mexico." *Journal of American Culture* 20, no. 2 (1997c): 19–29; 30–36.

———. "Isaac's Dream." *Anything That Moves* (April-May 1991b): 56–57.

———. *The Island of Floating Women and Other Stories.* San Diego: Clothespin Fever, 1993a.

———. "Matriarchal Music Making." In *Sounding Off!* edited by Ron Sakolsky and Fred Wei-han Ho, 41–51. New York: Autonomedia, 1995b.

———. "Music, Dance and Song: Women's Cultural Resistance in Making Their Own Music." *Heresies* 22 (1988): 18–21.

———. *Pictures of Patriarchy.* Boston: South End, 1984a.

———. "Race and Color Coding in Leslie F. Stone's 'The Human Pets of Mars': Reflections for the Repertoire of the Multicultural Classroom." In *Into Darkness Peering: Race and Color in the Fantastic,* edited by Elisabeth Anne Leonard, 57–70. Westport, Conn.: Greenwood, 1997a.

———. "Rainbow to the Moon Goddess." In *The Island of Floating Women and Other Stories.* San Diego: Clothespin Fever, 1993b. 87–101.

———. "Redefining the Question of Revolution." *Review of Radical Political Economics* 9, no. 3 (Fall 1977): 54–78.

———. *Sasha's Harlem*. Sylmar, Calif.: Pyx Press, forthcoming.

———. "Sex-Role Reversal in the Thirties: Leslie F. Stone's 'The Conquest of Gola.'" *Science-Fiction Studies* 73 (November 1997b): 471–482.

———. "Twin Oaks: A Feminist Look at Indigenous Socialism in the United States." In *Women in Search of Utopia: Mavericks and Mythmakers,* edited by Ruby Rohrlich and Elaine Hoffman Baruch, 157–167. New York: Schocken, 1984b.

———. "Women in Transition to Socialism: Perspectives on the Chinese Case." *Review of Radical Political Economics* 8, no. 1 (Spring 1976): 34–58.

———. "The Women Who Won the World: A Playful Segment." In *The Island of Floating Women and Other Stories*. San Diego: Clothespin Fever, 1993c. 169–175.

Wells, H. G. *The Island of Dr. Moreau*. 1933. New York: Berkeley, 1979.

———. *The Sea Lady*. 1902. Westport, Conn.: Hyperion, 1976.

———. *War of the Worlds*. 1898. Mineola, N.Y.: Dover, 1997.

Wheelwright, Julie. *Amazons and Military Maids: Women Who Dressed as Men in the Pursuit of Life, Liberty and Happiness*. London: Pandora, 1989.

Williams, Raymond. *Marxism and Literature*. Oxford: Oxford University Press, 1977.

Winner, L. "Do Artifacts Have Politics?" *Daedalus* 109 (1980): 121–136.

Wolf, Eric. "The Virgin of Guadalupe: A Mexican National Symbol." In *A Reader in Comparative Religion: An Anthropological Approach,* edited by William A. Lessa and Evon Vogt, 149–152. New York: Harper, 1965.

Wood, Susan. "Women and Science Fiction." *Algol/Starship* 16, no. 1 (Winter 1978/1979): 9–18.

Wright, Celeste Turner. "The Amazons in Elizabethan Literature." *Studies in Philology* 37, no. 3 (July 1940): 433–456.

Wright, Richard. "Five Episodes." Excerpt from *Island of Hallucination*. Unpublished novel. Reprinted in *Soon, One Morning: New Writing by American Negroes 1940–1962,* edited by Herbert Hill, 140–164. New York: Knopf, 1963.

Yocom, Margaret R. "Waking Up the Dead: Old Texts and New Critical Directions." In *Feminist Theory and the Study of Folklore,* edited by Susan Tower Hollis, Linda Pershing, and M. Jane Young, 119–129. Urbana: University of Illinois Press, 1993.

Young-Bruehl, Elisabeth. *Mind and the Body Politic*. New York: Routledge, 1989.

Yule, Colonel Henry C. B. *The Book of Ser Marco Polo, The Venetian* [1553?]. London: Murray, 1903.

Zipes, Jack, ed. *Arabian Nights*. [942?] New York: New American Library, 1991.

Index